Date Due

THE PRINCIPLES

AND METHODS OF DISCUSSION

THE PRINCIPLES
AND
METHODS OF DISCUSSION

by

JAMES H. McBURNEY, Ph.D.

Associate Professor of Public Speaking,
School of Speech, Northwestern University

and

KENNETH G. HANCE, Ph.D.

Professor of Speech,
Albion College

HARPER & BROTHERS PUBLISHERS

NEW YORK   LONDON

TABLE OF CONTENTS

PREFACE

This book is designed to present the working principles and the methods of discussion in terms of a democratic philosophy. The basic concepts implicit in every line and chapter are *criticism, cooperation,* and *communication*. The work is an attempt to implement the reflective deliberation of face-to-face and coacting groups. As such, it deals with group discussion, panel discussion, the dialogue, the symposium, the forum-lecture, and the forum, and their applications to both learning and policy-determining groups.

One of the important contributions of the book, we hope, will be the analysis of reflective thinking in relation to the problems of discussion. Discussion, we believe, involves much more than arranging chairs in a circle. While we have considered methods of preparing for discussion, participating in, and leading discussion, all this has been brought into close juxtaposition with an analysis of the logical pattern of discussion, the modes of reasoning in discussion, and the common obstacles to reflective thought. Such an approach, we feel, gives to discussion the form and substance which can make of its study and practice a stimulating and productive educative process. Especially is this true in a society whose schools and colleges are dedicated to the democratic way of life.

Throughout this work we have sought to avoid pedantry and formality which might operate to destroy the spontaneity of live, vigorous discussion. We have tried to provide a functional treatment which can be used to guide experiences in discussion and to serve as a basis for the criticism of these experiences. While the book has been designed primarily for college and university courses in discussion, it may be of service to any person or group interested in acquiring knowledge about the principles and methods of discussion, and proficiency in their use.

We are indebted to Professor Lyman Bryson, Teachers College, Columbia University, for permission to include his lecture on "Discussion in the Democratic Process," to Professor Gordon W. Allport, Harvard University, for permission to quote excerpts from his lecture "Social Control through Language," and to Professor Elwood Murray, University of Denver, and Professor Milton Dickens, Syracuse University, for permission to reprint materials. We also are indebted to Professor Emeritus John Dewey,. Columbia University, Professor Harrison S. Elliott, Union Theological Seminary, Columbia University, Professor Thomas Fansler, New York University, Professor J. M. O'Neill, Brooklyn College, Professor Lew Sarett, Northwestern University, and the several authors of the Inquiry Publications, for the background and stimulation which their writings have brought to this work.

Excerpts from copyrighted books and other printed materials are included by permission of the following publishers, whose courtesies are hereby gratefully acknowledged: The American Association for Adult Education; The Association Press; The University of Chicago Round Table; The Columbia University Press; Harcourt, Brace and Company; D. C. Heath and Company; Henry Holt and Company; Houghton Mifflin Company; The Institute for Propaganda Analysis, Inc.; The Macmillan Company; The National Occupational Conference; G. P. Putnam's Sons; and Simon and Schuster, Inc.

J. H. McB.
K. G. H.

Evanston, Illinois
October 8, 1938

THE PRINCIPLES

AND METHODS OF DISCUSSION

CHAPTER I

AN INTRODUCTION TO DISCUSSION

I. DISCUSSION AND PERSUASION

The workers in the plant had been out on a strike for more than thirty days when Smith, a representative of the Department of Labor, arrived in town. It was a conflict over union recognition and all efforts to come to some kind of agreement had failed. Smith realized that the only possible method of reaching a peaceful settlement lay in arranging a conference between representatives of the plant and representatives of the men. This he did. A group of six key men in the controversy spent the most of two full days with him talking over the issues at stake. The grievances of both parties were explained frankly and openly, the whole problem was analyzed, and the experiences of other plants under similar circumstances were considered. In the end a working agreement was reached.

This conference did not end the job, however. It remained to persuade both the strikers and the stockholders to accept the agreement reached in conference. At Smith's suggestion one of the strikers who had been active in the deliberations was asked to present the proposition to the workers at a mass meeting the following morning. A similar representation was made to the governing board of the plant. The acceptance of the agreement by these groups resulted in the termination of the strike and the reopening of the plant.

While attempts to resolve social conflicts are usually less simple and direct than this case might suggest, we have illustrated here what are probably the two most important kinds of situations in which speech takes place. What was the nature of this conference? Wherein did these deliberations differ from the later pleas and arguments which secured the results of the conference? Additional illustrations may help to answer these questions.

The Committee on Highway Construction and Maintenance of the State Senate was confronted with the problem of mounting repair costs on certain state roads caused by heavy truck transportation. What could be done about it? They discussed the question as a committee and reached a conclusion which was framed as a bill and later introduced on the floor of the Senate. Here Senator James, a member of the committee, presented the bill, argued its merits and defended it in debate. The bill was passed with some modifications.

We may consider one more illustration:

At the suggestion of the mayor of Elton, a group of citizens was called together to consider the growing delinquency rate among the youth of the city. Several meetings were held in which the causes of the problem were discussed and various proposals considered. It was the consensus of the group that a city recreation center under a competent director would help as much as anything that could be done. Such a center, however, would require a building and the building would necessitate a special bond issue which would have to be voted upon by the people. With the cooperation of the mayor and two of the service clubs of the city a campaign was launched which resulted in an endorsement of the bond issue at the next election.

It is not difficult to see that in each of these cases two essentially different kinds of speech activities were at work, that of meeting a problem, analyzing it, and working out what appeared to be the best solution, and secondly, that of prevailing upon others to accept this solution. The first of these activities in each case was *discussion*; the second was *persuasion*, and in the case of Senator James, *debate*. Whereas the discussions were inquiries motivated primarily by the desire to find answers to problems, the task of securing acceptance was in each case one of skillful advocacy. Herein lies the principal difference between discussion and all types of persuasion and debate. The difference, as we shall see, is one both of purpose and of method.

II. CONSTRUCTIVE AND INTENTIONAL REASONING

We have seen that in the first deliberations in each of the cases given the persons concerned were attempting to think together reflectively. They were confronted with a problem and were seeking to discover a solution. The kind of reasoning or thinking employed in situations of this sort we shall call *constructive*, or *reflective*.

After conclusions had been reached by constructive thought, it was then necessary to persuade others to adopt these conclusions. This was the attempt of the labor representative at the mass meeting, of Senator James on the Senate floor, and of the group trying to "sell" the idea of a recreational center to the electorate of Elton. The kind of reasoning involved in these situations we shall call *intentional*. It is reasoning designed to secure, justify, or defend a predetermined proposition.

Eugenio Rignano says of these two kinds of reasoning in his *Psychology of Reasoning*:

In constructive reasoning it is the object of the reasoner to discover truths yet unknown, that is to say new derivations of one group of phenomena from another. . . .

In such reasoning, the reasoner has at the outset no intention or desire to maintain certain points at the expense of certain others. He wishes only to discover *the truth*, whatever it may be. The "intentional" reasoner, on the other hand, starts reasoning in order to try to demonstrate the accuracy of definite assertions in which he has a par-

ticular interest. In one case the reasoner does not know in advance the final result of the new series of imagined experiments any more than the experimentalist knows the result of certain experiments which he sets himself to perform for the first time. The second, on the other hand, already knows the result of his reasoning *because he desires it.*
. . . It is clear that such "intentional" reasoning must, on account of this different function, present aspects and peculiarities very different from "constructive" reasoning.[1]

The methods of discussion are designed to implement the constructive thinking of groups of people. Discussion is an attempt on the part of a group to think together reflectively. It is on this basis most clearly distinguished from the reasoning of the advocate who sets out to defend a proposition to which he is committed either by desire or by the nature of the situation in which he finds himself.

John Dewey has this distinction between constructive and intentional reasoning in mind when he refers to the *process* and *product* of thought.[2] Reflective thinking is *thought in process* arising out of a state of perplexity, hesitation, or doubt, and proceeding to a search or investigation for the purpose of resolving this difficulty. The *product* or *outcome* of thought is the conclusion reached. It may be phrased as a proposition for the debater or persuader to defend and project.

Schiller distinguishes between the reasoner's actual procedure, or the process of discovery, and the reasoner's "own *ex post facto* version, rearranged as a logically cogent 'proof' . . ."[3] Sellars likewise distinguishes between *discovery* and *proof.*[4]

---

[1] Eugenio Rignano, *The Psychology of Reasoning* (New York: Harcourt, Brace and Company, 1927), pp. 209-210.

[2] John Dewey, *How We Think* (Boston: D. C. Heath and Company, 1933), Chapter V.

[3] F. S. C. Schiller, *Logic for Use* (New York: Harcourt, Brace and Company, 1930), p. 321.

[4] R. W. Sellars, *The Essentials of Logic* (Boston: Houghton Mifflin Company, 1925), pp. 15-16.

III. CRITICISM AND PROPAGANDA

We have contrasted discussion and persuasion, constructive reasoning and intentional reasoning; a third distinction which parallels these in many respects and contributes further to an understanding of the nature of discussion is that between criticism and propaganda. The critical analyst attempts to examine a problem objectively and impartially. He makes an effort to face all the facts at his disposal frankly and honestly. All aspects of the problem are considered with bias or prejudice toward none. While this description probably presents an ideal which is seldom if ever perfectly achieved, it may be accepted as a useful working conception. The principles and methods of discussion attempt to achieve for group deliberation such critical analysis in as large a measure as the nature and usual circumstances of such deliberation will permit.

Consider the following explanations of propaganda:

As generally understood, *propaganda is expression of opinion or action by individuals or groups deliberately designed to influence opinions or actions of other individuals or groups with reference to predetermined ends.*

Thus propaganda differs from scientific analysis. The propagandist is trying to "put something across" good or bad, whereas the scientist is trying to discover truth and fact. Often the propagandist does not want careful scrutiny and criticism; he wants to bring about a specific action.[5]

Gordon Allport states:

A satisfactory psychological definition of propaganda is the following: *Propaganda is an organized attempt to influence public opinion in behalf of some special interest by means of suggestion.* This definition has three parts. Propaganda must attempt to influence *public* opinion (which means the opinion of many people) . . . Secondly, some *special interest* always motivates propaganda. Usually it is

[5] Institute for Propaganda Analysis, Inc., *Monthly Letter: Propaganda Analysis*, Vol. I, No. 1, October, 1937, pp. 1-2.

a selfish financial or political interest held by the propagandist himself. But the special interest may be altruistic in
character as in a safety campaign or in propaganda for
peace. Nevertheless it is a special interest in the sense that
it represents an emotional goal of great personal importance
to protagonists of the cause. Lastly, and most significant for
psychology, propaganda always depends upon the use of
suggestion. Open argument and presentation of all the
facts of the case are not propaganda. A conclusion reached
in the light of all available evidence on both sides of a question is not the product of suggestion. Suggestion, rather, is
the process of reaching a conclusion with only part of our
mental equipment. . . . In short, suggestion is the absence
of complete self-determination.[6]

These definitions of propaganda may be profitably
studied with great care, if for no other reason, to indicate
what discussion is not! Discussion does not "attempt to
influence public opinion" or any other kind of opinion
except as the critical analysis of problems causes people
who have participated in such criticism to change their
opinions without pressure or coercion of any kind. Discussion, if it is true discussion, is not motivated by "some
special interest"; protagonists in the usual sense of that
term have no place in critical deliberation. And above
all, discussion does not "depend upon the use of suggestion"; it proceeds "through open argument and presentation of all the facts of a case"; it attempts to reach conclusions "in the light of all the available evidence on both
sides of a question"; it respects the intellectual integrity
of the individual and seeks to foster "complete self-
determination" with all of "our mental equipment at
work."

IV. THE RATIONALE OF DISCUSSION

In this introductory chapter we have contrasted discussion and persuasion, constructive reasoning and inten-

[6] Gordon Allport, "Social Control Through Language" (unpublished lecture, *Symposium in Public Speaking, Northwestern University,* June, 1938), p. 12.

tional reasoning, criticism and propaganda, in an effort to shed some light on what discussion is and what it is not. Discussion, constructive reasoning, and criticism have many things in common as do persuasion, intentional reasoning, and propaganda. While we have emphasized these common elements in order to provide an orientation with respect to discussion which we believe is sound and fundamental, it is only fair to add that these terms are by no means identical. Persuasion, for example, may develop from reasoned discourse which cannot be classified as propaganda under the usual definitions of this term. The best persuasive speeches do not rely upon suggestion to the exclusion of sound argument.

What is more important for a clear understanding of discussion and its relations to these conceptions is the fact that no one of the three parallel comparisons represents a mutually exclusive or completely dichotomous distinction. Discussion and persuasion are different, but the difference may be largely one of degree. Constructive reasoning can and should be distinguished from intentional reasoning, but there are instances of reasoning which partake of the nature of both. Criticism and propaganda are as different as day and night in many of the situations in which they operate, but here again we must recognize the presence of a *continuous variation* which admits of degrees of objectivity and degrees of suggestion.

Nor are these comparisons meant to imply preferences. Both discussion and persuasion are tremendously important social tools. The cases which we presented at the beginning of this chapter were intended to illustrate some of the differences, suggest some of the values and limitations of both, and to show how they often play complementary roles in the solution of social problems.

The principles and methods of discussion aim to achieve constructive reasoning and critical analysis in group deliberation. Most discussion groups will probably not accomplish these goals completely, but to the degree that those who take part can escape affective identification with the proposals they present and the substitution of suggestion for reason, the more nearly will the group approach what we consider true discussion to be. The three fundamental bases of discussion are *criticism*, *cooperation*, and *communication*, with criticism understood as constructive group-thought of which cooperation and communication are necessary concomitants.

EXERCISES

1. Bring to class three examples similar to those given in the first section of this chapter designed to show the relationship between discussion and persuasion.
2. Write a 400-500 word essay comparing discussion and propaganda and discussing the place of each in a democratic society. Be certain to read the discussions in Appendices B and C and the lecture included in Appendix D. Consult the bibliography at the close of this chapter for additional references. Read some of these essays in class and discuss the questions which they raise.
3. Collect definitions of the following terms and compare and discuss them in class: discussion, debate, persuasion.

SELECTED BIBLIOGRAPHY

Dewey, John, *How We Think*. Boston: D. C. Heath and Company, 1933. Chapters I, II, and V.

Doob, Leonard, *Propaganda, Its Psychology and Technique*. New York: Henry Holt and Company, 1935. Part III.

Childs, H. D., "Propaganda and Pressure Groups," *The Annals of the American Academy of Political and Social Science*. Vol. 179, May, 1935.

Ellis, Elmer, "Education Against Propaganda," *Seventh Year Book*. National Council for the Social Studies, 1937.

Institute for Propaganda Analysis, *Monthly Letter: Propaganda Analysis*. Vol. I, No. 1, October, 1937.

Lumley, Frederick E., *Means of Social Control*. New York: The Century Company, 1925. Chapters I, V, and VIII.

Lumley, Frederick E., *The Propaganda Menace*. New York:

Harcourt, Brace and Company, 1936. Chapters I, II, V, and VI.

Rignano, Eugenio, *The Psychology of Reasoning.* New York: Harcourt, Brace and Company, 1927. Chapter X.

Sarett, Lew, and Foster, William T., *Basic Principles of Speech.* Boston: Houghton Mifflin Company, 1937. Chapter XVIII.

CHAPTER II

THE NATURE AND PURPOSE OF DISCUSSION

I. A WORKING DEFINITION OF DISCUSSION

Discussion may be defined as *the cooperative deliberation of problems by persons thinking and conversing together in face-to-face or co-acting groups under the direction of a leader.* There are four parts to this definition which we shall need to explain.

A. DISCUSSION AS THE REFLECTIVE DELIBERATION OF PROBLEMS.

Much of what was said in Chapter I will help us at this point. We know that discussion is concerned with reflective thinking rather than intentional reasoning and with critical analysis rather than propaganda. We know also, in a general way at least, what is meant by reflective thinking and critical analysis. The question with which we are primarily concerned here is: What form does this problem-solving type of thinking naturally tend to take in group deliberation?

Dashiell, reporting a number of experimental studies in discussion and closely related fields, notes that "qualitatively, group discussion seems to be adequately characterized by the traditional analyses of individual thinking, as, e.g., stated by Dewey . . .".[1] In other words, we may say that the reflective thinking of a group of individuals in its total, over-all pattern or form appears to correspond very closely to that of the solitary thought of a single individual. Professor Dewey states:

> Upon examination, each instance [of reflective thought] reveals more or less clearly, five logically distinct steps: (1) a felt difficulty; (2) its location and definition; (3) suggestion of possible solution; (4) development by reasoning of the bearings of the suggestion; (5) further observation and experiment leading to its acceptance or rejection; that is, the conclusion of belief or disbelief.[2]

For purposes of analyzing and directing thought in group discussion we have found the following adaptation of Professor Dewey's analysis most helpful:

1. *Defining and Delimiting the Problem.*—All reflective thinking has its inception in some kind of felt difficulty, perplexing situation, or problem. This suggests that the first logical task for the group is that of *locating* the problem as definitely as possible. Not much can be accomplished until the members of the group reach some understanding as to what the problem is and what its limits are. This is aided by an attempt to state the problem as clearly and definitely as possible and to define the terms involved in such a statement.

2. *Analyzing the Problem.*—When the problem has been located it is then possible to diagnose the difficulty. In other words, attempt to find out what is wrong and what is causing the trouble. Here is involved the discovery of underlying cause and effect relationships which

---

[1] J. F. Dashiell, "Experimental Studies of the Influence of Social Situations on the Behavior of Individual Human Adults," *Handbook of Social Psychology*, edited by Carl Murchison (Worcester, Massachusetts: Clark University Press, 1935), p. 1131.

[2] John Dewey, *How We Think* (Boston: D. C. Heath and Company, 1910), p. 72.

must be known and understood before any progress can be made in the solution of the problem. The doctor's diagnosis of a patient presents a simple illustration of this step. First he gets from the patient an account of his symptoms (effects) and then conducts an examination to discover other possible symptoms and to determine if possible what the cause of the ailment is.

In discussion the process of analysis involves a second step. Not only must the nature of the problem be understood in terms of these causal relationships, but it is important as well to know what the group wants any proposed solution of this problem to do. In other words, what are the purposes and motives of the persons concerned? By what criteria is the group to measure the proposed solutions? In the case of the doctor this is not likely to present a problem; the obvious value in the situation is the restored health of the patient. If we have a flat tire on the road, however, what our purposes are will have a significant bearing on the solution to the problem. If the important thing is to get to our destination as quickly as possible, certain solutions may appeal to us which would not be considered seriously were the main concern that of getting the tire fixed as cheaply as possible. Until the purposes and values in the situation are clarified by the group, there is little hope of reaching understanding. Such a clarification of values is an important aspect of analysis.

3. *The Suggestion of Solutions.*—The third logical step in group deliberation is the suggestion of possible solutions. While this process grows out of analysis naturally and easily, it is important to diagnose the problem carefully before attempting to prescribe a remedy. By a solution we mean simply an hypothesis or proposal which is offered tentatively by some member of the group as a possible explanation or way out of the difficulty. Needless to say, perhaps, the success of the entire reflective process hinges on the capacity of the group in evolving and suggesting apt solutions.

4. *Reasoned Development of the Proposed Solutions.*—
The next task of the group is that of thinking through
the various solutions given. When the implications of
each hypothesis are known it is possible to weigh and
compare their relative merits in terms of the causes of
the problem they are offered to correct and in terms of
the aims and purposes of the group affected by the problem. On the basis of such mental experimentation the
group may reach a tentative conclusion.

5. *Further Verification.*—Probably the best test of any
proposal is to try it out and observe the results. Quite
obviously such verification usually involves methods and
facilities other than discussion. However, it is possible
for a discussion group to review carefully the steps that
will need to be taken in putting the proposed solution
into operation. Such deliberation serves to check the
thinking of the group and often brings to light practical
matters which might otherwise escape notice.

The steps in reflective thinking as they relate to discussion will be developed in considerable detail in Chapter X. This preliminary explanation is offered here in an
effort further to define and explain the nature and purpose of discussion.

B. Discussion as Persons Thinking and Conversing
   Together Cooperatively.

Discussion implies cooperative effort as well as reflective thought. On this basis it may be helpfully distinguished from debate. Whereas debate consists of a competition between opposing or differing outcomes of
thought, discussion attempts to move cooperatively toward some conclusion which will represent the consensus of the group. This should not be construed to
mean that there is no difference or conflict in discussion.
There is. As a matter of fact, it is difficult to conceive
of any very profitable discussion taking place without
difference of opinion among the members of the group.
The distinction turns on the method of dealing with

conflict rather than on its presence or absence in the deliberations. Debate draws the lines of conflict in terms of a specified proposition, motion, or resolution, and creates a situation in which opponents "work against each other" in a competitive effort to achieve their respective proposals or, at least, to salvage as much of them as the circumstances will permit. Discussion attempts to deal with conflict by creating a situation in which two or more persons can "work together" toward a solution. Cooperation is implicit in the philosophy of discussion, and all the techniques and methods are designed to facilitate this "working together" in the group.

C. Discussion in Face-to-Face or Co-acting Groups.

The face-to-face group is the typical situation for discussion. By this is meant simply a group of such size and arrangement that each person can face every other person without moving to the front of the room. Such a group may be seated around a table or in any other circular or semicircular arrangement. Every person is privileged to contribute and as he speaks he may see everyone present and be seen by them. The thread of conversation is taken up by members of the group as they have something to say. The stimulus-response pattern is thus constantly changing as attention is directed from one speaker to another.

The physical requirements of a face-to-face group quite obviously limit the number that can participate on this basis. To obviate this difficulty, methods have been devised to facilitate discussion in larger groups of the co-acting type. By a co-acting situation we mean one in which all the members of the group are responding or reacting to some single, central source of stimulation. The ordinary public speaking situation is of the co-acting type. As a matter of fact, practically all auditoriums, lecture rooms, classrooms, and assembly halls are designed to accommodate co-acting groups. The seats are arranged so that the audience can see and hear the speaker on the platform. While such groups present special problems for discussion which are not present in the face-to-face group, it is possible nevertheless to secure cooperative group thinking and contributing if appropriate methods are applied. The panel, dialogue, symposium, and forum are especially designed to meet this type of situation. We shall consider these methods in later chapters.

D. Discussion as a Directed Activity.

Discussion typically takes place under the direction of a leader. In anything but very small and informal face-to-face groups this leadership is indispensable, and it is generally helpful even there. The function of the leader is that of directing a cooperative activity. The occasion is not one for him to exploit for his own purposes. He is there, rather, as one skilled in discussion leadership for the purpose of helping the group realize its full potentialities in the group thinking process.

II. THE GROWTH AND DEVELOPMENT OF DISCUSSION

A. The Background of Discussion.

Modern students of discussion should know that they are dealing with an art which has been practiced and written about for centuries. Mahaffy says of the ancient Greeks:

When we inquire into the causes that made politics so developed a feature among the Greeks, we shall in the first place find, even in Homer's societies, the habit of open discussion a leading fact in everyday life. There is a sort of instinct to have things talked over and reasoned out, so much so that the very king, who has come to a decision with his council, and has ample authority to fulfil it, will not do so without calling together an assembly of the soldiers in the camp or the free citizens in the market-place, and seeking to obtain their approval by acclamation. This assembly, called together to approve, without any power of voting or of reversing the prince's decision, is regarded by all historians as the embryo of the long-subsequent sovran assemblies of citizens in every Greek democracy.[3]

The ancient historian Thucydides and others give us descriptions of the Athenian general assembly or *Ecclesia*; later writers tell us about the practices in the Roman *Forum*. The general picture is one of stormy public debate with the popular demagogues of the day playing a conspicuous role. It is undoubtedly true that public debate and oratory occupied an importance place in ancient Greek and Roman life. Training in rhetoric and dialectic was emphasized in the schools, and treatises on these subjects which remain classics today were prepared by teachers and philosophers of the time.

What the ancients called *dialectic* was probably the closest approximation of modern discussion. Developed and practiced by Plato, it was perhaps given its most complete and systematic treatment in Aristotle's *Topics*. Here it is explained as a method of discussion (or debate) operating chiefly through question and answer for the purpose of intellectual training, casual encounters, the study of the philosophical sciences, and the investigation of the principles used in the other sciences.[4] Of some interest to us is the distinction which Aristotle makes between discussion in the spirit of competition and, to use his own words, "those who discuss things together in the spirit of inquiry." Says he, "The principle that a man who hinders the common business is a bad partner, clearly applies to argument as well; for in arguments there is also a common aim in view, except with mere contestants, for these cannot both reach the same goal; for more than one cannot possibly win. . . ."[5]

In so far as dialectic meant a group of people discussing things together "in the spirit of inquiry," we may

---

[3] J. P. Mahaffy, *What Have the Greeks Done for Civilisation?* (New York: G. P. Putnam's Sons, 1909), pp. 182-183.

[4] *Topics*, I, 2.

[5] *Ibid.*, VIII. 11.

liken it to discussion. We have reason to believe that many of the dialectical discussions in both ancient and medieval life were conducted with this end in view. On the other hand, to the extent that dialectic amounted to a competition in which opponents attempted to force one another to acknowledge conclusions by skillful questioning, marshaling of argument, and clever subterfuge, it cannot be said to have been in the spirit of discussion as we have defined the term. While such disputation may have been an illegitimate offspring of the true dialectic, it is nevertheless true that many dialecticians conceived of their art in this way and practiced it on this basis. So much was this the case that in the early part of the seventeenth century Francis Bacon and some of his contemporaries complained bitterly that the dialectical method was simply one of disputation actually adverse to discovery and the search for truth. Bacon's plea was for a logic of discovery. Says Professor Dewey:

Bacon brought his charges against the Aristotelian method itself. In its vigorous forms it aimed at demonstration and in its milder forms at persuasion. Both demonstration and persuasion aim at conquest of mind rather than of nature. Moreover they both assume that some one is already in possession of a truth or belief, and that the only problem is to convince some one else, or to teach. In contrast, his new method . . . would be a logic of discovery, not a logic of argumentation, proof, and persuasion.[6]

Out of this impatience with the authoritarianism of the past came what we today know as *scientific method.* The advances which this method has brought in the physical sciences during the last two centuries are a commonplace. And yet, through it all, the equally (if not more) important problems of policy in the realm of practical affairs have been left very largely to methods grounded in force, creed, and dogma. "The essential need

[6] John Dewey, *Reconstruction in Philosophy* (New York: Henry Holt and Company, 1920), pp. 28-29.

[today] is the improvement of the methods and conditions of debate, discussion, and persuasion." "That," says Professor Dewey, "is *the* need of the public."[7] Perhaps it is not too ambitious to say that the principles and methods of discussion attempt to bring the problems of practical policy in our society under the surveillance of an approach comparable in many ways with the method of science. At least, as we have seen, discussion finds its focus in the critical deliberation of such problems.

These are the essential phases of scientific method: a problem, hypothesis, deduction, and verification. These also are the common features of any intelligent discussion. The discrepancy between the method of science and that of discussion varies with the degree of definiteness with which problems are formulated; with the degree of vagueness with which hypotheses or suggestions are made; and with the degree of accuracy with which consequences are deduced and verified. But the difference is one of degree, not of kind.[8]

While the roots of the discussion method must be sought in ancient theory and practice, it is probably safe to say that it stems more directly from the conceptions of scientific method which have developed in the last few centuries. In fact, the attempts to apply the principles of scientific method to group deliberation are for the most part developments of the present century. This is not to deny the probability that men in all ages have attempted to solve their common problems critically and reflectively, nor to minimize the significance and vitality of the tradition of free public discussion dating back to the old New England town meeting which is the heritage of the American people. It is meant rather to emphasize the importance of renewing, extending, and improving these facilities.

[7] John Dewey, *The Public and Its Problems* (New York: Henry Holt and Company, 1927), p. 208.

[8] Philip Paul Wiener, "Scientific Method and Group Discussion," *Journal of Adult Education*, Vol. IX, No. 2, April, 1937, p. 136.

B. CONTEMPORARY INTEREST IN DISCUSSION.

That there has come a renewed interest in methods of discussion in the last fifteen years there can be no question. A group for social study and research known as the *Inquiry*, which was organized in 1923 and continued its work until 1933, has done much to shape our present conceptions of discussion and to call attention to its social significance.[9] In the last few years discussion has probably received most attention in the field of adult education, where workers have recognized its educational values and have developed discussion techniques suitable to this field. A development of considerable interest is the Forum Program of the United States Office of Education, which at the time of this writing has been responsible for the establishment of nineteen governmentally sponsored community forums. Hundreds of private forums under various auspices have been organized throughout the country. Discussion appears to be playing an increasingly important role in various types of social work, agricultural extension programs, radio, and in the programs of conventions, conferences, and institutes. Educators are emphasizing its importance in the schools.

During the five years following 1929, the number of public forums and discussion groups throughout the country doubled. Many observers were inclined to regard the increase in forums as a consequence of unsettled political and economic conditions, aspects of which formed the chief topics for discussion at these meetings. But when data show a continuing demand for such facilities of public discussion, and when in all sections of the country new forum groups are constantly being organized, even the doubting Thomases must recognize that the forum movement is neither a passing fad nor a temporary excrescence

[9] For an account of the activities of the Inquiry see Eduard C. Lindeman, *Social Education; An Interpretation of the Principles and Methods Developed by the Inquiry During the Years 1923-1933* (New York: The New Republic, Inc., 1933). See pages 207-226 for list of Inquiry publications.

of political and economic unrest, but a vital feature of our national life.

During the last year and a half the Office of Education has received thousands of letters requesting information and guidance in the organization of community forum groups. Thirty-six per cent of these letters came from principals and superintendents of schools, 17 per cent came from college and university officials, and 46 per cent came from civic leaders. More than five hundred requests have been received from individuals and groups in forty-four states asking that their communities be included in the federal program of forums. In many instances the correspondence reflects a public demand for the educational opportunities that forums provide to the adult population and a desire that these opportunities be offered as a regular part of the public school program in the community.[10]

C. Relations to the Social Scene.

Much of the recent literature dealing with discussion has been more concerned with arguing its role in a democratic society than it has been with expounding the methods of discussion. If democracy means anything, it must mean the active participation of the individual in the choices and policies of the group. In its best sense, it means action of this sort on the highest possible plane of intelligence with relative freedom from exploitation and violence. Democracy by its very nature must place a premium on group intelligence, since its values are realized in the degree that the members of the group participate competently in the solution of group problems and the formulation of policies. Democracy is thwarted in the degree that passivity and domination supplant such intelligent participation. By facilitating the critical examination of problems and suggested plans and policies, and the exercising of intelligent choice among them, discussion offers an important means of democratic participation. It works toward the creation of articulate,

[10] John W. Studebaker, United States Commissioner of Education, "Public Forums: An Evaluation," *Journal of Adult Education,* Vol. IX, No. 3, June, 1937, pp. 393-395.

alert, active groups and communities, and through these, a public habituated to reflective thinking and responsible acting.

Communication plays an important role in any society. If democracy is to exist in a society as complex as ours, it is imperative that there be abundant opportunity for free, open communication. Freedom of choice is the very essence of democracy, and no choice can be free or intelligent which is denied access to the facts. But the problem involves more than freedom of speech; it demands honest speech. Too much of our writing and speaking has degenerated into a confusion of propagandist tongues. It attempts to short-circuit critical, reflective thinking by resorting to emotionally loaded platitudes, mass suggestion, and half-truths. One has only to witness a political campaign, tune in on the radio, or read the average daily newspaper to appreciate the truth of this statement. To be sure, not all propaganda is dishonest; nevertheless it is true that an honest cause and sincere advocacy invite a hearing on the level of intelligent deliberation. Certainly, those who resort to these tactics must face the presumption that their cause cannot stand critical analysis and reflective consideration. The important point, however, is that a public educated to respond to propagandism is constantly in danger of exploitation. Programs and policies do not have to stand on their own merits. Issues are settled in terms of promotional skill and intrigue. The way is open for special interests and their schemes. The individual is lulled into mental inertia and ultimate submergence and disillusionment.

There is probably no type of communication less favorable to extravagant propaganda than that which takes place in a face-to-face group. Especially is this true if the members of the group have had some experience in reflective group thinking. Such a situation strongly militates against the more obvious tactics of the propagandist and makes even his subtle methods much more difficult. What is more, each individual is encouraged to share in the process in such a way that his own powers of critical judgment are sharpened and developed.

D. Relations to Speech.

Much of what has been said in this chapter explains the relations of discussion to speech. Discussion, like other speech skills, must be learned, and the best way to learn it is through guided experiences in discussion. This book is designed to supply the basis for such experiences. Every person has a responsibility to himself and to society to develop knowledge, attitudes, and skills which will enable him to grow to his full stature in ability to cooperate with others for the attainment of common and reciprocal ends. Speech is the great medium through which human cooperation is brought about. The principles and methods of discussion are offered to implement speech in what is probably its most normal and useful function, that of promoting better understanding and mutuality in purpose and conduct.

Exercises

1. Conduct a class discussion on the question: What is the role of discussion in a democratic society?
   a. Appoint from three to five members of the class to do special reading on the subject and to report their positions in five-minute forum talks.
   b. Follow the talks by a short period of class discussion under the direction of a student leader.
   c. Try to come to some conclusions, but do not attempt to force group consensus; if you do not agree, understand why you disagree.
   d. Have someone keep a record of the number of times each person contributes in the discussion.
2. Conduct a class discussion on some campus problem. Organize the discussion in terms of the steps in reflective thinking, proceeding from the first step through the fifth in the order in which they are explained in this chapter. Arrange the class as a face-to-face group and appoint a leader. Criticize the adequacy with which

each step in the reflective process is worked out by the group.

3. Write a 300-400 word paper illustrating the five steps in reflective thinking. Select some simple problem with which you are familiar for purposes of this analysis. State the problem and explain the process. Read Chapter VI in John Dewey, *How We Think* (1910 edition), and/or Chapter IV in Edwin A. Burtt, *Principles and Problems of Right Thinking*, in connection with this exercise.

4. Appoint three members of the class to act as a committee to prepare a report on the nature and purpose of scientific method and its relations to discussion. The committee is expected to investigate this topic (see selected bibliography), prepare a report, and designate one of its members to present this report in class. Undertake this assignment as a cooperative project and discuss the report in class.

5. Discuss the following statements in relation to what has been said in this chapter:

a. "Discussion is the highest form of conflict. It may sink into physical combat or rise to the heights of reasoning based on the results of the ablest research. Discussion may take the form of debate where two sides are pitted against each other and where each strives for status by winning. Each debater therefore distorts the truth, giving his side of the case undue advantage and minimizing the opposing side, or even misrepresenting by insinuation. In debate the best talker often wins. A poor side may be presented as the better by a skillful debater and a strong side fail of deserving presentation. An able lawyer may win for social injustice against a poor lawyer representing justice, and hence injustice be written into legal records and become the precedent for future decisions.

"Discussion may remain on the gossip level and give rise to many false myths. It may consist of endless talk, commonplace remarks; it may deal chiefly with opinions based on biased interpretations of a few experiences. On the other hand, it may reach the heights of scientific, impersonal presentation, diagnosis, and prognosis. At its best it creates a consensus opinion, a moving unity out of destructive disharmonies. A discussion group is at its best when all who participate come prepared to contribute the findings of research and to integrate the meanings with other research contributions."—Emory S. Bogardus, *Contemporary Sociology*, pp. 260-261.

  b. "Group discussion is not an argument nor a debate. In an argument the persons representing each side usually have their minds made up. Their purpose is to convince or defeat their opponents. In genuine discussion, on the other hand, folk come with open mind and with problems, expecting to get new light on their problem in working with others in search for a solution. In debate, one desires to know what another person thinks in order that he may devise arguments to convince him he is wrong. In discussion, one wishes to know what the other person thinks in order that he may get more light on his own problem or may cooperate with the other persons in solving their common problem.

  "The ordinary methods of argument and debate, carried on in deliberative groups, are really a denial of a true democratic process. Usually, such deliberations represent a contest in which one side is trying to defeat the other, or the pleading of a case, in which the person or the committee making the presentation is seeking to win the group. Indeed, the whole procedure is one of contest. Care is taken to present only the facts which support one's position, and to ignore or minimize the weight of the considerations in opposition. Anything which withholds important information or tends to put a peculiar construction on facts defeats the democratic process at the start."
—Harrison S. Elliott, *The Process of Group Thinking*, pp. 18-19.

Selected Bibliography

Burtt, Edwin Arthur, *Principles and Problems of Right Thinking*. New York: Harper and Brothers, 1928. Chapters I, II, and IV.

Clarke, Edwin Leavitt, *The Art of Straight Thinking*. New York: D. Appleton and Company, 1929. Chapter XIV.

Dewey, John, *How We Think*. Boston: D. C. Heath and Company, 1910. Chapter VI.

Dewey, John, *Logic, the Theory of Inquiry*. New York: Henry Holt and Company, 1938. Chapter XXIV.

Dewey, John, *Philosophy and Civilization*. New York: Minton, Balch and Company, 1931. Pp. 318-331.

Elliott, Harrison S., *The Process of Group Thinking*. New York: Association Press, 1932. Chapter I.

Russell, Bertram, *The Scientific Outlook*. New York: W. W. Norton and Company, Inc., 1931. Chapters I, II, III, and XI.

Saidla, Leo E., and Gibbs, Warren E. (Editors), *Science and The Scientific Mind*. New York: McGraw-Hill Book Company, Inc., 1930. Chapters I, V, VII, VIII, XXI, and XXIII.

Sheffield, Alfred Dwight, *Creative Discussion* (2d ed. rev.). New York: Association Press, 1927. Pp. 6-31.

Sheffield, Alfred Dwight, *Joining in Public Discussion*. New York: George H. Doran Company, 1922. Pp. v-xv.

Studebaker, John W., *The American Way*. New York: McGraw-Hill Book Company, Inc., 1935. Chapters I, II, and III.

Walser, Frank, *The Art of Conference*. New York: Harper and Brothers, 1933. Chapters I and VI.

Wiener, Philip Paul, "Scientific Method and Group Discussion," *Journal of Adult Education*. Vol. IX, No. 2, April, 1937, pp. 136-140.

Wolf, Abraham, *Essentials of Scientific Method*. London: G. Allen and Unwin, Ltd., 1928.

CHAPTER III

THE VALUES AND LIMITATIONS OF DISCUSSION

I. The Values of Discussion
  A. Value in supplementing solitary thought
  B. Value as an investigative technique
  C. Value as a learning technique
  D. Value as a policy-determining technique
  E. Esthetic and therapeutic values
  F. Social values
II. The Limitations of Discussion
  A. Limitations imposed by persons
  B. Limitations imposed by method
  C. Limitations imposed by matter
  D. Limitations imposed by time

I. THE VALUES OF DISCUSSION

With a working definition of discussion and some consideration of its growth and development before us, we are now in a position to assess its values and limitations, at least in a preliminary way.

A. VALUE IN SUPPLEMENTING SOLITARY THOUGHT.

Some writers have attempted to develop a concept which they call the *group mind*, the *group will*, or *group consciousness*. This, they appear to argue, is a sort of supermental entity which exists in the group apart from the individuals who compose it. It is an attempt to personify the group. The result is a more or less mystical concept which we believe is neither useful nor necessary. All the thinking that is done in a group situation is done by the individuals who compose the group. "One fails to see what need there is in this reference for a social mind in any other sense than that of several individuals' minds working in cooperation."[1] The only question we raise here then is: How productive is the group situation for individual thought?

The more obvious values of group-thought are those which arise from pooling experiences and sharing ideas. Whether this thought is as penetrating and thorough as private thinking appears to depend on the nature of the problem under consideration, the situation, and the individuals involved. It seems fair to say that cooperative thinking *may* "produce results superior to anything any individual could have produced by himself."[2] "If one is not too impervious to social stimuli, something great and even *new* may be produced by putting two or more heads together. . . . The stimulation of new ways of conceiving old facts represents the profitable side of discussion."[3]

No one would seriously propose discussion as a *substitute* for solitary thought. The value of cooperative thought lies in its ability to *supplement* and extend private thinking. The occasion for discussion may provoke preparatory thought, and participation in good discussion almost always develops ideas which stimulate thought long after the discussion is over.

B. VALUE AS AN INVESTIGATIVE TECHNIQUE.

The investigative function of discussion is not wholly distinct from its use as a learning technique. When we speak of this function of discussion we are thinking of the role that it plays in assembling facts on a problem and (in some cases) placing interpretations on these facts which provide a clearer insight into the problem. Under such circumstances learning, in the sense of individual improvement, is only incidental to the main purpose of the discussion. A typical example of this is the special

[1] Morris Ginsberg, *The Psychology of Society* (London: Methuen and Company, 1921), p. 64.

[2] *Ibid.*, p. 131.

[3] Floyd H. Allport, *Social Psychology* (Boston: Houghton Mifflin Company, 1930), p. 289.

committee appointed to investigate a problem for the purpose of preparing a report. The report is the end product in such a case, and the success or failure of the committee turns on the adequacy of this report.

A discussion group obviously does not offer facilities for fact finding in the sense of observing phenomena directly. It does, however, provide an opportunity for investigators to pool their information, to check the findings of one against another, to uncover aspects of the problem which need further study, and to work out at least the broad outline of the report. While the functions of any investigator are, first, to find out and, second, to report what he has found, it is commonly necessary to make some interpretations of the facts, and in some cases to make specific recommendations. Interpreting facts in terms of a specific problem is the primary function of reflective thinking. At this point it is perfectly possible for a group to originate suggestions that might not have occurred to independent investigators had they not had the benefit of the discussion. An idea developed orally will usually take on more definite form in the process, and new ideas often emerge from the exchange of experiences and opinions in discussion.

C. VALUE AS A LEARNING TECHNIQUE.

Learning has at least two aspects of which we should take notice: first, the growth or development of the learner as an individual, and second, what is probably a corollary of the first, the acquisition of knowledge. To speak of the growth of the individual in connection with learning naturally raises the question, growth in what? Participation in discussion offers an opportunity for development along at least two lines, which few will deny are important criteria of growth, the ability and disposition to approach problems on the level of reflective deliberation, and the ability and disposition to cooperate with others in the solution of group problems. Herein probably lies the greatest contribution of discussion to the learning process. While discussion may not be the quickest or most spectacular method of imparting information, participation in the group thinking process leaves a residue in the experience of the learner in terms of socially desirable skills and attitudes which quite conceivably may have greater educational values than the knowledge which might be acquired by other methods in the same amount of time.

Investigations of the relative merits of discussion and other teaching devices, notably the lecture method, as means of imparting information in different fields of thought, do not indicate any unanimity of opinion. It seems reasonable to conclude that the experiences and predilections of the teacher, the nature of the subject matter, and the type of group being taught will determine the answer to this question. Lecture and discussion may be, of course, and commonly are used as complementary methods in teaching. More is said about this in Chapter XIV.

D. Value as a Policy-Determining Technique.

By an action group is meant simply one whose primary responsibility is the determination of programs and policies which may be used as a basis for action. Most committees, boards of directors, and legislative bodies of all sorts, large and small, are examples of such groups. The traditional method of the action or policy-determining group is that of parliamentary debate conducted under the time-honored rules of parliamentary procedure. It should be emphasized here that such deliberation is not discussion in the sense in which we have defined the term. It is debate. As a matter of fact, such legislative debate is by all odds the most common and the most significant kind of debate.

An action group, unlike most learning groups, must reach some decision which the group is willing to accept as the basis for action. Failing in this, it has failed in the very purpose for which it was created. Under the rules of parliamentary debate a majority vote is usually taken as the will of the group. The discussion method, on the other hand, achieves a basis for action only through group consensus, except where special procedures are invoked. Herein lies the practical weakness of the method so far as the policy-determining group is concerned. Anyone who has had the slightest experience with such groups knows how easy it is for the proceedings to reach an impasse unless the rule of the majority is invoked.

Notwithstanding this weakness, the discussion approach has a much wider application in this field than is commonly realized. In the small, closely knit policy-determining body, where the members of the group are accustomed to cooperative procedures, it is often possible to reach a working consensus through discussion. In such groups it is at least wise to make the attempt before drawing the battle lines in formal motions and votes. The practical values of an action program cooperatively achieved recommend the effort in this direction. Group harmony, an understanding of the program which comes from having a hand in its making, and enthusiastic cooperation in the execution of the plan are the important dividends. Special suggestions for the use of discussion methods in policy-determining groups are given in Chapter XV.

E. Esthetic and Therapeutic Values.

We would be remiss not to observe that discussion in many situations offers a pleasant intellectual experience of some esthetic value. There are possibilities for artistic satisfactions in lively, stimulating discussion which have values in and of themselves. Informal discussion is a close neighbor to social conversation. In the hands of good conversationalists discussion can be deft, sparkling, and witty, as well as penetrating and informational. It stimulates thought and provides the opportunity for the expression of this thought, an experience which is not wholly without its own rewards.

As a means of getting people who believe differently to talk together and to arrive at understandings (if not agreements), discussion helps greatly in building up healthy mental attitudes. It acts to relieve tension, to increase sociability, and to make for wider and deeper appreciation of one's own beliefs and feelings in relation to those of others. By developing habits of reflective thinking and cooperation it serves as a helpful therapeutic to dogmatism, prejudice, introversion, and other factors which often contribute to emotional instability.

F. SOCIAL VALUES.

We have already pointed out the relations of discussion to a democratic society. Most of its values, social and otherwise, find their focus here. Professor Bryson develops this thesis in his lecture "Discussion in the Democratic Process" which appears in Appendix D of this book. He concludes, "If democracy has become difficult we can make it work only by clarifying the process which is its essence." *That process is discussion!*

II. THE LIMITATIONS OF DISCUSSION

A. LIMITATIONS IMPOSED BY PERSONS.

If discussion is to lay claim to democratic values it must suffer the limitations which democracy imposes. General participation means the inclusion of mediocrity in both intelligence and language competence. While groups can be constituted in such a way as to minimize the difficulty, the problem is nevertheless inherent in the method. Individual differences are inevitable no matter how the groups are selected; what is more, any rigorous attempt at homogeneous grouping will in itself vitiate many of the democratic claims of discussion.

Those who like quick action, order, precision, and efficiency will at times be impatient with discussion. At its worst it can be exasperatingly slow, pedestrian, confused, and dull; and even at its best it must be admitted that the seeds of these problems are ever present. The primary purpose of a study of the principles and methods of discussion is to develop knowledge, attitudes, and skills which will make the process as efficient as possible.

The ultimate alternative of the democratic process is the dictatorial and authoritarian method. Such a method in the hands of honest, enlightened individuals has certain advantages. It moves more rapidly and usually more efficiently, at least from the standpoint of immediate results. But it too presents difficulties, dangers of a different sort for both learning and action groups. In both cases it may sacrifice the integrity of the individual and leave him open to exploitation by those who are not honest and enlightened.

B. Limitations Imposed by Method.

We have defined and explained discussion as group-thought in process. Discussion methods, we have said, are designed to foster situations favorable to creative group thinking. If we accept this conception realistically, we must here again recognize the limitations which it imposes. Introspect your own reflective processes at their best. Are they orderly? Are they sure and definite? Do they make uninterrupted progress toward a clear objective? Seldom is this the case. Is it likely, then, that a group which is faced with the additional problem of communicating thought can avoid these same difficulties? Reflective thinking is not easy. It involves trial and error; we find ourselves in blind alleys and have to retrace our steps; ideas which hit us at the moment may be nebulous in conception and difficult of expression, but if they appear to be productive they must be nurtured and developed. Periods of maturation and plateaus in which little progress is made are inevitable in group thinking just as they are in individual thinking. For these reasons even good discussion is apt to lack the polish and sureness of movement which one has reason to expect of a finished piece of thought of any kind.

If discussion is to be condemned on this basis, however, so must we condemn all reflective thought and all creative processes. This does not mean that hesitation and confusion are to be taken as signs of good discussion, nor does it mean that we should not seek methods which will obviate these difficulties so far as it is possible to do so. The important thing is that we clearly understand that discussion is not and does not pretend to be a finished, completed result of thought which people can stand off and admire; the main purpose of discussion is to provide a working situation in which people can tackle vital life problems. It is only fair that it be judged by standards of thought and language applicable to this kind of use.

The *method* of discussion admittedly limits its usefulness in many situations where speech must play a part. The mass meeting, the political rally, large group gatherings of all kinds where the spirit is high, where action is demanded, or where the group is not ready or prepared to deliberate, do not lend themselves to discussion. Here is where persuasion finds its full play and social usefulness. As pointed out in Chapter I, discussion and persuasion are often complementary processes; discussion may be used in the small planning group, but when the results of these deliberations have to be carried over to the larger public, persuasive techniques will often be the only practical method of getting results. Persuasion, *properly understood and employed*, is an essential aspect of large-scale democracy.

C. Limitations Imposed by Matter.

All reflective thinking has its inception in problems, but not all problems by any means lend themselves to profitable discussion. The nature of the problem, the persons involved in the problem, and the time available for its solution are all relevant to the success with which discussion may be applied and the wisdom of its use.

In Chapter V we shall point out the kinds of problems in which discussion has special value. We may say here, however, that it has definite limitations in dealing with questions of fact. Facts may be worked over, clarified, and interpreted in conversation, but they can seldom be discovered by conversation. This does not mean that good discussion can get along without facts. Nothing is further from the truth. It means rather that discussion must rely on facts which are brought in by members of the group, facts which have been got by direct observation, by practical experience, and by experimentation. These are the methods by which we tackle nature directly and wrest therefrom the facts and materials which must continually be forthcoming if discussion and deliberation by and large are to escape stagnation and sterility.

Scientific method and discussion are in a very real sense complementary processes. Scientific method supplies the facts; discussion interprets and applies these facts in questions of value and practical policy in the realm of social, economic, and political affairs. The scientist may discover that a certain combination of chemicals will produce the most powerful explosive man has ever known, but when it comes to deciding whether or not this should be used as an instrument of warfare, in his capacity as chemist he does not pretend to be able to give an answer. While honesty and intelligence are surely as important to civilization in determining whether or not this explosive is to be used to blow up men and nations as it is in the discovery of the explosive, the fact remains that questions such as these seldom receive the same objective treatment. However difficult it may be, discussion as we are studying it attempts to take a step in that direction.

We have spoken of the limitations of discussion in dealing with questions of fact. There are further limitations which apply in the case of questions of value and policy. Not all such problems can safely or wisely be submitted to group deliberation and decision. Consider, for example, the relationships between parent and child, teacher and student, employer and employee, and so on through the whole gamut of human experience. Do not these relationships commonly present problems which must be handled directly by the parent, the teacher, the employer, or whatever responsible person is in authority? The question presents a tremendously difficult and dangerous dilemma. If you answer it affirmatively, you run the risk of sanctioning an undesirable extension of authority and domination in these relationships. If you answer it negatively, you are apt to deny a proper place to the ability and maturity of judgment which responsible authority should carry. The truth of the matter is, it is probably impossible to answer this question helpfully in the abstract; it depends upon circumstances, cases, and individuals. Whatever the answer may be, however (and it appears to lie somewhere between the two extremes), we are disposed to affirm our faith in the capacity of the group to work out its own problems in more situations than is commonly allowed, if given the proper kind of opportunity. In Chapter IX we shall consider ways and means of employing the best expert opinion and the most mature judgment in the process of group deliberation without sacrificing democratic decision.

D. Limitations Imposed by Time.

Action cannot always wait on group deliberation. "For when there is panic in the air, with one crisis tripping over the heels of another, actual dangers mixed with imaginary scares, there is no chance at all for the constructive use of reason, and any order soon seems preferable to any disorder."[4] An emergency may be a matter of hours, and discussion requires time. In such situations quick persuasion or even commands and force may have

[4] Walter Lippmann, *Public Opinion* (New York: Harcourt, Brace and Company, 1922), p. 414.

to supplant deliberation. The dangers lie in "imaginary scares" and trumped-up emergencies which are used as an excuse for short-circuiting the critical process, and in the difficulty of regaining democratic privileges once surrendered.

EXERCISES

1. To what extent can the problems arising in parent and child, teacher and student, employer and employee relationships be handled democratically? What role can discussion play in this process?
2. Display a picture which involves considerable detail in color and design. Observe this picture carefully for two or three minutes and then make a list of the items which you observed, all the detailed aspects of the picture of every kind which you can recall. Put these lists aside and discuss the picture as a group, itemizing as many details as possible. Then compare the group report with the individual reports. Is any individual report superior to the group report in the number of items observed and in the accuracy of observation?
3. Discuss the lecture on "Discussion in the Democratic Process" (Appendix D) in relation to the values and limitations of discussion set forth in this chapter.
4. Conduct a class discussion on the problem: What form of student government should this college adopt? Think this problem through carefully before coming to class (it may be wise to prepare a discussion outline; see Chapter VI), appoint a leader, and conduct the discussion on a face-to-face basis following the steps in reflective thinking.

SELECTED BIBLIOGRAPHY

Bennett, H. Arnold, "Limits of the Discussion Method," *Educational Method.* Vol. 10, November, 1930, pp. 104-109.

Bryson, Lyman, "The Limits of Discussion," *Journal of Adult Education.* Vol. IX, No. 3, June, 1937, pp. 261-264.

Elliott, Harrison S., *The Process of Group Thinking.* New York: Association Press, 1932. Chapter II.

McKean, Dayton D., "Debate or Conference," *Quarterly Journal of Speech.* Vol. XX, April, 1934, pp. 223-236.

Morgan, Rita, "The Technique of Cooperation," *Quarterly Journal of Speech.* Vol. XX, April, 1934, pp. 236-241.

Mueller, A. D., *Principles and Methods in Adult Education.* New York: Prentice-Hall, Inc., 1937. Chapter VI.

Needham, I. B., "Uses and Limitations of the Discussion Method," *Journal of Home Economics.* Vol. 27, 1935, p. 514.

Sheffield, Alfred Dwight, *Creative Discussion* (2d ed., rev.). New York: Association Press, 1927. Pp. 50-53.

CHAPTER IV

OCCASIONS FOR DISCUSSION

I. TYPES OF OCCASIONS WHERE DISCUSSION IS USEFUL

In classifying occasions for discussion it is helpful to distinguish large and small learning groups and large and small action groups. This classification will have value in the explanation of special methods for these groups in later chapters.

A. TYPES OF LEARNING GROUPS.

Discussion is probably best adapted to small learning groups such as classes, study clubs, seminars, and informal group meetings of the occasional type. Here, as we have said, the purpose of the discussion is the development of the individual members in socially desirable skills and attitudes and the acquisition of knowledge about the question under consideration. Where physical conditions permit, the best organization for such groups is on the face-to-face basis.

In groups such as these, discussion has a wide application in the teaching of specific subject-matter fields. Many classes in history, social problems, philosophy, and literature can and do employ the discussion approach. Seminars in all fields of study are usually conducted on the discussion basis. Here the group deals with reports on specialized problems followed by critical discussion of the methods, materials, and conclusions of the report. Study clubs of all sorts, interested in book reviews, art, literature, and contemporary social, economic, and political problems, find values in discussion for their programs.

Much is being said today in the field of professional education about the activity or integrated curriculum. Many elementary schools, some secondary schools, and a few colleges are modifying their traditional programs in terms of these newer conceptions. Without any attempt to appraise this development here, it is important to take notice of the integral part which discussion plays in this type of curriculum. An integrated activity program is organized in terms of large areas of interest or core fields, such, for example, as the social sciences, thus breaking down departmental lines and course divisions as we commonly know them. Within such an area the work of the group is organized around problems and student activities growing out of these projects. Discussion operates in any such program at its most central and crucial point, the point where the problem is being determined and analyzed, and the activity is being planned. The situation calls for cooperative group discussion, and the success of the activity, indeed the values of the entire program, cannot help but be importantly conditioned by the nature and method of the deliberations which take place.

Large learning groups of thirty, a hundred, five hundred, or more people also present occasions on which discussion can be used if special adaptations are made. The size of the group necessitates a co-acting organization, and the typical procedures, as we have seen, are the dialogue, panel, symposium, or lecture followed by open-forum discussion. In many large, regularly scheduled classes these procedures or some variation of them are displacing the traditional lecture method. Occasional meetings of large learning groups are usually organized as institutes or conferences. Such meetings are often held over a period of two or three days or even a week or two weeks. Usually some special problem or theme is adopted for consideration. While the older institutes were largely speechmaking affairs with the prospective learner in the role of listener, the more progressive conferences today seek to provide active participation for all. Often this can be accomplished by alternating small group discussions with general conference meetings and by providing some opportunity for audience participation in the general meetings.

B. Types of Policy-Determining Groups.

Committees and boards of one kind or another constitute the typical policy-determining group. With a membership of from three to twelve persons, these bodies are usually appointed or elected by some larger group and charged with special duties. In the case of committees, these duties may consist in attention to some phase of regular business over a long period of time (standing committee), or to a specific task to be performed and reported back to the group (special committee). Their function commonly combines investigation and the recommendation of policy based on their findings. Examples of policy-determining boards are boards of county commissioners, school boards, trustees, and the boards of directors of business and commercial concerns.

The legislative assembly is the best example of the large policy-determining group. It is exemplified in our state legislatures and national Congress. To an increasing extent the work of such assemblies has been delegated to committees, with most of the important policy-determining discussion taking place in these smaller groups. Legislative debate under parliamentary procedure, however, remains the usual method of the assembly.

The convention is another type of action group. While conventions are often conducted on the institute or conference plan, and consist largely of an instructional program, they usually attempt to pass on at least a few plans and policies. In this latter capacity they commonly proceed as legislative assemblies under parliamentary procedure. Here again a large part of the real policy-determining discussion is turned over to committees of special designation.

Groups charged with a special judicial function, such as our regularly constituted courts and arbitrational tribunals, are also situations in which discussion plays some part. Judicial debate is the time-honored procedure in our courts of adjudication, and some variation of this is commonly employed in cases of arbitration. Industrial disputes boards, agencies for collective bargaining, and other comparable tribunals vary considerably in their modes of procedure, but they too are for the most part modeled after the usual court room methods with such adaptations as are necessary. A recent tendency toward freer round-table discussion in dealing with industrial disputes in some trades and industries should be noted and may be regarded as salutary and progressive. It may be said in general that there is a growing field served by quasi-judicial tribunals in which cooperative discussion may well play a much larger part than it now assumes.

II. PHYSICAL EQUIPMENT FOR DISCUSSION

Physical surroundings and equipment mean more for discussion than is commonly appreciated. Often they set the atmosphere and determine the character of the discussion. Straight-backed chairs nailed to the floor in precise rows may warm the heart of the legendary schoolmaster, but the warming effect seldom gets as far as the occupants of the chairs. Fortunately, the requirements of a discussion group are modest and in most cases can be met easily and simply.

A. REQUIREMENTS OF FACE-TO-FACE GROUPS.

If the group is small enough to be seated around a table, this is probably the best arrangement for a face-to-face group. If the size of the group precludes com-

fortable seating space at the table for everyone, it is best
to dispense with the table and simply arrange the chairs
in a circle. In any event, the arrangement should be such
as to make each person feel that he is a part of what is
going on. Avoid end seats, corners, and stragglers; do
everything that is physically possible to bring each person into the discussion circle. Any experienced public
speaker knows how difficult it is to do much with an
audience that is scattered all over the room. These difficulties are even more acute in the discussion situation.
It is normal and natural for people to look at each other
when they are conversing. So far as it can be accomplished the seating should be arranged to make this
possible.

Care should also be taken to provide convenient facilities for the leader. It is of first importance that he be
seated within easy conversational range of every person
present and where he can face each member of the group
without difficulty. His place should be focal and accessible without being prominent in the sense of dominating
the group. The leader, after all, is a member of the
group; and while his duties require that he be placed
where he can handle the situation easily, it is a mistake
to remove him from the group any more than is necessary. A leader is very apt to find himself in the role of
a public speaker with his group as a nonparticipating
audience if he erects too many barriers between himself
and the others. Platforms, teachers' desks, speakers'
stands, and other such properties should ordinarily be
dispensed with for this reason. The leader should be
provided with simple facilities for taking such notes as
he cares to make and be seated where he can lead the
discussion as a member of the group.

Under most circumstances it should not be difficult to
secure these simple accommodations for a discussion
group. If an informal, congenial room with reasonably
comfortable chairs can be added to these specifications,

experience has shown that it will pay dividends in the quality of the discussion.

B. Requirements of Co-acting Groups.

Where the size of the group prohibits the face-to-face arrangement, the ordinary facilities of a good auditorium, lecture room, or classroom will serve for discussion. It should be emphasized again that these facilities are not ideal for discussion and should be resorted to only when the size of the group necessitates them. Both the leader and the members of the panel or symposium should be seated in front of the group, preferably on a platform where they can be seen and heard easily. Special suggestions for the arrangement of panel and symposium speakers and their leaders are given in Chapter XVI. In Chapter XVII attention is given to the matter of handling discussion from the floor in the co-acting group.

III. ATMOSPHERE DESIRABLE FOR DISCUSSION

Informality, friendliness, and vitality best characterize the atmosphere desirable for discussion. While congenial physical surroundings can do much to provide this atmosphere, the spirit of the group as reflected in the attitudes of the members and the leader is unquestionably the most important factor. Undue formality, overly strict discipline, tension, and stiffness all militate against free discussion. Where these conditions exist, the ice must be broken if much is to be accomplished. Most groups will "unlimber" if given the opportunity and a little encouragement. The leader can do much in his handling of the situation to break down reserve. Sometimes a short explanation of what is expected of the group will help. In small face-to-face groups people should be made acquainted with one another. In large conferences one or more social meetings of an informal type can well be included on the program.

Such an atmosphere can be established without jeopardizing in any way the decorum and seriousness of purpose necessary to the discussion of important problems. A friendly, cooperative group spirit, as a matter of fact, is the most effective antidote against those who are disposed to take advantage of the situation. Group disapproval is more subtle in curbing undesirable behavior than is rigorous discipline exercised by the leader, and certainly much less disturbing to the deliberations of the group.

EXERCISES

1. Appoint a committee of three or four students interested in education to investigate the relations of discussion to Progressive Education, the committee to proceed as follows:
   a. Do individual reading on the subject in the literature of Progressive Education. Attempt to draw your own conclusions even though you do not find much material dealing directly with discussion.
   b. Meet to draw up the outline of the report. This report should be the product of group work and discussion. Consider questions such as these: What are the objectives and methods of Progressive Education? How do they compare with those of discussion? What is the nature of the Progressive curriculum? What part can discussion play in such a curriculum?
   c. Select a member of the committee to present the report to the class. Follow the report by a brief class discussion led by one of the other members of the committee.
2. Appoint a committee of three or four students interested in law to investigate the relations of discussion to legal and quasi-judicial tribunals.
   a. Proceed as in Exercise 1.
   b. Consider questions such as these: To what extent does discussion enter into our regular courts? How about the deliberations of the jury? To what extent is it feasible to establish agencies designed to handle disputes out of court, e.g., arbitration tribunals? How might discussion operate in such tribunals? What is

the procedure in industrial disputes boards, boards of mediation, and the like? What are the possibilities of discussion in employer-employee relationships?

3. What are the physical advantages and limitations for discussion of the room in which this class meets?

4. What occasions for discussion now exist or might profitably be developed in your fraternity or residence hall? On your college campus? In your home community? Make this exercise the basis for a systematic survey of your college community in terms of the discussion facilities now available. Arrange to visit and observe these discussion groups or forums.

SELECTED BIBLIOGRAPHY

Columbia Associates in Philosophy, *An Introduction to Reflective Thinking*. Boston: Houghton Mifflin Company, 1923. Chapter XI.

Coyle, Grace L., *Social Process in Organized Groups*. New York: R. R. Smith, Inc., 1930. Chapters I, II, III, and VIII.

Dewey, John, *Philosophy and Civilization*. New York: Minton, Balch and Company, 1931. Pp. 126-141.

Follett, Mary P., *Creative Experience*. New York: Longmans, Green and Company, 1924. Chapters II, XIV, XV, XVI, and XVII.

Follett, Mary P., *The New State*. New York: Longmans, Green and Company, 1926.

Lindeman, Eduard C., *Social Discovery*. New York: New Republic, Inc., 1925. Chapters VI, X, and XII.

Lindeman, Eduard C., *Social Education*. New York: New Republic, Inc., 1933. Chapters VI, VII, VIII, IX, X, XI, and XII.

Overstreet, H. A., *Influencing Human Behavior*. New York: W. W. Norton and Company, Inc., 1925. Chapter XIV.

CHAPTER V

PROBLEMS FOR DISCUSSION

I. TYPES OF PROBLEMS FOR DISCUSSION

The advocate begins his speech with a proposition. Either he has formulated a judgment which he wishes to present or he is called upon to defend a proposition which someone else has formulated for him. In any event, it is his task to win acceptance for a predetermined proposition. The discussion group begins with a problem or felt difficulty and undertakes the process of formulating a judgment. There are three general types of problems with which the student of discussion should be familiar, those of fact, value, and policy.

A. PROBLEMS OF FACT.

A factual problem raises the simple question: Is this true? It is probably safe to say that most questions of this type do not lend themselves to profitable discussion. It is futile and senseless to spend much time discussing a question which can be settled simply and accurately by observation, measurement, classification, or experimentation. If there is question about the average winter temperature in New Orleans or the distance between New York and Chicago, the best way to settle such problems is to take temperature readings and to measure the distance, or else consult authorities who have already done so.

It should not be concluded hastily, however, that discussion serves no useful purpose in dealing with factual problems. We have already mentioned the values of pooling findings and critical discussion of materials and methods. Especially is this true of questions of fact requiring extended investigation and research. Apart from specialized research in which discussion serves this auxiliary function, there are also some general questions of popular interest which lend themselves to discussion. Consider as an example the question: *Is the United States heading toward Fascism?* Here is a question of fact which presents several issues that can be deliberated upon by a group: *What is Fascism? What factors in the American scene can be called Fascistic? Are these factors on the increase? Are there counteracting influences?* These issues and others would need to be considered.

B. PROBLEMS OF VALUE.

If, instead of the average winter temperature in New Orleans or the distance between New York and Chicago, we were asked to consider whether New Orleans is a good place to spend a winter vacation, or whether the New York Central is the best route to take between New York and Chicago, we would have problems at least somewhat more amenable to discussion. These problems as stated raise questions of value, so characterized because they attempt to assess the goodness or badness or rightness or wrongness of persons or things. It is on this basis that they are to be distinguished from questions of fact into which this evaluative element does not enter.

If anyone wishes to determine whether New Orleans or any other place offers desirable winter vacation facilities, he is confronted with the necessity of determining first what constitutes desirable winter vacation facilities. Having made this decision, it is then possible to apply the standard to the case in question in terms of the available facts. In the matter of the travel route it would again be essential to set up standards before attempting to decide which is the best route. This setting up of standards commonly opens a wide range of personal preference which does not occur in the formulation of a factual judgment. This element of personal preference is implicit in all problems of value. In some cases, of course, standards are pretty well established and generally recognized, thus reducing the discretionary element; in others, because of the absence of accepted standards, they must be established out of a matrix of widely divergent opinion and feeling.

Discussion is a highly useful approach in the formulation of evaluative judgments. If such judgments are to be rationally made and rationally held, they must be submitted to the reflective processes. Where group preferences and group evaluations are involved, discussion serves a function that probably cannot be performed as well by any other method.

The following are examples of problems of value which have been used by discussion groups: *Is mercy killing justified? Are craft unions better than industrial unions? Is Japan justified in her attack on China? Did the United States make a mistake in recognizing Soviet Russia? Was Senator Black's appointment to the Supreme Court wise? Has the Federal Theater Project been helpful to the American theater? Is the sit-down strike justifiable?*

C. PROBLEMS OF POLICY.

The most usual and probably the most valuable problems for discussion are those of policy. Here the typical question raised is: What should be done? or, Should this action be taken? Policy-determining groups are concerned solely with questions of policy and it is the type of question most frequently considered by learning groups.

It should be noted that problems of policy are closely related to those of value and fact. Policy judgments must of necessity be premised on factual and evaluative judgments. For example, consider the question: *What would constitute a desirable reconciliation between the American Federation of Labor and the Committee for Industrial Organization?* It would be necessary here to assess the values of the aims and purposes of both these organizations, and to determine the factual question: What have been their accomplishments thus far? In other words, the discussion of a question of policy involves the group selection, determination, and interpretation of those factual and evaluative factors which enter into the policy under consideration. A course of action is decided upon in terms of the facts and values involved in the situation. Discussion assists in this process by assembling the facts, assessing the values, and interpreting both facts and values in such a way as to enable the group to make an intelligent decision on policy.

Problems of policy may be raised for discussion at two different levels, that of a general problem area and that of a specific solution. A group may discuss what course of action the United States should take in the present Sino-Japanese conflict, or some specific proposal for our action in the controversy, such as invoking the neutrality act recently passed by Congress. It can discuss ways to world peace, or some definite proposal such as the League of Nations. The nature of the problem and the interests of the group should determine the level at which any question of policy should be approached. Sometimes there are advantages in discussing a particular solution. If some such proposal occupies the center of attention, is pending adoption, or is of special interest to the group, it may be wise so to phrase the problem. On the other hand, there is real danger in directing the discussion toward a specific proposal prematurely. It is apt to prejudice the group and may also serve to divide it into affirmative and negative camps in such a way as to make cooperative discussion exceedingly difficult. Careful analysis of the problem followed by the deliberation of possible solutions to the problem is the desirable procedure in discussing questions of policy no matter how they are phrased. Since questions raised on the level of a general problem area lend themselves to this approach more easily and naturally than those in which some one proposal is singled out, it seems wise generally to phrase policy questions this way unless there is some special reason for doing otherwise.

II. ENCOUNTERING OR SELECTING THE PROBLEM

Having analyzed the types of problems for discussion, we turn to the questions: How are the problems for discussion determined? How are they encountered or selected? Why is it that some groups have trouble finding enough time to deliberate adequately the many problems which present themselves and others appear to have just about as much trouble finding something to talk about? The answer lies in part at least in the nature and function of the group. In the case of the action or policy-determining group, the problems for discussion usually present themselves in the ordinary course of the business with which the group is concerned. Committees, boards of directors, and the like seldom have to look around for something to talk about. The problems are implicit in the work of the group, and they are met and deliberated upon as they arise or as they appear to require the attention of the group. The only realistic justification for the creation or continuance of any action group is the existence of immediate or potential problems with which they can and should deal.

Groups assembled for the purpose of learning, on the other hand, commonly determine their problems for discussion by deliberate selection. A community forum or a discussion class, for example, often must cast around for those questions which seem most suitable for their purposes. While the necessity for selection in this manner cannot be wholly obviated, there is much to be said in favor of setting up a learning program in such a way that problems will be encountered in the process of learning very much as they are in the case of the action group. Such problems almost always give rise to better motivated, and consequently, to more stimulating and profitable discussion than do those subjects which are dug up and dusted off for the occasion. This is probably the best answer to the problem of determining the question for discussion. Wherever possible, avoid the necessity of arbitrary and artificial selection by adopting a field of study which presents its own problems. In this way the questions for discussion will arise naturally and normally from the activities of the group.

III. REQUIREMENTS OF A GOOD DISCUSSION QUESTION

No matter how the problems to be discussed are encountered or selected, there are a number of simple specifications for discussion questions which should be observed.

A. INTERESTS OF THE GROUP.

First of all, the question for discussion should be one that people want to talk about, one that is close to the real, vital problems with which they are concerned. While all sorts of considerations may enter into the selection of the question, it is certainly sound psychological advice to "take off" from the interests of those who are expected to do the discussing. It should normally be a question on which members of the group have opinions and feeling, one that is likely to strike fire because of its very vitality. Do not avoid a subject because it is controversial; rational difference is the lifeblood of significant discussion. On the other hand, do not go out of your way to secure bizarre topics or those which are apt to stir up needless difficulty. There is no inherent merit in controversy except as it represents a frank and genuine confrontation of opinions on issues which ought to be faced squarely. Discussion of matters which are not important and realistically significant to the group, if the leader is able to get any discussion on such subjects, is invariably forced, desultory, and inconsequential.

The suggestion that questions for discussion be kept within the interests of the group often draws the objection that this is likely to limit seriously the possible selections. Granting that this may be the case with certain groups, it still holds that problems outside the circle of interests of the participants cannot be expected to elicit stimulating discussion. By all means, work to widen, deepen, and enrich these interests, but begin with existing interests. Discussion is a helpful way of bringing about these enlarged horizons. A series of discussion meetings will often lead from the more immediate and sometimes superficial aspects of living to an extended perspective which invites reflection on fundamental values and policies.

B. Capacities of the Group.

The capacities of the individuals composing the group should also be considered. We have reference here both to capacity for discussion and to capacity for reflective thinking, which, in the light of what we have already said, may be seen to be closely related. As in the case of interest, discussion can be a means of developing powers of reflective deliberation, but the composition of the group in terms of age and intelligence must nevertheless be a determining factor in selecting questions for discussion.

C. Knowledge of the Group.

Closely related and equally important in this connection is the knowledge of the group. Regardless of interest and capacity, people cannot be expected to make significant contributions or be expected to get much out of a discussion where they know little or nothing about the question. Only ignorance and misunderstanding can result from misinformation or no information. To be sure, the pooled contributions of the group may add to the general store of knowledge, but pooled ignorance can hardly be helpful to anyone. When we speak of knowledge, however, it should be understood that we do not necessarily mean technical, abstruse, or sophisticated information. There are countless problems which can be considered profitably in the light of the most homely philosophies and simple experiences, problems dealing with immediate personal relationships, community, state, and national affairs, which most mature persons have experienced and about which they have ideas. Problems such as these can ordinarily be approached by a group of laymen in terms of their own experiences with profit to both the individual and the group. To the extent that expert information is needed, it can and should be secured either by special investigations or by calling in a qualified expert. On the other hand, questions of a specialized nature, regardless of the field, should be approached only in those cases in which the group has substantial information about them. Nothing can do more damage to the cause of discussion than to assemble a group of people to talk about something that they know little or nothing about. What is more, there is a real danger that the participants in such affairs will establish unfortunate habits

of reasoning and of approaching problems on the basis of
flimsy and inadequate information.

D. Purposes of the Group.

In so far as selection is exercised in determining questions for discussion, certainly a criterion of importance
is the purpose of the group. Is it the purpose of the discussion to develop understanding and information concerning a specific body of knowledge? Is it the primary
purpose to provide experiences in cooperative group
thinking and speaking? Is it the purpose to develop group
esprit de corps and congenial contacts? In any event,
know what the purpose or purposes of the discussion
are and choose the question that will best serve the end
in view. Be sure, however, that it is the group purpose
that is being served and not that of someone who wishes
to *use* discussion to accomplish his own ends. The best
way to avoid such perversions is frankness and honesty
in the consideration of purposes. The group has not only
a right but an obligation to insist on such frankness and
honesty. Discussion is not immune to manipulation, and
one way to circumvent the method is to substitute ul-
terior purposes for the real group purposes in determining the problems to be discussed.

E. Preferences of the Group.

It follows from what we have said that it is generally
wise to consult the wishes of the group in choosing the
questions for discussion, in so far as a deliberate choice
needs to be exercised. Certainly it is unwise and out of
harmony with the whole spirit of discussion to be dictatorial in this matter. While guidance and advice from
the leader or some responsible person are necessary with
many groups, especially immature or beginning learning
groups, they should be encouraged to make their own
decision in the matter of choosing the problem as well as
in other matters which arise during the course of the
discussion.

IV. PHRASING THE QUESTION

A. USE THE QUESTION FORM.

Questions for debate are usually stated as propositions, resolutions, or motions. The best way to state a problem for discussion is in the form of a question phrased as a complete sentence. A question tends to start the discussion off in the pattern of reflective thinking more easily and naturally than will any other form of statement. It invites inquiry rather than dogmatic assertion, avoids any appearance of prejudice in advance, implies the necessity of diagnosis before prescription, and tends to arouse attention and interest. Moreover, as we have said, the question should be phrased as a complete sentence. Fragmentary expressions or terms such as *War or Peace?*, *The Farmers' Plight*, *Whither America?*, or *Fascism* are not in and of themselves discussible matters. The adoption of a mere term as a subject for discussion is both logically and psychologically bad. It fails to raise a clear issue, if any issue at all, and, as might be expected as a corollary of this, it invariably fails to elicit discussion. The inevitable result is considerable milling around and lost effort which is shaped into constructive deliberation only when someone is wise enough or sufficiently fortunate to get some issue stated and opened up for discussion.

B. DELIMIT THE FIELD OF DISCUSSION.

The question for discussion should be as clearly indicative of the area for discussion as possible. In other words, it should state the problem for discussion as clearly and accurately as it can be done in advance of the discussion and thereby indicate what is expected of the group. It should be emphasized, however, that there is nothing, under ordinary circumstances at least, to prevent the group from modifying this statement during the progress of the discussion if it seems wise to do so. Here is another respect in which discussion differs from debate. In most debates it would be sheer heresy to attempt any change in the proposition after the debate started. This often results in much sparring over terms and minute, legalistic interpretations and definitions designed to secure a strategic advantage which, fortunately, can be avoided in discussion. While it is unwise indiscriminately to alter the question for discussion, it certainly is not unreasonable to expect that the problem can be conceived more clearly after some deliberation. As a matter of fact, the first step in reflective thinking normally consists in an attempt to define and delimit the problem. If it seems wise to modify the original question in the light of this preliminary reflection, by all means do so. There is surely nothing to be gained by proceeding with an inadequate statement merely because it happens to be the one given to the group at the outset.

V. PROBLEMS FOR DISCUSSION

A recent survey of the United States Office of Education (in which questionnaires from two hundred forums had been returned at the time of this report)[1] indicates that the five most popular general areas of discussion during the fall of 1934 and the spring of 1935 were the international situation, economic recovery, fascism and war, New Deal legislation, and liberty and democracy. The following are some of the problems discussed in the demonstration forum centers sponsored by the Office of Education:[2]

Must the West Get Out of the East?
Where Will Our "Good Neighbor" Policy Lead Us?
How Can We Buy More Goods?
What Is the Place of Women in Industry, Business, and the Professions?
Should the Power of the Supreme Court Be Curbed?

[1] See *School Life*, April, 1936; reprint with additional information available at the United States Office of Education, Washington, D. C.
[2] See *A Step Forward for Adult Civic Education: The Story of Ten Forum Demonstration Centers*. United States Department of Interior, Office of Education, Bulletin No. 16, 1936, pp. 24-26.

Should the United States Maintain Strict Neutrality in all
  Future Wars?
Is War Inevitable?
Is the New Deal Socialistic?
Do We Need a New Political Party?
Should We Establish a System of Government-Supported
  Medical Care?
Should Capital Punishment Be Abolished?
Can a Democracy Plan Its Economic Life?
Should the Nations of the Western Hemisphere Found a
  League of Nations?
Is Propaganda a Menace?
Did the United States Make a Mistake in Recognizing
  Russia?
What Should Be the Place of Consumers' Cooperatives in
  the United States?
Should Organized Lobbying Be Prohibited?
Is the Townsend Plan Practicable?
Do We Pay Our Executives too Much?
Do Company Unions Help Labor?
Is a Labor Party Desirable?
Are Free Speech, Free Press, and Free Assemblage in Danger
  in America?
Has the South Hurt New England?
Who Are the War Makers?
1914 versus 1937—Is the Danger of War as Great Today
  as Then?
What Is Society's Duty to the Unfortunate?
Why Do We Have Depressions?
Can We Make Private Industry Self-Regulating?
Can We Manage Money and Credit?
Will Unstable Government Budgets Stabilize Business?
Can Government Service be Made a Career?
Is Public Utility Regulation a Failure?
What Happens When Government Goes into Business?
What Is America's Role in World Affairs?
What Are the Underlying Causes of Fascism and Bolshe-
  vism?
Do We Need a New Liberal Party?
What Constitutes Capacity to Pay Taxes?
What Is the Status of Women in Germany and Russia?

Is Government Participation Desirable in the Housing Problem?

What Is the Role of the Family in Developing Democracy?

What Can Be Done about the Southern Sharecropper Problem?

While social, political, and economic questions are decidedly in the majority in this list, there is no reason why discussion needs to be confined to problems in these fields. Questions for discussion can be raised in the fields of religion, art, music, literature, science, education, in short, wherever problems of interest to the group exist. Interesting and profitable discussion can be organized on questions relative to specific books, plays, motion pictures, and works of art. Policy-determining groups, of course, encounter problems for deliberation of every conceivable kind and variety in terms of the business with which they are concerned.

EXERCISES

1. Phrase a question for discussion on some recent book you have read. State the question in such a way that it will raise for discussion what you consider to be the most significant contribution of the book.
2. Take the current issue of some magazine such as *Harpers* or the *New Republic* and see how many good questions for discussion you can phrase in terms of the problems discussed in the magazine.
3. Phrase a suitable question for discussion in each of the following fields: music, art, literature, science, philosophy, economics, history, psychology, journalism, sociology, political science. Add to your list representative questions in as many other fields as possible.
4. Phrase a suitable question of policy on the level of a general problem area and another on the level of a specific solution or proposal for each of the following subjects: school policy relative to play production, intercollegiate athletics, the school paper, the grading system, library regulations, student housing, student-faculty relations, student government.

5. Phrase questions of fact, value, and policy in any two of the fields listed in Exercise 3. Phrase them in such a way that they deal as nearly as possible with the same general problem in each case and yet illustrate the three types of questions.

6. Work out a series of discussion questions in some field or area of interest. Try to make these questions suitable for the study of a given field over a period of time through the means of several discussions. Take some such general field as international relations, labor problems, agricultural problems, or money and banking. Select the field which you think the class might most profitably consider.

SELECTED BIBLIOGRAPHY

Burtt, Edwin Arthur, *Principles and Problems of Right Thinking*. New York: Harper and Brothers, 1928. Chapter XIV.

Evans, D. Luther, and Gamertsfelder, Walter S., *Logic, Theoretical and Applied*. New York: Doubleday, Doran and Company, Inc., 1937. Chapter VI.

O'Neill, James M., and McBurney, James H., *The Working Principles of Argument*. New York: The Macmillan Company, 1932. Chapter II.

CHAPTER VI

PREPARING FOR DISCUSSION

I. HOW MUCH PREPARATION IS NEEDED?

There is no such thing as too much preparation for discussion. The more that is known about the problem by the members of the group, other things being equal, the better and more profitable will be the discussion from every point of view. When we say that discussion is "thought in process" or the constructive thinking of groups, we do not mean to imply that the group should approach the problem without any previous study or thought. To be sure, it is a mistake to come to a discussion with the idea of fighting for some predetermined conclusion, but there is no reason why careful preparatory study needs to have this result. If you reach conclusions as a result of your preparation, hold them tentatively and report them tentatively, subject to any change which may be indicated by the deliberations of the group. In other words, do as much thinking and studying on the problem as is reasonably possible, and then come to the discussion prepared to "rethink" with the other members of the group. The contribution of discussion comes in this rethinking process in the way of a clarification, refinement, and integration of ideas. What is more, it presents an opportunity for new and original thinking which carries the group beyond the point reached by any individual in his preparation.

This does not mean that a person needs to be an authority on a subject before he attempts to discuss it with others. There are obviously many situations for discussion in which it is unreasonable to expect much direct preparation. This is often the case in public forums and occasional groups which are not a part of some regular program or curriculum. We do not mean to imply that such groups serve no useful purpose. They offer opportunities for acquiring additional information, and what is more important, the chance for people to share experiences in such a way as to produce better understanding and more tolerant attitudes. Especially is this true where the problems approached are those with which the members of the group have had considerable experience and on which they have done some general reading.

Our point here has been to emphasize again the danger of superficiality and mere talk. It is on this score that discussion is most often attacked. For these reasons we are disposed to emphasize the values of preparation and to set forth ways and means of getting ready for discussion which may be used when and where they have an application.

II. WHAT KIND OF PREPARATION IS NEEDED?

A. DIRECT AND INDIRECT PREPARATION.

A distinction between direct and indirect preparation will enable us further to clarify our position in the matter of preparing for discussion. By direct preparation we mean that study and thought which are undertaken in terms of a specific problem for a specific occasion. We shall discuss such a method in this chapter. Indirect preparation consists of general knowledge and experience which may be brought to bear on the problem without having been assembled or undertaken with any particular occasion in mind. The importance of such preparation for discussion cannot be overemphasized. The person who is active mentally day by day, reads widely, and in general keeps himself informed on the problems of the day is incomparably better prepared to take part in discussion than one who does not keep himself so informed. It is probably safe to say that no amount of direct preparation will compensate adequately for the meager background and limited perspective which come from a failure to establish regular reading habits.

Let us take a specific example. A student at Northwestern University has at his command a great library containing thousands of volumes with new books being added daily. The periodical reading room places at his disposal the leading magazines and newspapers from all over the world. The reference reading room, under the direction of a trained reference librarian, contains encyclopedias, dictionaries, statistical publications, and standard reference books in most fields of knowledge. The University, through the several Schools and Departments, brings to the campus each year a group of distinguished lecturers, leaders in the life and thought of the nation. The Y. M. C. A. and the Y. W. C. A. sponsor a series of class and all-university conferences in which contemporary problems are discussed by students, faculty, and guest lecturers and discussion leaders. This is not to mention the programs of many other groups and the regular course offerings of the various divisions of the University.

Facilities such as these are available in a greater or lesser degree to every college student in America. If you are a college student, plan your regular daily or weekly program in such a way that you can take advantage of a reasonable number of these opportunities. Readers of this book, presumably at least, are interested in improving their ability to take part in discussion. While there are values in the study and application of the principles and methods of discussion, any such study is bound to be limited and more or less barren unless those engaged in such a study have something to contribute in discussion. Apart from such direct preparation as may be made for the discussion of special problems, adopt now a systematic program designed to keep you apace with contemporary thought in the fields in which discussion most commonly takes place. The following may be taken as the minimum for such a program: (1) Read some good newspaper regularly; the *New York Times* is available in most college libraries. (2) Read regularly two magazines such as *Harpers* and the *New Republic*. (3) Read at least two general, nontechnical books in the field of economics, politics, or sociology each year. Your selections may be guided by the book review sections in the magazines and newspapers you are reading. (4) Attend at least once a month some lecture or public discussion in which current problems are being considered.

B. The Role of Reflective Thinking in Preparation.

The distinction which we have made between reflective thinking or constructive reasoning and intentional reasoning also has an application in the preparation for discussion. The advocate who has selected or has been given a definite proposition to defend usually spends his time searching for reasons and evidence which will support his particular thesis. If the circumstances of the case are such that he is committed to a specific proposition, there is not much else that he can do. Discussion, however, imposes no such commitments. The preparation for discussion can and should be conducted in the pattern of reflective thinking. Define and delimit the problem; analyze the problem; canvass the advantages and disadvantages of the different solutions; try to evolve a solution which seems most likely to meet the situation; and give thought to ways and means of putting this solution into operation. In terms of these steps, assemble the available information on the subject, read what others have written about it, talk it over with those who have had some experience with the problem, and what is perhaps most important, bring your own reflective powers to bear on the problem.

The application of reflective thinking in preparing for discussion will be aided by the following suggestions for study:

1. *Adopt a Tentative Rather Than a Fixed Attitude toward Knowledge.*—Do not investigate a problem with the idea of validating certain preconceived notions about it. Keep your mind open. Be prepared to abandon conceptions which are not borne out by the facts. Be willing to entertain new ideas if they appear to be indicated by your study. There is a very human tendency to attempt to adapt the facts and views of others in such a way as to make them appear to conform to some pet ideology or pattern of ideas of your own. Guard yourself against this tendency. Make an effort to be fair and objective in your study.

2. *Judge the Soundness and General Worth of Statements.*—Adopt a sound, critical attitude in your study. Not everything that is printed or spoken from a public platform can be accepted by thinking persons. Give careful consideration to what is said, but do not feel obligated to accept it merely because you found it in a book. Guard the integrity of your own convictions and ideals. Be willing to entertain ideas with which you do not agree and try to understand them, but adopt them only when

you are convinced of their soundness and general worth.

While it is wise to adopt a cautious, questioning attitude, do not try to set yourself up as a judge in fields where you are not competent to judge. Be willing to grant a reasonable presumption at least to an expert or specialist when he is writing or speaking in his own field. It is no mark of intelligence to criticize or object simply for the sake of objecting. As a matter of fact, it is one of the surest ways of making a nuisance out of yourself.

3. *Turn to Yourself First When Reflective Thought Is Required.*—When confronted with a problem, make an attempt to think it through for yourself before turning to others. This practice has the advantage of bringing to bear on the matter all of your own experiences and serves at the same time to give direction to your further study of the problem. It is a poor economy of time and effort to start investigating a problem without first getting it as thoroughly in mind and as much of a perspective on it as is possible through your own reflective consideration.

4. *Organize and Systematize Your Study.*—Perhaps the best way to organize the investigation of a problem is to follow the steps in reflective thinking. The following section presents suggestions for preparing a discussion outline which is planned in terms of these steps. Whether or not it seems advisable to record your investigation in written form, the several steps in the outline may well serve as guides to direct your study.

III. THE DISCUSSION OUTLINE

A. Purposes and Uses of the Discussion Outline.

The discussion outline is designed to systematize and direct the preparation for discussion and to serve as a record of the preparation that has been made. Both the leader and the members of the group can profitably prepare such outlines. The making of the outline serves to stimulate investigation, clarify thinking, and prepare the individual to express his ideas in discussion with a minimum of confusion and lost effort. It serves to conserve the time and energy of the group and ordinarily paves the way for more productive group thinking.

The discussion outline should not be thought of as a speaker's outline or brief. Members of the group most certainly should not attempt to speak from such outlines nor should they feel bound by them in any way during the discussion. The outline has served its purpose if it has caused the individual to investigate the problem and do some thinking on it before the discussion takes place.

B. Specifications for Making Discussion Outlines.

Because of the nature and purpose of the discussion outline, there is no reason why it should be made to conform in all particulars to a set of hard and fast rules. On the other hand, the outline should not be a hit-and-miss, formless document if it is to serve a useful purpose. The greatest variation comes in the extent to which the reasoning is refined and factual material is included. Perhaps the best that we can say here is that the outline should be reasonably complete; at least, it should be sufficiently developed so that another person can follow the thinking recorded in the outline and see what materials have influenced the conclusions. Since the conferee will need to make himself understood in the discussion, it is not unreasonable to expect as much of the outline.

Begin the outline with a statement of the problem phrased as a complete sentence in question form. Make provision for five main divisions labeled as follows: I. Definition of the Problem; II. Analysis of the Problem; III. Possible Solutions; IV. Tentative Conclusion; V. Suggestions for Putting Solution into Operation. Using Roman numerals to designate these main divisions, indicate further subordination by capital letters, Arabic numerals, small letters, Roman numerals in parentheses, capital letters in parentheses, etc. Coordinate series of points should be indented consistently, and explanatory interpretations may be interpolated parenthetically as required to make the thought clear. Complete sentences should be used except in the headings of the five main divisions of the outline and in the citation of statistical material and other points where topical statement conveys the meaning adequately. The sources of the material should be given in complete bibliographical references entered in the margin of the outline, as footnotes, or stated parenthetically after the statements which are to be documented. Observe the following suggestions in developing the several divisions of the outline.

1. *Definition of the Problem.*—Include definitions of any terms appearing in the statement of the problem which seem to need clarification. Define also any terms appearing in the outline which might be misunderstood or misinterpreted. See Chapter X for an explanation of the methods of definition and their role in discussion.

2. *Analysis of the Problem.*—Analysis of the problem involves two steps which are usually closely related. These are a diagnosis of the problem in terms of effects and causes, and a consideration of the standards or criteria by which the proposed solutions may be evaluated. Here again it may be advisable to turn to Chapter X for a more complete discussion of these matters than is given in this section. Notice also the specimen outline included in this chapter.

Set forth the existing evils, effects, or symptoms of the problem together with such interpretations and evidences of these symptoms as have significantly affected your thinking. Follow this with a statement of the cause or causes of these symptoms as you understand them. Subordinate to the statement of each cause, give your reasons for believing it to be a cause and the factual materials upon which these reasons are based.

Next present a concise statement of the standard or standards which in your opinion should be considered in judging the possible solutions. While any proposal will, of course, be judged by the adequacy with which it solves the problem as diagnosed, it is advisable to give special attention to the formulation of reasonably definite criteria for this judgment. These standards should represent the values which you think are important in the situation and which should be conserved by the solution. For example, consider the question: *Should college athletes be paid?* Any one or some combination of the following statements might constitute standards for evaluating the possible solutions: We must preserve the amateur status of college athletics; we must do the thing that will give us the best teams, gate receipts, and athletic prestige for the college; intercollegiate athletic contests serve no important educational purpose of the college and might as well be abolished or at least greatly curtailed; the important thing is to get a set of rules governing amateur status which can and will be enforced honestly and impartially; I am a college athlete and wish to capitalize upon my athletic ability as much as possible. This list is by no means exhaustive, but it indicates what is meant by standards of evaluation, and should serve to make it clear how important it is that consideration be given to such matters before attempting to deliberate solutions. It is impossible to reach any realistic understanding of proposed solutions without understanding the purposes and values of those who propose the solutions. The presentation of these standards in the discussion outline should be accompanied by such interpretative material and evidence as appears to be necessary.

3. *Possible Solutions of the Problem.*—Set forth in this division of the outline the different solutions to the problem which you think merit consideration. This list should include the leading proposals which have been revealed by your investigation of the problem and which have entered into your thinking on the problem. Under each of these list briefly what you consider to be the chief advantages and disadvantages of the proposal. While these points do not need to be elaborated at length, they should be sufficient to indicate what your reaction is to each proposal and to give some explanation of this reaction.

4. *Tentative Conclusion.*—From the list of solutions presented in Section III of the outline, select and set forth here the one which you have tentatively concluded to be the most satisfactory proposal, the one which appears to deal with the causes of the problem most adequately and which measures up best in terms of the standards, criteria, or values which you believe to be important. This proposal should be developed in some detail in terms of the reasons and facts which have caused you to favor it. Be equally frank and forthright, however, in stating what you consider to be possible disadvantages. You are under no obligations to present a case for this proposal. Your only responsibility is to explain how you feel about it and why you feel as you do.

5. *Suggestions for Putting Solution into Operation.*— It is wise generally to give special consideration to ways and means of putting the proposed solution into operation. This gives your thinking a more realistic relation to possible action and serves at the same time as a further check on your thinking. Is your solution workable? Can it be applied practically in the situation which gives rise to the problem? What steps must be taken to put it into operation in this particular situation? Set forth these steps together with such factual materials and interpretations as have significantly affected your thinking on these matters.

C. A Specimen Discussion Outline.

The following outline is presented to exemplify the suggestions given in the preceding section. It is designed to present a reasonably complete record of the thinking done by a member of a discussion group in preparation for discussion. While the outline could easily be expanded in terms of further evidence and interpretations, it is sufficiently comprehensive for all ordinary purposes as given.[1]

[1] Prepared by James A. Rahl, student in the School of Speech, Northwestern University.

DISCUSSION OUTLINE

Question: What Should Be the Policy of the United States with Regard to the Present Sino-Japanese Conflict?

I. Definition of the Problem
   A. "Should be" is taken to mean not only that policy which would be most desirable and theoretically valid, but also that policy which would be most reasonable and practicable in the light of all important considerations.
   B. "Policy" may mean definite action of any sort, definite inaction, or some variation between these extremes.
   C. "The United States" refers to the federal government in all departments which deal with foreign affairs.

II. Analysis of the Problem
   A. Causal relationships.
      1. Evidences and symptoms of this conflict.
         a. For several years, relations between China and Japan have been strained.
            (1) Japan has made repeated thrusts into Chinese territory, and both nations have pursued policies which are incompatible with amicable relations.
         b. This summer (1937) Japan began an offensive which has as its apparent goal the complete conquering of all China.
            (1) The principal objectives have been along the northern front.
            (2) Shanghai, Nanking, and other important cities have been constant scenes of battle, while several other points along the front are being attacked by Japanese forces.
               (a) For maps of the principal lines of march and battle, see *Time* magazine, October 9, 1937.
            (3) Many thousand soldiers have been killed with prospect of further slaughter on both sides.
            (4) Countless civilians together with their

property and cities have been wiped out.

(a) In the small city of Changshu alone, over 800 civilians were killed and 2,000 injured by Japanese bombers.— These and further figures may be found in the *New Republic*, November 3, 1937, pp. 373-374.

c. Japan's progress has not been entirely successful.

  (1) China has given unexpectedly strong opposition.

  (a) Fighting warlords have joined to battle the common enemy.

  (b) Chiang Kai-shek's nationalist movement has gone far to prepare the Chinese for this event.

  (2) The length of the war is costing Japan tremendously in physical terms and in prestige.

  (a) She has placed herself in great jeopardy with regard to Russia.

  (3) The war gives prospect of being a lengthy one.

  (a) See the *New Republic*, October 13, 1937. "What's Ahead in China" by N. Pfeffer, p. 319.

d. This war inevitably raises political, economic, and moral questions in the United States.

  (1) Japan is clearly an aggressor nation; is America morally bound to aid the oppressed nation?

  (2) Will our interference or lack of participation reduce the human misery and suffering involved?

  (3) How imminent is the possibility of our involvement in the conflict?

  (4) American exports to Japan in 1935 amounted to $203,000,000. Imports were $151,000,000. Exports to China in 1935 were $38,000,000. Imports were $64,000,000.

(a) See *World Almanac*, 1937, pp. 308-309.

(5) These figures, coupled with the fact that Japan is our third most important trading nation, show that any action of the United States will be greatly influenced by economic considerations.

e. The question of American action in this conflict was brought sharply to the fore on October 5 in Chicago when President Roosevelt changed the American attitude from a position of passive neutrality to a position of "an active searcher for peace."

(1) He stated that aggression by selfish nations must be stopped if peace-loving countries are to remain safe.

(2) This must be done, he said, by a "quarantine" of the guilty nations.

(a) For the text of the speech, see *International Conciliation*, November, 1937, p. 711.

f. A few days later, the American State Department issued a note approving the action taken by the League of Nations in condemning Japan as an aggressor nation, guilty of violating the Nine-Power Treaty signed at Washington in 1922, and the Kellogg-Briand Pact of 1928.

(1) See *supra*, p. 716.

2. Causes of these conditions.

a. The reasons for Japan's aggression are clouded by propaganda.

(1) Ostensibly, she is intervening because of several Chinese assaults in Manchukuo, in order to crush anti-Japanese groups in China, and to destroy communistic movements.

(a) See *supra*, p. 720.

(b) See also *Current History*, November, 1937. "Japan's Case Against China; China responsible for forcing Nippon's hand" by K. K. Kawakami, pp. 35-41.

    (2) Further, Japan states that she wishes to modernize China and secure cooperation between the "sister" nations.

    (3) Most economists and political observers state, however, that the real reason is apparent; Japan is a "have-not" nation with a real need for territorial expansion if she is to survive; China is the logical territory.

  b. The nature of Japan's attack has been the employment of all the weapons and methods of real warfare. This has brought stiff resistance from China. It has further brought extreme apprehension in the peaceful nations.

  c. The implications of all this to America are apparent.

    (1) We are morally involved simply because of the extent of our relations in numerous ways with the rest of the world.

    (2) We are economically involved because of the size of our foreign trade in the Orient.

    (3) We are politically involved simply because the government must obviously maintain a position of some sort.

  d. The cause of the sudden change in the administration's attitude is not known.

    (1) Speculation will lead us nowhere.

B. Criteria by which to judge proposals.

  1. Our first and most important objective is to keep America out of warfare with all its evils.

  2. The second objective is to pursue that plan which will secure the quickest settlement of the conflict.

  3. The third objective is to be as just and fair as possible to both sides.

  4. It is of course necessary to choose that plan which will be the most practicable and which will best serve the interests of the greatest number of our citizens.

5. Further, any chosen plan must be judged with an eye to its future consequences and precedents as well as its immediate results.

III. Possible Solutions of the Problem (These solutions may be graded according to the *extent* of American participation in the conflict; the plans suggested here may be supplemented by others which fall in between them)

A. The first possible solution is one of complete isolation.

1. The United States as a nation would be officially unaware of a state of war in the Orient.
2. Shipping and trading would continue as before, at the entire risk of the trader; the government would accept no responsibility.
3. America would refuse to enter into any agreement, parley, cooperative action, or other proposal made by other nations in dealing with the conflict.
4. The policy of the nation would thus be one of *inaction*.
5. This policy would probably aid the traders temporarily although they would not be assured of federal protection.
6. It would favor Japan rather than China, since the latter nation needs more help.
7. Issues:
   a. Could this policy be maintained for very long?
   b. Is this policy just to China, the attacked nation?
   c. Is this policy consistent with the Nine-Power Treaty?
   d. Is this the best policy to keep us out of war?

B. A second solution would be one of moderate isolation in which the neutrality law is enforced upon both nations at war.

1. This infers participation, for it gives recognition to the conflict.
2. The President would invoke the neutrality statutes.
   a. This law prohibits the shipment of all contra-

band war materials as defined by the President to either party.

b. Contraband goods may not be shipped indirectly to these nations through neutral countries.

c. If the nations desire trade in other materials, they must send their own ships to our shores, pay cash upon receipt, and transport the goods back at their own risk.

d. American loans and investments in the warring nations are prohibited.

3. This law would work a hardship on both China and Japan.

4. China would be injured since her shipping facilities are inadequate. Japan would suffer because of her great dependence upon American trade.

a. See *International Conciliation*, November, 1937, p. 721.

5. This policy would not be desirable to the traders since their shipping would be considerably injured.

6. The policy would require action by the President.

7. Issues:

a. Is this policy practicable in the light of the extent of our foreign trade?

b. Is this policy just to China? to Japan?

c. Will the plan shorten the war?

d. Will it endanger us?

C. The third possible solution would be one of mild action against Japan.

1. This would mean a willingness on the part of the government to call a Nine-Power parley.

2. It would mean the voicing of our disapproval (as the President has done) of the course of action taken by Japan.

3. It would probably mean the boycotting of Japanese products, and an embargo on goods to Japan.

4. Such a policy would be one of cooperation rather than isolation.

5. It would undoubtedly incur the ill-will of Japan and injure greatly our Oriental trade.

6. Issues:

    a. Will this policy shorten the war?

    b. Is this policy just to Japan?

    c. Will this policy set any dangerous precedents for the United States?

D. A fourth possibility would be one of active participation in attempts to force a peaceful settlement of the dispute.

1. This would mean leading the nations of the world in the movement to end the war.

2. It would mean the application of all the measures in Plan C with stiff economic sanctions against Japan.

3. It would probably mean the alignment of the United States with other nations in a threat to stop the conflict with armed measures if necessary.

4. Such a policy would be a definite concession to China, and might possibly involve a war with Japan.

5. This policy would greatly reduce our Oriental trade.

6. Issues:

    a. Will this policy lead us into war?

    b. Will this policy set any dangerous precedents?

    c. Is this policy just to Japan?

    d. Is this policy compatible with American ideals?

E. A fifth possibility would be one of direct action against Japan with armed means, but this is so far removed from the stated objectives that it is not considered here.

IV. Tentative Conclusion

A. It appears that Plan B would be the best policy.

B. This plan is one of moderate isolation in which the

neutrality laws are enforced upon both nations at war.

C. Reasons for this choice:

1. This policy is the most likely to keep us out of war.
   a. If the United States becomes a party to active attempts to end the conflict, she will likely become involved, and may find it necessary to engage in war in order to save her "national honor."
   b. This policy will hold us aloof.
      (1) It will keep our trading interests from becoming involved, and will not place the United States in a jeopardized economic position.
   c. This plan will involve no endangering entanglements.
2. This plan is a definite peace move and is most likely to aid in ending the conflict quickly.
   a. Japan is intent upon defeating China; she must gain a victory or fight the war to a finish because of the great extent to which she is now involved; she cannot back down.
      (1) See *Foreign Affairs*, October, 1937. "Price of Japanese Imperialism" by Nathaniel Pfeffer.
   b. Therefore, she will resist all attempts to stop the war, regardless of the strength of those attempts.
   c. Therefore, the participation of the United States would only prolong the conflict.
      (1) It would likely call forth allies for Japan and China.
      (2) This would precipitate a world conflict.
   d. The first obligation of the nation is to its own citizens and their lives and happiness. Therefore, though we sympathize with China, we must look to American welfare first.
3. This policy is justifiable.
   a. True, it would mean a refusal to aid a guiltless nation which is being attacked.

   b. But, this policy takes cognizance of possible guilt on both sides.

   c. Further, it is less likely to lead us into war.

  4. The plan appears to be practicable.

   a. It has already been enacted in essence into law by Congress.

   b. Trading would be injured, but not so much as by the other suggestions.

    (1) It will still permit trading with both sides provided they send their own ships for the goods.

    (2) There is no danger to American shipping.

   c. This policy is in line with past American precedent.

  5. The suggested policy will not involve future difficulties, since no entanglements or dangerous precedents are made.

 D. Disadvantages of this policy of neutrality.

  1. This plan is apparently not in harmony with President Roosevelt's views on the situation.

  2. This policy will incur the ill-will of both parties to the conflict.

  3. It will not be met with approval by Great Britain and France who desire to see the United States help them in protecting their interests.

  4. This policy will be difficult to enforce upon some traders whose interests will be hurt.

  5. Such a plan goes against the great body of Chinese sympathizers in America.

  6. Such a policy may easily be washed away by propaganda, since it is always difficult to sit still, rather than to move in some direction.

V. Suggestions for Putting Solution into Operation

 A. The neutrality law should be revised and brought up to date by Congress.

 B. The law must be strictly enforced.

  1. If the President refuses to do so, Congress must take the task in its own hands.

  2. The citizens must make their wishes known and see that their demands are heeded.

  3. Those who enforce the law should lay the mat-

ter before the people and fully explain the reasons for this action.
4. Violators of the law must be uncompromisingly
punished.

C. Any demands by other nations to the contrary must
be disregarded.

D. Our position, once taken, must be inviolably maintained.

E. The purpose of this action should be made clear
to the world.

D. LIMITATIONS OF DISCUSSION OUTLINES.

The chief danger of the discussion outline is that the
maker will feel that he is under some sort of responsibility
to defend the proposal specified in his outline. He does
have a responsibility to explain and interpret his thinking
on the problem, and presumably the outline represents his
feeling on the problem when the discussion begins. So
long as these convictions are honestly held, by all means
stay by them. On the other hand, be willing to change
your mind and modify your position as the discussion
develops whenever the logic of the situation convinces
you that such is indicated. A participant in discussion has
absolutely no responsibility to defend any predetermined
proposal unless that proposal continues to represent his
convictions. Even then he should treat the proposal as
impersonally as possible and confine his arguments to an
honest attempt to make the others understand why he
feels as he does about the problem.

We have said that the pattern of thought in discussion
is typically that of individual reflective thinking. The five
main divisions in the discussion outline are the usual steps
in such thinking. Another possible misuse of the discussion outline occurs when an attempt is made by the conferee to force the group to follow the pattern of his own
thinking. To be sure, the same formal steps will be followed (definition, diagnosis, suggestion of solutions,
reasoned development of solutions, and consideration of

ways and means of putting into effect the proposal adopted), but there is no reason to expect that the group will conform to any prearranged thought pattern. in terms of the data of the problem under consideration. If each member of the group has done some preparatory thinking, we should expect the group effort to represent a collaboration of the several participants. The pattern of the group-thought should take form as the discussion progresses. For the leader or any member of the group to insist on some predetermined substantive pattern would be to vitiate any possibility of originality on the part of the group.

IV. SOURCES OF INFORMATION

There are a few common sources of information with which every student of discussion should be familiar. Knowledge of these sources and ability to use them intelligently may very well be one of the important outcomes of a study of discussion. Certainly anyone who plans to participate in discussion should know how to investigate problems for discussion.

A. REFERENCE BOOKS AND BIBLIOGRAPHIES.

One of the best places to start the investigation of a problem is with reference books and any available bibliographies on the subject or related subjects. Most libraries have a separate reference department where materials of this sort are assembled for use. The librarian in charge is prepared to give you assistance. Encyclopedias, dictionaries, statistical publications, handbooks, bibliographies, and standard treatises in the various fields are usually included in the reference collection.

B. BOOKS.

Books are available in your school and community library on most of the problems adopted for discussion. These are usually catalogued by author, title, and subject.

It is a good practice to jot down the subjects suggested by the problem under which you might reasonably expect to find material. With this as a guide, check through the library catalogue, making a record of the books which appear to be useful references. Many books will contain bibliographies which can be used to extend your investigation.

It is often a problem to know how to use books for the purpose of informing oneself on a special problem. Much time and effort can be wasted on reading through material which has little or nothing to offer on your problem. It is wise generally to scan the available books before spending too much time with any one of them. Study the table of contents, chapter headings, subheadings, index, and bibliography. Having made this preliminary inventory, you can then return to the books or parts of books which appear most likely to yield information on the problem you are investigating.

C. PERIODICALS.

Periodical literature should not be neglected in the investigation. The problems most commonly discussed are those of current interest and very often the periodicals offer the best source of information. The *Reader's Guide* may be used as an index to popular and general publications. Published monthly, it serves as an index to all but the current issues of magazines. The *Reader's Guide* has been published since 1900. *Poole's Index*, covering the period from 1802-1906, may be used for the older magazine material. The *International Index*, published since 1920, is devoted to the more special and technical journals in the humanities and sciences. Several special indexes are also available such as the *Industrial Arts Index*, *Agricultural Index*, and *Educational Index*. All of these are arranged alphabetically by author and subject and sometimes by title. Uniform subject headings are employed with numerous cross references.

D. NEWSPAPERS.

Newspapers often supply valuable information in investigating problems for discussion. Reports of events, texts of speeches, and the like are sometimes available only in the files of newspapers. The *New York Times Index* may be used for the *Times*, and by getting the dates of events from this source, it is possible to use it to check the files of other papers.

E. PUBLIC AFFAIRS PAMPHLETS.

A bulletin published by the United States Office of Education entitled *Public Affairs Pamphlets* supplies a useful index to inexpensive pamphlets on social, economic, political, and international affairs. The pamphlet publications of some eighty different organizations are listed in this index. Since the tabulation was prepared primarily to meet the needs of the public forum demonstrations and their programs of public discussion, it is especially valuable for our purposes. The bulletin emphasizes the importance of "making use of pamphlet material as an auxiliary to public discussion."[2] Another useful index to such materials is the *Public Affairs Information Service* published by the H. W. Wilson Company, New York.

F. UNITED STATES GOVERNMENT DOCUMENTS.

Lists of government publications may be secured from the Superintendent of Documents, Washington, D. C. Many of these publications can be found in the larger libraries. The *Congressional Record*, containing the speeches, debates, and proceedings of Congress, is especially useful. The index to the *Record* makes these materials readily accessible. Congressional *Hearings*, other documents of the Senate and House, including speeches and special reports, and reports from the sev-

[2] *Public Affairs Pamphlets*, February, 1937. For sale by the Superintendent of Documents, Washington, D. C. Price 10 cents.

eral executive departments are also useful sources of information.

G. Selected References, Handbooks, and Digests.

In recent years a considerable number of specially prepared collections of pro and con articles on current topics have been published for the benefit of school debaters and others who wish to get in one place a concise summary of points of view on these topics. The *Reference Shelf* series of the H. W. Wilson Company is one of the best sources of this type. Each volume contains outlines, bibliography, and reprinted articles on a single problem, such as federal aid to education, international traffic in arms, and collective bargaining. Another source of this type is the *Debate Handbook*, published annually by the National University Extension Association. The *Congressional Digest*, published monthly except July and August, contains bibliographical data and pro and con discussions of topics before or pending in Congress. Digests of opinions on current topics, bibliography, and a special forum section may be found in *Counterviews*, a monthly publication.

V. RECORDING DATA

An extended investigation of any problem necessitates some systematic method of recording information.

A. Reference Cards.

Perhaps the best method of note-taking consists in recording items of information on separate file cards. Each of these cards should be given an appropriate heading and carry an exact bibliographical reference. The headings may be used as a basis for the alphabetical arrangement of the cards in a file box. In preparing for discussion it has been found helpful to use the several divisions of the discussion outline or some variation of them as a basis for organizing the filing system. Thus the cards dealing with matters of definition may be assembled together. A section of the file can be given over to analysis, with cards on the nature and extent of the problem, causes of the problem, and standards for evaluating solutions. Cards dealing with the merits and demerits of possible solutions and facts relating to them can likewise be filed under special headings. If the extent of the investigation warrants it, these larger divisions may be broken down into subdivisions appropriate to the problem under consideration.

The following form is suggested for reference cards. This particular reference was included with others in preparation for a class discussion on the question: *What should the federal government do to relieve the present business recession?*

Suggested Solutions: Inflation or Deflation
John T. Flynn, economist and journalist
"This Setback in Business," Harpers Magazine, No. 1052, January, 1938, p. 204.
"The choice is a simple one, even though it be an appalling one for a political government to make. We must make up our minds either to inflate or deflate. If we decide that we want to hold up prices we must decide to inflate. The government must make an end of talk about balancing the budget. . . . If we decide that inflation by government credit is too dangerous— which is the fact—then we must decide to move down to a lower price level."

B. BIBLIOGRAPHY.

The record of an extended investigation may also include a bibliography. If such is needed, the bibliography on discussion included in Appendix E may be taken as an example of a satisfactory form for recording bibliographical materials.

1. Prepare a model discussion outline on a problem suitable for discussion. Select your own problem, but be certain that it is one which lends itself to library investigation. Exchange outlines in class, raise questions about them, and discuss any problems which may remain about the method and purpose of such outlines.

2. Adopt a problem for discussion which lends itself to considerable library investigation. Prepare model discussion outlines on this problem. Conduct a discussion on this problem and follow it with a period of criticism in which the logical pattern of the discussion is compared with that of the several outlines. Which outline most nearly resembles the pattern of the discussion? Did the person whose outline most nearly corresponds with the pattern of the discussion dominate the discussion? Consider the relations of the outlines to the discussion in terms of participation.

3. Employing the problem used in Exercise 1 or 2, prepare five reference cards on each of the following topics: (a) definition of the problem; (b) analysis of the problem; (c) possible solutions to the problem; (d) the solution tentatively adopted; (e) suggestions for putting the solution into operation.

4. Prepare reference cards on a problem for discussion in which you make use of the following materials and sources: (a) two references from two different encyclopedias; (b) five references from five different books; (c) one reference, if possible, to a bibliography on the subject; (d) five references from five different periodicals, with at least one from a periodical published before 1906; (e) three references from newspapers, with at least one from the *New York Times*; (f) two references to pamphlets; (g) two references to United States Government Documents; (h) and three references taken from at least two different sources of the type listed in Section IV.G of this chapter. Collect these references on more than one subject or problem if you find it impossible to fulfil the assignment using only one topic;

but be certain to consult each of the sources indicated and otherwise meet the specifications given above.

SELECTED BIBLIOGRAPHY

Baird, A. Craig, *Public Discussion and Debate*. Boston: Ginn and Company, 1937. Chapter III.

Elliott, Harrison S., *The Process of Group Thinking*. New York: Association Press, 1932. Chapters VI, VII, and VIII.

O'Neill, James M., and McBurney, James H., *The Working Principles of Argument*. New York: The Macmillan Company, 1932. Chapter III.

Walser, Frank, *The Art of Conference*. New York: Harper and Brothers, 1933. Chapter III.

CHAPTER VII

PARTICIPATING IN DISCUSSION

I. INDIVIDUAL DIFFERENCES AND FITNESS FOR DISCUSSION

Discussion often brings together people with very different abilities and capacities, both in kind and in degree. That there are individual differences in native capacity or intelligence, understood as the ability to think reflectively, there can be no doubt. So far as discussion is concerned, however, this factor can easily be overemphasized. *Other things being equal*, the most intelligent person, measured by standard intelligence tests, can in all probability make the most significant contribution in discussion. These other factors, however, are seldom equal! "Intelligence" is not a completely undifferentiated element; it includes not only ability to make associations in reasoning, but also powers of observation and constructive imagination. Equally intelligent people will differ in type of intelligence. Some have the peculiar ability of making snap judgments of considerable value; others are superior in more deliberate thought. Allport distinguishes between *soundness of judgment*, the capacity for making a mature decision in a crisis, and *general adaptability*, including adjustment to the social group, its persons, and its laws.[1] In addition, there are many other factors affecting one's fitness to participate in discussion, such as emotional stability, personality, and speech, to say nothing of individual differences in knowledge and experience relative to the problem under consideration.

Great caution should be exercised in excluding people from discussion or limiting it to a select group. The typical discussion calls for many types of ability, and one of its more important values lies in the opportunity which it presents to bring these different types together in a cooperative undertaking. While there are, of course, many situations in which groups should be constituted in terms of special ability and information, discussion, in many of its most useful applications, should be viewed as an opportunity to assemble persons of all kinds and degrees of ability for the purpose of securing whatever contribution they are able to make. Herein lies its greatest claim to democratic values.

This does not mean that we are placing a premium on mediocrity. The discussion process, properly conducted, is not one of leveling down, but rather one of integrating at the highest possible level. In a very important sense a solution to a group problem is not a desirable solution unless the members of the group have participated in its formation; "if ideals are to be expressed in action that is

[1] Floyd H. Allport, *Social Psychology* (Boston: Houghton Mifflin Company, 1924), p. 105.

sustained and resourceful, then those who *do* the doing must themselves have done the *thinking*."[2]

II. PROCEDURE IN DISCUSSION

Procedure refers to the decorum and rules governing participation. Procedure in discussion varies with the type of discussion and the purposes of the group. Later chapters dealing with the forum, panel, policy-determining groups, and other special types point out variations in procedure peculiar to these situations. *In no case, however, should the procedure be made an end in itself.* Procedural devices and techniques are justified only as they aid the group in the reflective thinking process. A good general rule to follow is the fewer formal procedures and rules of decorum the better. Self-discipline and the ordinary courtesies of good conversation with some guidance from a leader will usually suffice. Deliberations which are truly cooperative do not require the formal rules of procedure, such as parliamentary procedure or rules of order which must be invoked in certain types of debate.

A. SECURING RECOGNITION.

As we have said, the typical situation for discussion is the small learning group, preferably eight to fifteen persons and not more than twenty or twenty-five. In groups of this kind it is good policy for the leader to reserve the privilege of requesting members to address him before speaking. Often it is wise to invoke this rule at the outset of the discussion (especially with inexperienced groups) and gradually relax it as the discussion "warms up." In this way, certain essential habits, such as one person speaking at a time, are established in the beginning and the discussion can then proceed on a somewhat freer basis. To insist throughout the discussion that all ques-

[2] *A Cooperative Technique for Controversy* (New York: Association Press, 1924), p. 5.

tions and remarks be sent through the chairman is almost always a mistake. In good discussion there will be conflicts and differences which result in spirited exchanges of opinion and series of questions. Often two or three persons in whose thinking the particular issue under consideration is a pivotal matter will be the focal points in such an exchange. The discussion at this juncture may consist of a series of short contributions, questions, replies, and observations of one kind or another. For these people to address the leader each time they wish to speak would be a needless and stultifying formality. On the other hand, these exchanges should not be allowed to get out of hand. The leader may need to caution those most actively involved to speak "one at a time"; if others appear to want to say something, he may need to intervene in their behalf; and in no case should such exchanges be allowed to continue to the point of tedium for the group as a whole.

Members who wish to speak may address the leader as "Mr. Chairman" or "Mr. Leader" or get his attention by raising their hands or simply "getting his eye." In cases where the leader is not insisting on recognition before speaking, a member may come in whenever the opportunity presents itself. *The member always has the privilege, however, to address the leader and request permission to speak!* In general the leader should give preference to persons who have not as yet spoken *when they wish to speak on the point that is then before the group.* If the member wishes to introduce a new aspect of the problem, he still has the privilege of addressing the chair, and whether or not he will be permitted to speak at that time is a matter for the leader to decide through recourse if necessary to the wishes of the group. The member who intentionally or inadvertently digresses from the point at issue in his contribution may be asked by the leader to defer it until the present matter has been settled to the satisfaction of the group.

B. Invoking the "Rule of the Majority."

The discussion belongs to the group. Within certain limits it should be made what they wish to make of it. Perhaps the most noteworthy exception to this rule is the group that is learning how to participate in discussion, such, for example, as a class in discussion. Here in the interests of learning some deference to the teacher, who is presumably an expert in the technique of discussion, may need to be made. On other occasions it may likewise be wise to give considerable latitude to an experienced leader. In general, however, this rule holds; discussion is a democratic method and the decisions should be made by the members of the group. The question we raise here is, when and how should the wishes of the group be expressed?

The following situations may warrant or even require an expression of opinion from the group: (1) Should a time limit be imposed upon speakers (see below)? (2) Should the group move on to another aspect of the problem? (3) Should a certain definition be tentatively adopted for purposes of this discussion? (4) Should a certain point be referred to a committee or to an expert? (5) Should the statement of the problem for discussion be modified? This list is meant to be suggestive only. These are merely some of the situations in which the group-will *may* need to be ascertained. Ordinarily, however, even these matters will take care of themselves in the usual course of the discussion without calling for a vote or expression of opinion. Such a vote should be taken only when an impasse has been reached or when time is being wasted in attempting to settle procedural problems which might better be decided without delay.

The taking of a vote is usually initiated by the leader who may simply say, for example, "We do not have much time left. Perhaps it would be wise to limit contributions to thirty seconds. Does this meet with the approval of the group? All those in favor of such a limitation raise your hands"; or "We can't seem to agree on this definition. Why not adopt the one most acceptable to the group for our present purposes and proceed? Will all those favoring definition A raise their hands? Definition B?" It is assumed that the wishes of the majority will prevail when such votes are taken. The leader ordinarily will not vote except where his vote is needed to break a tie.

We are not suggesting here a form of parliamentary procedure for group discussion. It is of utmost importance that the suggestions given on taking votes *not* be so interpreted. In parliamentary debate all deliberation is conducted in terms of motions; no debate takes place until a motion is made and seconded and the vote on this motion is recorded as the will of the group, thus terminating the debate. A vote to determine the wishes of the group in discussion is taken merely to speed up the process, to stop unnecessary bickering, and to avoid what might on rare occasions develop into a complete impasse. It is applied primarily to questions of procedure.

C. LIMITING DISCUSSION.

The necessity of limiting discussion sometimes arises where definite time limits are imposed on the group. Ordinarily this can be handled informally by the leader without imposing arbitrary limits. Our experience has been that this is usually the best procedure. If the leader will keep an eye on the clock, it is possible for him to "push" the discussion along without making a point of it or appearing to do so. Other ways of handling this problem are to impose time limits on individual contributions or to allocate definite amounts of time for the consideration of the several aspects of the problem.

Of course, the group may prefer to proceed leisurely and get as far as it can even if the time available does not permit completion. This often is the best procedure to follow especially if it is possible for the group to continue the discussion at some later date.[3] Depending upon the circumstances, however, it may be more satisfying to cover the entire problem in the time allotted than to have to stop in the middle of things. If this is the case, the suggestions we have made about time limitations will prove helpful.

III. ATTITUDES AND BEHAVIOR DESIRABLE IN DISCUSSION

The attitudes of the individuals composing the discussion group are as important as, if not more important than, any other factor. No amount of attention to procedure can achieve cooperative group thinking if the attitudes of those doing the discussing are competitive, self-centered, and individualistic. You cannot *make* people cooperate. The best that can be done is to create a situation favorable to such cooperation. There can be no question that an understanding of the attitudes and behavior desirable in discussion and a serious attempt to develop such attitudes should be the constant goal of anyone who seeks to develop proficiency in discussion.

A. CONSIDER THE COMMON GOOD.

If an individual is to be helpful in any cooperative undertaking, he must have some concern for the welfare of the group. If one's conduct in discussion stems wholly from selfish purposes, it is almost inevitable that the group process will suffer as a result. There is some analogy with the football player and his team. No matter how brilliant he may be, he must work with the other players if the team is to be successful; and what is more, his own personal success as a player is so identified with

[3] The classes in discussion at Northwestern University met three days a week for one hour when they were first organized. Experience has shown that the problems discussed cannot ordinarily be handled adequately in a one-hour period. Considerable improvement in the course has been effected by scheduling it for one one-hour meeting and one two-hour meeting each week. The one-hour meetings are given over to a consideration of discussion methods and the two-hour meetings to discussions of contemporary problems and criticisms.

that of the team that he will usually find it wise, even from a selfish point of view, to cooperate with the other members of his team. The same may be said of the members of a business concern, a fraternity, or any other group. Anyone who attempts to capitalize upon a group undertaking to further his own ends at the expense of the group is not only an impediment to the group, but is likely to lose personally as a result of the attempt.

The implications of this philosophy can be reduced to a few simple suggestions so far as discussion is concerned. Try to discover what should be the group purpose in the situation at hand. Work honestly and faithfully to get this purpose understood and achieved. Be tolerant of other points of view. Be frank and aboveboard in your conduct. Put all your cards on the table and do all you can to get the others to do the same. If your personal interests appear to be inconsistent with the best interests of the group, be honest with yourself and with the group in your appraisal of the situation.

B. Assume Your Share of Group Responsibility.

When a leader is designated to conduct a discussion there is often a tendency on the part of the group to place all the responsibility on him. This conception of the leader's function is wholly incorrect. He is not there to give a lecture or to put on a show for your entertainment. His only responsibility is to do what he can to create a situation that will enable you to contribute to the best advantage of the group. He is largely helpless if members of the group persist in taking a passive attitude. The failure of the discussion to accomplish anything under these circumstances is as much your failure as it is his. Each member of the group should be as concerned about the success of the discussion as he has a right to expect the leader to be. If each member has this conception of his responsibility and conducts himself accordingly, there is little chance that the discussion will become a dull, listless, lethargic affair.

C. THINK BEFORE YOU SPEAK BUT DO NOT THINK TOO LONG.

We have repeatedly emphasized the importance of careful preparation for discussion. Most certainly thought should precede utterance. The point we make here, however, is that this utterance cannot be held in abeyance indefinitely. No one will deny the importance of having something worth while to say before attempting to speak, but there is such a thing as being too cautious about stating your views. I have a competent friend who seldom says anything in the early part of a discussion or conference of any kind. He lets everyone else do the talking and then comes in with his contribution after he has the benefit of what everyone else has said. By this time he sees pretty clearly what the issues are, his own thinking has taken more definite form, and it is possible for him to make a safe, orderly statement which, incidentally, is usually helpful and to the point. While this technique sometimes enables one to play a sage role in the discussion, it is not difficult to see what would happen to the conference if everyone attempted to follow the same procedure. There would be no discussion. It is impossible for everyone to wait until all the facts and opinions are in; someone has to do the preliminary work.

Do not be afraid to express your ideas in discussion even if you are not perfectly sure of your ground. Throw the idea into the discussion for what it is worth. If it proves to be wrong or of little value, be perfectly willing to recognize and acknowledge that fact. Let the group know what you are thinking about. It is only in this way that real group thinking can take place. If you were to try to conduct your private thinking on the basis that no new ideas were to be admitted until they were fully matured, you would do no thinking. Group thinking becomes equally sterile under these circumstances. While ideas should be definitely beyond the "half-baked" stage before they are contributed, it does not follow that one should try to wait upon complete certainty and finality. Especially is this true of discussion, since its very purpose is that of developing ideas. It is a group of persons thinking "out loud"; it is "thought in process." Any composition, oral or written, which presumes to report the finished results of thought as a basis for controlling the behavior of others, must be measured by somewhat different standards, but discussion is an attempt to work over ideas, to think problems through. It can succeed only as people contribute these ideas.

D. CONTRIBUTE OBJECTIVELY.

In contributing ideas in discussion seek to avoid any personal identification with them which will make it difficult or impossible for you to treat these ideas objectively. There is a very human tendency, once a position has been taken, to personalize the matter in such a way that you feel moved to defend it under any circumstances, and even to feel a tinge of resentment if someone disagrees with the position. We like to "save face." We feel that we suffer a loss of prestige and respect if our ideas do not meet with acceptance. Such face saving can obviously become a serious impediment to group thinking. By all means defend a position in which you honestly and seriously believe, but be certain that this belief has its basis in the merits of the position and not in the fact that you happened to be the one to introduce the idea. It is said that parents have difficulty in appraising their children as other people see them. This is perhaps as it should be, but in the realm of ideas there is much to be said for the advice that you try to treat your contributions as impersonally and objectively as though they had been begotten by somebody who sits across the table from you.

This objectivity is not always easy to achieve. In the first place, be on your guard against making your contributions personal issues. An attitude toward discussion which grows out of an appreciation of the dangers in this direction will help as much as anything else. It is also wise to use language which avoids the appearance of irrevocable commitment and categorical finality. One can introduce his point by saying: "My present feeling in the matter is this"; "I think that we ought to consider this point of view"; "From what I have seen, this seems to be the case"; "I keep coming back to this conclusion. Am I wrong?"; "I wish that you people would tell me what you think of this idea"; "I'm just thinking out loud here, but this seems to me to be the case."

Expressions such as these need not be the introduction to devitalized, unenthusiastic statements. Most certainly they should not be if the discussion is to be alive, stimulating, and productive. Contributing objectively should not mean apathetic detachment. Vigor and enthusiasm are essential to good discussion, but they should spring from real sincerity and honest conviction rather than from attempts to "save face." When the latter motivation operates, the result is invariably rancor and bad feeling.

E. LISTEN TO UNDERSTAND.

A good listener is as important in discussion as a good contributor. Give as careful attention to the other fellow as you would like to have him give to you. And what is most important, make an honest attempt to understand the point he is trying to make. Deliberate misinterpretation is inexcusable. Almost as disruptive to group thinking, however, is the person who is so occupied with his own thoughts or so concerned about what he is going to say next that he fails to get the point of the man who is speaking. Another habit to be guarded against is that of listening to someone solely from the standpoint of refuting what he has to say. If you think that you do not agree with a position, it is all the more important that you be certain that you understand it thoroughly. It is almost impossible to appreciate an explanation if the whole focus of your attention is given over to an attempt to refute what you think the speaker is trying to explain. Give the speaker your undivided attention, especially if you think you disagree with him, until you are certain that you understand him. There is time enough for refutation, if such is necessary, after an understanding has been reached.

The best test of understanding is the ability to state another person's position in such a way that he will accept your statement as a fair summary of his position. If you do not understand, ask questions until you do.

IV. SPEAKING IN DISCUSSION

One person communicates his ideas and feelings to another through visible and audible symbols, i. e., through sounds, words, and bodily action. Good speech is as important in discussion as in any other activity in which speech plays a part. Sarett and Foster set forth six basic principles underlying effective speech: "(1) Effective speech is not for exhibition but for communication; (2) Effective speech commands attention in order to win response; (3) The technique of effective speech is unobtrusive and therefore disarming; (4) Speech is effective, other things being equal, in proportion to the intrinsic worth of the speaker; (5) Impressions of the speaker are derived largely from signs of which the audience are unaware; (6) Effective speech results in part from free bodily action."[4] If you have not read *Basic Principles of Speech*, in which these principles are developed, we suggest that you do so. We shall explain here three requisites of good speech which are of special importance to the participant in discussion.

A. UNDERSTANDABLE AND MEANINGFUL SPEECH.

Considerable experience with discussion prompts the simple advice: Speak loudly enough to be heard easily by all present. Few things are more aggravating in discussion

---

[4] Lew Sarett and William Trufant Foster, *Basic Principles of Speech* (Boston: Houghton Mifflin Company, 1936), p. 12.

than individuals who continually and persistently fail to make themselves heard. The reason for special difficulty with this matter in discussion seems to lie in the fact that participants often are engaged in a dialogue with the person next to them or at least close at hand. As a result they unconsciously adjust the volume or loudness to meet this situation, forgetting that the other persons present wish to hear what they have to say. If members will constantly keep in mind that the entire group is their audience, this problem will be largely eliminated. In this same connection it should be emphasized that clearly articulated speech is as important in discussion as in any other situation. Bad enunciation and other slovenly speech habits are in no way excused by the relatively informal nature of the occasion.

The purpose of speech in discussion is to convey one's ideas to others with maximum accuracy and economy of time and effort. Understandability in communication must ultimately be reduced to a consideration of the symbols we use to convey our meanings. It is a matter of fact that the symbols which we must of necessity use in ordinary speech do not have fixed, completely negotiable meanings. Not only do words have different meanings for different individuals, but the meanings attaching to a symbol may vary widely for the same individual on different occasions. All this is tremendously complicated by the symbolic significance of the vocal inflections and bodily activity which accompany the spoken word.

Ogden and Richards, after distinguishing broadly between the purely scientific or symbolic and the evocative functions of language, describe five separate characteristics of symbols which we shall mention here: (1) strict or scientific symbolization in which no attitude is conveyed; (2) the expression of attitude toward listener ("such as amity or hostility of the speaker to his audience"); (3) the expression of attitude toward the referent, or the thing we are talking about; (4) the promotion

of effects intended or the effects which we wish to promote by our utterance; and (5) an indication of the
speaker's own clearness or vagueness in relation to the
reference or thing he is talking about.[5] The following
conclusion of practical importance to the participant in
discussion is stated:

Most writing or speech then which is of the mixed or
rhetorical kind as opposed to the pure, or scientific, or
strictly symbolic, use of words, will take its form as the
result of compromise. Only occasionally will a symbolization be available which, without loss of its symbolic *accuracy*, is also *suitable* (to the author's attitude to his public), *appropriate* (to his referent), *judicious* (likely to
produce the desired effects) and *personal* (indicative of
the stability or instability of his references). The odds are
very strongly against there being many symbols able to do
so much. As a consequence in most speech some of these
functions are sacrificed.[6]

The pertinent question for us is, which of these functions should be sacrificed in choosing our words in discussion? Is it our primary concern to attempt to convey
to the group exactly what we mean, to indicate by our
choice of words an attitude toward the group, to indicate an attitude toward the thing we are discussing, to
attempt through our selection of symbols to promote the
acceptance of our idea, or to indicate the adequacy of
our grasp of the idea? We suggest that the first responsibility of one contributing in discussion is symbolic accuracy. Use those words which most carefully and
faithfully convey your meaning to the group. Even
when the greatest of caution is exercised our best efforts
will only approximate such accuracy; they will at best
be a compromise with true symbolization.

The question as to whether evocative or emotionally
toned words are desirable in discussion is probably one

[5] C. K. Ogden and I. A. Richards, *The Meaning of Meaning* (New
York: Harcourt, Brace and Company, 1930), pp. 224-227.
[6] *Ibid.*, p. 234.

of the most perplexing questions we shall have to face. The use of such language in persuasive speech is an accepted and necessary practice; but what position are we to take in speech which attempts to implement reflective thought and critical analysis? The question is not whether ordinary language symbols contain emotional elements. They do. We know that. The point is that some terms have more emotional coloring than others. Hence we must determine some principle or principles of selection. Working with Ogden and Richard's classification of the functions of language, we have the following suggestions to offer: (1) As we have said, the first aim should be symbolic accuracy. (2) We see no harm in words which indicate an attitude toward the group so long as that attitude is one of friendliness, amity, respect, and goodwill. (3) We feel that words expressing attitudes toward the referent (the thing to which the word refers) should be used carefully, honestly, frankly, and with great care that they do not beg the question (i.e., do not use them as a substitute for reasoning). (4) Words which promote the acceptance of the idea being developed should be avoided so far as possible. Such words are purely question begging and have no place in discussion wherever they can be avoided. (5) Words indicating the speaker's degree of clarity and grasp of the subject are in no sense objectionable so long as they are honestly used.

We have gone into this matter of words in some detail because we do not wish to be put in the position of saying that language in discussion should be coldly scientific and devoid of emotional elements; nor do we wish to endorse the exploitive use of evocative language. We see values in certain emotional coloring and warmth of expression. Such language can be stimulating and helpfully provocative. We have sought to indicate the kind of attitudes which can accomplish these purposes without seriously compromising fidelity of meaning. *What we are after is an honest, fair use of language!*

There is another problem in the use of language with which students of discussion are concerned. Aside from the use of emotionally toned words, how is one to know that the word he uses means the same thing to the group that it means to him? Here is one of the most prolific sources of confusion and misunderstanding. Other people will understand us only in terms of their own experiences. This observation suggests at least a partial answer to our question. Relate what you have to say to the experiences of those to whom you are speaking. *So far as it is possible to do so, reduce the explanation of your position to common experiences, concretes, and observables.* Later in this chapter we outline a method of contributing in discussion; this will give further help on this point. The section on definition in Chapter X presents additional suggestions. The very awareness of the problem, an appreciation of the dangers of misunderstanding and ambiguity, will in itself help to correct the naïve assumption that people understand exactly what we mean when we use words which have reasonably definite meaning for us.

B. Direct and Communicative Speech.

Speech in discussion should be direct and communicative as well as understandable and meaningful. We have in mind here principally physical directness and eagerness to communicate. To achieve this directness look at the people you are addressing. The group is your audience. Include everyone present when you speak. Make each person feel that you are talking to him. Direct a few sentences to one member of the group, then to another, and then to someone else. Even though certain of your remarks are designed primarily for the leader or some member of the group, do not neglect the others. As we pointed out earlier in this chapter, often an exchange of opinion will develop between two or three members of the group involving a number of questions and replies without anyone else contributing for several minutes. Such exchanges are typical of discussion (at least of small groups) and if they appear to be advancing group-thought they should be encouraged by the leader. The speakers, however, have the responsibility of making the entire group feel that they are a party to these conversations. Isolated dialogues tend to destroy the unity and solidarity of the group.

The person who wants to talk and manifests this desire in his mode of speech, bodily action, and vocal inflections usually achieves what we have called *communicativeness*. He is interested, alert, and anxious to get into the fray. There is a significant vocal variety, in force, pitch, quality, and time which holds attention to his ideas and adds meaning to them. The communicative member is usually an active speaker. Gestures, movements of the head and body during speech, tend to free the individual and, if controlled and coordinated, like vocal variety, add to the total effect of the communicative act.

C. ANIMATED AND SINCERE SPEECH.

Animation is probably an aspect of the point we have just been making. Dullness, lethargy, listlessness, even on the part of a few members, operate like a wet blanket on discussion. Participants have a responsibility at least to act interested.

Sincerity is probably the most helpful personal quality in discussion. If a speaker is genuine and honest in what he has to say, one can forgive and forget many shortcomings. Avoid exhibitionism. Be your best self and view experiences in discussion as an opportunity for further self-improvement.

V. A METHOD OF CONTRIBUTING IN DISCUSSION

In this chapter we have considered procedure, attitudes and behavior, and speaking in discussion. While all this is closely related to the method of contributing, it remains to be pointed out what rhetorical form contributions should take. How should a conferee organize or "put together" his contributions in discussion in order best to make his position clear, and at the same time stimulate cooperative thinking? This is the question which we wish to answer here. It should be kept in mind that a contribution in discussion may vary from a single sentence (or even a word) to a speech of considerable length, such, for example, as those given in a symposium or a forum-lecture. The advice we are offering applies to any contribution, regardless of length, in which a position is taken on some issue or proposition.

A. The Truth-Claim of a Proposal in Discussion.

What claim to truth and group consideration does a proposal have? Presumably, any position reported by a member represents a conclusion (even though it may be quite tentative) which he has reached through some reflective thought. Not infrequently in creative discussion one has the experience of having an idea "grow" considerably, or at least become much clearer, while he is in the very process of explaining the idea. Granting this possibility, we say that *any proposal's truth-claim consists in the reflective processes which the individual making the proposal has gone through* (or is going through) *in reaching the conclusion which the proposal reports: Where several people collaborate in a proposal, its truth-claim then consists in their combined reflective processes.* Any proposal in discussion has exactly this claim to truth, no more and no less. To be sure, someone may quite accidentally (unreflectively) reach a conclusion which *later thought* (*or the thought of others unknown to the present thinker*) may prove to have a much stronger claim to truth than the present thinker's reflective processes would indicate; but for purposes of the present discussion it must stand on its own merits. And these merits are exactly equal to the worth of the thought that has "gone into" the conclusion or is "put into" it by someone in the present discussion.

In the above analysis of the truth-claim, the term "reflective processes" should be understood to include the *facts* and *authoritative opinions* considered, as well as the definitions used, the analyses made (including standards of value), the hypotheses considered, the reasoning gone through, and any further verifications employed. The truth-claim of the proposal, then, resides in these factors.

B. THE EXPLANATORY, DENOTATIVE, OR EMPIRICAL METHOD.

When a scientist reports the conclusions of his research in a paper or scholarly journal, how does he go about it? He explains as carefully as he can what his problem has been and exactly what thinking and procedures he went through in reaching his conclusions. The report amounts to an invitation for someone else to pose the same problem and go through the same procedures, with the implied assumption that he will reach the same conclusion. In other words, the scientist sets out the factors in which reside his conclusion's only legitimate claim to truth. If he is a true scientist he does not go beyond these factors. It is not his function to persuade those who listen to his paper or read his article, except as they are "persuaded" by this kind of account. Presumably, they will be "persuaded" (assuming that his audience is equally objective) to accept his conclusions unless they can point to some discrepancy in his report—some factors that he has omitted or misinterpreted. For purposes of scientific reporting, this is the only kind of audience in which he is interested. This same scientist may on another occasion be confronted with the necessity of persuading some audience *to act* upon his conclusions—to buy, sell, build, declare war, or do anything else that he believes to be sensible in terms of his conclusion. To accomplish this he may resort to all the "persuasive appeals" at his command; and when he does so he steps out of the role of scientist into that of advocate.

The good scientific report presents no more and no less than the legitimate truth-claim of the conclusions it sets forth. The contributor in discussion, we believe, will do well to emulate this kind of reporting in most respects. Nothing difficult or abstruse is involved in this advice. It means simply that whenever the speaker in discussion takes a position on some issue (it may be on a single aspect of definition or analysis or an explanation of a proposed solution) he should explain frankly and honestly *what* his position is and *why* and *how* he arrived at it. It may be called the explanatory, denotative, or empirical method, because the speaker attempts to describe the path that he followed in reaching his conclusion. Says Professor Dewey:

The empirical method points out when and where and how things of a designated description have been arrived at. It places before others a map of the road that has been travelled; they may accordingly, if they will, retravel the road to inspect the landscape for themselves. The scientific investigator convinces others not by the plausibility of his definitions and the cogency of his dialectic, but by placing before them the specified course of experiences, searchings, doings, and findings in consequence of which certain things have been found. . . . Dialectic thereby itself receives a designated status and office. . . . All the wit and subtlety of reflection and of dialectic find scope in the elaboration and conveying of directions that intelligibly point out a course to be followed.[7]

This is what we mean, then, by the explanatory, denotative, or empirical method. The speaker gives others an account of the reflective processes which he went through in reaching his conclusion. In so far as it is necessary for understanding, he presents the facts and expert opinions, the definitions, analysis (including his purposes and values), hypotheses considered, and what his reasoning has been on these hypotheses—in short, the

[7] John Dewey, *Experience and Nature* (Chicago, London: Open Court Publishing Company, 1925), p. 11.

factors which determine his proposal's claim to truth and group consideration. This method should be distinguished from the usual procedure of the persuader and debater. The advocate, even in the so-called logical approach (confirmation), attempts to demonstrate or prove a predetermined proposition by arraying in its support a syllogistic "trestlework," the premises of which have been *selected* not because they are the factors which influenced his acceptance of the proposition, but because he thinks that they will persuade or compel someone else to accept his conclusion. Unfortunately such a structure lends itself admirably to concealment and suppression, at least in its usual rhetorical forms.

C. ADVANTAGES OF THE EMPIRICAL METHOD.

We shall mention four advantages for discussion of this empirical method. First and foremost, the method is *conducive to critical, cooperative thought*. If the contributor tells the group frankly *what* he believes and *why* and *how* he reached his conclusion, the members can enter into his thinking, agree with him, disagree with him, but in any event they will understand him. Understanding him, they can, in turn, show *why* and *how* they disagree with him (if they do), at the precise point where they differ, in such a way as to make their difference intelligible (if not acceptable) to him. This *is* reflective group thinking.

Second, as a corollary of what has just been said, the method *encourages frankness in the statement of the purposes and values which are influencing thought*. It is impossible really to enter into a contributor's thinking until we know what purposes, wishes, desires, motives, values-are operating in his thinking. Granting that he may not be wholly conscious of these factors himself, and that often he may be reluctant to state them even when he is aware of their presence, the empirical method at least encourages an explanation of purpose, and prompts others to inquire into the values upon which the speaker is operating.

In the third place, the empirical approach *makes possible interesting and stimulating contributions*. The method gets away from the barren syllogistic demonstration which so often characterizes argumentative speech. But someone may object that there is nothing very interesting about a scientific report. Such reports are tremendously interesting to those who are capable of understanding them. Some of these reports are fascinating even to the lay listener or reader. Recall, for example, Paul de Kruif's dramatic description in *Microbe Hunters* of the work of Major Walter Reed of the United States Army, Dr. James Carroll, and others who went to Cuba in 1900 with a special commission to "give special attention to questions relating to the cause and prevention of yellow fever."[8] He describes the tremendous problem which these men faced and how they went about the business of solving it. This method of contributing conceives of thought as an aspect of experience and reports it with all the richness and warmth of the actual experience. What is more, the speaker in discussion ordinarily deals with questions in the realm of value and policy; while this will admittedly make his reporting less objective than that of the scientist, he will be dealing with experiences which are more immediate and vital to the average listener than those with which the scientific investigator is most often concerned.

A fourth advantage of the empirical method is *its ease and naturalness*. The five steps in reflective thinking describe a typical act of thought. In reporting one's thought in discussion one finds these same five steps at least suggestive of an organization which can be followed. This advice applies whether the speaker is presenting a complex set of experiences in a sixty-minute lecture or a brief observation on some specific point, let us say in analysis.

[8] Paul de Kruif, *Microbe Hunters* (New York: Harcourt, Brace and Company, 1926).

In each case he has met a problem and has thought his way through to a conclusion. The most simple and natural way of contributing his idea to the group is through an explanation of the steps in thought which led him to adopt this conclusion.

VI. EVALUATING AND CRITICIZING DISCUSSION

For groups which are using this book as a basis for directed experiences in discussion designed to develop proficiency in discussion, it is important that standards of evaluation and criticism be developed. The old saying that "practice makes perfect" is only a half-truth; much depends on the kind of practice. Much truer is the statement that "practice makes permanent." The repetition of errors and mistakes only serves to reinforce these mistakes and establish them as habits. Class discussions should be followed by periods of criticism in which the work of individuals and the group is evaluated and suggestions for improvement made.

One of the most useful purposes of this treatment of the principles and methods of discussion is to develop standards of criticism. The following criticism blank has been used to advantage in discussion classes. Our procedure has been to mimeograph this material on two sides of an 8½ x 11 sheet and place it in the hands of the instructor or an appointed observer during the discussion. This person is seated just outside the discussion circle where such note taking as needs to be done will not interfere with the progress of the discussion.

Check List for Group Discussion

Instructor .... Section No. ...... Date ....
Problem Discussed ....
  I. Conclusion Reached by Group ....
     (Here space is provided for a brief statement of the exact conclusion reached by the group or what appears to be the concluding position of the majority. Any well-developed minority position may be noted.)

II. The Pattern of the Discussion ....
    (Here is given a very brief outline of the progress of
    the discussion with attention given to the steps in re-
    flective thinking.)
III. Leadership ....
    (The observer writes a paragraph criticizing the leader
    of the discussion. See Chapter VIII, especially the check
    list at the end of the chapter.)

The above headings, without the parenthetical material, of course, are properly spaced and placed on one
side of the criticism blank. On the other side, running
the long way of the sheet, we suggest the headings and
columns shown in the accompanying figure.

Name	Number of Participations		Information on Problem			Attitude Toward Group				Attitude Toward Solution Favored by Majority					
										Before			After		
	Running Score	Total	Well-Informed, Thoughtful	Considerable Material, but Undigested	Poorly Informed	Cooperative	Argumentative	Dogmatic	Hostile	Pro	Doubtful	Con	Pro	Doubtful	Con
Smith		12	X			X						?	X		
Jones		15		X		X				X			X		
Brown		4			X			X		X				X	
etc.															

The information provided by this blank, together with
the discussion outlines prepared by members of the
group, can provide a helpful basis for criticizing and
evaluating the work of each person in the group. Additional standards of criticism can be developed in terms
of the special purpose of the discussion under consideration.

Where facilities are available, it has been found helpful to record one or more discussions and then play
them back to the group for purposes of criticism and
evaluation.

EXERCISES

1. Prepare a five-minute talk on some problem of your own choice. Plan this as a contribution in discussion in terms of the suggestions given in this chapter. Organize the talk on the basis of the five steps in reflective thinking. Consider questions such as these in criticizing the contributions: Was the speech clear and understandable? Was the contribution satisfactorily organized? Did the speaker appear interested, animated, and sincere, at the same time avoiding affective identification which his proposal? Were the attitude and manner of the speaker favorable to cooperative group deliberation? Was the thinking of the individual reported in such a way as to keep the thinking of the group in process? Was the speaker adequately informed? Following each talk, ask some member of the class to state in one minute what he has understood the position of the speaker to be. If the speaker has not been understood, let the class ask questions until such an understanding has been reached.

2. Study the discussions in Appendices A, B, and C from the standpoint of the contributions. So far as they are applicable, apply the questions in Exercise 1 to these contributions.

3. Conduct a class symposium on some suitable problem for discussion. From three to five members of the class representing different views on the problem may present five-minute contributions. The symposium may be opened by a student leader and followed by a face-to-face discussion in which all members of the group participate under the direction of the leader. In criticizing the symposium give special attention to the nature and method of the contributions, both of the symposium speakers and of those in the discussion period which follows.

4. Conduct a panel discussion followed by a period of general group discussion. Criticize the nature and method of the contributions.

5. Criticize the report of some experimental study such as can be found in journals reporting such studies. Out-

line the report in terms of the steps in reflective thinking and write a brief critique of the method.

6. Make a recording of a class discussion. Study the record carefully from the standpoint of the nature and
method of the contributions.

7. Conduct a practice discussion on some problem with
which the group is familiar. Experiment with procedure, giving each member an opportunity to lead
the group for a few minutes. Practice securing recognition, invoking the rule of the majority, limiting discussion. Criticize the way in which these procedural
problems are handled.

8. Write out five sample contributions in discussion dealing with different aspects of some problem with which
you are familiar. Make these from 50 to 75 words in
length. Plan them as examples of ways of dealing with
different situations which arise in discussion. Read these
contributions in class. Criticize the choice of words, the
attitudes indicated both by the composition and by the
manner of reading, and the clarity and vitality of the
contribution.

9. Conduct a class discussion in which the criticism blank
given in this chapter is used. Consider the discussion in
terms of the data on the completed blank. What do these
data reveal concerning your work in the discussion?

10. Divide the class into groups of two and conduct dialogues before the class. Let each pair choose its own
subject. Criticize the dialogues from the standpoint of
contributing. Consider pattern, continuity, spontaneity,
the form and method of contributing, attitudes and
manner of speaking, and general conversational ability.
Continue this drill with people who have difficulty in
contributing.

SELECTED BIBLIOGRAPHY

Elliott, Harrison S., *The Process of Group Thinking*. New
York: Association Press, 1932. Chapters III and IV.

Courtis, S. A., *Cooperation*. Ann Arbor, Michigan: Brumfield and Brumfield, 1934. Chapters V and XII.

Chase, Stuart, *The Tyranny of Words*. New York: Harcourt, Brace and Company, 1938.

Ogden, C. K., and Richards, I. A., *The Meaning of Meaning*. New York: Harcourt, Brace and Company, 1930. Chapters I, II, and VI.

Saidla, Leo E., and Gibbs, Warren E. (Editors), *Science and the Scientific Mind*. New York: McGraw-Hill Book Company, Inc., 1930. Chapter XXI.

Sarett, Lew, and Foster, William T., *Basic Principles of Speech*. Boston: Houghton Mifflin Company, 1936. Chapters II, IV, V, VIII, and XX.

Thouless, Robert, *Straight and Crooked Thinking*. New York: Simon and Schuster, 1932. Chapter I.

CHAPTER VIII

LEADING DISCUSSION

I. The Conceptions of Leadership
   A. The general attitude which the leader should take
   B. The degree of freedom which the leader should permit
   C. The general method which the leader should use
II. The Functions of the Leader
   A. What the leader should do
   B. What the leader should not do
III. The Qualities of the Leader
   A. Intellectual equipment
   B. Character and personality equipment
   C. Communicative equipment
IV. The Leader's Preparation for Discussion
   A. Personal preparation
   B. The preparation of the group
V. The Methods of Leadership
   A. Methods useful in fostering the usual processes of discussion
   B. Methods useful in handling difficult or unexpected situations
VI. Appraising Leadership

As was pointed out in Chapter II, discussion ordinarily takes place under the direction of a leader. In most situations the leader plays an indispensable role in discussion, and some semblance of leadership is usually helpful even in small, informal groups. Knowledge of the proper functions of the leader and skill in the leadership of discussion should be one of the primary objectives of study in this field.

I. THE CONCEPTIONS OF LEADERSHIP

Any consideration of the functions, qualities, and methods of the leader presupposes an understanding of the desirable type of leader and of his relationship to the discussion group. Three factors should be considered: (1) the general attitude which the leader should take toward the group; (2) the degree of freedom which the leader should permit the group; (3) the general method which the leader should use in conducting the discussion.

A. The General Attitude Which the Leader Should Take.

Three general attitudes are possible: (1) the leader understood as a dictator, who has thought through the problem and is convinced that his duty is to coerce the group to reach the same conclusion he has reached; (2) the leader understood as a group-instructor, who thinks it is his duty to overrule the wishes of the group if necessary in order to arrive more quickly at the conclusion which he feels certain it desires to reach; (3) the leader understood as a constructive guide, who by serving as a coordinator of the group has the obligation of helping each person to do his own thinking.[1]

We believe that the effective discussion leader is not a dictator or even an instructor, but a guide who is trying to arrange conditions so that each conferee can do his best in creative thinking and contributing. We believe this to be the ideal type of leadership both because it is the democratic way and because it is the means of most fully achieving the cooperative deliberation which is characteristic of good discussion. Whereas the other types of leaders may conduct orderly and neat semblances of discussion, it is only the democratic leader who can inspire confidence and stimulate each member to do his best.

B. The Degree of Freedom Which the Leader Should Permit.

Three degrees of freedom may be permitted by the leader: (1) He may plan the course of the discussion in

[1] See Emory S. Bogardus, *Leaders and Leadership* (New York: D. Appleton-Century Company, 1934), pp. 20-23.

advance and force the group to follow it; (2) he may give the group almost complete latitude to explore the problem as it wishes; (3) he may cooperate with the group in analyzing the problem, making contributions, and formulating conclusions, his suggestions being largely related to procedure rather than to subject matter.

We believe that wherever possible the leader should follow the third course and permit the maximum of freedom but should make his influence as a sympathetic guide felt when the occasion demands. He should think through the problem in advance, and he should give the group the benefit of his careful preparation; but he should not impose his thinking upon the discussion. After all, the discussion belongs to the group; and he should not be regarded as a subject-matter expert to the point where he can restrict the group's freedom of exploration and interpretation.

C. The General Method Which the Leader Should Use.

Three methods are also available in conducting the discussion: (1) There is the method in which the leader controls the discussion by issuing orders and making positive, didactic statements, viz., "The next point will now be taken up," or "We shall accept Mr. Smith's definition"; (2) contrasted with this is the method where the leader never makes a positive suggestion and confines himself to a few desultory questions or innocuous, devitalized expressions such as, "Has anyone anything to say?" or "Do you suppose I ought to try to sum this matter up?"; (3) there is the leader who asks discerning, thought-provoking questions and leads the discussion positively by occasional creative questions and suggestions such as, "Hadn't we better get this problem analyzed before talking about solutions?" or "Can someone give an example of Mr. Smith's point?" or "Shouldn't this point of view be considered?" We recommend this third method of leadership. The leader is a positive, stimulating force in the group situation; he is not a dominating factor nor is he a mere figurehead or non-entity.

II. THE FUNCTIONS OF THE LEADER

A. What the Leader Should Do.

The broad functions of the leader are five: (1) to secure the process of reflective thinking according to the procedure outlined in Chapter II and in harmony with time limits available and with the wishes of the group; (2) to secure the most cooperative type of participation on the part of each conferee; (3) to provide for the introduction of facts or expert testimony when needed; (4) to keep the discussion clear and well summarized; (5) to handle conflict creatively.

1. *To Secure the Process of Reflective Thinking.*— The leader is responsible for the broad outline of the procedure and for the orderly development of the logical pattern. Consequently, he should encourage the group to begin at a well-defined point and proceed with as few digressions as possible. He should also try to reconcile demands for protracted analysis of a certain point with those for progress to other steps in the pattern. He should try to adjust the development of this pattern to the time limits available for the meeting and to the wishes of the group. In attempting to secure the orderly development of the logical pattern, however, he should be careful to avoid pedantry and trifling insistence upon the "machinery" of the discussion. While we have pointed out that the typical organization of discussion is that of the steps in reflective thinking, it is a mistake to assume that these always occur, or should occur, in the sequence in which we have discussed them. These steps are suggestive of the logical pattern of discussion, but the leader should not be dogmatic in attempting to apply them. They should be used as a flexible guide rather than as a strait-jacket.

2. *To Secure the Most Cooperative Type of Participation.*—The leader should keep his eyes upon all members of the group in order to secure representative participation. Using the methods which are described later, he should try to elicit contributions from every person who has something of value to present. Likewise he should encourage friendly and cooperative participation in the spirit of good reflective thinking.

3. *To Provide for the Introduction of Information.*— The leader needs to be ready to detect the difference between informed and uninformed opinion and to note the points at which the group is in need of information. While the leader is not necessarily a subject-matter expert, he is obligated to sense the need for such information as an expert can provide, lest the discussion become but a series of uninformed opinions.

4. *To Keep the Discussion Clear and Orderly.*—The leader has an obligation to provide a perspective of the thinking process for the benefit of those so engrossed in it that they cannot see the whole pattern of the deliberation. He needs to be a part of the discussion and at the same time an observer surveying it from a distance. He needs to detect the time and place for a correlating or a summarizing statement, and the proper point for urging the group to progress to another step in the logical pattern.

5. *To Handle Conflict Creatively.*—The leader needs to know the different types of conflict, the motives underlying them, and the best means of dealing with them. He needs to study carefully the analysis of conflict which we provide in Chapter XIII and to be able to relate each type of conflict to the most satisfying deliberation on the part of the group.

The ideal leader is thus both a participant and an observer. He understands the meaning of every stage of the discussion, even taking notes if it seems advisable concerning the most important contributions and points of view. He realizes the part which each conferee is playing in the discussion and attempts to encourage him to make his most complete contribution. He needs to be able to steer the discussion around or through danger points caused by misunderstanding or by a belligerent or overzealous manner of participating.

B. What the Leader Should Not Do.

To this list of functions of the leader several cautions should be added. First, while leading and encouraging the group thinking process, he should not dominate it or control it autocratically. Second, he should not insist where the discussion should begin or make the "machinery" superior to spontaneous responses from the participants. One leader, for example, destroyed spontaneity and stifled participation by insisting that the discussion begin at a point of little interest to the group at the moment, even though the conferees were eager to contribute on another phase of the problem. He should have permitted the discussion to begin at the point of interest, then have brought the group around to the more logical starting point by inviting other contributions upon that phase of the problem. Third, he should not talk every time some member contributes. Fourth, he should not assume the role of an authority in the subject being discussed unless he has special qualifications other than that of being a discussion leader. Fifth, he should not summarize the progress of the discussion to the point of intruding or of slowing down the group process. Sixth, he should not be a protagonist or proponent of a point of view, but should be an objective interpreter of contributions from all members of the group.

III. THE QUALITIES OF THE LEADER

The functions of the discussion leader which we have just considered imply that he possess certain qualities which are fully as important as those required in an expert in any other field. These qualities may result in part from native capacities and in part from training and practice. We shall discuss these qualities under three heads: (1) intellectual equipment; (2) character and personality equipment; (3) communicative equipment.

A. INTELLECTUAL EQUIPMENT.

To meet the demands placed upon him, the leader should possess the following five qualities pertaining to intellectual equipment: (1) knowledge of discussion; (2) alertness of mind; (3) ability to diagnose; (4) objectivity; (5) knowledge of people.

1. *Knowledge of Discussion.*—Knowledge of discussion is needed if the leader is to realize the first function—that of securing the process of reflective thinking according to the pattern of group discussion. If he possesses this quality, he knows how to plan the sequence of "moves" and how to maintain a perspective of the process through which the group is moving under his guidance.

2. *Alertness of Mind.*—This quality is essential both because of the leader's position and because the group may very well include persons with keen and alert minds who are making contributions which he must be able to understand and to interpret if necessary. He must be able to sense the direction of the discussion, anticipate situations created by agreement or conflict, and adapt his remarks to these new situations. In this position the slow, deliberate thinker is unsatisfactory, because he will too often slow down and even destroy spontaneous group participation. The person who thinks rapidly and who "sees the point" quickly is the ideal discussion leader—provided, of course, that the other qualities also are present.

3. *Ability to Diagnose.*—Rapid thinking, however, is not enough. The leader must be able to analyze and synthesize, to diagnose the process of group thinking. He must sense causal relationships and think according to logical patterns. More than this, he should see the problem in perspective and sense the interrelations of the various contributions. This requirement demands keen ana-

lytical and synthesizing abilities lest the discussion be to him but a mass of statements and illustrations without order or pattern. Elliott describes this ability in these words: "It is this combination of analytic and synthetic capacity which the chairman of the discussion must develop. He brings out every detail in the situation, every individual contribution of the group members, but he sees each in its relation to other contributions and to the total picture of the situation or to the conclusions as to what to do. He must be able to see the bearing of various contributions to the progress of the discussion."[2]

4. *Objectivity.*—The leader must be objective, because the opinionated or prejudiced person will only with the greatest of difficulty create a cooperative attitude in the group. He should serve as a referee or interpreter, not as a protagonist of some point of view. He should appraise each contribution fairly, not maximize or minimize according to his predetermined opinions.

5. *Knowledge of People.*—This ability will enable the chairman to understand the characteristics of the persons in his group as well as the motives underlying their contributions. In other words, the leader who knows human beings can survey intelligently and classify accurately the members of the group according to personality types, background, ability to contribute, and point of view. Seeing the group as more than an aggregate of individuals, he can secure balance and progress by varying his methods of encouraging contributions and by reacting sympathetically and constructively to individual differences. Furthermore, the leader who knows human beings can appraise intelligently the probable motives actuating contributions, separating prejudiced observations from well-founded comments, and undesirable conflict from that which results from a clash of rational points of view. To this type of leader there will

[2] Harrison S. Elliott, *The Process of Group Thinking* (New York: Association Press, 1932), p. 80.

be meanings in tones of voice, facial expressions, and phraseology.

B. Character and Personality Equipment.

The effective leader should possess the following three qualities pertaining to character and personality equipment: (1) patience and self-restraint; (2) stimulating personality; (3) sense of humor.

1. *Patience and Self-restraint.*—The leader needs this quality in order to avoid becoming disconcerted by seemingly inadequate contributions or by conflicts. He should also restrain himself from rushing to straighten out a phase of the discussion which seems to him to be involved. He should be patient and restrain himself, realizing that the values of discussion will ordinarily be achieved only if the participants resolve the conflicts or advance the thinking process through their own contributions—under his wise guidance, of course. He needs to remember that effective group deliberation may be slower than individual thinking, but that the meeting of many minds may ultimately produce a superior product.

2. *Stimulating Personality.*—Normally the effectiveness of the leader may be in direct proportion to the warmth of his personality and to his interest in the group and its problems. The leader can make the group dull and uninterested by a cold, I-don't-care attitude, or he can make it eager and interested by alertness and responsiveness to his task and to the contributions of the participants. Frequently the leader with this quality is able to stimulate spontaneous contributions almost at once from a group which otherwise would be reticent and reserved.

3. *Sense of Humor.*—The leader can do much to avoid irritations by making use of a sense of humor. Just as a "soft answer turneth away wrath," so a humorous allusion may soften a dogmatic statement or an emotionally charged situation. The destructive effects of a heated

remark may thus be minimized and the discussion restored to a plane of cooperation.

C. COMMUNICATIVE EQUIPMENT.

In group discussion attention must necessarily be given to the problem of communication. Important as this may be for the average participant, it is doubly significant for the leader, who is required to coordinate and evaluate contributions from many sources. For this reason he will need facility in phrasing and proficiency in oral expression. The leader who cannot clothe his thoughts in adequate language can only with great difficulty keep the discussion clear. Conversely, the leader who can express himself, who can adeptly phrase and rephrase questions, and who can do so pleasingly and clearly will be of great assistance to the group process.

We realize that the concept of the effective leader which we have here presented may be too ideal or impossible of attainment. If this be true—and we hope that it is not—we justify our point of view on the grounds that the ideal should be emphasized in order to make group discussion as effective as possible. We realize that persons of various backgrounds, abilities, and kinds of training are serving as discussion leaders with some degree of success; but it is our hope that through this description of certain ideal qualities we can encourage people to become even more successful leaders. In order to assist prospective leaders, we are including in this chapter a section devoted to the preparation of the leader and one devoted to a practical treatment of methods of handling specific problems likely to arise in discussion.

IV. THE LEADER'S PREPARATION FOR DISCUSSION

A. PERSONAL PREPARATION.

Before undertaking to lead a discussion, the leader should inform himself concerning the subject for con-

sideration and learn to recognize the dominant characteristics of the group which he will guide. Wherever
possible, this preparation should be carried on systematically and it should provide the leader with at least a
general knowledge of the subject and with the ability to
detect the nature of the group as well.

The preparation on the subject should be carried on
in the manner suggested in Chapter VI, embracing the
direct and the indirect preparation recommended for
the members of the group. The leader often will do well
to prepare a discussion outline in the same form as that
described for the participants. In some cases it may be
wise for him to annotate this outline in such a way as to
give him cues for his moves as a leader.

The leader's preparation with respect to the group
should include training in recognition of its nature, its
relation to the subject, and its readiness for the discussion. The leader should equip himself to recognize the
personality type of the group, its level of information in
general and with respect to the problem, its level of interest, and its point of view toward the subject.

Any good public speaker recognizes the importance
of knowing his audience and adjusting to it. For different reasons, but in the same general way, the leader
should be sensitive to individual idiosyncrasies and group
differences. This does not imply any mystical or clair-
voyant ability, but rather the capacity to size up people
intelligently and sympathetically.

While it is sometimes possible to study the group in
advance, what is more important the good leader should
bring to his task a mature knowledge of people, a warm
liking for people, and a fine ability to perceive and react
constructively to the many cues which he can get from
the behavior of the group as the discussion proceeds.

B. The Preparation of the Group.

In some cases the leader may wish to assist the group
in preparing for the discussion by making study-guides

and distributing them to the conferees. In doing so he should not step too definitely into the role of teacher and certainly not into that of dictator. On the contrary, he should merely make available a tentative outline of materials, suggest readings, and ask questions. Such a service to the group is especially valuable in cases where the members are not likely otherwise to have access to such materials.

To guide him in this phase of preparation, the leader will find abundant materials available. For example, the United States Department of Agriculture has a series of pamphlets prepared especially for use by discussion groups. These pamphlets contain reading lists, provide certain necessary factual materials, give points of view arising from the facts, and raise issues which may be developed by the group. One "Subject-Matter Pamphlet" entitled *Taxes: Who Pays, What For?* introduces the topic by enumerating the kinds of taxes, then asks such questions as: "Who pays taxes? Why have taxes? What limits taxes? How should a tax system be judged? For what purposes should tax money be used? What tax schedules would best fit current needs?" Several pages are devoted to brief discussions of these questions, to the presentation of facts, and to the listing of questions useful in discussion.

The Educational and Recreational Guides, Inc., issues each month a *Group Discussion Guide* and also *Photoplay Studies*, consisting of study-guides and materials for discussing photoplays. For example, the guide to Maxwell Anderson's *Winterset* includes a discussion of the playwright, of the background of the play, of the play and the photoplay, together with questions and readings.

The Institute for Propaganda Analysis assembles its *Monthly Letters* into annual volumes (see Volume I, 1938) to which are added "Suggested Activities and Discussion Notes." The H. W. Wilson Company also has a *Discussion Series: Contemporary Social Problems.* This series is designed to provide analytical and background material on current problems.

Another useful set of outlines and study-guides has been prepared by the Inquiry.[3] Included in the nearly fifty such outlines are the following: "Attitudes Toward Unemployment—Outline for Group Discussion for National Federation of Settlements" in *Occasional Papers*, May, 1929; "The Worker and His Job" (three outlines) in *Occasional Papers*, April-May-June, 1925; "What Use Can We Make of the Peace Pacts?" in *Occasional Papers*, February, 1929; "The Social Worker and His Job" in *Occasional Papers*, May, 1927.

It is a common practice in certain groups for the leader to mimeograph study-guides and bibliographical materials for the benefit of the group. He may use materials already in print so far as they are applicable, or he may work out guides of his own, using these materials as models.

V. THE METHODS OF LEADERSHIP

A. METHODS USEFUL IN FOSTERING THE USUAL PROCESSES OF DISCUSSION.

We are here concerned with some methods for meeting the following six problems: (1) how to get the group acquainted; (2) how to get the discussion started; (3) how to help all members contribute their best; (4) how to keep the discussion moving and at the same time clear; (5) how to determine whether to introduce otherwise unconsidered material in order to keep the pattern adequate; (6) how to bring the discussion to a satisfying conclusion.

1. *How to Get the Group Acquainted.*—Various suggestions concerning the getting-acquainted process may be made. Informal introductions under the guidance of the leader may well precede the discussion. Informal seating and informal speaking will do much to secure what several observers have termed the "clublike" attitude. A recess in a long discussion may be useful in en-

[3] These and other materials of the Inquiry are published by the Association Press, New York.

couraging casual conversation and in developing friendliness. A postdiscussion period of getting together
informally has in some cases been useful in groups whose
sessions continue for several days.

2. *How to Get the Discussion Started.*—Several ways
of starting the discussion may prove useful. The leader
should attempt to learn whether the group is of the "self-
starting" type or whether it needs artificial means of getting under way. If it is of the former type, the leader is,
of course, not confronted with a problem of stimulating
discussion. If, however, it needs the assistance of the
chairman, he may well use one or a combination of the
following means. He may make a brief introductory
statement concerning the purpose of the group and the
nature of the problem. He may define the problem and
make it vital by relating it to the experiences of the conferees. He may follow the statement of the problem with
a brief explanation of the nature of group discussion,
outlining the plan of reflective thinking and proposing
the general use of it. He may present a case or incident
which will prompt the group to discuss it, the problem
which it presents, and the possible solutions of the problem. He may present in bold contrast two points of view
concerning solutions of a problem in the hope that the
contrast will start discussion. He may ask for incidents,
observations, or experiences of a kind which most of the
group have had and about which they will talk freely.
If he wishes to be less direct and use the statement-
question or question approach, he may throw out a
question or two designed to stimulate response. Another
method is to ask some member to present his view as a
starting point for the discussion.

3. *How to Help All Members Contribute Their Best.*
—In order to help all members contribute their best, the
chairman should try to recognize different persons from
time to time, encouraging contributions from all parts of
the group and all types of personalities. The manner of
the leader can also be an influential factor in helping the

conferees to do their best. If he thinks clearly and contributes in a cooperative spirit, he may encourage a like attitude and like habits in the others of the group.

4. *How to Keep the Discussion Moving and at the Same Time Clear.*—The leader should maintain a "happy medium" between tedious movement and too-rapid progress, avoiding petty digressions, and summing up wisely and succinctly. He may save time and keep the discussion clear by supplementing his oral summaries with blackboard notations and graphs indicating progress. Wherever possible, he should try to avoid deadlocks by securing either tentative conclusions acceptable to all members or an agreement to suspend judgment until further information is available. Furthermore, he should encourage every person to speak to the issue at hand, and he should be ready to point out irrelevancies or suggest the advisability of withholding certain contributions until a more appropriate time. Finally, he should be careful to recognize the time for movement to another step in the thinking process. To secure this movement he may simply direct the group to another matter. Should certain members insist upon continued discussion of a point which the leader feels has been adequately handled, he may request a majority ruling of the group, as pointed out in Chapter VII. In some cases the group may wish to impose time limits upon contributions or upon certain phases of the discussion.

5. *How to Determine Whether to Introduce Otherwise Unconsidered Material in Order to Keep the Pattern Adequate.*—In many cases the leader will be justified in introducing material which he knows is pertinent and believes to be essential. It is necessary, however, that he be careful lest he dictate excessively to the group or distort the discussion according to his own point of view. We believe that any of the following methods will be satisfactory. He may invite a member to introduce the material. He may prompt its introduction by asking pertinent questions. Or he may change his role from that of

chairman to ordinary participant—making his temporary change clear in order to avoid misunderstanding—and introduce the material himself. In any event, he should not impose himself or his point of view but should show the importance of this new material to orderly thinking.

6. *How to Bring the Discussion to a Satisfying Conclusion.*—Here lies the crux of much adverse criticism of discussion. Many participants become dissatisfied because they cannot see any tangible results, and they regard discussion as merely aimless talking with no visible outcomes. Here the leader can perform a service to both the members of a particular group and the cause of discussion. For the learning group he can provide a summary and interpret the results, showing the progress that has been made. It may be well for him to reconstruct briefly the pattern of the group's deliberation in order to systematize the summary. For the policy-determining group he may try to effect a consensus to bring the process to a satisfying conclusion—in this case, the basis of subsequent action. Failing of this, he may take a vote to determine the size of the majority and the probable reasons for the point of view of the majority. (See the chapters on "Learning Groups" and "Policy-determining Groups" for more specific suggestions.)

B. Methods Useful in Handling Difficult or Unexpected Situations.

Frequently the leader will be confronted with such disturbing and difficult situations as that presented by: (1) the ready-talking, interrupting conferee; (2) the nonresponsive member; (3) the too-assertive member; (4) the member who is overanxious to settle the problem; (5) the antagonistic member; (6) extrinsic conflict.

1. *The Ready-Talking, Interrupting Conferee.*—This type of person, who often kills interest in creative discussion, must be handled politely but firmly by the leader. One means that has been found useful is to interrupt him pleasantly and ask him to state his point briefly.

Another is to interrupt, sum up his contribution, and ask for contributions from other members; and a third method is to ask him to yield to the other members. As an extreme measure the leader may request that members be recognized by him before speaking. He can then control those who appear to be dominating the situation. If there is any question about the imposition of this requirement, he may ask for a confirmation of his ruling by a majority vote.

2. *The Nonresponsive Member.*—This may be a difficult problem to diagnose because the failure of any member to contribute may be the result of natural reticence or the fact that the member thinks more slowly and deliberately than the others. If the member is reticent, the leader should not force any contribution at the outset but should eventually direct a question at him and finally bring him fully into the discussion. If the person appears to be a deliberate thinker, the leader should give him time and permit him to contribute when he desires. It may be well for the leader to suggest occasionally that those who have spoken most often should give an opportunity for comment to those who have not done so. Sometimes an informal conversation outside the group discussion or a special assignment calling for a specific contribution may elicit responses from the person who does not enter easily into the discussion.

3. *The Too-Assertive Member.*—This person, who makes a dogmatic statement without qualification or adequate support, may be handled by asking him to repeat his assertion and to explain it. Frequently his explanation will include important qualifications which modify his original dogmatic position, or it may include supporting material which he was previously unwilling to present.

4. *The Member Who Is Overanxious to Settle the Problem.*—This person, who wishes to use short cuts in thinking, may be encouraged to use the pattern of reflective thinking and thus remain in step with the group. For

instance, the leader may convince him of the need for greater deliberation by asking him some questions on steps which the member wishes to omit, or the leader may point out wherein the group avoided misunderstanding at earlier stages in its thinking by using a more systematic procedure. Continued interruption on this member's part may also be met by the method proposed for the handling of the interrupting member.

5. *The Antagonistic Member.*—This person, who is fiery and caustic, may well be handled by the three methods suggested by Sheffield. First, the leader should divert any caustic or angry remarks from the group to himself, then ask the maker of the remark to explain it to him. This should cause both the caustic person and the group to regain composure. Second, the leader should sum up in a quiet voice and in less "charged" words the apparent reasons for anger. Third, the leader should remind the group that frank discussion requires self-control and that if the group is to progress it must exercise self-control even if provoked by caustic remarks.[4]

6. *Extrinsic Conflict.*—The whole problem of conflict, especially that which we call *extrinsic*, is so important and requires so much care in handling that we have chosen to give it treatment in a separate chapter. Detailed suggestions for both the leader and the conferee are provided in Chapter XIII.

VI. APPRAISING LEADERSHIP

In addition to understanding the functions, qualities, and methods of the successful leader, we should consider certain criteria by which his work may be judged. A check list of tests may serve to correlate the various principles and methods described in this chapter and also to aid the leader in measuring his effectiveness. We suggest that the leader ask himself the following questions at the close of a discussion:

[4] Alfred D. Sheffield, *Creative Discussion* (New York: Association Press, 1933), p. 62.

1. Did I state the problem fairly and clearly?
2. Did I stimulate spontaneous participation at the outset and maintain it throughout the discussion?
3. Did I guide the discussion in the pattern of reflective thinking without making the pattern too obvious?
4. Did I succeed in guiding the group without intruding or assuming the role of dictator?
5. Did I succeed in getting all members of the group to participate?
6. Did I encourage the statement of all different points of view?
7. Did I clarify and summarize adequately without impeding the spontaneous progress of the discussion?
8. Did I adequately handle the problem of expert information by detecting the need for it and providing for the obtaining of it?
9. Did I tactfully and constructively handle troublesome individuals and unexpected situations?
10. Did I successfully handle the various types of conflict?
11. Did I keep the spirit of the discussion cooperative and creative?
12. Did I maintain the proper pace for the group, unobtrusively speeding up or slowing down the progress as the materials and the responses of the members warranted?

If the meeting has gone badly, the leader will probably find the reason in a negative answer to one or more of these questions. Conversely, affirmative replies will almost certainly be signs of successful leadership and profitable discussion in so far as the leader has the power to make it such.

Exercises

1. Analyze the work of the leader in the discussion reprinted in Appendix A. How did he phrase his contributions? How often did he contribute? How far did he impose himself? Apply to his work the tests given in Section VI of this chapter.

2. Study the "Round Table" reprinted in Appendix B. Who served as leader? How do you know? What did he contribute? Was a separate leader needed? Why?

3. Analyze the work of the chairman in the forum reprinted in Appendix C. How did he introduce the discussion? How well did he do it? How often did he contribute? How far did he impose himself? Apply to his work the tests given in Section VI of this chapter.

4. Analyze the work of the leader in each of the following discussions in *Discussion Methods for Adult Groups* by Fansler: (a) forum dialogue, pp. 29-51; (b) group discussion, pp. 71-80; (c) group discussion, pp. 82-99; (d) panel discussion, pp. 111-132. How did he phrase his contributions? How often did he contribute? How far did he impose himself? Apply to his work the tests given in Section VI of this chapter.

5. Analyze the work of the leader in each of the seven discussions in the *Journal of Adult Education* and each of the two discussions in *Religious Education* cited in the bibliography at the end of this chapter. How did he phrase his contributions? How often did he contribute? How far did he impose himself? Apply to his work the tests given in Section VI of this chapter.

6. Write 250-350 words on one or more of the following: (a) the functions of the leader; (b) discussion without a leader; (c) the qualities of the good leader; (d) the preparation of the leader; (e) the leader of discussion vs. the chairman of debate; (f) a successful leader whom I have observed. In preparing these essays, use material found in the bibliography at the end of this chapter.

7. Select a topic for discussion and prepare an adequate study-guide for the use of the group. Organize the material under useful headings.

8. Prepare a discussion outline upon a selected topic. Annotate it so that it will serve as a guide to the leader in conducting a discussion. Indicate points at which the leader will probably need to make contributions, at which troublesome situations may arise, and at which special information may be needed.

9. Write brief statements using the language which would be appropriate for the leader in dealing with the following situations; imagine a specific situation and write as though you were the leader: (a) a group which ignores the logical pattern of discussion; (b) a situation in which the requirements of time or material demand that the group proceed to another phase of the pattern; (c) a situation in which a summary is needed; (d) a proper closing of the discussion.

10. Write brief statements using the language which would be appropriate for the leader in dealing with the following situations; imagine a specific situation and write as though you were the leader: (a) a talkative member; (b) a reticent member; (c) a member who wishes to make a short cut in the procedure; (d) a sarcastic or antagonistic member.

11. Prepare and present a five-minute speech introducing a discussion. (This exercise can profitably be performed by each person in the class.)

12. Conduct a class discussion with a member of the class acting as the leader. At the next meeting of the class each person should present a summary of the discussion.

13. Conduct a class discussion. Each member of the class should then prepare a critique of the work of the leader.

14. Conduct a discussion in which each member of the class is prepared to act as the leader. When the group convenes, call on one person to start as the leader; after a few minutes call on a second person; etc.

Selected Bibliography

Artman, J. M., and Others, "The Problems Brought to Religious and Character Education by the Socio-Economic Debacle," *Religious Education*. Vol. 29, June, 1934, pp. 266-270. (A panel discussion.)

Bogardus, Emory S., *Leaders and Leadership*. New York: D. Appleton-Century Company, 1934. Chapters I and II.

Bryson, Lyman, *Adult Education*. New York: American Book Company, 1936. Chapter V and pp. 83-90.

Bryson, Lyman, and Others, "Recent Trends in the American Movement for Adult Education," *Journal of Adult*

Education. Vol. 5, June, 1933, pp. 265-270. (A panel discussion.)

Charters, Jessie A., "The Training of Leaders for Adult and Study Groups," *Journal of Adult Education.* Vol. 2, January, 1930, pp. 16-21.

Courtis, Stuart A., and Others, "The Function of Education in Achieving and Maintaining a Social Order of Integrated Persons," *Religious Education.* Vol. 29, June, 1934, pp. 271-281. (A panel discussion.)

Elliott, Harrison S., *The Process of Group Thinking.* New York: Association Press, 1932. Chapters V, VI, VII, VIII.

Ellis, A. Caswell, and Others, "Education for Citizenship," *Journal of Adult Education.* Vol. 4, June, 1932, pp. 260-265. (A panel discussion.)

Garland, J. V., and Phillips, Charles F., *Discussion Methods.* New York: H. W. Wilson Company, 1939. (A collection of discussions with suggestions on method.)

Johnson, Roy I., "Standards in Round-Table Discussion," *School Review.* Vol. 37, January, 1929, pp. 44-48.

Lawrence, James C., and Others, "Unemployment Educational and Guidance Problems," *Journal of Adult Education.* Vol. 4, June, 1932, pp. 266-278. (A panel discussion.)

Leigh, Robert D., *Group Leadership.* New York: W. W. Norton and Company, 1936. Pp. 82-86.

Lindeman, Eduard C., "Social Methods for Social Problems," *Progressive Education.* Vol. 10, May, 1933, pp. 253-255.

Mueller, A. D., *Principles and Methods of Adult Education.* New York: Prentice-Hall, Inc., 1937. Chapters VII and VIII.

Overstreet, Harry A., and Others, "Education for Culture," *Journal of Adult Education.* Vol. 4, June, 1932, pp. 249-259. (A panel discussion.)

Overstreet, Harry A., and Others, "To What Extent Does Radio Broadcasting in the United States Need Public Regulation?" *Journal of Adult Education.* Vol. 6, June, 1934, pp. 278-285. (A panel discussion.)

Russell, James E., and Others, "Occupational Education," *Journal of Adult Education.* Vol. 4, June, 1932, pp. 279-284. (A panel discussion.)

Scott, Elmer, and Others, "Social Values in Adult Education," *Journal of Adult Education.* Vol. 4, June, 1932, pp. 240-248. (A panel discussion.)

Sheffield, Alfred D., *Creative Discussion.* New York: Association Press, 1927. Pp. 31-46. (See 1933 ed. also.)

Tead, Ordway, *The Art of Leadership.* New York: Whittlesey House, McGraw-Hill Book Company, Inc., 1935.

Walser, Frank, *The Art of Conference.* New York: Harper and Brothers, 1933. Chapter IV.

CHAPTER IX

THE ROLE OF FACTS AND EXPERT OPINIONS IN DISCUSSION

A city council spent some time at one of its meetings in a discussion of the alleged failure of a manufacturing company to live up to its agreement concerning the employment of local labor. One member said that more of the company's employees lived outside of the city than inside. One said that a person who "should know" had said so. Another said that similar reports had come to him. The discussion continued with charges of broken faith and with suggestions concerning means of correcting the condition. Finally, the suggestion was made that the facts be secured and that the discussion be continued only when the rumors had been verified.

When consulted, the president of the company said that the payroll on that day showed a total of 148 employees and of this number 116 were residents of the city, 25 lived on rural routes of the city, and 7 lived in other communities. The seven, he said, included persons in administrative positions who could not well be replaced by local labor.

This case illustrates several problems of interest to students of discussion. It shows how futile and wasteful of time and effort discussion can be without facts. It shows how even allegedly expert testimony can be misleading. It shows how facts can alter the course of a discussion which has ignored them. It shows, also, how dependent we are upon facts, and consequently how carefully we should test them before finally accepting them. For example, were these facts submitted by the president wholly valid, and did they completely represent the situation?

Thus facts and expert opinions have an important role in discussion even though it may sometimes be an impromptu and unprepared conversation. In this chapter we shall first consider the nature of facts and expert opinions, then observe their relation to the preparation of the participants in discussion. Next we shall consider their uses, their sources and means of introduction into the discussion, and the suitable tests for them.

I. THE NATURE OF FACTS AND EXPERT OPINIONS AND THEIR RELATION TO THE ORDINARY AND THE EXPERT WITNESS

By facts we mean statistics and cases the nature and existence of which are not subject to opinion. They are phenomena which are observed, described, classified, and reported. They are subject to errors through human frailty only in so far as there are deficiencies in gathering and describing them. For example, facts may consist of data concerning the population of the United States, the number of persons, racial affiliations, or places of residence. Or they may consist of such instances as those in a list of universities having field houses, student union buildings, or dormitories for men.

By expert opinion we mean a point of view held by a person who through training, position, or special experience is peculiarly able to interpret or criticize phenomena. This opinion may consist of an expert's testimony concerning the meaning of data about population, for example, or about the value of the dormitories for men.

Facts and expert opinions must also be considered with respect to the ordinary and the expert witness. To the student of discussion the term "witness" may be confusing, suggesting as it does a person in a court of law. To us at this point it has the following meaning: The ordinary witness is that observer and reporter of facts or purveyor of information who possesses no special equipment for compilation, interpretation, and criticism of phenomena. The expert witness, on the other hand, should possess this equipment.

Facts are customarily reported by ordinary witnesses. Facts thus given are normally accepted even though the qualifications of these witnesses are only honesty, reasonable intelligence, and care in observation. But ordinary witnesses are not infallible reporters even if they are honest, intelligent, and careful. Powers of observation and classification of phenomena may be subject to "expertness," which consists of training, position, or special experience in addition to these other capacities. For instance, any normal person can "count noses," make observations, and report his findings quite satisfactorily. But when fine distinctions among phenomena are required, the ordinary witness is quite likely to fail even as an observer. At this point the expert witness must be called upon.

Authoritative opinion is rarely accepted from ordinary witnesses, because special competence is normally regarded as the first requisite of the interpreter and critic of phenomena. Consider, for example, the fact that whereas we accept only rarely the average person's interpretation of reasons for shifts in centers of population, we more readily accept the interpretation of such data by a trained sociologist.

II. THE RELATION OF FACTS AND EXPERT OPINIONS TO THE PREPARATION OF THE MEMBERS OF THE GROUP

The question is often asked: Shouldn't discussion be reserved for those people who possess "all the facts" or who are experts in the problem being considered? We answer in the negative. We believe that, while facts and expert opinions are needed for intelligent discussion, it is unnecessary to wait until all the facts are in and a group of experts has been marshaled. It is true that from many points of view the ideal situation for discussion is one in which all the facts are present and the participants are experts—that, for example, experts connected with departments of state and foreign affairs should be the only ones to discuss problems of treaties. It is also true that persons with broad training and backgrounds will ordinarily accomplish more with group discussion than will those with more limited resources. It is likewise very true that specific preparation for the deliberation of a problem is usually helpful and should be encouraged. But in the absence of the ideal condition, the most useful position to take, we believe, is to encourage the best deliberation in the light of the available information, then to secure additional data by the best means possible. Especially is this true when you consider that the values of discussion lie not only in the adequacy of the answers provided, but in the opportunities for growth which it affords to the individual participating.

This point of view seems tenable for several reasons. While realizing that persons of limited background often attempt to discuss with few facts and sound opinions available, we believe that to exclude the average person is to deny him the opportunities which discussion presents. After all, discussion does not presume to be an instrument for scientific exploration, but a means of fostering critical and cooperative thinking. Furthermore, we believe that it is better to create through the medium of discussion uses for information and to make provision for securing it than to deny any opportunity for discussion merely because a complete stock of information is not available in advance.

Discussion should also help persons to watch their own experiences and to draw conclusions from them, as well as to form their own points of view based upon facts and expert opinions. What is more, discussion can be useful in demonstrating the futility of attempting to proceed far without securing adequate information.

III. THE USES OF FACTS AND EXPERT OPINIONS IN DISCUSSION

A. What They Should Do.

Facts and expert opinions are useful to discussion in supplying information upon which to construct good reasoning, in clearing away blockades created by disputes over matters of fact, and in providing authoritative conclusions upon which the less expert thinking of the participants can rely.

The introduction of such information should serve to add validity to the group's thinking. It should also serve to prevent the continuing of an argument on a point which could be settled quickly and finally by stating a fact or even an expert opinion. If a fact is introduced, argument should terminate at that point and be taken up elsewhere. To argue over a fact implies a misunderstanding of what facts are, a disagreement over the reasonableness or source of the facts, or a disagreement over the meanings of the facts in question. If there is misunderstanding as to what facts are, argument over them is beside the point, because facts are found not through argument but through investigation. If, on the other hand, there is disagreement over the reasonableness or the source of the facts, or over the meanings of the facts, discussion may take place concerning these matters but not concerning the facts themselves. The discussion then deals with the means of arriving at the facts or with the meanings of the facts.[1]

The introduction of expert opinions may enable the participants in discussion to project their thinking more readily into new realms. This can often be done because they can use the expert opinions to short-circuit lines of thought less comprehensible to them and thus proceed to a point which they can profitably consider. This process is open, of course, to the danger of stifling creativeness and independence in thinking, and hence must be used carefully.

The second major purpose served by facts and expert opinions is to suggest possible charts of discussion. Because the expert has the benefit of knowledge, training, and experience not available to the members of the group he is able through his opinions to open up vistas of thought which would not ordinarily occur to them. His influence may be felt in several ways. He may, as Elliott says, place "the immediate problems in their wider setting" by bringing "to the group instances of the problem in areas of life with which the members are unfamiliar." He may also "open problems not felt by the group." He may present "a point of view by one whose experience is recognized as significant."[2]

B. What They Should Not Do.

The value of facts and expert opinions to discussion should not blind us, however, to the dangers in their indiscriminate use or to the possibility of their misuse. There are three unjustifiable uses of them: (1) the use and acceptance of *purported* facts as material not open

---

[1] See Mortimer J. Adler, *Dialectic* (New York: Harcourt, Brace and Company, 1927), Part I, Chapter 2.

[2] Harrison S. Elliott, *The Process of Group Thinking* (New York: Association Press, 1932), pp. 139-142.

to question; (2) the use of facts to supersede reasoning on points which might profitably be thought out; (3) the use of expert opinions to dictate the group's point of view or to supersede critical reasoning, except in certain aspects of the problem where the group is not equipped to deal with them reflectively.

To protect himself against the first misuse, a participant in discussion should be alert to inspect what are represented as facts, and inquire whether these facts are made available by an ordinary or an expert witness and whether the method of transmission affects their validity. He should assure himself that they have been gathered properly and have not been subjected to distortion and coloring. In other words, he should apply those tests suggested in Section V of this chapter before permitting the facts to serve as conclusive bases of thinking.

To protect himself against the use of facts to supersede reasoning, a conferee should guard against stopping short upon learning of certain data which may be perfectly acceptable. He should continue the reasoning process by giving meaning to the facts if that can profitably be done. If he simply and naïvely defers to the facts, discussion becomes but a series of steps from one fact to another instead of being the process of reasoning implicit in the very nature of discussion.

To avoid permitting the opinions of authorities to dictate his course unduly, the participant in discussion will do well not to accept blindly the opinions of experts, but to use these opinions merely as means of carrying his own thinking further. He should guard against being told how to think, even though the substitution of such opinions may be the easy way out of certain difficulties. Except in those aspects of the problem where he and the others in the group are not equipped to deal with them reflectively, independence of thought should be preserved even though assistance from authorities may be secured and wisely used.

IV. THE MEANS OF SECURING AND INTRODUC-ING FACTS AND EXPERT OPINIONS

The members of a discussion group will be constantly confronted with the problem of securing facts and expert opinions and of making them available at the most advantageous time. This situation presents two problems and questions: (1) What are the sources available? (2) What are the ways of introducing the information?

A. SOURCES OF FACTS AND EXPERT OPINIONS.

The sources of information are three: (1) the indirect preparation of the members of the group; (2) their direct preparation; (3) reports made by one or more authorities meeting with the group. The first two are described in detail in Chapter VI, which considers preparation for discussion, and will be only mentioned again here.

The indirect preparation of the members, which consists of everything in their background, is a useful and probably the most widely employed source of information for discussion. For example, a group of parents at one time carried on an effective discussion of problems of bringing up children. No member was a technical expert or had prepared himself specifically for this discussion. The fathers were businessmen and teachers, one mother had done some general reading in the literature of child care, and all the parents had had, of course, many experiences with their children. Out of the pooling of experiences and the reasoning from the facts and opinions there came a sizable body of material which was useful as the basis of deliberation. The point is that, while the pooling of ignorance will not result in profitable discussion, the resources of a group through its background may be surprisingly great. Furthermore, the richer and fuller the background of any member of the group is, other things being equal, the more competent is he as a witness.

The direct preparation of the members, which consists

of specific reading and possibly directed experiences for the discussion, is useful in supplementing the background preparation. This may take the form of reading materials suggested by a study-guide or bibliography, or of reading or experiences undertaken by the participant because he sees the usefulness of such preparation for this discussion.

The third source of facts and expert opinions consists of reports made by one or more authorities meeting with the group. These persons will presumably be the expert witnesses referred to earlier in this chapter. They need not necessarily be authorities in the sense of technical experts but in the sense of persons whose training and experience peculiarly fit them to present facts or opinions bearing upon the problem being discussed. Technical experts may be no more useful in this capacity than are persons whose experiences, combined with normal intelligence, honesty, and care in observation and interpretation, are close to the problem under discussion. A capable farmer, for example, may be a most satisfactory source of facts and competent opinions concerning certain problems of agriculture; and a labor union leader may provide information useful to a group considering labor problems.

B. Ways of Introducing Facts and Expert Opinions.

We now face the question: By what means can these facts and expert opinions be introduced into the discussion? This problem involves three variables: (1) *Who* can introduce the information? (2) *When* can the information be introduced? (3) *How* can the information be made available?

The facts and expert opinions can be presented by the members of the group or by the authorities who are meeting with the group. The information can be introduced at almost any time, as, for example, in a report or a lecture preceding the discussion proper, or in a contribution made at a point late in the deliberations when it is needed to develop the process of reasoning. The information can be submitted in the form of a carefully prepared lecture, a book report, a systematic report of an experience, or an impromptu contribution made at the point of need in the discussion. This last is, of course, the most usual and customary method. These variables do not necessarily affect the validity of the facts and opinions; they merely relate to the means by which the information is made available. Comparative advantages of a lecture by an authority or an impromptu contribution by a member of the group, for example, cannot be determined categorically, but depend upon circumstances which we shall mention later.

The following methods, embracing the *who*, *when*, and *how*, suggest ways of introducing information to the group. These methods are arranged according to their relation *in time* to the progress of the discussion.

First, the information can be introduced by one or more lectures preceding the group discussion proper. This method is used in many conferences conducted by the Y.M.C.A. and similar groups and is designed to provide data and points of view likely to be used in the subsequent discussions. It is useful in supplying this information in advance of the discussion proper and also in supplying it systematically and by an authority. The weakness in this method lies in the fact that the information is provided at a time when its usefulness may not be fully appreciated by the group and also that the lecture may too strongly dominate the course of the group's thinking.

Second, the information can be introduced by having the members of the group report upon their reading done in advance of the discussion. This serves essentially the same purpose as the preliminary lecture, the only difference being in the person or persons doing the reporting. The values and weaknesses of this method are the same as those of the lecture, the influence of the points of view of the authors of the books being comparable to the influence of the lecturer.

Third, the information can be introduced by the members of the group during the discussion. Either voluntarily or at the suggestion of the leader, some person assists the group by reporting the facts and opinions gained from some special reading done in advance of the session. This method and the second differ only in the time element; in one case a member who has done some special reading gives his factual report in advance of the discussion proper, and in the other case it is introduced during the course of the discussion. Both methods may be used to advantage, but ordinarily the information will be more useful if introduced at the time of need rather than as a preface to the discussion.

Fourth, there is the normal and most commonly used method—that in which the members introduce the material as needed and in an impromptu manner without having made any special factual study for purposes of this report. Some person, for example, knows the facts concerning the sales tax returns in his state and presents the data when the group needs such information to think its way through a phase of the taxation question. He does it informally, not in a prepared speech or report, drawing upon both his indirect and his direct preparation. This method has merit in that it is timely and uses resources possessed by the group. Its weakness lies in its reliance upon the memory of an ordinary witness, who may be in error in recalling or handling the factual material. Also, if the group relies exclusively upon this method, it is running the risk of lacking the information when it is needed. This is, of course, not an adverse criticism of the method but of the sole use of this method. In any event, it is the normal method; and upon it the average discussion group relies for the bulk of its information.

Fifth, the information can be introduced by an authority who is meeting with the group, but who—theoretically at least—takes no active part until called upon. The group may ask for facts or expert opinions to enable it to proceed to another line of thought. If the authority enters into the discussion only in response to a need felt by the group, this method is useful. It is timely, it provides for the use of an expert witness, and it gives the group an opportunity to cooperate with the authority in the development of its thinking. The weakness lies in the absence of the systematic array of material probably found in the lecture and in the possibility that the authority will dominate the group.

The sixth method is similar to the fifth, the only difference being in the fact that the authority is not meeting with the group throughout the discussion, but is called in when the group is confronted with the need for information. The usual procedure is for the group to take a recess until such time as the members and the expert can meet together. This method has all of the advantages of the fifth, where the authority is present at all times; but of course has the disadvantage of interrupting the process of group thinking, an interruption which may at times seriously affect the continuity of the logical pattern of thought.

The seventh method is similar to the sixth in that it requires a recess in order to secure the needed information. This consists of the delegating of one or more members of the group, as a committee, to secure facts or expert opinions through reading or direct observation. For example, the group may take a recess to permit a member to consult books in a library or to investigate certain phenomena so as to aid the group concerning the point in question. This method may, like the sixth, inconvenience the group or interrupt the train of thought; but as an expedient it is useful, especially if the information serves to break a deadlock or to conserve the group's time.

Needless to say, no group will limit itself to any one of these methods. While they are mutually exclusive as explained here, they frequently overlap in the normal course of discussion. We have described them separately merely because it is a convenient way of suggesting the availability of the several methods. There probably is no one *best* method. While we have offered some appraisal of the several methods, the important thing undoubtedly is to see to it that the facts and expert opinions necessary to the deliberations of the group are made available.

V. THE TESTS OF FACTS AND EXPERT OPINIONS

A knowledge of the tests governing facts and expert opinions is fully as important as a knowledge of their nature. It is essential to know whether a fact or opinion introduced into the discussion has validity and can be used as described in Section III. To determine this validity there are two major tests of both facts and opinions: (1) the test of the facts and the opinions themselves and (2) the test of their sources (witnesses).

Probably the most important use of these tests is in helping an individual to understand what facts and expert opinions are and what conditions their usefulness. He should use these tests to check up on himself before the discussion begins—to free his own thinking from uncritical judgments concerning facts and expert opinions. Frequently, also, these tests may be applied in the discussion in the interests of accuracy and fair play.

A. TESTS OF FACTS.

There are two tests of facts: (1) tests of the facts themselves and (2) tests of the sources of the facts.

1. *Tests of the Facts Themselves.*—These tests appraise the facts themselves, irrespective of their source. Two questions present themselves: Qualitatively are the facts acceptable? Quantitatively are the facts adequate? The first of these questions inquires into the accuracy and the consistency of the facts.

a. Are the Facts Definite and Clear?—Before accepting the facts too hastily, a member of a discussion group should inquire as to their definiteness and clarity. It is futile to deal with inexact, nebulous data—with statistics which are only the roughest approximations and are not clearly arrayed; reasoning can be little more than useless when based upon such material.

b. Are the Facts Documented?—Here we are concerned with the identification of the book or other source from which the facts are obtained. For instance, did certain facts on unemployment come from the *World Almanac*, the *Monthly Labor Review*, or a campaign handbook of a political party? While complete documentation is probably unnecessary in discussion, it is well to require definite enough citation to establish a presumption as to the authenticity of the facts. This test is useful, not so much in enabling a person to check on the facts at a later time as in discouraging loose handling of facts.

c. Are the Facts Correct?—One can inquire first whether the facts as reported are true representations of an experience. For example, we seek to learn whether the facts concerning students' attitudes about campus social affairs square with the experience of the person who made the observation upon which the facts are based. Next we inquire whether the facts are reported correctly from a record, such as a book or chart. We also inquire as to the accuracy of the record from which the facts are secured—whether this is a correct statement of the facts in the case. For example, a table may have a typographical error in composition, with the result that the data taken from it are invalid. Finally, this test questions the correctness of the classification of the facts. For instance, it asks whether a table giving the occupations of the members of Congress as lawyer, farmer, etc., or classifying these persons according to occupation is based upon correct classifications. It inquires whether a person who is both a farmer and a lawyer is properly classified as a lawyer. This test assumes that important differences in facts and their meanings can result from different systems of classification and tabulation of data.

d. Are the Facts Consistent?—While this test of

consistency is different from those concerning accuracy, it can also be regarded as a "handle" by which to get hold of inaccuracies. In other words, a person who says "That doesn't sound consistent with logic" is using this test of consistency as a means of getting at an inaccuracy which may be the reason for the inconsistency. This test raises four questions: (1) Are the facts consistent with other facts presented on the same point by the same witness? (2) Are the facts consistent within themselves? (3) Are the facts consistent with known facts? (4) Are the facts consistent with reason?

It is important to inspect the facts in order to determine whether one statement is inconsistent with another. This does not mean consistency with known facts, but consistency with other facts being introduced to the group. For example, let us assume that the record of a university in intercollegiate athletics introduced at one time in the discussion differs from that introduced at another by the same witness. An alert member of the group, noting this discrepancy, interrupts: "Let's see, didn't you give us figures on this a short time ago? You appear to have different facts? How about this inconsistency?"

Equally important is the question of consistency of facts within themselves. Consider a simple instance: A person says that businessmen comprise fifteen per cent of the membership of Congress, farmers five per cent, lawyers eighty per cent, and other professional persons five per cent. An observer applying this test will detect the fact that the total is more than one hundred per cent, and will use this question of consistency to reach the inaccuracy which is the cause of the discrepancy.

Similarly, the test of consistency with known facts places the recently introduced data alongside data known by a conferee or by the group, and inquires as to the reason for the difference. This test has values in detecting false data in terms of the certain data which have been verified by the group.

The wisdom of applying the test of consistency with reason—of inquiring whether the facts "sound reasonable"—lies in the fact that a person's reasoning ability is frequently his only available means of testing data. If he subjects the data to a comparison with his thinking in the realm of cause and effect, or generalization and analogy, he may detect an inconsistency which will lead to a checkup on the accuracy of the facts. For instance, data concerning the relative expenditures for education, armaments, and waterways may appear to be highly improbable or unreasonable. The application of this test may raise doubts concerning their accuracy; then the use of some of the tests of accuracy may ultimately disclose an error, for example, in reporting or classification.

e. Are Enough Facts Presented?—To these qualitative tests there is added one which is a purely quantitative consideration and should not be confused with the tests of accuracy and consistency. While we do not presume to suggest here the amount of factual material required to pass the test of adequacy, we do suggest that too little data should not be permitted to stand as representative or conclusive. Ordinarily the answer to the question of adequacy is dependent upon either the group's satisfaction with the amount submitted or the ability of the individual member to produce enough data to permit good discussion on the point in question.

2. *Tests of the Source (Witness) of the Facts.*—These tests go beyond the facts themselves and ask four questions about the person who is responsible for the facts: (1) Is the witness physically qualified? (2) Is he mentally qualified? (3) Is he morally qualified? (4) Did he have the opportunity to get all the necessary facts?[3] *It is important to understand that the witness of which we*

[3] See James M. O'Neill, Craven Laycock, and Robert L. Scales, *Argumentation and Debate* (New York: The Macmillan Company, 1928), Chapter 6. Also, see James M. O'Neill and James H. McBurney, *The Working Principles of Argument* (New York: The Macmillan Company, 1932), Chapter VII.

speak in this section may be either a conferee acting in this capacity or some person quoted by a conferee.

a. Is the Witness Physically Qualified?—The test of physical competence is important because facts are secured by means of the five senses of the witness. While this test is rarely used in discussion (in contrast to the courtroom), it is true, nevertheless, that the detection of a physical defect which has a bearing upon the ability to gather facts can invalidate the facts coming from this witness. The test consists simply in asking whether the witness possesses the eyesight, powers of hearing, or other requisites to make the necessary observations.

b. Is the Witness Mentally Qualified?—This is a useful test, because even in the case of the fact-witness the mental abilities may vitally affect the accuracy of his powers of observation, organization, or transmission of the facts. The first test of mental powers applies to the memory of the witness. If the memory is defective, a presumption of error is at once raised; and the facts made available by this witness will thereby be discredited. The second test of mental powers applies to the person's accuracy, both in expression and in freedom from the tendency to exaggerate. It is important to ascertain whether the witness has the ability to phrase his thoughts so accurately that he says what he intends to say and is easily understood. This test serves to free the discussion from purported facts which may not truly represent actual phenomena or what the witness intended to say or write. It is also well to determine whether the witness is prone to exaggerate. If his habits of mind are so slovenly that he does not observe and express himself accurately but constantly exaggerates, his testimony of even a factual nature will be discredited. Intentional exaggeration will, of course, mean even more rapid and final discrediting. The best means of detecting exaggeration is to investigate if possible the accuracy of the witness concerning other testimony produced by him.

c. Is the Witness Morally Qualified?—The test

of moral qualification includes an investigation of motive and of general fitness to be trusted even on matters of fact. This inquires whether the witness has some sympathy with, or interest in, the question at issue. If he has, his testimony will, of course, be questioned and probably rejected. Similarly, the general moral character of the witness is tested to learn whether he is reliable and trustworthy. This test can, of course, be carried to absurd lengths, especially in discussion; but it serves as a good means by which the group can protect itself against the dangers of witnesses who may otherwise be perfectly capable.

d. Did the Witness Have the Opportunity to Get All the Necessary Facts?—This test is concerned with the relation of the witness's report to the breadth of his observation. It provides a means of exposing witnesses who have observed only a few phenomena or exceptional phenomena—those witnesses whose opportunities for observation are too limited to be useful. It checks up on those persons who make only a superficial survey and then disseminate facts purporting to be conclusive.

B. Tests of Expert Opinions.

There are two tests of opinions: (1) tests of the opinions themselves and (2) tests of the sources of the opinions.

1. *Tests of the Opinions Themselves.*—These tests appraise the expert opinions themselves, irrespective of their source. As in the testing of facts, both the qualitative and the quantitative questions are raised.

a. Are the Opinions Needed?—This test seeks to inquire whether facts are available and preferable to opinions. Certainly even expert opinions should not be admitted as substitutes for facts when these facts are available and can be interpreted by the group. For example, it is unwise to rely upon an opinion as to the costs of maintaining the highways in a certain state when facts are available and can be easily interpreted. Or it is folly to accept the opinion of the most capable labor leader, industrialist, or government official as to the amount of unemployment when data on this are available in official documents.

b. Are the Opinions Clearly and Definitely Stated?—Because much fruitless discussion may result from a misunderstanding of the meaning of testimony, it is well to inquire as to the exact phrasing of the statements. Ambiguity may arise from both the original statement and the reproduction of it, and the discerning participant in discussion will be quick to determine whether meanings are affected by words or constructions which may be easily misunderstood.

c. Are the Opinions Documented?—This test inquires as to the place where the statements of opinion were made or found. Especially in order to discourage the loose handling of testimony, this should be frequently invoked.

d. Were the Opinions Actually Expressed?—This test is not concerned with the uses of documentation and clear phrasing, but asks whether, by chance, the testimony was "manufactured" by the person who reports it. For example, a statement by the Secretary of State concerning an aspect of the nation's foreign policy may be introduced into the discussion. The quotation contains clear and definite statements, and all the requisites of documentation are apparently attended to. It is possible, however, that the quotation is the opinion of a person other than the Secretary of State and should be carefully scrutinized. This test makes such scrutiny possible. It is obvious that the use of this test can easily create a quibble; and any person applying it should always assume the honesty of the witnesses unless there is some reason for doing otherwise. The most common application of this test comes in cases of "hearsay" evidence where a conferee is reporting the opinions of other persons, second or third hand. Such opinions may be mere rumor or gossip. Many honest persons quite unwittingly aid and abet whispering campaigns which might be checked by a little healthy skepticism.

e. Are the Opinions Consistent?—This test asks whether the testimony "sounds reasonable," and in so doing it may be a means of checking up on the accuracy of the testimony itself. This test raises five questions: (1) Are the opinions consistent with other opinions by the same witness upon the same point? (2) Are the opinions consistent within themselves? (3) Are the opinions consistent with opinions of other witnesses? (4) Are the opinions consistent with reason? (5) Are the opinions consistent with known facts?

With the exception of the third and fifth questions, these specify the same kind of testing process as that described in the case of facts, and need not be discussed further here. The third question asks whether the opinions being tested harmonize with other expert opinions, especially those which may have been accepted by a group in a discussion. The fifth question asks whether the opinions submitted are consistent with known facts. It is useful in arraying the opinions against the knowledge possessed by those persons to whom they are submitted. For instance, if a statement is made that the United States is open to armed attack along the Atlantic coast, and apparently reliable facts point to almost insurmountable difficulties facing any aggressor, difficulties making such an attack highly improbable, this test may disclose a defect in the opinion.

f. Are Enough Opinions Presented?—This is fully as useful as the corresponding quantitative test of facts. It is true that no specified number of opinions on a particular issue can be required categorically. As a matter of fact, one really competent opinion will be better than several less competent opinions. This test is useful, however, in discouraging generalizations from inadequate testimony.

2. *Tests of the Source (Witness) of the Expert Opinions.*—These tests go beyond the opinions themselves and ask two questions concerning the person who stated the opinions: (1) Is the witness mentally qualified? (2) Is the witness morally qualified?

a. Is the Witness Mentally Qualified?—The test of mental competence, which for the expert includes inquiry concerning knowledge and experience as well as powers of observation and reasoning, is probably more important than in the case of fact-witnesses. This is true because of the reliance upon special knowledge and experience, together with interpretative and critical powers, in the opinion-witness. It is necessary to understand whether the witness is ordinary or expert and whether his training and experience qualify him to use his interpretative and critical powers in the matter in question. One of the most flagrant abuses of expert testimony is the use of opinions by an expert in one field on the assumption that he is an expert in all fields. For instance, a distinguished chemist is not necessarily an authority in the field of economics.

b. Is the Witness Morally Qualified?—This test, which includes an investigation of motive and general fitness to be trusted, is likewise even more important in opinion than in fact testimony. If it is advisable to inquire into a person's fitness to observe and report facts fairly, it is much more important to test his moral fitness to formulate opinions. Especially is this true in discussion when the opinions may influence the group's point of view or even supersede critical reasoning upon some occasions. The witness's special sympathy with the opinion expressed (prejudice) and his general moral character (integrity and reliability) should, therefore, be tested.

We have submitted what may appear to be a formidable array of tests. We do not wish the discussion to degenerate into a quibble over adequacy of facts, competence of witnesses, or use of facts and expert opinions; but we do wish the participants in discussion to make critical judgments on facts and opinions. Altogether too many people are exceedingly naïve in these matters and are too willing to bow to what appears to be a fact or an expert opinion. We must realize that in discussion, as in any other kind of speaking and reporting, facts and opinions are adduced by persons with purposes and motives and who are subject to the same human frailties as we ourselves are.

A mastery of these tests will give the member of a discussion group an understanding of the factors determining the adequacy of facts and opinions. Intelligently, courteously, and sympathetically applied in the interests of honesty and fair statement, these tests will make discussion a more useful social tool and a more satisfying experience.

AN OUTLINE OF THE TESTS OF FACTS AND EXPERT OPINIONS

Tests of Facts

I. Tests of the Facts Themselves
    A. Are the facts definite and clear?
    B. Are the facts documented?
    C. Are the facts correct?
       1. Are the facts as reported true representations of an experience?
       2. Are the facts reported correctly from a record?
       3. Is the record correct?
       4. Are the facts properly classified?
    D. Are the facts consistent?
       1. Are the facts consistent with other facts presented on the same point by the same witness?
       2. Are the facts consistent within themselves?
       3. Are the facts consistent with known facts?
       4. Are the facts consistent with reason?
    E. Are enough facts presented?
II. Tests of the Source (Witness) of Facts
    A. Is the source (witness) physically qualified?
    B. Is the source (witness) mentally qualified?
       1. Has he a reliable memory?
       2. Is he accurate?
          a. Is he accurate in expression?
          b. Is he free from exaggeration?
    C. Is the source (witness) morally qualified?

1. Is he unduly interested in the question?
2. Is his general moral character good?
D. Did the source (witness) have the opportunity to get all of the necessary facts?

Tests of Expert Opinions

I. Tests of the Expert Opinions Themselves
   A. Are the opinions needed?
   B. Are the opinions clearly and definitely stated?
   C. Are the opinions documented?
   D. Were the opinions actually expressed?
   E. Are the opinions consistent?
      1. Are the opinions consistent with other opinions by the same witness upon the same point?
      2. Are the opinions consistent within themselves?
      3. Are the opinions consistent with opinions of other witnesses?
      4. Are the opinions consistent with reason?
      5. Are the opinions consistent with known facts?
   F. Are enough opinions presented?
II. Tests of the Source (Witness) of Expert Opinions
   A. Is the source (witness) mentally qualified?
      1. Has he adequate knowledge and experience?
      2. Has he adequate powers of observation and reasoning?
   B. Is the source (witness) morally qualified?
      1. Is he unduly interested in the question?
      2. Is his general moral character good?

Exercises

1. Criticize the use of facts and expert opinions in the discussion in Appendix A. In what form do they appear? How are they introduced? By whom? How useful are they? Apply the appropriate tests to these facts and expert opinions.
2. Criticize the use of facts and expert opinions in the "Round Table" in Appendix B. In what form do they appear? How are they introduced? By whom? How useful are they? Apply the appropriate tests to these facts and expert opinions.
3. Criticize the use of facts and expert opinions in the

forum in Appendix C. In what form do they appear? How are they introduced? By whom? How useful are they? Apply the appropriate tests to these facts and expert opinions.

4. Criticize the use of facts and expert opinions in the following discussions in *Discussion Methods for Adult Groups* by Fansler: (a) forum-lecture, pp. 7-25; (b) forum-dialogue, pp. 29-51; (c) group discussion, pp. 71-80; (d) group discussion, pp. 82-99; (e) panel discussion, pp. 111-132. In what form do they appear? How are they introduced? By whom? How useful are they? Apply the appropriate tests to these facts and expert opinions.

5. Criticize the use of facts and expert opinions in the discussions in the *Journal of Adult Education* and the discussions in *Religious Education* cited in the bibliography at the end of Chapter VIII.

6. Under what circumstances would each of the following be an expert witness: (a) a chairman of a discussion; (b) a college professor; (c) a farmer; (d) an historian; (e) a banker; (f) a druggist; (g) a newspaper reporter; (h) a chemist; (i) a member of Congress; (j) a president of a steel corporation. Explain.

7. Bring to class any kind of argumentative article. Criticize the facts and their use, applying the appropriate tests of the facts and the sources of the facts.

8. Bring to class any kind of argumentative article. Criticize the expert opinions and their use, applying the appropriate tests of the expert opinions and the sources of these opinions.

9. Conduct a class discussion or observe an outside discussion and appraise it with respect to the use of facts and expert opinions.

10. Conduct a class discussion in which facts and expert opinions are introduced in the following manner: (a) by having one or more lectures preceding the group discussion proper; (b) by having the members of the group report in advance of the discussion proper upon some special reading; (c) by having the members present these reports as needed during the discussion; (d) by having the members introduce the information as

needed and in an impromptu manner; (e) by having an authority who is meeting with the group introduce the information as needed; (f) by having an authority who is called in at a particular time introduce the needed information; (g) by having a committee which has been delegated to secure the information introduce it when needed. In performing the first, fifth, and sixth methods, invite if possible an expert to sit with the group. Possibly some member of the college or university faculty may be secured. Criticize all of these seven methods.

11. Write 250-350 words on one or more of the following: (a) the nature of facts and expert opinions; (b) the ordinary vs. the expert witness; (c) the relation of facts and expert opinions to the preparation of the members of the group; (d) the use of facts and expert opinions in discussion; (e) the means of securing facts and expert opinions; (f) the means of introducing facts and expert opinions; (g) the tests of facts and expert opinions. In preparing these essays, use material found in the bibliography at the end of this chapter.

Selected Bibliography

Clarke, Edwin L., *The Art of Straight Thinking*. New York: D. Appleton and Company, 1929. Chapters X, XI, XII.

Elliott, Harrison S., *The Process of Group Thinking*. New York: Association Press, 1932. Chapters IX and X.

Follett, Mary P., *Creative Experience*. New York: Longmans, Green and Company, 1924. Chapter I.

O'Neill, James M., Laycock, Craven, and Scales, Robert L., *Argumentation and Debate*. New York: The Macmillan Company, 1928. Chapter 6.

O'Neill, James M., and McBurney, James H., *The Working Principles of Argument*. New York: The Macmillan Company, 1932. Chapter VII.

Sheffield, Alfred D., *Creative Discussion*. New York: Association Press, 1927. Pp. 46-50.

CHAPTER X

THE LOGICAL PATTERN OF DISCUSSION

In Chapter II we outlined briefly an adaptation of the five steps in reflective thinking explained by Professor Dewey in *How We Think*. These steps have been referred to many times in subsequent chapters. The discussion outline is planned in terms of these steps and they are helpful in organizing one's contributions in discussion. Here we shall analyze these steps in some detail. From two points of view these steps in reflective thinking constitute the logical pattern of discussion: (1) as the over-all pattern of discussion and (2) as independent acts of thought within this over-all pattern. For example, let us say we are discussing the problem: *Should the United States form a military alliance with Great Britain?* Here the larger pattern of thought, or the so-called over-all pattern, will be definition, analysis, hypothesis, reasoned development of hypothesis, and further verification. It is perfectly obvious, however, that just as soon as the group begins to think about this larger problem it will immediately run on to many other problems which must be thought through. Each step in the over-all pattern will precipitate such questions, and these questions lend themselves as readily as does the larger problem to the five-step form. Thus, in the analysis step in the matter of a military alliance with Great Britain, the group might encounter questions such as these: Is it likely that the United States will become involved in war in the near future? Is the United States capable of protecting herself in the event of war? What relations, agreements, or understandings, military or otherwise, do we now have with Great Britain? Is there merit in an alliance of the so-called democratic powers? This list is by no means complete, but it does make clear the point that the larger problem must be deliberated in terms of many other problems. And what is more, these "other problems" will in turn break down into further questions. Thus, the quest for the answer to the original problem leads the group into the consideration of a veritable hierarchy of questions, each in itself calling for thought which may be broken down into a five-step unit.

We have in the discussion of a complex problem, then, a pattern of many related acts of thought combining to form the over-all structure of the thinking. Both the larger structure and the contributing units may be analyzed on the five-step basis. We shall assume that the normal pattern of any problem-solving discussion will be these five steps in reflective thinking. As the group proceeds through these stages in thinking it will encounter many pertinent problems whose solutions are demanded by the larger problem under consideration. The thought given to each of these secondary questions will in turn follow this five-step analysis. It is the purpose of this chapter to consider the nature and method of each of these steps in thought in considerable detail. While we shall have the over-all pattern primarily in mind in most of our references, we shall assume now that the reader will see the application to the many problems which arise within this larger pattern.

In studying the logical pattern of discussion as here presented it is important to keep in mind that this pattern ordinarily is and should be more flexible than a systematic analysis of it is likely to indicate. It is not our wish to prescribe "steps" into which all discussion must fall nor to make of discussion a formal, stereotyped technique. This analysis of the reflective thinking of groups is offered in the same spirit in which other writers have presented analyses of the solitary thought of individuals. The sequence in which the steps in reflective thinking are explained is not an infallible guide to the order of their appearance in discussion, nor should it be thought that these steps always appear as wholly distinct and separate entities in group-thought. Nevertheless, experience has shown the pattern here presented to be generally typical of good discussion and an understanding of this pattern to have functional values in the preparation and conduct of discussion.

I. DEFINITION

A. The Role of Definition in Discussion.

We have repeatedly pointed out that all reflective thinking has its inception in problems. In Chapter V we went into the kinds of problems which lend themselves to profitable discussion and offered suggestions for the phrasing of suitable discussion questions. Let us assume that the group begins with such a question at least tentatively phrased. The first logical task is that of clarifying this question, perhaps revising it, and thereby delimiting the area of discussion. There must be a meeting of minds on what the question is and as clear a conception of its meaning as is possible before going on to analysis. Definition aids in this process. While the desires of the group or the exigencies of the occasion will dictate very largely what is to be discussed, definition is required to secure understanding and further progress. Definitions established at the outset will also serve a useful purpose in the later stages of the discussion.

We have two suggestions to make concerning the process of definition in discussion. First, it should be recognized that the *definition will (or should) take form depending on the main purpose of the group in making it.*[1] Nothing is to be gained by working for absolute finality in definition. The group may agree that for purposes of this discussion the term under consideration will mean a certain thing. Such definition enables members to use the term as defined and to be sure that the group knows what they are talking about when they use it. This conception of definition also makes protracted quibbling about definitions unnecessary. Even though John Jones does not especially like the definition, at least for purposes of this discussion he can use language and take positions in terms of the meaning agreed upon. Second, *definitions should be tentatively adopted and changes in meaning allowed as the discussion progresses.* This does not mean that language should be used ambiguously, but rather that meanings should be allowed to grow. Such changes in definition or conception can be made deliberately when more adequate meanings are suggested by the deliberations. Growth in meanings and conceptions should be viewed as goals and important outcomes of discussion.

B. METHODS OF DEFINITION.

For our purposes here we shall explain the two basic kinds of definition operating in discussion and merely indicate a few other types which may be of some value.

1. *Definition by Classification.*—The traditional method of definition is that by classification. Here the term being defined is identified with or "placed in" a larger class of which it is a member and then differentiated

[1] See Edwin A. Burtt, *Principles and Problems of Right Thinking* (New York: Harper and Brothers, 1928), pp. 157-159.

from other members of the class. Thus a horse is a mammal with certain unique characteristics which distinguish it from other types of mammals. The more general class in such definition is commonly called the *genus* and what we have here referred to as the "member" (or the term being defined) denotes one of its *species*. The factors which distinguish one species from the other species in any given genus are known as the *differentia*.

Most of the specifications or rules for such definition follow rather obviously from this explanation of the method: (1) a term should be defined in relation to the genus which most accurately and helpfully (in terms of purpose) identifies it for use in the discussion at hand; (2) the differentia should clearly demarcate the term from other species in the same genus; and (3) the definition should not employ the term being defined or mere synonyms of it except where such synonyms are adequate for the purposes at hand.

2. *Definition by Gradation.*—With a little thought one can see that not all terms and conceptions lend themselves helpfully or even accurately to definition by classification. Perhaps if we could assume complete liberty in choosing a *genus* for purposes of definition and if we could assume a vocabulary which provided us with a much larger number of usable and understandable *classes* than now obtains we might not encounter this difficulty. As it is, we sometimes do violence to meaning by classifying terms where they do not belong. Especially is this true in the case of phenomena which exhibit what we shall call the principle of *continuous variation*. Consider, for example, these paired opposites, black and white, sane and insane, conservative and radical, work and play, intelligent and unintelligent. Shall we say that this paper is black or white? In fact, it is neither; it is "some" white and "some" black; it is somewhere between the two extremes. Is writing this book work or play? Perhaps we should not commit ourselves on this, but at the moment it appears to be a little of both. This principle of con-

tinuous variation is exhibited in the colors of the spectrum, one color merging into the other. It is impossible to draw hard and fast lines between the colors without being wholly arbitrary. In Chapter I we distinguished between discussion and persuasion, constructive and intentional reasoning, and criticism and propaganda. Each of these distinctions exhibits the principle of continuous variation which we are discussing here. While discussion and persuasion are different, it is not possible to distinguish between them categorically. Their true differences are better exhibited by constructing a continuum in which discussion is placed at one pole and persuasion at the other, with the differences understood as a graded series shading gradually from one pole to the other.

Such mental constructions (the continuum) may be profitably used as substitutes for arbitrary classes (the genus) in many definitions. Thus, instead of assigning a term to a class or genus, one can refer it to a continuum, its place on the continuum indicating the extent to which it incorporates the meaning assigned to each of the two poles. Assuming that there is a continuous variation between criticism and propaganda with the degree of objectivity as the principal variable, it is possible to place any speech experience in which this variable is involved some place on a continuum between the two poles represented by these two concepts. The necessity of classifying the experience in question as either criticism or propaganda is thus obviated. The position of the referent on the continuum will be determined by the degree of objectivity which it represents. Thus one may indicate the extent to which it partakes of the nature of each pole. The more specific and accurate this quantitative index can be made, other things being equal, the more accurate will be the definition.[2]

Definition by gradation has certain important advantages in discussion. Many of the concepts in the fields

[2] See Boris B. Bogoslovsky, *The Technique of Controversy* (New York: Harcourt, Brace and Company, 1928), pp. 98-174.

where discussion most often takes place display this characteristic of continuous variation. Arbitrary classifications in these fields are likely to stir up needless disagreement and conflict. If one person insists that debate is a *species* of criticism and another insists that it is a kind of propaganda, their positions in the matter appear to be diametrically opposed. Should they be fortunate enough to observe that the principle of continuous variation applies in this case, however, they may discover that in reality their positions are very close together. An appreciation of this principle and its relation to definition often leads to more complete understanding and tolerance. We urge that members of discussion groups attempt to employ this method of definition. When conflicts over classifications arise, attempt to discover whether the difference is real or merely verbal by constructing a continuum and relating the term to this continuum.

3. *Other Methods of Definition.*—There are several other methods of definition, or perhaps we should say aids to definition, which are helpful in discussion. One may *compare* the term under consideration to more familiar terms which are synonymous or nearly synonymous with it. The term may be *contrasted* with other concepts which are likely to be confused with it. Those meanings which are not applicable may be *rejected* by excluding the term from certain categories and by pointing out that it does not possess certain attributes. *Illustrations* or *examples* are also useful aids to definition in certain cases.

II. ANALYSIS

A. The Function of Analysis in Discussion.

Analysis has been defined as "the mental process of perceiving within a proposition the parts of which it is composed" or "the process of discovering the issues."[3] While this conception of analysis is adequate for the

[3] J. M. O'Neill and J. H. McBurney, *The Working Principles of Argument* (New York: The Macmillan Company, 1932), p. 50.

debater or arguer who sets out to prove a definite proposition, it will need to be modified for our purposes here.
We are interested in analysis as a step in reflective thinking. In this process, as we have seen, analysis serves two
closely related functions: (1) the discovery of the nature
of the problem in terms of its symptoms, manifestations,
or effects, and the cause or causes which are producing
these effects; (2) the discovery of criteria or standards
of value which may be applied in the situation. Analysis,
as we are using the term here, does not concern itself
with solutions to the problem except as it aids in suggesting possible hypotheses. It surveys the past and present
situation, considering both causal relationships and motives and purposes. By doing this it prepares the ground
for the reflective deliberation of solutions and often calls
to mind possible solutions, but it does not itself go into
these matters. These are later steps in the process of
reflective thought. Just as diagnosis precedes prescription,
so should analysis precede attempts at solution.

One of the most common mistakes in discussion is that
of beginning the discussion with a consideration of solutions to the problem or, at least, jumping ahead to these
matters prematurely. It is nothing short of foolhardy to
attempt to solve a problem without analyzing it first.
Until one knows what the problem is, what is causing
it, and what purposes and motives are operating in the
group, it is impossible to consider solutions intelligently.

It should be pointed out that there is considerable
reciprocity between the two phases of analysis. An
understanding of the causes and effects of the problem
is almost essential to a deliberation of standards of value,
and the determination of values, in turn, enables the
group better to interpret positions which members have
taken on causes and effects. Sometimes the classification
of purposes will serve to resolve conflicts which have
arisen in the causal aspect of analysis. While a group
may proceed directly from definition to standards of
value and thence to a consideration of causes and effects,

the more usual sequence is definition, cause-effect relationships, and then values. The grasp of the problem which comes from dealing first with the analysis of the causal relations involved is usually of sufficient help in the discussion of purposes to warrant any reconsideration of causes and effects which may be required. Thus, in terms of the total pattern of discussion, the deliberation of values enables the group to look backward on its work with new insight and to move forward to a consideration of solutions with greater understanding.

B. Causal Relationships in Analysis.

In the next chapter we shall study the methods of causal reasoning. Suffice it to say now that such reasoning is of first importance in analyzing the problem. The first function of analysis is the discovery of the effects and causes of the problem. By *effects* we mean what we have previously called symptoms or manifestations of the problem. They might be referred to as evidences of the problem or, in the language of the school debate, existing and potential evils. The difficulty with "existing and potential evils" is that it implies in advance of analysis that something is wrong. While it is the observation of what is thought to be existing evils or a belief that difficulties are ahead which usually gives rise to discussion, analysis may reveal that such evils do not exist and that these fears were ungrounded.

We are here using the notion of *cause* in the traditional and popular sense to mean the event or events which produce or bring about the effects, these events preceding the effects in point of time. With respect to the consideration of causes by the group, it is the ordinary procedure to get a clear picture of the effects of the problem in mind first and then inquire into the causes. This sequence is suggested by the fact that it is usually the effects which are nearest the surface, the things we feel, and the factors which first bring the problem to our attention. On the other hand, where the problem is chiefly one of impending evils, it is possible to begin with an analysis of the causes which are operating and which may give rise to difficulties in the future. In either case it is essential to work out the entire causal picture with considerable care.

An example of this kind of cause-and-effect analysis is presented in the discussion outline on "The policy of the United States with respect to the Sino-Japanese conflict" in Chapter VI. This analysis may profitably be studied in this connection.

C. STANDARDS OF VALUE.

We are using the term "value" to mean the *ends* which are motivating the members of the group with respect to the problem at hand. A standard of value is the end or ends determined upon as *criteria* for measuring possible solutions to the problem. For example, let us say a family is contemplating the purchase of a new car. Price, comfort, economy of operation, appearance, a vague desire to surpass the next-door neighbor, the desire for other things which may have to be denied if a car is purchased—these and many other possible ends may compete for a place in the standard which will ultimately be applied in making a decision. Such values, ends, and standards of value are tremendously complex things and difficult to deal with reflectively even in one's own private thinking, to say nothing of the group situation. Certain motives may be operating which one hesitates to admit even to himself, and others may be essentially subliminal in nature, vague and unanalyzed.

Scientific method escapes the perplexing problem of values largely by confining itself to questions of fact into which purposes, desires, and motives do not enter, at least not to the extent that they do in questions of value and policy. Discussion, dealing as it does with social, economic, political, and religious questions, and other matters of practical policy, finds itself right in the middle of this whole complex problem. The contribution which it makes to any single group and to social thinking as a whole will be determined to a great degree by the extent to which it is able to deal with these values reflectively.

We consider the determination of standards of value in any given discussion to be an aspect of analysis. The group has met to solve a problem. Before the members can consider solutions intelligently they must know what ends they are after, what purposes and desires they wish to satisfy. An understanding of these factors will contribute to the establishment of criteria by which solutions may be evaluated, aid in the suggestion of solutions, and make comprehensible in a way that would otherwise be impossible the thinking of individual members on these solutions.

The reflective deliberation of values calls for special methods in discussion which may profitably be considered here. Professor Burtt sets the problem clearly when he distinguishes between two questions: *What is the cheapest way to travel to England?* And in the case of a man who has been offered a new position of a somewhat different sort than the one he now has: *Shall I accept this offer?*

What is the fundamental difference between these two thought-situations? Clearly, that in the first case a specific purpose governs the entire piece of thinking; . . . In the other case, a specific purpose emerges into being only as a result of the thinking itself; the goal of the latter is just to bring that purpose into being. In different terms we may put the matter thus: In the first case we know what we want all the way through the act of thought, a certain definite value is taken for granted; while in the second case we are trying to determine by the act of thought what we want, no value is taken for granted except the abstract one of making the best decision, but the controlling value is to be created by the thinking upon which we engage. We express this in technical terms of value-theory by saying that in the former situation the *end* of thought is clearly known and assumed, the purpose of the thinking being merely to select appropriate *means* for its attainment, whereas in the latter situation the end itself is in question, and the purpose of the thinking is precisely to give it shape and make it known. I assume that I definitely want to know the cheapest route to England; what I want to do about the offer of this new position is exactly what my thinking tries to decide.[4]

The question concerning the cheapest way to travel to England is a purely factual problem into which the question of purpose does not enter as a discussible issue. The matter of deciding upon the advisability of accepting a new position, however, given the facts concerning one's present position and the one that is offered, is largely a question of purpose and value. The question we raise here is: How may these purposes and values be dealt with reflectively?

There are four steps in the method of dealing with values reflectively: (1) discover what values are operating; (2) discover how these values are weighted by members of the group; (3) seek to establish an integration of values; (4) probe into deeper and more fundamental values. The first aspect of method is clear from what has already been said. Get before the group the purposes which are influencing the thought of the members. The leader may do this by directing the group to a consideration of the criteria or standards by which possible solutions are to be judged and urging each member to indicate clearly what he believes the important values in the situation to be.

Very often essentially the same values will be operating in the thinking of each member or at least most members of the group, but with different emphasis and weighting. The second aspect of method, then, is the attempt to discover how these different values are appraised. For example, there is an old tree in our back

---

[4] Edwin A. Burtt, *Principles and Problems of Right Thinking* (New York: Harper and Brothers, 1928), pp. 436-437.

yard which some members of the family think should be cut down. Despite the fact that others oppose this action, we find essentially the same values operating. All of us have a sentimental attachment to the tree which makes us reluctant to see it go; and all of us know that it shades the house too much and that its roots are damaging the foundation. Those who think that the first consideration is more important than the second believe that the tree should be spared; and those who are more concerned about the house prefer to have it removed. We are agreed on the values, but not on their relative importance.

Values and different weightings of values are often shifted and revised during discussion. New values are sometimes discovered. When differences exist the group should make an effort to bring about these shifts in the direction of a consensus or commonly accepted standard. This is the third step in method. In the case of the tree the group decided that the house had better be the first consideration; but in deference to sentiment for the tree it was decided to save it if possible. We therefore proceeded to a consideration of solutions with these standards of value agreed upon. One solution considered was that of cutting the roots of the tree next to the house. After consultation with a tree specialist this was the course of action taken.

Where differences in values persist, the group may attempt to relate the more immediate purposes and motives to more fundamental goals and ends. Very often, ends can be examined reflectively only when they are considered from the standpoint of still further ends to which they may contribute. This process of elaborating conflicting preferences in the light of more basic values usually leads the group into philosophical speculations and sometimes to a final agreement on a standard of value. Often these deliberations are stimulating and educative quite apart from the problem under consideration. The total effect of continued and widespread discussion may be the emergence of general principles of value of considerable social significance.

The failure of a group to reach a consensus on values need not stop the discussion. While it does make any agreement on solutions improbable, at least these solutions can be deliberated in the full light of the purposes and motives which are at work in the group. Say the Columbia Associates in Philosophy:

> If two men would reach no agreement whatsoever upon any thing that both considered good, then, of course, it would be impossible to choose reflectively between their proposals; the final choice would needs be based upon their irrational preference for one of the alternatives. Frequently reflection does find itself thus impotent to effect any agreement; and in such cases of conflict, when the circumstances preclude an agreement to disagree, it may become necessary to appeal to unreasoning force, either through a majority vote, or through recourse to arms.[5]

III. THE SUGGESTION OF HYPOTHESES

The third step in reflective thinking is the suggestion or calling up of hypotheses or possible solutions to the problem which has been defined and analyzed in steps one and two.

A. THE ROLE OF HYPOTHESES IN DISCUSSION

Clarke defines the term "hypothesis" as "a preliminary guess at the truth, based on limited evidence or even on mere suspicion, but which its maker intends to subject to rigid tests."[6] Throughout this work we have used the terms "proposals" and "suggested solutions" with this same meaning. These latter terms are especially applicable to problems of policy where the hypotheses suggested are in a literal sense suggested solutions. The hypothesis, then, may be understood as a tentative expla-

[5] Columbia Associates in Philosophy, *An Introduction to Reflective Thinking* (Boston: Houghton Mifflin Company, 1923), p. 219.
[6] Edwin L. Clarke, *The Art of Straight Thinking* (New York: D. Appleton and Company, 1929), p. 210.

nation of the phenomenon under investigation or a possible solution to the problem designed to be used as a basis for further reasoning, experimentation, or investigation. In other words, it is a guess or theory concerning the problem under consideration, formulated for the purpose of directing further discussion. One or more such hypotheses may be injected into the deliberations of the group. It, of course, goes without saying that the success of the discussion is vitally conditioned by the aptness, depth, and discernment of these hypotheses.

B. The Requirements of a Good Hypothesis.

More important than any formal requirements of an hypothesis is its adequacy with respect to the problem at hand. Guesses based on "mere suspicion" may bear fruitful results at times, but it is to be hoped that the preliminary definition and analysis in the discussion will supply a more solid basis for suggestion.

While any hypothesis in discussion should be stated as clearly and concisely as possible, it should be kept in mind that the idea may be in the process of development and that it is altogether too much to expect final formulation at this stage of the reflective process. The hypothesis should be submitted to the group as a tentative proposition which may be used as the focal point for the reasoned development of its implications for the problem.

C. Aids for the Calling up of Hypotheses.

While the ability to call up apt hypotheses is determined to a considerable extent by the natural fertility of the mind and what is sometimes called *creative ability*, there are a few simple aids which can be given. First and foremost is a thorough knowledge of the broad field in which the question for discussion arises and a mastery of the problem under consideration. Both the direct and the indirect preparation of which we have spoken apply here. Careful preliminary definition and analysis in the discussion are also invaluable in suggesting solutions. As a matter of fact, the careful deliberation of these matters may lead the group to the answer to the problem with compelling cogency; at times the solution is almost indicated by the analysis. A further aid is the recollection and consideration of experience with similar problems. If the group is discussing the relief problem in Chicago, the experiences of other cities with this problem may be of great help in suggesting possible solutions for Chicago.

Experience in the formulation of hypotheses is also helpful. People who have disciplined themselves to approach problems reflectively both in their private thinking and in groups will grow in the capacity to call up solutions to problems.

IV. THE REASONED DEVELOPMENT OF HYPOTHESES

The hypotheses suggested by the members of the group must be "reasoned out" or "thought through." In this process the implications of the hypotheses will be developed; and if more than one solution has been proffered, the proposals will be compared and contrasted in relation to the problem. A solution to the problem has been offered; before committing ourselves to it and putting it into operation, we try to foresee what the consequences will be. We conduct series of *mental experiments* in an effort to bring to bear on the proposal all the accumulated experiences of the group. We are seeking the solution which will most nearly solve the problem in conformity with the standards of value held by the group. The modes of reasoning developed in the next chapter explain this process and supply the methods for carrying it out.

V. FURTHER VERIFICATION

The fifth step in reflective thinking, called by Professor Dewey "further observation and experiment leading to acceptance or rejection," is applied to the solution which our thinking has indicated to be most satisfactory. The most adequate test for any proposal quite obviously is putting it into practice and observing the results.

Thus, for example, if several people come to a fork in a road and must choose between two possible courses to take, the ultimate test of the validity of any decision they may reach in the matter is subject to the subsequent experiences that they have in taking the route which seems most likely to bring them to their destination. If they take one route after reflective consideration, and then find it does not take them to their destination, their hypothesis has been proved wrong. On the other hand, if the route does bring them to their destination, their hypothesis has been thereby confirmed. This simple case illustrates the pragmatic importance of acting upon thinking; it is the action which gives the ultimate test to the deliberative process. Thus, the scientist will test out his hypothesis in a laboratory under as controlled conditions as he can create, and this process of verification becomes one of the important steps, if not the most important step, in his whole procedure.

To continue our illustration, let us suppose that the people at the fork in the road take the wrong route and fail to reach their destination. In this case, the error often may be rectified by retracing their steps and taking the other fork. This is, of course, what the scientist does when his hypothesis proves to be incorrect; he revises it in terms of his experience and tries again. At the same time, it must be recognized that action on a wrong hypothesis may in many situations prove fatal to the actors, or at least cause irreparable damage and inconvenience. If our friends start merrily off on the wrong road and wind up in a bottomless pit or something equally catastrophic, any benefit which ensues from this experience must at best be reserved for their posterity. In other words, our point is that many choices once made cannot readily be revised. It is needless to multiply examples to this effect. This is true in many, if not most, of the serious problems which men must deliberate; and acting on a wrong hypothesis is seldom a satisfying experience even though one may live to profit by the experience.

What application do these considerations have for discussion? Certainly they emphasize the practical importance of thorough definition and analysis and careful deliberation of solutions before any decision is made. All of this we have explained in preceding sections. Quite obviously a discussion group cannot conduct experiments and make tests as does the scientist, at least not through the agency of discussion. Perhaps the best that can be done in the way of further verification *is to review the steps that would need to be taken in putting the solution* (which has now been tentatively adopted) *into operation*. If this final review confirms the previous conclusion of the group, the discussion must then give way to action.

EXERCISES

1. Prepare in writing five examples of definition by classification and five by gradation. Discuss these definitions in class.
2. Analyze three problems, one each of fact, value, and policy, with respect to the causal relationships which you think are essential to an adequate diagnosis. In each case list the effects and the causes separately and give your reasons for believing them to be the significant effects and the real causes. Consider these examples in class. Ask of each analysis given: How do you know these are the effects and causes? Why do you think they are? Does this analysis explain the problem adequately? In what way, if any, do the analyses differ in form with respect to the different kinds of problems?
3. List the values which you think are important in each of the three questions considered in Exercise 2; in other words, what criteria or standards of value do you think should be kept in mind in attempting to solve these problems? In each case explain why you feel that these

values should be conserved by the solution; press this "why" question as far back as you can; try to discover the fundamental, basic values upon which your purposes and motives rest in each case. Does your total list of values, for all three problems, represent a consistent philosophy or set of values? Should they be consistent? Are they consistent within each problem? Discuss these matters in class in relation to some of the problems.

4. Phrase two or three hypotheses for each of the problems analyzed in Exercises 2 and 3 and explain in each case which hypothesis you prefer. Give reasons for your preference in terms of the causal relations and values worked out in the preceding exercises.

5. To what extent can each of your preferred hypotheses in Exercise 4 be verified reflectively, i.e., in discussion? What individual or group action would need to be taken to test these hypotheses pragmatically?

6. The following sequence of thought was suggested by Harrison S. Elliott for the discussion groups at the 1938 Geneva Conference of the Y.W.C.A.: "What is the situation? Why? What particular aspects of the situation should be discussed? What various solutions have been proposed by sincere people? Why? What solutions seem to be the most in line with Christian ideals? Why? In light of our differences and agreements, what next steps do we in the group want to take?" Conduct a discussion in which you use this plan. How does this sequence compare with the thought pattern explained in this chapter?

7. Study the logical pattern of the discussion reported in Appendix A. Write a 300-word criticism of the logical pattern of this discussion.

8. Record a discussion and play it back to the class for purposes of analyzing the logical pattern.

SELECTED BIBLIOGRAPHY

Boas, George, *Our New Ways of Thinking*. New York: Harper and Brothers, 1930.

Bogoslovsky, Boris B., *The Technique of Controversy*. New York: Harcourt, Brace and Company, 1928.

Burtt, Edwin A., *Principles and Problems of Right Think-*

ing. New York: Harper and Brothers, 1928. Chapters IV-VIII and XIV.

Clarke, Edwin C., *The Art of Straight Thinking.* New York: D. Appleton and Company, 1929. Chapters IV-X.

Cohen, Morris R., and Nagel, Ernest, *An Introduction to Logic and Scientific Method.* New York: Harcourt, Brace and Company, 1934. Chapters XI, XII, and XVIII.

Columbia Associates in Philosophy, *An Introduction to Reflective Thinking.* Boston: Houghton Mifflin Company, 1923. Chapter IX.

Dewey, John, *How We Think.* Boston: D. C. Heath and Company, 1910. Chapter VI. See Chapter VII in 1933 ed.

Jastrow, Joseph, *Effective Thinking.* New York: Simon and Schuster, 1931. Chapters I and II.

Robinson, Daniel S., *The Principles of Reasoning.* New York: D. Appleton and Company, 1928. Chapters V and XXIV.

Wallas, Graham, *The Art of Thought.* New York: Harcourt, Brace and Company, 1926. Chapter IV.

CHAPTER XI

THE MODES OF REASONING IN DISCUSSION

I. THE "GROUP THINKING" AND THE "SOLITARY THINKING" OF INDIVIDUALS COMPARED

Discussion is a thinking process, and we have examined the logical pattern which this thinking should normally take. The thinking that enters into discussion must of necessity be that done by the members of the group before or during the discussion and *reported* by them, or the thinking of others as it is represented in the *citation* of their opinions by someone in the discussion. The "group thinking" of individuals differs from their "solitary thinking" in the fact that it must, by the very nature of the situation, be shared with others. The reporting of thought to others, thus, becomes a special problem in discussion. In Chapter VII we considered this problem from the standpoint of procedure, attitudes and behavior, speaking, and a method of contributing in discussion.

All this advice was given in an attempt to help the participant make his thinking available to the group in the manner and form which would be most conducive to cooperative group thinking. The fact remains, however, that *the expression of thought must follow thought*; this is true even though we recognize that the expression of thought for others usually serves to clarify the thought of the speaker and that such expression may even result in wholly new ideas for the speaker. The peculiar problem of the speaker in discussion is that of presenting the *product* of his private thinking in such a way as to keep the thinking of the group in *process*; the crux of the problem, to paraphrase Professor Dewey, lies in communicating thought in such a way as to make of communication the establishing of cooperation in an activity in which there are partners and in which the activity of each is modified and regulated by this partnership.

The modes of reasoning which we shall consider in this chapter, *example*, *analogy*, *sign*, and *cause*, and the formal structure which they take, enter into every unit of reflective thought at every step in the process and are therefore elements of the unit which must be reported and described when the thought is contributed in discussion. A refinement of the comparison made between constructive and intentional reasoning in Chapter I will further explain this point.

II. A COMPARISON OF CONSTRUCTIVE AND INTENTIONAL REASONING

As we pointed out in Chapter I, the most obvious difference between constructive reasoning and intentional reasoning lies in the *purpose* of the reasoner. Whereas the intentional reasoner begins with a predetermined proposition to which he is committed either by desire or the nature of the circumstances and seeks to secure the acceptance of this proposition, the constructive reasoner begins with a problem and seeks to discover a solution to this problem. Of more significance to us here are the *formal* differences between these two types of reasoning. In the preceding chapter we studied the logical pattern of constructive thought as it relates to discussion. In elaborating this thesis in relation to the modes of reasoning operative in discussion (the function of the present chapter) it is helpful to examine briefly for purposes of comparison the structure of intentional reasoning in which these same modes of reasoning operate.

The task of the intentional reasoner is that of supporting his propositions with reasons so selected and arranged that the acceptance of his basic premises (evidence, i.e., facts and expert opinions) will *imply* his conclusion. Thus, if he can establish by facts and opinions or otherwise get you to admit that all men are mortal; and if he can establish that Socrates is a man, then you find yourself in the position of having to admit that Socrates is mortal or else run the risk of being put down by your fellow men as ignorant or obstinate or both. The uninitiated may not recognize that this "winning" argument happens to be one from *sign*, and that it is expressed in a *categorical syllogism* in the *first figure*. The argument of the intentional reasoner becomes much more complex when, instead of contenting himself with a single syllogism, he advances several and supports the premises of these with still further syllogisms until he brings together an elaborate structure of propositions which "hooks up" at one end to his basic premises (facts, expert opinions, or assumptions) and at the other to the conclusion that he wishes to prove. Such an argumentative structure consists of examples, analogies, causes, and signs presented as reasons and "subreasons" thrown into syllogistic forms for the purpose of compelling assent to the proposition which they are designed to support. To be more accurate, the typical rhetorical argument presents these reasons in the form of *enthymemes*, which may be broadly differentiated from the syllogism in the fact that their premises are only probable and their formal structure is often defective measured by the rules of the syllogism, yet convincing and acceptable rhetorically.[1] We need not press this point here, however. The important thing to see is that the modes of reasoning which we propose to explain in relation to discussion in this chapter, example, analogy, cause, and sign, together with the syllogism (and/or enthymeme), also serve a useful function in the argument of the advocate.

The constructive or reflective thinker reasons in terms of examples, analogies, causes, and signs and employs the syllogism for certain purposes, but all this is done in the "setting" or "frame" of the steps in reflective thinking outlined in Chapters II and X; and when the constructive reasoner reports his conclusions in discussion he should present these examples, causes, signs, and syllogisms as aspects of the total act of thought which led him to his conclusion. Thus they will be given to the group in the form in which they *actually* operated to influence the thinking of the speaker, rather than in a structure, specially designed to prove, convince, or compel acceptance. This, of course, is the method of contributing in discussion explained in Chapter VII. The group, if it wishes, *after the discussion is over*, for the purpose of persuading others, may marshal arguments to support the conclusion which it has reached, but for a member of the group to argue his conclusions in this manner *in the discussion* is to impair the proper functioning and jeopardize the success of the entire process.

[1] The common conception of the enthymeme as an elided or truncated syllogism is false and misleading. While the enthymeme *usually* appears with one proposition of the three-proposition form suppressed, this is not the true distinction between the enthymeme and the syllogism. The recognition of this fact has important implications for the application of the syllogism in argumentation and for an understanding of the structure of argument. See James H. Mc-Burney, "The Place of the Enthymeme in Rhetorical Theory," *Speech Monographs*, October, 1936, Vol. III, No. 1, pp. 49-74; also, "Some Recent Interpretations of the Aristotelian Enthymeme," *Papers of the Michigan Academy of Science, Arts and Letters*, Vol. XXI, 1935, pp. 489-500.

There are those who believe that all speaking and writing which presents a position or proposal should follow the pattern of reporting which we have suggested for discussion. This position, of course, would deny any place for persuasion, debate, and propaganda. As stated in Chapter I, *we do not subscribe to this position.* All that we say is that discussion should be conducted on this basis. This is what distinguishes discussion from other forms of communication. Whatever limitations this conception imposes on discussion as a useful social tool, these are limitations which it must suffer; and whatever values may be found in this process are values which society may realize through the use of discussion.

III. TYPES OF REASONING

A. Example.

Reasoning from example is the simple process of inferring conclusions from specific cases or instances. The following precautions should be observed: (1) beware of generalizing from too few cases; (2) make certain that you sample fairly the phenomenon about which you are generalizing, i.e., examine typical cases—get a fair cross section of the whole; and (3) exceptions to what appears to be the general rule should be noted and your conclusion modified or qualified in terms of these exceptions. Exceptions do not *prove* the rule; they *test* the rule. These rules should be observed by the group in drawing generalizations from cases cited by members and should be complied with by individuals reporting generalizations in discussion.

It is important to note that a generalization need *not* be a categorical statement, i.e., a statement which asserts that *all* members of a given class exhibit certain characteristics. Quite the contrary, the thinker should report precisely what he discovers to be the case. To be sure, it is not very helpful to say, for instance, that *some* university students operate automobiles. *Quantify* your statement as accurately as you can. The best generalization would report the exact percentage, twenty per cent, eighteen per cent, or whatever it is. In the case of students operating automobiles in any given university such a percentage might be obtained by questioning all the students. In many cases this is not possible and the investigator must employ a sampling technique; this technique is typical in reasoning from example.

The American Institute of Public Opinion has conducted referenda on political questions throughout the United States by a sampling method. What it says of its method explains this technique.

The crucial factor in the entire undertaking is the nature of the cross-section used in the survey. If the cross-section is properly chosen, a very small sample will accurately represent the larger body of public opinion from which it is taken, and great increase in the number of voters will bring no impressive increase in accuracy. This fact, which can be demonstrated mathematically in a variety of ways, is empirically confirmed by the Institute's own experience and by that of other measures of public opinion.

On national questions, the number of voters interviewed runs from 3,000 to 50,000, depending on the problems involved. Whatever the size of the sample, the cross-section is so constructed that residents of Montana, for example, have the same proportional representation in the sample as in the nation as a whole; income groups in the sample are proportional to income groups in the body of the nation; and so on through various classifications of special interests or characteristics. Every Institute sample is tested for its proportional accuracy with respect to six factors: (1) representation by states, (2) men and women, (3) urban-rural distribution, (4) age, (5) size of incomes, (6) political partisanship. A very small sample of this sort gives a better result than even a tremendous sample in which there is a disproportion under any of the six heads.[2]

[2] George Gallup and Claude Robinson, "American Institute of Public Opinion—Surveys, 1935-38," *The Public Opinion Quarterly*, Vol. 2, No. 3, July, 1938, pp. 373-374.

B. ANALOGY.

An analogy is a comparison between two cases, in one of which a certain factor is known to exist while in the other this same factor is under question. It employs the following line of reasoning: If two cases are alike in all essential respects, they will (in all probability) be alike in the respect under question. An analogy is *literal* when the two cases compared fall in the same general category, two cities, two counties, two automobiles. The analogy is *figurative* when the compared cases are generically different, as for example in the following: You should not change horses in the middle of a stream; you should not therefore change generals in the middle of a campaign. Figurative analogy has no probative force; it is useful only for making points clear and suggesting lines of reasoning which might not otherwise occur to the group. Literal analogies are chiefly valuable in relating other experiences to the case under discussion. If the advisability of adopting the quarter system by a certain university now employing the semester plan is being discussed, the group will find it profitable to consider comparable institutions in which the quarter system is being used.

The important precaution to observe in all analogies is that the cases being compared are actually analogous— that they are alike in all respects which affect the comparison in any significant way. Nonessential differences, of course, do not invalidate such reasoning.

C. CAUSE.

Reasoning from cause to effect and effect to cause enters into much of the thinking in discussion. In analysis, as we have seen, the group attempts to get before it a clear picture of the problem in terms of the effects, or symptoms, and the causes operating to produce these conditions. Again, when one proposes a solution to a problem of policy he is suggesting that a cause or set of causes be placed into operation and it is up to him to consider the probable outcomes (effects). Whether causal reasoning proceeds from cause to effect or effect to cause depends largely on which of these factors (cause or effect) is better known and understood; we reason from the known to the unknown or less known. The direction of causal reasoning (cause to effect or effect to cause) does not greatly affect the rules governing its use in discussion.

We suggest that the following precautions be observed in causal reasoning: (1) beware of a causal argument in which the connection between the cause and effect is broken or incomplete; (2) consider the possibility of causes other than those under discussion operating to prevent or alter the relationship in question; (3) observe the extent to which the effect in question is the result of the cause under consideration; and (4) consider what effects other than the one in question are (or will be) produced by the cause.

When one reasons that a broken mirror will produce bad luck or that the drouth was visited upon us because the government caused the farmers to plow under some of their crops and kill some of their pigs, we have cases in which the causal connection is broken, i.e., no causal relation exists.

C ——————   —————— E
(Causal connection is incomplete)

The operation of other causes to prevent the causal relation in question is illustrated by cases in which our calculations are upset by factors which we neglected to consider. Thus the government's crop control scheme was badly shaken by the unprecedented drouth in the Middle West. Here another cause operated to prevent a result which might otherwise have occurred. "If a man takes a dose of deadly poison, the chances are that it will cause his death; but it may be shown that this effect will not naturally follow in this case, by showing that the man took an antidote."[3]

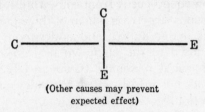

(Other causes may prevent
expected effect)

Errors in causal reasoning often arise in a case where several causes are operating to produce a single effect, and the reasoner makes the mistake of assuming that one of these causes is wholly responsible for the effect. The resulting fallacy has been called that of *part cause*. The fact that college graduates on the average earn more money than persons who do not hold a college degree is doubtless due in part to their college education. On the other hand, there can be little question that the very ability and initiative which enabled them to secure a college education are also contributing causes to their greater earning power.

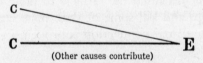

(Other causes contribute)

Just as other causes may be neglected, so may a reasoner fail to consider other possible effects of a cause which has operated or which he proposes to put into operation. Thus the invention which proposes a machine that will do the work of five men sounds attractive until we learn that it will take at least six men to operate the machine. The fact that a given cause will produce a certain effect may be wholly correct and yet present a very incomplete and inadequate picture. A proposal may produce other effects which very largely, if not com-

[3] J. M. O'Neill, Craven Laycock, and R. L. Scales, *Argumentation and Debate* (New York: The Macmillan Company, 1917), p. 144.

pletely, vitiate the desirable effect; or a proposal charged with evil consequences may be placed in a more favorable light by pointing out advantages which have been neglected.

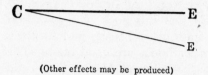

(Other effects may be produced)

The whole point of these rules is to enable the discussion group to see the entire causal picture. The failure to recognize the interrelations of causes and effects such as those suggested by the diagrams above can lead only to error and disillusionment in reflective thought.

D. SIGN.

When I infer that Wheaties are nourishing because they contain "toasted whole wheat flakes deliciously flavored with sugar, salt and malt syrup," I reason from *cause*; when I infer that they are nourishing because (so I am told) they are "the breakfast of champions," I then am reasoning from *sign*. A cause offered as a reason is a *ratio essendi*, a reason for the being of a fact; a sign is a *ratio cognoscendi*, a reason for acknowledging the being of a fact. Reasoning from sign involves all the associations and correlations which are not truly causal in nature. On countless occasions we infer the existence of things from the presence or absence of other things without meaning to suggest that any causal relationship is involved. The method or line of reasoning in making inferences from sign, then, is this: If two things are always or usually associated in some manner (other than being causally related) the presence of one may be taken as an indication of the presence or absence of the other, i.e., a reason for acknowledging its being or not being. The certainty with which such associations can be accepted in reasoning depends upon two things: (1) the *way* in which these two things are related and (2) the *degree* to which they are related.

The relationships involved in reasoning from sign may be either reciprocal or nonreciprocal. For example, if we reason that this book is a good book because it carries the imprint of Harper and Brothers, we assume that all Harper books are good books. This assumption asserts *a relation* between Harper books and good books which (if proved) warrants our conclusion. This relation is *not* reciprocal, however, because we cannot with equal cogency infer from the presence of a good book that it is a Harper book. This latter inference makes necessary a very different assumption, viz., all good books are Harper books. The only assumption which would make possible complete reciprocity between Harper books and good books would be: All Harper books are all good books. This statement asserts a perfect correlation (reciprocal relation) and from it we can take any Harper book to be a good book and any good book to be a Harper book.

In the matter of these nonreciprocal relations it is often impossible to assert that *all* members of a given class (e.g., Harper books) belong to another class (e.g., good books). Especially is this true of the kinds of subjects with which discussion ordinarily deals. Sometimes the best that we can say is *most* or *many* or even *some*. The fact remains, however, that the more exact we can be in quantifying these relations (by expressing them statistically, if possible) the more accurate we can be in the reasoning from sign based on these relations.

When phenomena vary reciprocally they are said to be *correlated* with each other. The degree of relationship is indicated by what is known as the *coefficient of correlation*. Employing this measure, the degree of correlation is indicated on a scale ranging from + 1.00 through 0.00 to − 1.00. A perfect positive correlation has as its coefficient of correlation + 1.00; this means that the presence of one variable may always be taken as a sign of the presence of the other. No correlation is indicated by 0.00 and a perfect negative correlation by − 1.00.

These matters enable us to suggest certain precautions which should be observed in reasoning from sign: (1) so far as possible premise your inferences from sign on carefully quantified relationships—percentages and coefficients of correlation; (2) where it is impossible to assign an exact mathematical index (which is usually the case in discussion), indicate the degree of relationship as carefully as possible, using such words as *many, most, practically none, about seventy-five per cent*; (3) beware of using *all* or implying *all* in reasoning from sign where something less than *all* is indicated by your data; (4) avoid the use of signs which do not establish significant degrees of probability—random, accidental associations are not significant; and (5) do not take mere association or correlation to mean causal relationship—variables which are related or show some correlation *may* or *may not* be causally related, but these relationships are none the less significant as *signs* in interpreting phenomena and inferring useful conclusions.

IV. THE FORMAL STRUCTURE OF REASONING

A. THE SYLLOGISM.

When two propositions are so formulated and laid down that a third proposition necessarily follows from these two propositions we have a syllogism.[4] All the principles, devices, and rules of the syllogism are designed to show how propositions can be combined in such a way as to yield other propositions by a process of reasoned interpretation. Any syllogistic reasoning must begin with certain *given* propositions; it then proceeds to combine and relate these given propositions in an attempt to see what they mean and to what they lead. The syllogism as such is not concerned with the *material truth* of the prop-

[4] Aristotle, *Prior Analytics*, I, 1.

ositions with which it deals, but rather with the *formal truth* or validity of the inferences made from these propositions. Thus, from the propositions, *All men have red hair*, and *Smith is a man*, we may infer syllogistically that *Smith has red hair.* Here our first premise is patently false (from a material point of view), our second one may be, and our conclusion in point of fact may or may not be, but the conclusion does follow necessarily from the propositions laid down; the reasoning is *formally* valid. All that you can say of a valid syllogism is that *if* the premises are true, then the conclusion also is true.

B. RELATIONS OF THE SYLLOGISM TO EXAMPLE, ANALOGY, CAUSE, AND SIGN.

If the syllogism may be depended upon to yield conclusions which are *materially true* only when the premises from which it proceeds are true propositions, and if the syllogism in and of itself has no reference to material truth, we may well ask how do we get propositions which are materially true in the first place? Much of what was said in the preceding section about example, analogy, cause, and sign applies at this point. *Example* was defined as the process of inferring conclusions from specific cases or instances, and *analogy* was explained as the process of bringing to bear related cases or instances through a method of comparison. Here, then, are two types of reasoning which deal not with given propositions, but with the raw data of human experience. They attempt to "gather it into" propositions which are materially true and which will meet the tests of observation and experience. In this capacity example and analogy are not syllogistic arguments in any helpful sense.[5] They are frequently referred to as *inductive* modes of inference

[5] Aristotle does speak of the inductive syllogism and makes example a species of enthymeme (see *Prior Analytics* II, 24, and *Rhetoric* II, 25); when examples and analogies are included in *ex post facto* reports such subsumption may be justified, but this point need not be pressed here.

for this reason, i.e., methods of drawing conclusions from experience.

Inferences from *causes* and *signs* are inductive modes of reasoning in one sense and deductive in another, with *deduction* understood to mean reasoning from given propositions to a conclusion. If we infer from the propositions that *All fire causes heat*, that *This is a fire*, and therefore *That this causes heat*, we are reasoning deductively from cause to effect and the reasoning is subject to the tests of valid causal reasoning. If we conclude that *Wheaties are nourishing* because *All the breakfasts of champions are nourishing* and *Wheaties are breakfasts of champions*, we are again reasoning deductively, this time from sign, and the reasoning is subject to the appropriate tests of validity.

At the same time it may be asked: How do you know that all fire causes heat? or How do you know that all the breakfasts of champions are nourishing? Any ultimately satisfying answers to either of these questions must involve a reference to experience. If an adequate sampling of fire shows that all fire causes heat, and if an adequate investigation of the breakfasts of champions shows them to consist of nourishing foods, we may then assert this to be the case. Is it not clear that these inductive processes, that of sampling fires and that of champions' breakfasts, also involve causes and signs? In the case of each fire examined we had to establish a causal relation; and in the case of each breakfast of a champion we had to establish an association. The accumulation of samples representing a fair cross section of the phenomena under investigation is the basis upon which we hazard a generalization.

From these explanations it can be seen that reasoning from cause and sign in their deductive capacities has a peculiar relation to the syllogism which does not obtain in the case of example and analogy. The advantages and limitations of the syllogism with reference to the use of causes and signs in discussion are now the topics to which we must turn our attention.

C. USES OF THE SYLLOGISM IN DISCUSSION.

While the syllogism has its most obvious application in intentional reasoning, there are two functions which it can serve in constructive thought: (1) it can serve as an *ex post facto* check or test of inferences; and (2) it can be used to suggest experimental combinations of propositions.

1. *As an* ex post facto *Check on Inferences.*—When a reflective thinker has made a deduction, let us say quite without conscious reference to the syllogism (as is almost invariably the case), he may if he chooses check this deduction by throwing it into a syllogistic form. The same, of course, can be done by members of a discussion group. Thus the syllogism, which plays a primary role in intentional reasoning, can be made to serve this secondary, but none the less useful role in constructive reasoning.

Three types of syllogisms ordinarily distinguished are the *categorical*, the *hypothetical*, and the *disjunctive*. A brief explanation of these types will serve to indicate how the syllogism may be applied as a test in constructive reasoning. We have used the categorical form of the syllogism in several examples in this chapter. The classic illustration will serve our purposes here: *All men are mortal; Socrates is a man;* therefore, *Socrates is mortal.* The first of these statements is the major premise, the second the minor premise, and the third proposition is the conclusion. Every categorical syllogism consists of three propositions which serve to relate three *terms,* a major term (mortal), a minor term (Socrates), and a middle term (men). Each of these terms is thought of as constituting a *class* and it is the relation of these classes with respect to *inclusion,* one within the other, which comprises the inferential process of the syllogism. Since this does not appear to be the place to go into all the figures and modes of the syllogism, we shall merely present the rules governing the categorical syllogism. The reader who wishes further information on this subject may consult any elementary work in logic.

A syllogism is not valid if it violates any of the following rules: (1) a syllogism must contain three and only three terms, each of which appears twice in the syllogism; (2) a syllogism must contain three and only three propositions; (3) the middle term must be distributed (cover *all* members of the class) in at least one of the premises; (4) a term must not be distributed in the conclusion unless it is also distributed in one of the premises; (5) no conclusion can be drawn from two negative premises; (6) if one premise is negative, the conclusion must be negative; (7) no conclusion can be drawn from two particular premises (as distinguished from universal premises; the proposition *Some men are rich* is particular while *All men are rich* is universal); (8) if one premise is particular, the conclusion must be particular.

In the *hypothetical syllogism* the major premise is a hypothetical statement (e.g., *If Brown wrote the story, it is a good story*) in which the first or conditional clause is called the *antecedent* and the second clause is called the *consequent*. In a valid hypothetical syllogism the minor premise must either affirm the antecedent or deny the consequent. This may be taken as the special rule of the hypothetical syllogism.

In the *disjunctive* syllogism the major premise sets forth two or more possibilities (e.g., *Either Brown or Smith wrote the book*) and the minor premise makes a selection among these by affirmation or negation in the following manner: *Brown did write the book*, the conclusion then being that Smith did not; or *Brown did not write the book*, in which case we may conclude that Smith did. There are two important rules in the disjunctive syllogism which must be observed if valid conclusions are to be drawn: (1) the possibilities enumerated in the major premise must be *all inclusive*; and (2) they must be *mutually exclusive*.

2. *The Syllogism Used to Suggest Experimental Combinations of Propositions.*—In the preceding section we discussed the syllogism as an *ex post facto* device which the constructive thinker can use as a check on his reasoning as he goes along. If an inference does not conform to the syllogistic rules, there is at least a presumption raised against it. It raises a danger signal which the reasoner can heed by reconsidering the point in question.

It is possible for the syllogism also to play a somewhat more positive role in reflective deliberation. The reasoner is constantly dealing in propositions at all stages of constructive thought; for purposes of investigating a proposition he may (1) take it as a tentative conclusion and work out its implications syllogistically or (2) he may take it as a premise and combine it with other propositions experimentally to see where the reasoning will lead him. Schiller says of the first of these two procedures:

We may start with any proposition, and make it either a conclusion or a premiss. To take it as a conclusion means to explore its connexions with the body of recognised knowledge. We then look for two other propositions from which it can be deduced and which will support it and vouch for its truth. . . . In this way we can, by reasoning, build up a body of coherent truth-claims which stand and fall together and will not lightly be rejected. . . . Such trains of thought may discover new relations, but hardly new facts, and are fitly called recoils.[6]

Applying this procedure in the fourth step of the reflective thinking process, the reasoner may take his hypothesis as a tentative conclusion, and work out its implications through a series of these so-called *recoils*. By considering reasons for and against it, by refining these reasons through subreasons and thence considering facts and expert opinions, by checking the inferences syllo-

[6] F. C. S. Schiller, *Logic for Use* (New York: Harcourt, Brace and Company, 1930), pp. 285-286.

gistically, and by weighing the case for and the case against the proposition, he may be able to pass a more accurate and pragmatically useful judgment on the hypothesis than he would otherwise be able to do. The chief danger in this process lies in the possibility that the reasoner will *desire* to prove or disprove the proposition, in which case his reasoning may become intentional, specious, or even sophistical. The obvious, though by no means simple, advice is to avoid such emotional identifications wherever possible. We have said much about this matter already and shall have more to say about it in Chapter XIII.

Schiller calls the second method arguing *forwards* or making *advances*:

> We shall, then, take our first proposition as a premiss, and try to associate it with another from which conjoined together some interesting conclusion may be deduced. The process need not be "valid" and the conclusion may be "only probable" (as when it has involved an undistributed middle); but it is essential to observe whether it occurs in actual fact. Moreover, it is evident that we have an enormous freedom of choice in experimenting with premisses; for they may be derived from any quarter, and antecedently quite improbable conjunctions may prove fruitful.[7]

D. Limitations of the Syllogism in Discussion.

In this section we wish to point out certain limitations of the syllogism which affect its use in discussion. Broadly speaking, many significant inferences cannot be thrown into syllogistic forms and it would be a serious mistake to rule them out of group deliberation for this reason. We certainly should not view the syllogism as an end in itself, but rather as a tool which can serve a useful purpose within certain limitations.

1. *Limitations Imposed by the Principle of Continuous Variation.*—To make this first limitation clear it is necessary to examine the fundamental laws or assumptions

[7] *Ibid.*, p. 286.

upon which the syllogism rests. These so-called *Laws of Thought* are three, *identity, contradiction,* and *excluded middle.* All three of these laws are relevant to the relation of *class inclusion* with which the syllogism exclusively deals. We shall be concerned here primarily with the law of excluded middle which may be expressed: "A is either B or non B." The objection to this law of excluded middle is precisely the objection which was raised to definition by classification in Chapter X. In cases where the principle of continuous variation operates (e.g., black and white, sane and insane) it is impossible, without being wholly arbitrary, to draw a hard and fast line between B and non B. Yet this is precisely what must be done if these terms are to be used in a formally valid syllogism. The whole syllogistic doctrine is built upon the assumption that we can reduce the known universe to definite categories and that everything can be pigeonholed in terms of these categories. Definition by classification is implicit in the doctrine. To the extent that terms in discussion defy such definition (and many of them do) we cannot force them to behave according to the rules of the syllogism without sacrificing their true meaning and the real truth of the matter.

The practical advice which this limitation of the syllogism suggests is this: Do not accept the syllogism as the final authority in reasoning. Do not be dogmatic and arbitrary in applying it. Do not make a fetish of formal validity. Take the formal fallacy (violation of a rule of the syllogism) as a caution sign rather than a stop sign. Many difficulties in syllogistic inference can be bridged honestly and safely by the recognition that the differences between B and non B *may* be relative rather than absolute.

2. *Limitations Imposed by Probable Inference.*—The rules concerning the *distribution* of terms in the syllogism impose a second limitation on its use in discussion. We have seen that "the middle term must be distributed in at least one of the premises." Now a term is said to be

distributed if it refers to a class of things in its entirety, e.g., *all men, every person*. Thus, if the data indicate *some*, *many*, or anything less than *all*, one is estopped from using the syllogism, at least as a formally valid instrument. Yet, for example, the fact that most of the barbers in Chicago belong to a union establishes a *high degree of probability* that barber X belongs to the union. To be sure, the conclusion is not proved by the evidence offered; it is quite possible that barber X may not belong to the union, but it would be absurd to deny that the fact that most barbers belong to the union establishes a strong presumption that the barber in question likewise belongs.

Many of the inferences in discussion are of necessity *probable* rather than *certain*. Our explanation of argument from sign emphasizes this fact. These arguments are significant and helpful in reaching conclusions. While certainty in inference may always be regarded as salutary, it is sheer folly to insist that constructive reasoning in discussion either can or should wait upon such certainty. An accumulation of arguments establishing a high degree of probability may amount to zero measured by the standards of the syllogism. It is a serious misunderstanding of the syllogism to attempt to make a dictator of it in fields in which probable inferences have great practical significance and, in fact, may be the only kind of inferences which can honestly be made.

In brief summary of Chapters X and XI, we see that the total pattern of discussion is that of the five steps in reflective thinking. Each of these steps presents problems which likewise must be dealt with reflectively and which submit to this same five-step analysis. The modes of reasoning by which the thinker attacks these problems in all of their aspects are example, analogy, cause, and sign. Of these, example and analogy, and cause and sign as well, in certain of their applications, are means of drawing conclusions from facts and experience. These conclusions may then be used as premises from which to deduce further conclusions by reasoning from causes and signs. The syllogism may be used to test the formal validity of deductive inference and to suggest experimental combinations of propositions which may prove fruitful. In these roles, however, it is important to recognize that not all inferences of practical significance can be expected to meet the tests which the syllogism imposes.

Exercises

1. Bring to class five original examples of each of the following types of reasoning: example, analogy, cause, and sign. Be prepared to apply to each of your examples the appropriate tests of validity.

2. Bring to class five original examples of each of the three types of the syllogism. Be prepared to apply to each of your examples the appropriate tests of their validity.

3. Prepare a 500-word analysis of a problem in the pattern of reflective thinking. Annotate your paper marginally to indicate the modes of reasoning employed in each stage of the thinking process.

4. Conduct a class discussion with special attention to the modes of reasoning and possible applications of the syllogism.

5. Criticize the following statements in terms of what has been said in this chapter: .

   a. "It is quite true that syllogizing may prove a very interesting pastime, but we delude ourselves if we think it is likely to be of any real service in the serious business of reasoning."—F. W. Westaway, *Scientific Method*, p. 169.

   b. "Logic is of little use for the purpose of enabling us to reason; it rather enables us to know whether in a given case we *have reasoned* correctly, or at least to discover where the weak point in our reasoning must lie. Logic does not discover, but it tests discoveries which claim to be already made. It is also a useful instrument for combating fallacy and sophism.—F. W. Westaway, *Scientific Method*, p. 174.

6. Bring to class three examples of violations of each of

the rules governing causal reasoning. Select these so far as you are able from articles, advertisements, and the like.

SELECTED BIBLIOGRAPHY

Boas, George, *Our New Ways of Thinking*. New York: Harper and Brothers, 1930.

Bogoslovsky, Boris B., *The Technique of Controversy*. New York: Harcourt, Brace and Company, 1928.

Bridgman, P. W., *The Intelligent Individual and Society*. New York: The Macmillan Company, 1938. Chapter III.

Burtt, Edwin A., *Principles and Problems of Right Thinking*. New York: Harper and Brothers, 1928.

Chase, Stuart, *The Tyranny of Words*. New York: Harcourt, Brace and Company, 1938. Chapter XIII.

Clarke, Edwin C., *The Art of Straight Thinking*. New York: D. Appleton and Company, 1929.

Cohen, Morris R., and Nagel, Ernest, *An Introduction to Logic and Scientific Method*. New York: Harcourt, Brace and Company, 1934. Chapter XIV.

Evans, D. Luther, and Gamertsfelder, Walter S., *Logic, Theoretical and Applied*. New York: Doubleday, Doran and Company, 1937. Chapters VIII and X.

Jastrow, Joseph, *Effective Thinking*. New York: Simon and Schuster, 1931. Chapters III and IV.

Robinson, Daniel S., *The Principles of Reasoning*. New York. D. Appleton and Company, 1928. Chapters VIII, XVII, XVIII, XIX, and XXIII.

Schiller, *Logic for Use*. New York: Harcourt, Brace and Company, 1930. Chapters XIV and XVI.

Symonds, Percival M., *Education and the Psychology of Thinking*. New York: McGraw-Hill Book Company, Inc., 1936. Part II and Chapter XXI.

Westaway, F. W., *Scientific Method*. London: Blackie & Son, Ltd., 1924. Chapters XIII, XX, and XXII.

CHAPTER XII

OBSTACLES TO REFLECTIVE THINKING

"The understanding of right thinking may be advanced by analyzing how thinking goes wrong. Logic has always included the study of fallacies. A helpful psychological approach is to consider that as there are impediments of speech which prevent the speaker from speaking plainly, so there are also impediments of thought which prevent the thinker from thinking effectively. These defects are in the nature of temptations to use the thinking machine wrongly."[1]

In these words Jastrow suggests the importance of a study of obstacles to good reasoning. We believe this to be particularly true in a study of reflective thinking, where by the very nature of the process successful outcomes require freedom from distortion, diversion, and undue "coloring."

This study of the obstacles to reflective thinking has important applications to several phases of group discussion. It relates to the work of participants and leaders, to the role of facts and expert opinions, and to modes of reasoning. More than this, it is implicit in the point of view of both this volume and reflective thinking. It bears

---

[1] Joseph Jastrow, *Effective Thinking* (New York: Simon and Schuster, 1931), p. 103.

upon the three requisites of good discussion: critical thinking, cooperation, and communication, because obstacles to thinking can operate through all these elements to destroy the fullest service which they can render to discussion.

In this chapter we shall first consider some of the causes of these obstacles, then briefly touch upon the logical fallacies, and finally analyze in some detail a number of obstacles to which we are attaching the name "stratagems."

I. SOME CAUSES OF OBSTACLES TO REFLECTIVE THINKING

One of the best means of knowing any phenomenon is through an understanding of its cause. For this reason we are here suggesting some of the causes of the obstacles to reflective thinking. These are presented in the major classifications called *personal* and *social*, which we believe most usefully represent the factors responsible for fallacies and stratagems.

A. Personal Causes.

The personal causes of obstacles can be conveniently considered from the point of view of the motives actuating them, whether they are unintentional or intentional. This classification provides an indication of the differences between the causes and also suggests the possible reasons for their existence.

1. *Unintentional.*—By the term "unintentional causes" we mean those factors which operate involuntarily, without the operation of the will. To the extent that a person cannot overcome such deficiencies he is prevented from participating efficiently in individual thinking or group discussion. To the extent, however, that a person can overcome some of these deficiencies by self-discipline or training, these variables are subject almost entirely to his desire to think effectively. They include

the factors preventing a person from reasoning logically, independently, concretely, and rapidly—and consequently preventing him from being free from at least some of the obstacles to good thinking.

Among the more important of these factors are the inability to observe, to remember, to organize, to analyze, to make hypotheses, to synthesize, and to appraise. Associated with these are mental inertia, lack of interest in "finding answers," gullibility, and stereotyped or tabloid thinking.

These factors vitally condition good discussion. For example, a group composed of persons with these disabilities can hardly develop the pattern of discussion satisfactorily. The first step in reflective thinking, for instance, will be virtually barren if clear observation, good memory, and the power to organize thoughts are lacking. Faulty analytical powers cannot provide a clear analysis of the problem or a determination of the values desired in the solution. Faulty powers of speculation, synthesis, and appraisal cannot do more than create blundering guesswork concerning the future. Conversely, keen mental activity and the ability to diagnose causes and effects are needed for constructive thinking which is free from errors.

Independent thinking, which is equally necessary, is frequently impeded by dependence upon other persons' ideas or one's previous thinking. If a person restricts his thinking to the channels previously cut, he is almost certain to be unreflective. He is likely to give undue weight to authority and become what Francis Bacon called a "slave to custom."

Furthermore, concrete and practical thinking—vitally needed in profitable discussion—can often be impeded by what we are calling *excessive intellectuality*. By this statement we do not mean that intellectuality is undesirable. If we did we should be inconsistent with our earlier observation concerning the need for logical and creative thinking. What we do mean is that a highly intellectual individual may, unless he exercises great patience, impede good discussion. The conferee of this type, who thinks clearly but often abstractly and very rapidly, may become irritated at the attempts of other persons to inject more concreteness into the discussion and to proceed more deliberately. He may perpetrate, perhaps unconsciously, some of the obstacles to group deliberation, such as manipulating unduly the thinking of the slower members or even attempting to make his ideas prevail by resorting to such stratagems as ridicule and irony.

On the other hand, slowness in thinking may at times be a cause of certain obstacles. The slow-thinking individual not only impedes progress but may easily be the cause of stratagems which victimize both himself and the group. He may, for example, be open to a number of the stratagems of diversion and direct attack because he is slow to comprehend new ideas. He may not be dull, and he may possess all the other requisites of reasoning, but the fact that things "dawn on him" slowly weakens his effectiveness.

Emotion, especially excessive emotion, is also a possible source of obstacles to reflective thinking. It may interfere with the processes of logical and independent reasoning and also influence the rapidity of one's thinking. It may blur one's vision, upset chains of reasoning, and make it impossible accurately to relate one's thinking to normal situations in life. It may intensify deficiencies in reasoning powers and upset even the best of mental abilities. It is a definite cause of a number of the obstacles arising from words, censorship, and diversions. We do not mean to imply that emotion has no place in the thinking process. To do so would be to ignore human nature and disregard the values of enthusiasm. What we are saying is that there should be a balance between feeling and thought in order to insure the most reliable individual and group thinking.

2. *Intentional.*—The intentional factors are those which

operate largely by a person's express desire. They include self-interest, self-esteem, dominance of low interests, desire to imitate, prejudice, desire to convert others, and the tendency to rationalize. Many of these are included by Bacon in his "Idols of the Cave," which cause a person to restrict his outlook, look at things exclusively from his own point of view, and persist in stating his own favorite notions.[2]

In part these factors arise from the unintentional causes which we have just considered, and in part they are products of other circumstances. The most brilliant mind, for example, may be so dominated by self-interest and self-esteem that it is made incapable of participating effectively in discussion. It may use as many stratagems as possible to make its interests prevail. Consider how self-interest and low interests affect standards of values and attitudes toward problems, and how a desire to imitate destroys independence. Consider how prejudice may warp thought in the direction of conservatism or radicalism, as the case may be. The desire to convert and propagandize is almost certain to put into operation such stratagems as censorship and diversion, and rationalization may also prompt the use of censorship.

As in the case of the intentional factors, emotions may also play a prominent part in giving rise to obstacles. Whether these emotions are intentional or unintentional, they have their subversive effects. In fact, they are probably more powerful when intentional because they are then consciously associated with such factors as self-interest and a desire to convert or propagandize.

B. SOCIAL CAUSES.

The social causes of obstacles may be either unintentional or intentional, but it is probably not profitable to press this distinction in this case. The term "group pres-

[2] See Francis Bacon, *Novum Organum*, translated by James Spedding and included in *The Philosophical Writings of Francis Bacon* (Boston: Houghton Mifflin and Company, 1857), ii, p. 77.

sures" expresses the essential nature of the social force operating upon a person to cause him to use, or to be the victim of, the various obstacles. Whether it is the conscious or unconscious pressure from a church, political organization, or family, the point is the same. The individual is thinking as the group pressure dictates; and if the pressure is great, he is almost certain to put into play such stratagems, for instance, as censorship, diversion, and the many obstacles arising from language which we shall explain later.

Again we find in Bacon some suggestions as to the nature and effect of these influences. The Baconian "Idols of the Forum," or "Market-Place," describe particularly the force of tradition; and the "Idols of the Theatre" refer to the allegiance to creeds, dogmas, and parties.[3] The person who is influenced by these pressures will quite naturally tend to make his thinking conform to these "idols" and may be prompted to put into operation any stratagem which will serve his purpose.

It is clear that there is force in Jastrow's statement that "These defects are in the nature of temptations to use the thinking machine wrongly." This is just the point we wish to emphasize. Whether personal or social, unintentional or intentional, many factors operate to influence a person's thinking ability and his point of view.

We believe that the best thing to do is to call attention to the causes of these stratagems and to the stratagems themselves so that they can be studied. We believe that by carefully outlining and describing them we can aid the student of group discussion to free his mind of these obstacles and to defend himself against their use by others. Our purpose is to secure good thinking.

II. LOGICAL FALLACIES

The first of the obstacles to reflective thinking which confront us are the logical fallacies, those associated with errors in the syllogism and in the example, analogy, cause,

[3] *Ibid.*, pp. 78-79.

and sign. It is not our purpose in this chapter, however, to discuss these in detail, because of their close relation to the materials of Chapter IX and Chapter XI. It is sufficient to recall that fallacies represent errors in the modes of reasoning described in Chapter XI. As pointed out there, the syllogism by its nature imposes certain rules governing the relations of its parts; and any violation of these rules gives rise to a fallacy. The example, analogy, cause, and sign also impose certain rules upon their respective processes; and violations of these rules give rise to further fallacies.

Closely associated with these fallacies are the errors which arise from the misuse of facts and expert opinions. As described in Chapter IX, these include errors in the facts and opinions themselves as well as errors in the sources of facts and opinions. The outline given at the end of Chapter IX suggests where these errors may arise and how they may be detected.

III. STRATAGEMS

In addition to the errors in the use of facts and expert opinions and in reasoning there is a body of obstacles to reflective thinking to which we have attached the name "stratagems." They represent a number of means which may operate to distort either the individual's thinking or the group's deliberations. Whether they are used intentionally by persons seeking an advantage or whether they creep in almost undetected, their effects are equally harmful. The name "stratagem" suggests their nature because they may be artifices or devices to obtain an advantage; they may include some of the elements of fallacies, and again they may exist even if the reasoning and the facts are otherwise satisfactory.[4]

[4] The term "stratagem" is used by Schopenhauer to designate a group of thirty-eight tricks of Dialectic which he describes in his essay entitled "The Art of Controversy." In this essay Schopenhauer makes no special effort to classify these stratagems, merely numbering them I-XXXVIII. We acknowledge our indebtedness to him for the term "stratagem" and also for the many suggestions provided by his treatment of the subject.

We are using the classifications "in language" and "outside of language" to designate two general areas in which the stratagems may appear and to suggest something of their general nature.

A. Stratagems in Language.

By this term we mean those obstacles to reflective thinking which arise from inexactness in the meaning of words or combinations of words and also from the use of "colored" or "loaded" words. While not in every sense exclusive, these classifications will be found useful.

1. *Inexactness in Language.*—The stratagems included in this category are those arising from unfixed meanings and confusion in terms. They give rise to misunderstandings which the lines of thought themselves do not warrant. The remedy in each case is the supplying of a more appropriate word or phrase to express the concept intended.

a. Ambiguity.—This stratagem arises from the use of a word or phrase with a double meaning. The word "cut," for example, may mean "sever" or "grieve"—and in the vernacular of the college campus may even mean "absent oneself from." Or the word "forum" may mean "a tribunal," "an institution where discussion may be conducted," or "a method of conducting discussion." The defense against this stratagem may be the context, but where that fails it is necessary to ask for a clarification of meaning or a substitution of words to provide for greater clarity.

b. Vagueness.—This arises from the use of a word or phrase with no well-defined meaning. Like the preceding stratagem, it may cause confusion and permit a thought to be misinterpreted or to enter the discussion with false credentials because nobody knows exactly what it means. Consider the rather frequent, uncritical use of such semi-technical words as "gestalt," "balance of trade," "due process," and "general welfare." The defense is to ask for a clarification by definition or a substitution of a more precise word.

c. Accent.—This arises from the use of a word whose meaning depends upon accentuation, or from the placing of an incorrect emphasis upon some part of a sentence. The unfair separation of a word from its context or the use of inflections of the voice in reading may create a false impression from a statement that is basically true. For example, the statement "The United States should not abrogate the rights of citizens in New York" may by a slight emphasis on the last words imply that the government could rightly abrogate the rights of citizens elsewhere. The defense is either a careful understanding of the meaning of a word or phrase irrespective of the peculiar accent, or an analysis of the meaning of each word in its context.

d. Amphiboly.—This stratagem arises from the use of an ambiguous grammatical construction in a sentence. The misconception results most commonly from confusion over antecedents and words of reference and from word order which makes the meaning ambiguous. An example of the confusion arising out of inadequate words of reference is seen in the sentence: "The foreign policy of the United States and England may not be wholly acceptable to all of our citizens." This sentence can mean either (1) the foreign policy of the United States and the foreign policy of England may not be acceptable or (2) the Anglo-American foreign policy may not be acceptable. These two meanings are, of course, widely different. Another example is seen in the sentence: "The apartment house and the community house being built on First Street will have two great values to the city either one of which is worth more than the cost of construction." This sentence can mean (1) that either building is worth more than the cost of construction or (2) that either value is worth more to the city than the cost of construction—in other words, that the cost of construction is more than offset by the values to the city.

An example of confusing word order is seen in the classic sentence: "That is equal to twice two and three," which may mean seven or ten.

The defense against this stratagem consists in a use of clear words of reference, or of a change in the order of the words. For instance, the insertion of "that of" just preceding "England" will clarify the meaning of the first illustration; and the placing of the clause "either one of which is worth more than the cost of construction" just following "First Street" will make the second illustration clearly mean that either building is worth more than the cost of construction.

To summarize, these stratagems involving the inexact use of language may pertain to a single word, a sentence, or a longer unit. They cause either needless discussion as to exact meanings or useless argument over misrepresented ideas. Worse yet, they make possible varying degrees of misrepresentation of a single thought or a long series of ideas. Consider, for example, how an argument could be needlessly prolonged because of confusion over the meaning of the term "liberal education" or the distinction between "personal rights" and "property rights." In the interest of clear thought these stratagems need to be avoided as well as detected and removed.

2. *"Coloring" in Language.*—The various forms of this stratagem arise from the fact that there are emotional meanings attaching to many words and phrases. It has been frequently said that virtual synonyms may be selected on the basis of three considerations: (1) to convey a strong favorable reaction to some person or thing; (2) to convey a meaning which is neutral; (3) to convey a meaning in strong antipathy to some person or thing.

Examples of words selected to produce strong "pro" or "con" responses are provided by two of the propaganda devices described by the Institute for Propaganda Analysis. "Glittering Generalities" is described as "a device by which the propagandist identifies his program with virtue by use of 'virtue words.' Here he appeals to our emotions of love, generosity, and brotherhood. He uses words like truth, freedom, honor, liberty, social justice, public service, the right to work, loyalty, progress, democracy, the American way, Constitution defender." "Name Calling" is described in these words: "Here the propagandist appeals to our hate and fear. He does this by giving 'bad names' to those individuals, groups, nations, races, policies, practices, beliefs, and ideals which he would have us condemn and reject. . . . Today's bad names include: Fascist, demagogue, dictator, Red, financial oligarchy, Communist, muck-raker, alien, outside agitator, economic royalist, Utopian, rabble-rouser, trouble-maker, Tory, Constitution wrecker."[5]

Ogden and Richards help us in understanding this stratagem in their comment upon four groups of words which should be avoided in discussion: Irritants, Degenerates, Mendicants, Nomads. They say that in thoughtful discussion both Irritants and Degenerates must be rejected: "Irritants because of their power to evoke disturbing emotions, and Degenerates because of the multiplicity of their associated referents." In other words, Irritants are "loaded," or emotionally colored, words connoting strong points of view. They may denote fairly objective meanings; but Degenerates, on the other hand, are ambiguous, inexact words lacking precise denotations of any kind.

Of the Mendicants they say: "There is another class of words which may profitably be placed beyond the range of legitimate dispute. Matthew Arnold speaks of 'terms thrown out, so to speak, at a not fully grasped object of the speaker's consciousness.' So long as the true function of these Mendicants, as they might be designated, is recognized, they will cause little trouble." The thought here is that these are words which "beg" their way around among half-formulated ideas attempting to find a place of attachment. They are not fully associated with any precise concept, but call up incomplete associations and imperfect meanings.

Nomads, which were first described by Locke, are those words used by persons who do not know the complete idea which they express, and which fill the "discourse with abundance of empty noise and jargon." Of these words Locke says: "Men take the words they find in use amongst their neighbors, and that they may not seem ignorant what they stand for use them confidently without much troubling their heads about a certain fixed meaning, whereby besides the ease of it they obtain this advantage that as in such discourse they are seldom in the right so they are seldom to be convinced they are in the wrong, it being all one to draw these men out of their mistakes, who have no settled notions, as to dispossess a Vagrant of his habitation, who has no settled abode."[6]

In some cases the same word may be at one time an Irritant, at another a Degenerate, at another a Mendicant, and again a Nomad. If this circumstance does exist, the difference lies in the use of the word and in its relation to the thought which it expresses. For instance, the word "patriot" may be an Irritant in the sense that it is an emotionally colored word, a "virtue word." It may also be a Degenerate in that it is somewhat ambiguous, failing to distinguish between blind love of country and wise, discerning respect for one's native land. It may also be a Mendicant in that it is used to represent a half-formulated idea which vaguely suggests "love of country," "willingness to die for one's country," and "good citizenship." The word "begs" its way around among these indefinite concepts and attempts to call up associations which are not warranted by the concepts themselves or by the word. Finally, it may be a Nomad in that it is a word of rather wide but at the same rather loose usage, being a handy

[6] C. K. Ogden and I. A. Richards, *The Meaning of Meaning* (New York: Harcourt, Brace and Company, 1930), pp. 136-137. Additional material is available in the edition of 1923, pp. 240-243.

word to fit into a particular situation even if the precise meaning is not known.

In some cases a particular word may be primarily an Irritant. For example, "communist" is emotionally colored and at the same time fairly exact in its denotation. "Due-process" and "manifest destiny" are very apt to be Degenerates in that they may be ambiguous, inexact, lacking precise denotations of any kind. "Utopian" and "open-minded" are Mendicants upon some occasions in that they are not fully associated with any precise concept, but call up incomplete and imperfect meanings. "Due process" and "liberal" may in some cases be Nomads in that they are widely used by people who are not certain of the meanings. The *sound* of the words may often supersede the *meaning* as the basis of selection.

Whatever the name of the particular device or the direction of its meaning, this stratagem of "colored" words has invariably but one essential effect—that of making thinking subjective rather than objective. This stratagem thus defeats the means and purposes of reflective thinking by distorting or stopping thinking and by giving undue "color" to a conclusion. It goes beyond the legitimate credentials of a statement or of the thought represented by a statement.

The defense against this stratagem lies in the habit of translating one's thoughts into emotionally neutral words and in searching behind "colored" words used by other persons to detect the real meaning which the facts or the reasoning may warrant.

B. Stratagems Outside of Language.

By this term we mean those obstacles to reflective thinking which arise from attempts to control the admission of materials into the discussion or to distort the materials in such a way as to interfere with critical thinking. For purposes of convenience in describing these stratagems we have placed them in four groups to which we have attached the names Censorship, Diversion, Manipulation, and Substitution.

1. *Stratagems of Censorship.*—The distinguishing feature of these stratagems is their attempt to keep the individual or the group in ignorance of the true situation—to convey a false impression. The means may be by control or interpretation of the materials with which the group is working.

a. Errors in Fact.—As its name implies, this stratagem serves to create false impressions by misrepresenting conditions. A person attempting to gain special advantage for himself in a discussion gives, for example, what purport to be facts concerning all the costs of operation of the army and navy but intentionally or otherwise presents erroneous information. Or recall the illustration of the city council and the apparently erroneous data which impeded logical thinking (Chapter IX). The defense is the most complete knowledge possible plus careful scrutiny of attendant facts to detect discrepancies. A further defense consists of a searching questioning of the person submitting the facts.

b. Half-Facts.—Fully as serious as the stratagem of errors in facts is the one which "tells only half the story." This stratagem of half-facts plays upon the disarming effect of the plausibility of the actual facts submitted, and proceeds to influence thinking by the untrue picture which results. It is seen in a report of a labor struggle wherein facts are provided concerning the number of laborers in the picket line, the number of picketers imported from other cities, and the amount of violence committed by the picketers. However, no mention is made of the composition of the group trying to break the picket line. The person submitting the information neglects to mention the fact that the police may be controlled by the owners of the plant, that the strikebreakers may be imported men, and that as much violence was perpetrated by one side as by the other. He may also neglect to state who provoked the conflict.

This device has been called "Card Stacking" by the Institute for Propaganda Analysis. In using this, the propagandist "stacks the cards against the truth. . . . He resorts to lies, censorship, and distortion. He omits facts. . . . He draws a red herring across the trail to confuse and divert those in quest of facts he does not want revealed. . . . He lets half-truth masquerade as truth."[7]

The defense against this stratagem is essentially the same as for errors in fact: the most complete knowledge possible, plus searching questioning of the person submitting the facts, together with verification if possible from another source. Often *time* is a good defense in that second reports may correct the false impression of the first.

c. Overstatement or Understatement.—This stratagem is concerned largely with the interpretation of facts. The person using it may deal with complete and true facts, but at the same time give a false impression by his interpretation of the facts. He may make certain contrasts more glaring than the facts warrant, or he may obscure differences which really exist. The censorship exists in the fact that suggestion is made to displace the facts, with the result that the facts are little more effective than if they had been stopped at their source. In the example of the labor conflict cited above the defect lies in the control of the facts. Essentially the same effect could be produced by maximizing and minimizing the data submitted, of appraising some facts as unimportant and irrelevant and others as significant. In another case a city administration could submit all the facts in its annual report but could so dilate upon some data and minimize other facts that an erroneous impression would be created.

The defense consists in rejecting interpretations of facts by persons submitting them until there is the oppor-

[7] *Monthly Letter: Propaganda Analysis,* Vol. I, No. 2, November, 1937, p. 3.

tunity to study the facts objectively. It consists of concentrating on the facts and relegating the interpretations to a subordinate position, as well as of refusing to let suggestion operate to obscure facts.

2. *Stratagems of Diversion.*—The distinguishing feature of these stratagems is their attempt to divert the discussion to another matter because the person using the stratagem believes he can succeed more easily upon other ground. There are two types of stratagems of diversion: (1) those diverting to another argument and carrying on the discussion there; (2) those diverting to other ground for the purpose of stopping argument.

a. Diversion to Another Argument.—This type of stratagem involves the attempted handling of a line of thought by the introduction of another point which does not prove the first one but which diverts the discussion to another one more easily defended by the proponent. This definitely implies the continuation of the argument but upon a different proposition. We shall describe ten such stratagems.

(1) Making a simple diversion.—This consists simply in leaving the topic under consideration and beginning on another. It is often called evasion or ignoring the subject. The defense is quite as simple as the stratagem itself, and holds good for both the proponent of the stratagem and the victim of it. It consists in detecting the diversion and insisting upon a return to the original proposition.

(2) Fastening on a trivial point.—This consists in ignoring the question under consideration and fastening on a trivial point, destroying that, and conveying the impression that the main point has thus been destroyed.[8] It may be called diversion to a side issue which for all practical purposes becomes a new argument. For instance, the discussion of a set of cases in support of a generalization may be diverted to a consideration of only one. Agreement upon that one case may supersede considera-

<hr/>

[8] See Robert H. Thouless, *Straight and Crooked Thinking* (New York: Simon and Schuster, 1932), p. 59.

tion of the others and the conclusion which they logically reach. If the opponent is forced to admit defeat on this one, he is made to look defeated upon all others and the conclusion as well. The same may occur when any unimportant point is given undue emphasis. The defense consists first in the detection of the diversion by seeing all of the points in perspective, and second in the holding of the argument to the relation of all points to each other and to the conclusion.

(3) Giving the matter a general turn, then talking against that.—This consists, as Schopenhauer points out, in saying that a particular hypothesis in the physical sciences, for example, cannot be accepted because of the fallibility of human knowledge. It is frequently found in discussions of principles of economics in which the thinking is diverted from a principle itself to a consideration of the predictability of human nature. If this new issue is not pertinent but is injected merely for the purpose of leaving the point under consideration, it is a stratagem. The defense is detection of the relation between the main proposition and the general turn, and the raising of an objection if the connection is not valid.

(4) Using an inconsequent argument.—In this stratagem one uses as the defense of a point a statement which does not actually relate to or prove the point but which can be easily defended.[9] For example, one may cite in defense of a certain foreign policy the fact that it is new and therefore good. While not discussing the relation of novelty to merit, one proceeds to dilate upon the novelty and invites argument there. He then conveys the impression that the main point has been established. The defense is perception of the logical relation between the main point and the supporting argument, and the rejection of the latter if no valid relation exists.

(5) Using a contrary instance.—This applies particularly to reasoning by example, wherein a number of instances are required to establish a generalization. The

[9] *Ibid.*, p. 62.

diversion consists in citing a single instance to which the proposition does not apply and then implying that the proposition is necessarily overthrown. For instance, the thesis that "the reciprocal trade agreements will benefit American industry" may be attacked by saying that the shoe industry may be harmed by the importation of low-priced shoes from abroad. In this case the implication is that the one example of the shoe industry is not only true but also disproves the main proposition. The defense consists of one or more of the following steps: (1) see if the instance is really true; (2) see if it is pertinent to the generalization; (3) see if it is really inconsistent with the generalization, because the alleged inconsistency may be only apparent. If it is not a contrary instance, the discussion may then be returned to the main point, which should be considered on the merits of the generalization. If it is a contrary instance, it should be accepted as such and the generalization qualified accordingly.

(6) Using an irrelevant objection.—This stratagem consists in using a fact or line of reasoning which is irrelevant to the point being discussed. For example, a person discussing the wisdom of adopting the city-manager form of government in Chicago may point out the success of the system in Cincinnati. His opponent may divert the discussion by objecting that Chicago is different from Cincinnati because it is located on a lake and is a focal point for many transportation systems. The concern with these irrelevant points of difference diverts the discussion, and the original point may be lost because of the seeming truth of the objection. The defense is detection of the distinction between relevant and irrelevant objections by means of an analysis of causal relations, associations, and correlations. Irrelevant objections can then be rejected.

(7) Appealing to interests or motives.—Here the discussion is diverted from a logical consideration of the merits of a proposition to a question of its merits in the light of the interests of one of the persons discussing

the proposition. For instance, a person says that the Federal Trade Commission is a good institution because it exemplifies the principle of social control. You reply that this principle may mean control of a person's right to buy what he wishes, then ask your opponent how he would like to be told by the government what automobile to buy and what price to pay. This stratagem diverts the thinking from the main point and fastens it upon the interests and prejudices of persons. The defense consists in distinguishing between logical discussion and thinking dominated by personal or group motives. It consists in letting the "merits of the question" have the right of way.

(8) Using a false syllogism to divert.—Schopenhauer describes this stratagem as follows: "Your opponent makes a proposition, and by false inference and distortion of his ideas you force from it other propositions which it does not contain and he does not in the least mean; nay, which are absurd or dangerous. It then looks as if his proposition gave rise to others which are inconsistent either with themselves or with some acknowledged truth, and so it appears to be indirectly refuted."[10] The defense consists in detecting the extent to which the new propositions are invalid and in reverting the discussion to the original proposition.

(9) Arguing *ad hominem.*—This stratagem is most likely to arise when a person finds himself at a disadvantage in discussing a certain point and feels that he must introduce an argument which he can more easily attack. If he introduces a point made earlier in the discussion by an opponent, a point only superficially related to the point at hand and only superficially contradicting the opponent's present point of view, he is using the stratagem of *ad hominem.* He has two purposes: (1) to divert the discussion to a point which he can more easily meet

[10] Arthur Schopenhauer, "The Art of Controversy," in *The Essays of Arthur Schopenhauer,* translated by T. Bailey Saunders (New York: Willey Book Company, no date), p. 27. This book is now handled by The Macmillan Company, with whose permission we are making these quotations.

and (2) to upset the opponent by using against him a statement which is inconsistent with, and appears to be vitally related to, the present point. In other words, he attempts to show his opponent to be inconsistent. If the inconsistency is really upon related matters, there is, of course, no stratagem. Rather, it is the "use of a person against himself" on superficial matters which constitutes the stratagem. For example, you may be saying that "Compulsory public education is a good policy." Your opponent, realizing that he cannot adequately meet your reasoning or facts and expert opinions, diverts the discussion to a statement which you made earlier to the effect that "privately-endowed colleges are vital influences and should be encouraged." He claims that you are inconsistent, that your earlier statement and your present position are contrary; and he proceeds to discuss the earlier statement. If you permit the discussion to proceed along the line of "privately-endowed colleges" you will inevitably find your main point lost sight of. Also, if your opponent can make the apparent inconsistency clear, he may be able to defeat you on your present point.

The defense is to show that the relation between the present point and the earlier statements is only superficial, and that thus there is no inconsistency, at least of any consequence. It should then be insisted that the discussion proceed upon the present point.

(10) Arguing *ad personam.*—This consists in passing from the point in question to the opponent himself, and in making an attack upon his character, ability, or personality when such an attack has no inherent relation to the main point. Schopenhauer carefully distinguishes this from the *ad hominem* stratagem, which, as we have seen, passes from the point under discussion to a superficially related statement or admission which one's opponent has made earlier. In arguing *ad personam*, one leaves the subject and turns to the person of his opponent.[11] This

[11] *Ibid.*, p. 40.

stratagem is seen in the statement that "even the most logical reasoning of a college professor on matters of business can't be accepted because he has never had to meet
a payroll" that "so-and-so can't be a good President of
the United States because he belongs to a certain church."
The defense consists in distinguishing between relevant
causes and irrelevant causes, in exposing diversions to a
person's character, ability, and personality if these factors
are irrelevant, and in restoring the discussion to the main
point.

b. Diversion to Material Which Stops Argument on the Point Under Consideration.—This
type of stratagem appears when a person who finds himself nearly defeated on a point introduces a statement
which is not likely to be open to discussion. This statement is not the basis of new argument—as in the case of
the stratagems just considered—but is of such a nature
that the opponent almost immediately concedes the main
point or defers to the influence of the statement to which
the diversion is made.

(1) Using technical language.—This consists in diverting the discussion to a point which neither proves the
main proposition nor is made the basis of discussion. It
consists in using profound words related to technicalities
only slightly pertinent to the main point. For instance,
a conferee may make such a remark as "That doesn't
agree with the law of undistributed middle." Either
because of total ignorance of the meaning of the term
"undistributed middle" or because of the belief that the
term carries weight, the other participants are often influenced to stop thinking on this point and proceed to
something else. This may, of course, be a valid reply;
but it is so only when the diversion is to a valid objection
which can be explained and which logically raises doubts
concerning the soundness of the main point. The defense
against this stratagem consists in detecting the diversion,
then asking for an explanation of the term introduced.
To do so may be to confess ignorance and to open oneself

to ridicule, but such a confession may often be less objectionable than being misled by a stratagem.

(2) Deferring to an authority.—Frequently called *ad verecundiam*, this consists in making an appeal to authority rather than to reason. The principle underlying this stratagem is that the average person may not question the truth of a proposition if an "authority" has made a pronouncement favorable to it. The stratagem may take one of two forms: (1) it may divert the discussion to some person, preferably a "great name," or to an institution and then imply that it would be presumptuous to discuss the subject further; (2) it may divert the discussion to what is called "universal opinion" or "universal prejudice" in the hope that people will readily accept the proposition as soon as they can be convinced that it is generally adopted.

The first form is seen in the "Transfer" device described by the Institute for Propaganda Analysis. This device "carries over the authority, sanction, and prestige of something we respect and revere to something he [the propagandist] would have us accept." It is also seen in the "Testimonial" device described by the Institute for Propaganda Analysis. This attempts by using testimony from a "name" to "make us accept anything from a patent medicine or a cigarette to a program of national policy." The second form is seen in the "Band Wagon" device, which tries to make us "follow the crowd" or be in line with universal opinion. The theme of this device is "Everybody's doing it." It hopes to divert thought from the capability of a political candidate, for example, to the fact that a "ground swell" is developing and that everybody will vote for him. It plays upon the power of universal authority.[12]

This stratagem is different from the valid use of authority or universal opinion. In the latter case the authority is introduced into the discussion and considered with

[12] *Monthly Letter: Propaganda Analysis*, Vol. I, No. 2, November, 1937, pp. 2-3.

respect to his competence and reliability. The defense against the stratagem is indicated in this distinction between it and the valid use of authority. First, detect the introduction of the appeal to authority; then appraise it with respect to its validity and its pertinency to the subject.

(3) Deferring to tradition.—This stratagem appeals to the prestige and wisdom of the past, or to the sentiments associated with the past. It includes the suggestion "to keep in line" or "to revere our ancestors," and it warns against starting a "new and dangerous precedent" because the past has existed for a long time and conditions are "not ripe for a change." It is designed to stop or modify thinking because of the influence—suggested or stated—of tradition. We should not, however, be misled into supposing that all appeals to the past are stratagems. In some cases there may be real weight in tradition and real wisdom in continuing in line with past actions. Also, sentiments connected with the past may be valid reasons for holding a certain point of view—see the illustration of "values" presented in connection with Analysis in Chapter X. The defense against the stratagem is the same as that for the preceding device. First, detect the introduction of the appeal to tradition; then appraise it with respect to its validity and its pertinency to the subject.

(4) Arguing *ad populum.*—This consists in making an appeal to the emotions or prejudices of people, and thus avoiding the real question. For example, a person in discussing immigration laws diverts the attention of his listeners from the merits of the subject to national prejudice. He is attempting to stop thought—at least rational thought—and to get response based upon prejudice or high feeling. His hope is that there will be no discussion of the prejudice, merely blind acceptance or rejection of the main subject.

This stratagem is seen in the "Plain Folks" device, described by the Institute for Propaganda Analysis, which plays upon the belief that because persons are "just plain folks" they are necessarily wise and good.[13]

The defense against the stratagem rests in detecting the diversion, then appraising the validity of the popular appeal. If the popular appeal has no bearing upon the merit of the main proposition, it should be rejected and the discussion should revert to the original subject.

(5) Arguing *ad ignorantiam*.—"You cannot prove that what I say is not true; therefore, it is true." Here is a stratagem of diversion from the subject to the lack of proof as to its validity. The confusion between positive proof and refutation of proof perplexes the opponent, and he frequently gives up. The defense is to realize that this diversion proves nothing positive and that it is in reality only negative.

(6) Arguing *ad auditores*.—This stratagem consists of stating an invalid objection to a proposition, an objection which only an expert knows to be invalid. Assuming your opponent to be an expert, you realize that he recognizes the weakness of your objection; and you thus know that some additional support is needed to win the point. Therefore, you play up the objection before your less expert listeners, who do not see its weakness; and because any attempt at explanation of your weakness would require too much of your opponent's time, he is placed at a disadvantage. This is described by Schopenhauer as follows:

For example, your opponent states that in the original formation of a mountain-range the granite and other elements in its composition were, by reason of their high temperature, in a fluid or molten state; that the temperature must have mounted to some 400 degrees Fahrenheit; and that when the mass took shape it was covered by the sea. You reply, by an argument ad auditores, that at that temperature—nay, indeed, long before it had been reached, namely, at 212 degrees Fahrenheit—the sea would have been boiled away, and spread through the air in the form

[13] *Ibid.*, p. 3.

of steam. At this the audience laughs. To refute the objection, your opponent would have to show that the boiling-point depends not only on the degree of warmth, but also on the atmospheric pressure; and that as soon as about half the sea-water had gone off in the shape of steam, this pressure would be so greatly increased that the rest of it would fail to boil even at a temperature of 480 degrees. He is debarred from giving this explanation, as it would require a treatise to demonstrate the matter to those who had no acquaintance with physics.[14]

By the nature of this stratagem it does not apply as readily to the discussion group in which all persons are participating directly as it does to the panel discussion, symposium, or dialogue, where there is an audience. It may, of course, apply to the discussion group in the sense that the conferees other than the two immediate participants of the moment constitute an audience; but in all probability the stratagem will ordinarily be used with an audience which is a separate body. The defense consists in doing what Schopenhauer believes to be almost impossible, i. e., in exposing the diversion to the invalid remark and to attempt to explain the reason for its invalidity. At the same time it should be pointed out that this invalid remark has been introduced to stop thinking and to make the listeners laugh at the ridiculous plight of the victim.

(7) Declaring yourself an incompetent judge.—This apparently paradoxical stratagem is regarded by Schopenhauer as being effective only when you are more highly respected than is your opponent. It consists in saying concerning the subject, "What you now say passes my poor powers of comprehension; it may be all very true, but I can't understand it, and I refrain from any expression of opinion upon it."[15] In this way the insinuation is made that the proposition is nonsense. The diversion to the ironical statement is designed to stop thinking in much the same way that diversion to authority does. The de-

---

[14] Schopenhauer, *op. cit.*, p. 29.
[15] *Ibid.*, p. 35.

fense is to expose if possible the ignorance on the part of the person using the stratagem, suggesting that he probably is incompetent but in a different sense than he had intended to imply. Then discuss the main proposition.

3. *Stratagems of Manipulation.*—The distinguishing feature of these stratagems is their attempt to dispose of a proposition by remaining "on point" but by manipulating it in such a way as to distort the argument. They may take two forms: (1) manipulating the argument clearly but strategically; (2) manipulating it by confusing the subject—by "throwing a smoke screen around it." These two categories are not mutually exclusive, but are useful in pointing out the differences in method.

a. Express Manipulation.—In this type of stratagem a line of thought is handled clearly and strategically in such a way that it is distorted, is made to appear to be what it is not, or is used to serve a purpose which its nature does not warrant.

(1) Using all and some.—This means the conveying of an erroneous impression through the introduction of a universal statement implying "all" when such a qualification as "there is a tendency" is really meant or at least should be meant. The manipulation enters in the attempt to convey an impression of universality when the subject itself warrants only qualification with such phrases as "in some cases," "some," or "indications point to." The defense rests in questioning the universality of the manipulated statement and in determining whether a qualification more accurately describes the real situation.[16]

(2) Extending an argument.—This consists in carrying a proposition beyond its natural and intended limits, in making it appear as broad as possible, then in attacking it because of the weakness in the extended form. The extension may take the form of urging your opponent on to an unreasonable position or of deliberately misrepre-

---

[16] See Robert H. Thouless, *Straight and Crooked Thinking* (New York: Simon and Schuster, 1932), pp. 35-47. This stratagem may also be associated with errors in the materials of the syllogism.

senting his statement and stating it more broadly. The converse of this stratagem consists in giving your proposition the most restricted sense possible so as to reduce the number of objections that can be leveled against it.[17] The defense consists in an accurate statement of the point in question and of a denial that the question necessarily permits of the extension. The same defense may be made against an attempt at diminution of the question.

(3) Saying that the exception proves the rule.—This stratagem consists of meeting an objection to the validity of one's generalization by saying, "The exception proves the rule."[18] For example, your opponent says that all attempts at municipal operation of utilities have been unsuccessful. You reply by citing an instance of success. He replies that your instance is the exception which proves the rule. He is not attempting to divert to another proposition but to maintain his position by manipulating the relation between an instance and a generalization. The defense rests in pointing out that the exception does not prove the truth of a rule, but rather that it shows the falsity of an unqualified rule.

(4) Making an arbitrary distinction.—This stratagem is especially important in the light of the point of view expressed in Chapters X and XI with respect to the principle of continuous variation. The stratagem insists that we always find sharp distinctions between phenomena, and that words of directly opposite meaning must be used to describe these distinctions. The error lies in the fact that we cannot make arbitrary distinctions between phenomena which are related by a continuum. For instance, we cannot arbitrarily say that this paper must be white or black or that a person must be radical or conservative. Obviously, no such sharp distinctions really exist; and to draw the line at a middle point and call one side black and the other white is to do violence to sound thinking. This has been called the Intolerance of "a mind accus-

[17] See Schopenhauer, *op. cit.*, pp. 13-15.
[18] See Thouless, *op. cit.*, pp. 56-57.

tomed to hard and fast demarcation-lines and to abso-
lutistic, unmodifiable judgments."[19] To this stratagem
Thouless has given the name "drawing the line."[20]

The defense consists in disclosing the continuous variation—perhaps by a simple analogy—and of providing a
substitute word or words which will most accurately
describe the true relations. For instance, such words as
"gray" or "liberal" may be most exact.

This stratagem may also take the form of denying the
existence of differences because there is continuous variation between the different phenomena. It says that there
is no difference between "radical" and "conservative,"
for example, because there is a continuous variation between the two extremes. Bogoslovsky describes this as
the Indifference which has arisen as a reaction against
Intolerance. He refers to it as "mental bonelessness" and
"indefiniteness."[21] The defense lies in carefully indicating
the extent to which any term referred to or placed on a
continuum incorporates the meanings represented by the
two poles of the continuum. In other words, quantify all
statements as accurately and specifically as possible.

(5) Using special pleading.—This stratagem consists
in using in one situation an argument which would not be
accepted in another.[22] For example, a person interested in
big business argues that a protective tariff is necessary to
protect American industry from foreign competition
even though the cost of goods may be higher than if
there were free competition. He is unwilling, however,
to concede that there should be protection for agriculture
when the same line of argument is advanced. Or, a person may argue that a traffic law is needed to control
motorists and pedestrians, but he takes exception to this
line of reasoning when it is applied to himself. The point
is that the person using this stratagem refuses to accept a

[19] Boris B. Bogoslovsky, *The Technique of Controversy* (New
York: Harcourt, Brace and Company, 1928), pp. 254-255.

[20] Thouless, *op. cit.*, p. 169.

[21] Bogoslovsky, *op. cit.*

[22] Thouless, *op. cit.*, pp. 208-211.

line of reasoning in one situation which he insists upon applying in other comparable situations. The defense lies in taking the general principle involved, getting the user to admit it, and applying it in the cases where he fails to do so. In this way he will be forced either to reject the principle or to admit the truth of the principle in all cases.

(6) Using the mean between two extremes.—This stratagem consists in calling a point of view valid because it is the mean between two extremes. This device may be effective because of the desire of many people to accept something which is moderate, which is not an extreme.[23] The error lies in the fact that every view can be, after all, the mean between two extremes, that the truth cannot necessarily be associated with any *one* mean. The error may also rest in the fact that the truth may be in the so-called extreme position. For example, a person may argue that a gray suit is preferable to a black one because it is the mean between the extremes of black and white, and is therefore ideal. The truth may be that it is not necessarily a mean but may be an extreme between the two colors gray and black, and by that token bad. Or the truth may be that in this case a black suit is the best one to buy.

This description of the stratagem should not imply that every attempt at comparison between two things or the use of a mean for purposes of illustration is crooked thinking. The error lies in assuming that there is validity in a mean. The defense against the stratagem lies in pointing out the possibility that this mean could just as logically be an extreme and in either case that it may be undesirable. Either defense serves to destroy the implication of necessary validity in the mean.

(7) Refusing to admit something from which the point under discussion immediately follows.—This often consists in declaring that the opponent who wants you to admit the proposition from which the main point will

[23] *Ibid.*, pp. 64-67.

follow is begging the question. You do this by insisting that the proposition which you won't admit is so nearly like the main point that it is identical with it. You thus prevent the making of the argument because you refuse to admit the last link in the chain of reasoning leading inevitably to it.[24] The defense lies in disclosing the difference between the two statements and the perversity of the opponent in refusing to follow the chain to the logical conclusion.

(8) Admitting the premise but denying the conclusion.—This is represented by the words, "That's all very well in theory, but it won't work in practice." This stratagem is a violation of a rule of the syllogism which says that to admit the premises is to admit the conclusion. It is also based upon an impossibility, because a good theory must work in practice or else it isn't a good theory. The defense is to show the reasonableness of the rule of the syllogism and to show by example how a good theory must work or else it isn't a good theory.

(9) Refuting the bad proof of a good proposition and claiming complete refutation.—A person advances an argument against war by saying that the outlawing of war will mean that there will be no interruption of social events or curtailment of entertainment. He argues that the "inconvenience" to which many persons are put by such customary curtailment during wartime will be entirely removed by the outlawing of war. His opponent destroys the support for the argument by proving it to be insignificant, then proceeds to claim refutation of the main point. This is frequently used by some persons when their opponents use poor reasoning, facts, or opinions to support their propositions. The defense is to show that the proposition is not necessarily refuted, and that other reasons or proofs can be advanced in support of it.[25]

b. Manipulation by Confusing the Subject.— This type of manipulation involves the attempted han-

---

[24] See Schopenhauer, *op. cit.*, p. 26.
[25] *Ibid.*, pp. 39-40.

dling of a line of thought by confusing the arguments in question or upsetting the opponent to the point where the proposition may be admitted.

(i) Transposing question and answer.—This is a trick of dialectic or questioning which arrays questions in an order different from that normally required by their substance. Instead of asking questions in a logical order of cause and effect, for example, a person asks one on a cause, one on an effect, two on a cause, one on an effect, etc., so as to confuse an opponent, who doesn't see the relationships and doesn't see the questions in perspective. Or, again, a person may ask a series of questions at random instead of using such a logical sequence as definition, brief background, cause for present discussion, the problem and its causes and effects, solutions and their causes and effects, and means of verification. The effect of this random series of questions will be to confuse an opponent and to make it impossible for him to detect connections.

The defense consists in taking each question and saying: "What does it mean?" "What is its logical place in relation to the others?" It also consists in asking of the questioner: "Where are you going with this series of questions?" In other words, the best defense is a refusal to consider a series of questions until the relationship among them and their ultimate objective are determined.

This stratagem also consists in the use of the answers of an opponent for different or opposite conclusions from those which their substance warrants. For example, it occurs when an affirmative answer to the question "Should the United States carry on diplomatic relations with Great Britain?" is used to show that the respondent has thereby admitted the proposition that "The United States thus becomes obligated to support Great Britain in any war in which she may become involved." The defense lies in carefully relating the questions and answers in showing that each answer means just so much and no more.[26]

[26] *Ibid.*, p. 21.

(2) Asking compound questions and making compound statements.—This stratagem consists in begging the question to the extent of asking questions or making statements with several meanings and quickly advancing the argument resulting from the admissions or inferred from the compound statements. The defense lies in separating the compound elements and in dealing with them singly, refusing to be hurried by the unwarranted combinations.

(3) Asking the converse of an intended proposition to mislead the opponent.—Schopenhauer says of this: "If you observe that your opponent designedly returns a negative answer to the questions which, for the sake of your proposition, you want him to answer in the affirmative, you must ask the converse of the proposition as though it were that which you were anxious to see affirmed."[27] A variation of this is to ask both affirmative and negative questions so that the opponent will not detect the answer you hope he will give. The defense lies in taking the questions and answers on their merits, ignoring the order, and providing such answers as the facts and the reasoning warrant.

(4) Drawing a conclusion before the opponent does to confuse him.—This consists in assuming that all the premises have been admitted—even if they have not—and in drawing the conclusion, or it may consist in hastening to phrase the conclusion which results from admission of the premises. In this way the user of the stratagem can phrase the conclusion to his own advantage or confuse the opponent by putting between the premises and the conclusion which he was about to submit another conclusion upon which the opponent will have to ponder. As a result he may in confusion accept the one advanced by the strategist. The defense is to insist upon the establishment of all of the premises and the phrasing of the conclusion by the person who admits the propositions from which the conclusion logically follows.

[27] *Ibid.*, p. 21.

(5) Meeting a superficial argument with a superficial argument for effect.—This stratagem consists in declining to meet a weak argument by exposing its weakness, but rather in using an argument which is just as superficial as the one being met. The purpose is to dispose of the opponent and at the same time to make him appear ridiculous. For example, as suggested by Schopenhauer, it may be advantageous to meet an *ad hominem* argument by a similar argument, so as "to take the force out of it."[28] Confusion is the major aim of this device; and to secure it, the user is willing to sacrifice the weight of a valid counter-argument. The defense consists in exposing the superficial counter-argument and in showing wherein it does not refute the original proposition.

4. *Stratagems of Substitution.*—The distinguishing feature of these stratagems is their attempt to substitute extraneous materials or a contentious manner for the usual materials and attitudes of critical thought. They may take two forms: (1) using materials extraneous to the discussion; (2) using a manner injurious to reflective thinking.

a. Using Materials Extraneous to the Discussion.—This type of stratagem uses humor, ridicule, and irony to distort the thinking process. The defense for each of the three which we shall describe is to expose the substitution of the irrelevant materials and to show that they do not prove or disprove the subject being discussed.

(1) Using humor.—This consists in ignoring the question and injecting a humorous remark either relevant or irrelevant. It is designed to make the proposition more acceptable because of the association with humor, or because the humorous sidelight tends to minimize the amount of serious thought that will be devoted to an appraisal of the proposition.

(2) Using ridicule.—This stratagem consists in ignoring the merits of the question and in poking fun at, deriding, mocking, or making sport of either the question

[28] *Ibid.*, p. 26.

or the person proposing it. It attempts to make the subject or the person absurd by ludicrous remarks or allusions. It is designed to reduce the prestige of the object attacked and thus to hasten its rejection irrespective of its validity or weakness.

(3) Using irony.—This stratagem has the same ultimate purpose as that just described—to make the proposition or the conferee look ridiculous. The method, however, is different. In this case the strategist uses words to signify the opposite of what they would normally express in order to ridicule under cover of praise or compliment. It attempts to lower the prestige of the object attacked.

b. Using a Manner Injurious to Reflective Thinking.—This type of stratagem attempts to support or undermine a proposition, as the case may be, by disregarding either valid or invalid materials of discussion and substituting a manner of voice and action designed to force the desired point of view. The defense for each of the two stratagems which we shall describe briefly is to expose the substitution and to show that the manner of speaking does not necessarily relate to the proposition being considered.

(1) Using a strong manner.—This consists in using a bombastic manner in voice and action to attempt to hasten the acceptance or rejection of a proposition. It operates on the theory that frequently an intense manner shows conviction and confidence in one's position. In this respect it is harmful to reflective thinking in two ways: (1) it supersedes thinking with manner of speaking; (2) it uses a manner of speaking which is undesirable for reflective discussion even if admissible, under certain conditions, in persuasion.

(2) Arousing anger.—This stratagem consists in using such a manner as to make your opponent angry in order to confuse him and to make him incapable of sound judgment while under the influence of anger. This may be accomplished, as Schopenhauer says, "by doing him

repeated injustice, or practising some kind of chicanery, or being generally insolent."[29] It is clearly a device of substitution both in the means used by the strategist and in the response which is desired. The user substitutes *manner* for the suitable materials of discussion, and the victim is led to form irrational instead of critical judgments.

IV. AN OUTLINE OF STRATAGEMS

We are including here an outline of stratagems in order to make this material available in brief and topical form. It should be useful for purposes of review and for purposes of ready reference.

A. Stratagems in Language
    1. Inexactness in language
        a. Ambiguity
        b. Vagueness
        c. Accent
        d. Amphiboly
    2. "Coloring" in language
B. Stratagems Outside of Language
    1. Stratagems of censorship
        a. Errors in facts
        b. Half-facts
        c. Overstatement or understatement
    2. Stratagems of diversion
        a. Diversion to another argument
            (1) Making a simple diversion
            (2) Fastening on a trivial point
            (3) Giving the matter a general turn, then talking against that
            (4) Using an inconsequent argument
            (5) Using a contrary instance
            (6) Using an irrelevant objection
            (7) Appealing to interests or motives
            (8) Using a false syllogism to divert
            (9) Arguing *ad hominem*
         (10) Arguing *ad personam*

[29] *Ibid.*, p. 20.

  b. Diversion to material which stops argument on the point under consideration
    (1) Using technical language
    (2) Deferring to an authority
    (3) Deferring to tradition
    (4) Arguing *ad populum*
    (5) Arguing *ad ignorantiam*
    (6) Arguing *ad auditores*
    (7) Declaring yourself an incompetent judge
 3. Stratagems of manipulation
  a. Express manipulation
    (1) Using all and some
    (2) Extending an argument
    (3) Saying that the exception proves the rule
    (4) Making an arbitrary distinction
    (5) Using special pleading
    (6) Using the mean between two extremes
    (7) Refusing to admit something from which the point under discussion immediately follows
    (8) Admitting the premise but denying the conclusion
    (9) Refuting the bad proof of a good proposition and claiming complete refutation
  b. Manipulation by confusing the subject
    (1) Transposing question and answer
    (2) Asking compound questions and making compound statements
    (3) Asking the converse of an intended proposition to mislead the opponent
    (4) Drawing a conclusion before the opponent does to confuse him
    (5) Meeting a superficial argument with a superficial argument for effect
 4. Stratagems of substitution
  a. Using materials extraneous to the discussion
    (1) Using humor
    (2) Using ridicule
    (3) Using irony
  b. Using a manner injurious to reflective thinking
    (1) Using a strong manner
    (2) Arousing anger

1. Discuss in about 500 words how a study of "right think-ing" may be advanced by analyzing "how thinking goes wrong." Illustrate.
2. Using specific cases (real or imaginary), show how the "unintentional-personal" causes of obstacles may actually obstruct clear thinking and good discussion.
3. Using specific cases (real or imaginary), show how the "intentional-personal" causes of obstacles may actually obstruct clear thinking and good discussion.
4. Using specific cases (real or imaginary), show how the "social" causes of obstacles may actually obstruct clear thinking and good discussion.
5. Select two examples of each "stratagem in language." Show wherein each is a stratagem. Show how it could obstruct clear thinking and good discussion.
6. Select two examples of each "stratagem of censorship." Show wherein each is a stratagem. Show how it could obstruct clear thinking and good discussion.
7. Select two examples of each "stratagem of diversion." Show wherein each is a stratagem. Show how it could obstruct clear thinking and good discussion.
8. Select two examples of each "stratagem of manipula-tion." Show wherein each is a stratagem. Show how it could obstruct clear thinking and good discussion.
9. Select two examples of each "stratagem of substitution." Show wherein each is a stratagem. Show how it could obstruct clear thinking and good discussion.
10. Analyze the discussion in Appendix A to detect any stratagems. List them and suggest proper defenses against them.
11. Analyze the "Round Table" in Appendix B to detect any stratagems. List them and suggest proper defenses against them.
12. Analyze the forum in Appendix C to detect any strata-gems. List them and suggest proper defenses against them.
13. Analyze each of the discussions in *Discussion Methods for Adult Groups* by Fansler to detect any stratagems. List them and suggest proper defenses against them.

14. Analyze each of the seven discussions in the *Journal of Adult Education* and each of the two discussions in *Religious Education* as cited in the bibliography at the end of Chapter VIII. Detect any stratagems and suggest proper defenses against them.

15. Prepare an outline of the best defenses against each stratagem. This outline may be similar in form to the outline of the stratagems which we have provided at the end of this chapter.

16. Select a newspaper editorial, political speech, or magazine article which in your opinion contains one or more of the stratagems. Analyze the stratagems and suggest proper defenses against them.

17. Conduct a class discussion in which each member will be prepared to perpetrate one or two stratagems, and the other members will be prepared to detect the stratagems and defend themselves against the stratagems. (The point of this exercise is to give practice in detecting and dealing with stratagems.)

SELECTED BIBLIOGRAPHY

Bacon, Francis, *Novum Organum*. Translated by James Spedding and included in *The Philosophical Writings of Francis Bacon*. Boston: Houghton Mifflin and Company, 1857. ii, p. 77.

Bridgman, P. W., *The Intelligent Individual and Society*. New York: The Macmillan Company, 1938. Chapters V, VI, VII.

Burtt, Edwin A., *Principles and Problems of Right Thinking*. New York: Harper and Brothers, 1928. Chapter III.

Chase, Stuart, "The Tyranny of Words," *Harpers Magazine*. Vol. 175, November, 1937, pp. 561-569.

Clarke, Edwin L., *The Art of Straight Thinking*. New York: D. Appleton and Company, 1929. Chapters II, III, XIII.

Dimnet, Ernest, *The Art of Thinking*. New York: Simon and Schuster, 1932. Parts II, III, and IV.

Doob, Leonard, *Propaganda, Its Psychology and Technique*. New York: Henry Holt and Company, 1935. Chapters III-XI.

Elliott, Harrison S., *The Process of Group Thinking*. New York: Association Press, 1932. Chapters XI, XII, XIII.

Evans, D. Luther, and Gamertsfelder, Walter S., *Logic: Theoretical and Applied*. New York: Doubleday, Doran and Company, 1937. Chapters III, V, VI, VII, VIII, IX, XIV.

Institute for Propaganda Analysis, *Monthly Letter: Propaganda Analysis*. New York: 132 Morningside Drive.

Jastrow, Joseph, *The Betrayal of Intelligence*. New York: Greenberg, Publisher, Inc., 1938.

Jastrow, Joseph, *Effective Thinking*. New York: Simon and Schuster, 1931. Chapters 7-15.

Lippmann, Walter, *Public Opinion*. New York: Harcourt, Brace and Company, 1922. Parts II and III.

O'Neill, James M., Laycock, Craven, and Scales, Robert L., *Argumentation and Debate*. New York: The Macmillan Company, 1928. Chapter 8.

O'Neill, James M., and McBurney, James H., *The Working Principles of Argument*. New York: The Macmillan Company, 1932. Chapter XVI.

Schopenhauer, Arthur, "The Art of Controversy," an essay in *The Essays of Arthur Schopenhauer*, translated by T. Bailey Saunders. New York: Willey Book Company and The Macmillan Company, no date.

Sidgwick, Alfred, *Fallacies*. New York: D. Appleton and Company, 1884. Part II.

Thouless, Robert H., *Straight and Crooked Thinking*. New York: Simon and Schuster, 1932.

Westaway, F. W., *Scientific Method*. London: Blackie & Son, Ltd., 1924. Chapter II.

CHAPTER XIII

RESOLVING CONFLICT IN DISCUSSION

Lest the title of this chapter be misunderstood, we wish to say in this first sentence that *conflict plays a necessary and important role in discussion.* Conflict implies disagreement, and without disagreement there is usually little point in discussion; at least, profitable discussion is likely to be short-lived. Typically, any live discussion involves a whole series of conflicts, and it is through the resolution of these conflicts that discussion makes its important contribution. Most of the things said in this book are designed to show how *critical analysis, cooperation,* and *communication* can be brought to bear on group conflicts and differences. In fact, that is largely what discussion is.

The recognition that conflict has a place in discussion, however, should not blind us to the fact that there are kinds of conflict which impede the progress of discussion, and may even destroy it unless they are properly handled.

This chapter attempts to distinguish among the different kinds of conflict and to suggest ways of dealing with them.

I. WHAT IS MEANT BY RESOLVING CONFLICT

A conflict in discussion may be resolved on the basis of *understanding, agreement,* or *both.* Unless a group is confronted with the practical necessity of reaching an agreement (e.g., a policy-determining group), the members may often agree to disagree. If this agreement to disagree is based on an understanding of differences, what they are and why they exist, the conflict may be said to be resolved in at least one sense of the word. Such understandings should certainly be one of the principal goals of all discussion. People cannot be expected to agree on all things, nor is it desirable that they should. Intolerance and prejudice are probably rooted more in misunderstanding than they are in disagreement. One of the best ways of reducing intolerance and prejudice is the bringing of people face to face with each other for the purpose of reaching better understandings, if not agreement.

Understanding, of course, does not preclude the possibility of agreement. As a matter of fact, many supposed disagreements are dissipated by discussions which bring understanding to the aid of the conflict. Nor does agreement necessarily imply understanding. Enormous differences in motives and understandings, for example, may be represented in the superficial agreement which appears to exist among persons who cast their votes for the same candidate or the same platform in an election. As a matter of fact, it is not an uncommon experience in discussion for persons who think that they agree at the outset to discover through better understanding that this agreement was quite superficial, if not wholly illusory. The kinds of agreements sought by discussion are those which are based on understanding. Censorship, subterfuge, and intrigue, which are so often used to secure at least temporary agreement, have no legitimate place in discussion.

Where differences persist after understanding has been reached, *if group action is required*, mutual concessions may have to be made and the rule of the majority invoked. But such votes should be viewed as a court of last resort even in policy-determining groups.

II. FACTORS CONTRIBUTING TO CONFLICT

A. PERSONAL AND SOCIAL FACTORS.

In explaining obstacles to reflective thinking in Chapter XII it was pointed out that a great variety of personal and social factors, both intentional and unintentional, may contribute to crooked thinking in discussion. Many of the conflicts in discussion have their roots in these same causes—personal deficiencies in ability to think reflectively, excessive emotion, self-interest, self-esteem, prejudice, and others, as well as social pressures arising from affiliations with other groups.

It is especially important that we recognize these social factors as a cause of conflict, because they create a peculiar problem in method. Take as an example the legislative bodies and committees of a representative democracy. The man who sits in these groups is there as a representative of a constituency, and under ordinary circumstances he is under certain obligations to this constituency. Often he feels that he must represent what *he thinks* their interests, desires, and convictions to be, quite apart from his own position in the matter. In a very real sense, then, what may be the hundreds or thousands or even millions of persons whom this man represents are "absentee participants" in this discussion. Conflicts which are introduced in discussion, but not represented directly by the person or persons whose interests or convictions create them, may be exceedingly difficult to resolve. In the first place, these conflicts may be wholly fictitious and used as a stratagem by the representative to protect his own selfish interests; and even where the representative is wholly sincere and honest, he may not feel that he has complete liberty of expression and action.

B. THE ROLE OF EMOTION.

In terms of their cause, factors contributing to conflict may be further classified as rational and emotional. If we understand rational to mean a conflict which is intellectual in character, and emotional to imply prejudice and unthinking feeling, we may readily judge the rational conflict to be one capable of yielding more productive discussion. However, the nature of conflict does not permit the drawing of any such hard and fast line. Such a separation of rational and emotional elements does not exist in human nature. Certainly in the field of social and political problems the notion of a purely rational conflict is little more than a myth.

The question, then, is not whether emotion should play a role in discussion, but rather, what role should it play? So long as emotion means enthusiasm, zest, and eagerness, so long as it does not result in prejudice and duplicity, emotion can act as a generative force in discussion. Especially is this true when the emotions of the group find their outlet in a desire to solve the problem under discussion. It is when emotion means blind allegiance to a cause that it becomes bad—whenever it tends to supersede reason or to beg the question at issue in any way whatsoever.

In another sense emotions, feelings, and desires must be looked upon as the very "stuff" with which discussion must work. Preferences are necessarily involved in questions of value and policy, and the determination of standards of value is a function of analysis in reflective thought. From any point of view, then, the problem is not one of trying to eliminate emotion from discussion, but rather one of harnessing it to serve reflective ends. The following statement by Professor Bryson bears on this point:

There are some who dislike the word controversy and prefer to disguise the controversial character of discussion, largely because they are afraid that rivalry among disputants will make the search for truth impossible. The danger is real but unless discussion is competition among opinions it is not likely to be anything. What we want to avoid is competition among persons—quite a different thing. For the sake of vigor, searching analysis, and the true use of our minds in a cooperative effort for the best possible opinions, we need the sharp conflict of an admittedly controversial situation. For the sake of a truth discovered and its willing acceptance, we need a spirit of good will and sportsmanship.[1]

In other words, a controversial situation in which reasoning is conducted with spirit and enthusiasm (emotion) need not be uncooperative. The method of contributing explained in Chapter VII is designed to provide "a competition among ideas" which avoids a "competition among persons."

III. INTRINSIC CONFLICT

A. THE NATURE OF INTRINSIC CONFLICT.

We shall avoid the danger of implying inadvertently that emotion has no place in discussion by classifying conflict as *intrinsic* and *extrinsic* rather than rational and emotional. The word "intrinsic" means "pertaining to the nature of a thing, inherent, contained or being within." By an intrinsic conflict, then, we mean *one which is inherent in an adequate discussion of any given problem by any given group.* The word "adequate" is here used to imply critical thought, cooperation, and communication. The conflicts which inhere in such an undertaking are caused principally by (1) different facts or conflicting expert opinions accepted as facts, (2) misunderstanding concerning facts and expert opinions, (3) different interpretations of facts and expert opinions (different

[1] Lyman Bryson, "What is Good Discussion?" (unpublished lecture, *Northwestern University Symposium in Public Speaking,* July, 1938), p. 8.

reasoning), (4) misunderstanding concerning interpretations, (5) different values, and (6) misunderstanding concerning values. In other words, the causes of conflict inherent in adequate discussion are any differences and misunderstandings concerning facts and expert opinions, reasoning, and standards of value which are relevant to the problem under consideration. No successful discussion group can or would wish to overlook, side-step, slide over, or otherwise avoid meeting such differences and misunderstandings as squarely and completely as possible. It is to be expected also that both rational and emotional elements will enter into these conflicts in varying degrees.

B. Resolving Intrinsic Conflict.

The most apparent aspect of any conflict in discussion is disagreement. Such disagreement may be taken as a sign of misunderstanding or difference with respect to one or more of the items we have mentioned. Usually the specific cause of this disagreement will not be clear, nor will it be made clear without some probing into the matter. Often the leader will need to assist the group in this investigation of causes. In any event, it is unwise to permit disagreements to persist and to generate unnecessary "heat" without some directed attempt to discover their cause.

Unless the source of the disagreement is rather clearly indicated by the nature of the discussion up to the point of the disagreement, it is ordinarily best to inquire into the facts and expert opinions first; if the cause does not lie here, then proceed to the interpretations and reasoning of the persons involved, and thence, if necessary, to their standards of value. If the conflict is intrinsic (and it is always wise to assume that it is until an investigation demonstrates it to be otherwise), the cause of the difference or misunderstanding will be found in a consideration of these factors.

If the disagreement proves to have been caused by a misunderstanding with respect to one or more of these factors, we may assume that a recognition of that fact will resolve the conflict. If the disagreement is caused by different facts or different expert opinions which the conferees are accepting as facts, pooling the resources of the group bearing on the point may serve to resolve the conflict. Applying the tests of facts and expert opinion may help to appraise their adequacy and make way for some choice among them. It may even be necessary to call in an expert or appoint a special fact-finding committee. If all these resources fail, the best that can be done is to agree to disagree on this particular matter and proceed with the discussion. The same essential procedure may be followed with reasoning and values, applying the methods and procedures appropriate to these matters. Subject to the limitations which we pointed out, the syllogism may sometimes be used to resolve conflicts in reasoning.

In the case of intrinsic conflicts arising during the course of the discussion, where the further progress of the discussion demands at least some kind of working agreement, the group may invoke the "rule of the majority." This should be done only when all other methods fail and should not be understood to commit anyone to the decision reached except as a working basis for further discussion at this time and place. Thus, for example, the group may vote to use one definition of a term in preference to another for purposes of the discussion at hand. If differences in values cannot be reconciled, they may adopt a certain standard tentatively and proceed at least to discover what solutions measure up most satisfactorily in terms of these values. Sometimes it is better to recognize disagreements which defy resolution and hold in abeyance any decision in the matter until later in the discussion, hoping that later developments will clear up the difference.

All efforts to resolve intrinsic conflicts should be characterized by tolerance, willingness to listen to the other fellow, and patience with what may appear to be an untenable position. Keep in mind that your interpretation may appear just as bad to the other fellow as his appears to you. Unless these attitudes are taken both by the members of the group and by the leader, intrinsic conflicts may very easily develop into extrinsic conflicts.

IV. EXTRINSIC CONFLICT

A. THE NATURE OF EXTRINSIC CONFLICT.

The term "extrinsic" may be understood to mean "outside of the nature of an object or case; foreign." Thus we may define extrinsic conflict to be *those disagreements which are foreign and unessential to the adequate discussion of any given problem by any given group.* They may occur and frequently do occur in discussion, but they should be viewed as foreign elements, unproductive and disruptive, largely personal in character.

While we have defined intrinsic and extrinsic conflict quite categorically, it should not be assumed that these are mutually exclusive conceptions. Quite the contrary, they present an excellent example of the principle of continuous variation to which we have referred in earlier chapters. In extreme cases the differences are marked, but any given instance of conflict is likely to contain elements of both the intrinsic and the extrinsic in varying degrees.

B. RESOLVING EXTRINSIC CONFLICT.

As we have said, the safe rule (and incidentally the wise rule) is to assume that any conflict in discussion is intrinsic until it is proved that it is wholly or largely extrinsic in nature. This very assumption on the part of the leader and the group not only reduces the possibility of misjudging a member's motives, but also acts as the most effective kind of discipline if the conflict proves to be extraneous and intentional. Very often extrinsic conflicts are precipitated by persons who do not fully understand the nature and purpose of discussion and who have had little experience in cooperative undertakings. The quiet assumption on the part of the leader and the group that their fervor must be motivated by some insight into the problem which has not as yet been made clear, will reward the group for its patience if this insight is given, and strip the protagonist of any protective halo if it is not.

When we say that extrinsic conflict is largely personal in character, we mean to say that it most often takes the form of a clash between individuals which has little or nothing to do with the problem at hand, or finds its cause in motives or prejudices which are essentially foreign to the discussion. We must note in this connection, however, that one of the important steps in reflective thought involves matters which are personal in many respects. Values and standards of value cannot be wholly divorced from personal preference. If I happen to prefer red neckties to blue neckties, I imagine that within certain limits at least that is my business. Nor can I necessarily be judged uncooperative or pathological because I insist on that preference. Doubtless my preference will appear much less unreasonable to others who may be affected by it if I will attempt to explain it to them. And in the case of preferences which impinge upon the rights of others, I have that responsibility. Certainly there can be no reflective consideration of values unless those who hold them are willing at least to attempt to explain them. The deliberation of values relevant to the problem under consideration is an inherent part of discussion, and conflicts arising in this area should not be taken as foreign and extrinsic any more than any other legitimate difference or misunderstanding.

When conflict arises, then, unless it is obviously extrinsic in character, the group may proceed as we have suggested in the case of intrinsic conflict. If the review of facts, interpretations, and values reveals no difference or misunderstanding commensurate with the character and seriousness of the conflict, and if the conflict persists, we may assume that it is extrinsic and act accordingly. The question, of course, is: What should be done? And this question is by no means purely academic, because the group and the leader must often face this very practical problem.

When extrinsic conflict arises from persistent dullness and intellectual incompetence or from something approaching a pathological condition, the keynote of the leader's approach to the problem should be patience and sympathy *tactfully administered*. Nothing but bad feeling, which disrupts the entire discussion out of all proportion to the importance of the conflict, can result from any other method. The best thing that can be done for all concerned is to move on to something else as quickly and deftly as possible. Certainly such conflict should not be allowed to waste the time of the group. Properly handled, such a move can be made without cutting or "hurting" the individual involved.

Conflicts which are essentially intentional in character, deliberately created and persisted in by persons who know what they are doing, may sometimes be bridged by a little good humor on the part of the leader or by some measure of deference to the ego of the protagonist in the interests of the group. After all, the appearance of a victory on some *extraneous point* need not dislocate thought on matters which are germane to the discussion, and the more discerning members of the group at least will not be fooled by such deference. This advice, of course, can be carried too far. No one wishes to be bullied even on irrelevant points, and though one may be willing to sacrifice himself in the interests of the group occasionally, there may come a time when the intentional disturber will have to be told a few things. It is to be hoped for the good of the group that this time will come between discussions in a private talk. Very often the leader or some member of the group can accomplish infinitely more in such a conversation than could be gained by any direct attempt at discipline during the discussion. In all attempts to deal with such conflict methods should be used which make the offending member or members feel the pressure of group disapproval.

V. DISCUSSION COMPARED WITH OTHER METHODS OF RESOLVING CONFLICT

Thus far in this chapter we have explained the types of conflict which arise in discussion, suggested some of their causes, and pointed out methods of dealing with them. We wish now to raise the question: How does discussion compare with other methods of dealing with conflict? We shall be concerned here with conflicts which preclude the possibility of agreeing to disagree and demand some kind of settlement.

A. CONFLICT INHERENT IN HUMAN EXPERIENCE.

E. C. Lindeman in his book *Social Education* postulates sixteen propositions which in their totality constitute an hypothesis with respect to basic social theory. They include the following: ". . . difference is a given datum in human experience, as in all nature, and therefore, tension, friction, and conflict in human affairs are always to be expected," and ". . . in spite of our differences, there exists a compulsion which obliges us to seek some form of cooperative and collaborative living."[2] We do not propose to enlarge upon either of these hypotheses here. Suffice it to say that experience would seem to confirm the first and that any adequate conception of civilized society would appear to require the second. If such is the case, we face the problem of how best to deal with conflict in organized society. An analysis of discussion in relation to this problem is relevant to our study.

B. FORCE, COMPROMISE, LEADERSHIP, AND INTEGRATION.

History can be studied in terms of human conflicts, political, economic, social, religious, and the methods

[2] E. C. Lindeman, *Social Education* (New York: The New Republic, Inc., 1933), pp. 195-196.

that have been employed in dealing with these conflicts. The contemporary scene is no exception; the methods range from domination by physical force and violence to action based on cooperative group-thought.[3] When interests come into conflict the difference is usually settled (1) *by the domination of one party over the other through force or the threat of force,* (2) *through compromise,* (3) *through the mutual acceptance of the opinion of a third party,* or (4) *through an integration of the conflicting interests.* When the parties to the conflict (nations, states, groups of individuals, or individuals) prefer not to resort to force or are otherwise kept from doing so, the next resort is that of bargaining and compromise. Compromise is the quantitative scaling down of competing claims to a point where both parties feel that they should or must accept. Such a settlement is typical of arbitration and parliamentary debate. In both cases each party exerts all the pressure that it can command to secure a decision which preserves as much of its original claims as is possible, without resorting to tactics which are reprehensible under the conventions obtaining in the situation at hand.

At other times the parties to a conflict will be willing to refer the settlement of their differences to a leader or to an expert whom they respect and trust. This leader's authority, then, comes not from domination or force, but from the mutual consent and delegation of the people he is expected to serve. Still another method of settlement, making even greater demands on the willingness of the parties to resolve their differences without the use of force, is the attempt through a discussion of their differences to achieve an integration which conserves the essential values in the conflict. Such an integration may take the form of an invention or creation which brings to the solution of the problem a wholly new pro-

---

[3] See S. A. Courtis, *Cooperation* (Ann Arbor, Michigan: Brumfield and Brumfield, 1934), pp. 4-11; and Mary P. Follett, *Creative Experience* (Longmans, Green and Company, 1924), p. 156.

posal. Whereas a compromise works with existing claims, attempting to scale them down to acceptance, an integration attempts to discover a solution which is qualitatively different from the proposals precipitating the conflict. For example, a chauffeur contended that he needed an increase in salary to take care of his family adequately. His employer replied that it was impossible to pay him more. An integration was reached when a mutually satisfactory plan was worked out whereby he could assist with the car at the house next door, thus increasing his salary as requested, and at the same time maintaining adequate service for his employer. The resort to force would have terminated the man's employment, and a compromise would have resulted in a wage somewhere between that paid and that demanded.

An integration which conserves the essential values and purposes of the group should be the aim of discussion. That this integration is not always possible in the resolving of social conflicts there seems to be little question. Nevertheless, except where expediency and practical necessity dictate the use of other methods, there seems to us to be no other reasonable preference.

EXERCISES

1. Write a 500-word paper explaining the concept of integration as it relates to discussion. Include examples of integration in your paper. See especially Mary P. Follett, *Creative Experience.*

2. Write a 500-word paper in which you analyze the role of discussion in any one of the following situations: racial conflict, employer-employee conflict, family conflict, political conflict.

3. Conduct a class discussion in which special attention is given to the methods of dealing with difference and conflict. Note the number of conflicts arising in the discussion and how each was resolved. What were the causes of the conflicts?

4. Study the discussion in Appendix A from the stand-

point of conflict and the methods used in dealing with these conflicts.

5. Conduct a class discussion on the question: When, if ever, is the resort to force justified in settling human differences?

SELECTED BIBLIOGRAPHY

Courtis, S. A., *Cooperation*. Ann Arbor, Michigan: Brumfield and Brumfield, 1934. Chapters X and XI.

Elliott, Harrison S., *The Process of Group Thinking*. New York: Association Press, 1932. Chapters XI and XII.

Follett, Mary P., *Creative Experience*. New York: Longmans, Green and Company, 1924.

Follett, Mary P., *The New State*. New York: Longmans, Green and Company, 1926.

Lindeman, Eduard C., *Social Education*. New York: New Republic, Inc., 1933. Chapters V, VI, and VIII.

Wallas, Graham, *The Art of Thought*. New York: Harcourt, Brace and Company, 1926. Chapter V.

Walser, Frank, *The Art of Conference*. New York: Harper and Brothers, 1933. Chapter V.

CHAPTER XIV

DISCUSSION IN LEARNING GROUPS

The most natural and perhaps the most useful application of the principles and methods of discussion is in learning groups. While most of what is said in this volume applies to the learning situation, it will be the purpose of this chapter to make such special observations as appear to be useful to these groups.

I. THE RELATIONS OF DISCUSSION TO LEARNING

Discussion may be used in the learning process with one or more of four different ends in view: (1) the development of knowledge about and skill in discussion *per se*; (2) the development of special skills, attitudes, and personality traits; (3) the imparting of knowledge; and (4) the discovery of knowledge. In this chapter we shall not be directly concerned with the first of these purposes; special attention is given to discussion as an aspect of speech education in Chapter XVIII. It should be noted, however, that the development of skill in discussion *per se* may very well be and often is a secondary objective in learning situations in which one or more of the other ends are the primary goals.

Nothing but confusion can result from any attempt to appraise or implement discussion in the learning situation unless these ends are understood and considered. By the development of "special skills, attitudes, and personality traits" through discussion, we have reference to such things as skill in reflective thinking, attitudes and skills useful in cooperative undertakings, social attitudes, and such personality traits as self-confidence and sociability. This objective has to do with the growth and development of the individual and as such, should be distinguished from the aim of "imparting knowledge." In this latter capacity discussion has often been compared with the lecture method as a tool for introducing the student to a definite body of knowledge. The main purpose here is to "get across" to the student as much information in as thorough a manner and in as short a time as is possible. The fourth aim, that of the "discovery of knowledge," differs from the others in the fact that the group is attempting a creative task, to make new and more adequate interpretations and discover new conceptions.

In any given situation the role of discussion must quite obviously be determined by the objectives of the group and the merits of discussion as a means of achieving these objectives. Discussion may do certain things better than the lecture method and be less effective in others. Little is gained in attempting to compare the relative effectiveness of discussion and other methods except in terms of specific objectives for specific situations. We do not mean to say that these objectives are wholly separable entities. They are not. No discussion approach can develop skills apart from the discussion of some body of knowledge, and discovery is hardly possible without contributing, through the process, to all these ends. But from the standpoint of knowing what is the main purpose of any learning group and the relation of discussion to the group, these distinctions are indispensable.

II. VALUES AND LIMITATIONS IN THE LEARNING PROCESS

There are not available adequate data upon which to appraise the worth of discussion with respect to some aspects of the learning process. Many of the experiments reported in this field seem to be colored by rather decided preferences either for or against the method, and in many cases the investigator has failed to specify the objective of the learning process in the specific situation in which the experiment was done. Further difficulty in appraising the usefulness of discussion arises from the differences in ability to handle the method. The fact that some writers report gratifying results while others find the method deficient in situations which appear to be substantially identical may be explained by this difference in ability. There are a number of points upon which there is rather general agreement, however, and we offer these together with our own opinions for what they may be worth.[1]

A. SKILL IN REFLECTIVE THINKING.

Many educators believe that teaching students *how* to think is more important than teaching them *what* to think. The discussion approach in the learning situation probably has its greatest claim to superiority over other

[1] For a useful summary of experimental work in group discussion see J. F. Dashiell, "Experimental Studies of the Influence of Social Situations on the Behavior of Individual Human Adults," *A Handbook of Social Psychology*, edited by Carl Murchison (Worcester, Massachusetts: Clark University Press, 1935), pp. 1097-1158; see especially pp. 1125-1140.

methods (e.g., the lecture method) on this score. As we have seen, discussion consists in the reflective deliberation of problems. Experiences in discussion, properly conducted, are experiences in reflective thinking which can be observed, criticized, and appraised in such a way as to stimulate growth and development. Individual problem-solving exercises and group-thought undoubtedly have many similar and reciprocal values, because the pattern of thinking is essentially the same in both cases. The reasonable position would seem to be that opportunities for experiences in both of these activities should be provided in the educative process. But since much of the reflective thought of the world must take place in group situations, whether we like it or not, there seems to be little basis upon which we can deny the value of discussion for those who hold skill in reflective thought as one of their primary objectives.

B. Ability to Cooperate with Others.

Here again the discussion approach to learning has definite advantages over other methods. Individuals are given the experience of working with others in a group undertaking. We have spoken of, or implied, the value of such experiences many times in this volume.

C. Development of Personality Traits.

The traits of extroversion and introversion have been observed in many investigations of personality. The extrovert is understood as the person who "directs his interests outward," and appears to give "more attention to things and persons in his environment"; the introvert tends "to turn within," and is more introspective. Professor Murray has distinguished two types of each of these traits on the basis of egocentricity and objectivity.[2] Thus, he speaks of the egocentric extrovert as the selfish, self-centered individual inclined to garrulity and osten-

[2] Elwood Murray, *The Speech Personality* (Philadelphia: J. B. Lippincott Company, 1937), Chapter 6.

tation. The objective extrovert is often a man of considerable social and persuasive power, self-confident and yet critical. The egocentric introvert is the self-centered individual who finds it difficult to get along with other people and is excessively retiring, disposed to rationalize his own deficiencies, and be jealous of people with more social power. The objective introvert is the thoughtful, conscientious person who is socially adjusted and yet not dominant or self-centered. Professor Murray finds the two most effective "speech personalities" to be the objective extrovert and the objective introvert. Our own experience has been that the former makes the best advocate, persuader, or debater, while the person most competent in discussion, other things being equal, is the objective introvert. In fact, experimental study in this matter in which the Noll tests in scientific thinking and the Bernreuter Personality Inventory were employed, appears to justify the conclusion that experiences in discussion tend to produce the traits which we have ascribed to the objective introvert.[3] The desirable traits which discussion appears to develop are "intellectual honesty, open-mindedness, suspended judgment, and criticism, including self-criticism."[4] The total effect seems to be gains in objectivity and a general leveling-out effect with respect to egocentricity. We may expect the dominant, self-confident individual to become more critical of himself and more cooperative; conversely, we may expect the egocentric introvert to become a more socially minded individual.

D. Attitudes Toward Social Problems.

An experimental study now in progress in which some of the Thurstone attitude scales were given to students before and after the discussion of social problems to

---

[3] Alma Johnson, "An Experimental Study of Group Discussion as a Method of Teaching Certain Fundamentals of Speech" (unpublished study, Northwestern University), p. 45.

[4] *Ibid.*

which these scales apply, shows a tendency for attitudes to "cluster" as a result of discussion; that is, there are fewer extreme and divergent attitudes toward the problem discussed. There is a tendency toward consensus on what might be called "middle ground." In discussions of capital punishment, for example, people who came to the discussion with strong "favoring-attitudes" tended to move toward less extreme positions, and those who had no use for the death penalty before the discussion were less certain of their position after the discussion.[5] Our observations also show a secondary tendency for attitudes to gravitate toward the position held by the more capable, critical individuals as a result of discussion. There is little tendency, however, for the group to be influenced by the overly dominant egocentric individual; as a matter of fact, the opinions of such members are likely to be discounted more than they deserve to be.

E. Immediate and Delayed Recall.

The typical subject-matter examination is usually a test of the student's knowledge of a subject in terms of his ability to recall what he has read or heard and to reproduce it on the examination paper. The studies of discussion as a means of getting information "across" in such a way that students can recall it when asked to do so show a great variety of conclusions.[6] Some investigators report the lecture method to be superior and others find the discussion method more effective. As we have said, these discrepancies are doubtless explained by the predilections and experiences of the teacher, and by the kinds of groups and subjects under consideration. These factors will in all probability determine the usefulness of discussion as a means of "imparting knowledge." We would expect the discussion approach to be more effec-

[5] Karl Robinson, unpublished studies in discussion, Northwestern University.

[6] Dashiell, *op. cit.*, pp. 1132-1133.

tive in classes in social studies and English than in physics and chemistry, and to be more effective with students and teachers who have had some experience with the method than with those who have not.

There is some evidence to show that the lecture method is superior for purposes of immediate recall and that discussion has advantages in cases of delayed recall.[7] In other words, while discussion may not "get across" as much knowledge, what it does impart appears to stay with the learner.

F. Functional Knowledge.

Knowledge is functional which can be applied and used. It is one thing to be able merely to recall information and it is another thing to know it in the sense that you can use it, apply it, and work with it. Except for certain recondite information, most of us would in all probability prefer that things be mastered in a functional sense. It seems reasonable to believe that discussion has certain values in this direction. As a matter of fact, this may be the explanation of the superiority of discussion in the matter of delayed recall. We rely less on sheer verbal memory in those things which we have worked out in discussion with others; we know them because we have experienced them in a fuller and more complete manner. This line of reasoning, of course, suggests the value of carrying our discussions over into activities designed to give additional support to the experience. We have no doubt that such activities have educative values in many situations.

G. Motivation In Learning.

Some approaches in the educative process enlist the interest and desire of students to learn more effectively than do others. When properly handled, discussion can be of value in stimulating study and reading, not only in preparation for the discussion, but after the discussion

[7] *Ibid.*, p. 1132.

as well. The fact that one knows that he is expected to participate in discussion and that what he has to say will be subject to appraisal by the group may not be the highest type of motivation, but it does stimulate preparation. What is more encouraging, however, is the tendency for students to continue reading on issues raised in the discussion after the discussion is over. Leaders in the Federal Forum Project, for example, report: "1. Increased reading of books, magazines, and pamphlets dealing with public affairs. 2. Increased enrollment or attendance at other adult education classes or groups. 3. Application of the discussion method in other organizational programs. 4. Formation of study groups and the inclusion of public affairs topics in other organizational programs."[8]

H. INDIVIDUAL DIFFERENCES.

We have already referred to the effect which intergroup differences in knowledge about and experience in discussion would likely have on the success of the discussion approach in any given situation. Here we have reference especially to intra-group differences in the intellectual capacities of the members. There is some evidence to show that the poorer members of a group gain more from discussion than do their more capable associates.[9] In any situation in which the problem for discussion presents rather definite limitations on the amount of information which can be got, one would naturally expect that the poorer members would show more improvement. They have the benefit of the thinking of the better members and the better members are restricted by the limitations of the problem. Given a problem with greater potentialities for development and

[8] J. W. Studebaker and Chester S. Williams, *Choosing Our Way*, United States Department of Interior, Office of Education, Bulletin 1937, Misc. No. 1, p. 96.

[9] Dashiell, *op. cit.*, p. 1128.

the resultant discussion on a correspondingly higher plane, we should expect that here the more capable conferees would show greater gains than the poorer members.

Whether or not discussion does relatively more for poor groups than for brilliant groups, speaking now of inter-group differences in intellectual ability, is a difficult question on which to venture an hypothesis. Of course, the nature of the problem would be a determining factor, but assuming that the problems were graded in difficulty in terms of the capacity of the group, we see no reason to believe that discussion would be any more helpful or any less helpful in one situation than in the other.

If we compare the relative effectiveness of the discussion method and the lecture method in relation to inter-group abilities, the following hypotheses may be ventured: (1) that the lecture is rarely as effective as discussion for poorer groups; (2) that brilliant groups can make progress under the lecture system much more readily than poor groups; and (3) that the lecture system is often the superior method for brilliant students, especially in advanced study.

I. LEVELS OF LEARNING.

It is probably safe to say that discussion has a wider application in the lower reaches of the educative process than it has in the upper. We do not refer here to the age level of the learners, but rather to the degree of advancement which their study has reached. In other words, we suggest that discussion as a regular classroom method may have a wider application on the high school level than on the college undergraduate level, and in turn, more opportunities for helpful use in undergraduate classes than in graduate study. These differences are purely relative, however, and many of the most advanced groups can and do use the discussion method profitably, e.g., the graduate seminar.

III. SPECIAL METHODS FOR LEARNING GROUPS

We may say here again that with few exceptions the principles and methods developed throughout this volume apply to learning groups in so far as such groups employ the discussion method. Our only purpose here is to note certain applications and a few special methods.

A. THE PROBLEM-SOLVING METHOD.

This method is the normal and natural procedure in all reflective thought and in all discussion. In Chapter X we discussed the five steps in reflective thinking as the typical over-all pattern in discussion. A class, let us say in social problems, employing the discussion method might well be supplied with a syllabus, this syllabus designed to raise a series of problems and to provide bibliography on each of these problems. The class would then do the readings, prepare discussion outlines if it seemed advisable (see Chapter VI), and carry on discussions under the leadership of the instructor or members of the class. Many classes in literature, sociology, economics, political science, and education can and do use this method profitably. As a matter of fact, it is difficult to conceive of many courses in which this method could not be used at least on occasion for some of the materials of the study.

B. THE DEVELOPMENTAL METHOD.

This method is one in which the group has as its goal the mastery of a specific body of knowledge or point of view which has been worked out by someone else.[10] For example, the group may be studying a specific book and the purpose of the discussion be that of uncovering or bringing to light and interpreting what has been said in the book. Here the problem before the group is what the author of the book has said. Likewise, in classes where

---

[10] The label "developmental" we take from Thomas Fansler, *Discussion Methods for Adult Groups* (New York: American Association for Adult Education, 1934), pp. 63-65.

the purpose is the understanding of a definite body of knowledge, such, for example, as American history, the approach may be developmental in character.

This method is usually employed with an expert in the field of study as the leader (not infrequently the instructor in charge of the class) who directs the discussion in terms of a prearranged outline. Such a discussion may follow the instructor's lectures on a unit of work in the course, or a textbook may be used as a guide and source of information. The method can very easily become little more than a recitation in which the instructor asks questions and the students *try* to give the "right answers."

C. The Case Method.

The case method is really a variation of the problem-solving method in which a hypothetical or actual case is taken as the basis of the discussion. The facts of the case are given to the group, and their problem consists in working out a solution. The usual steps in reflective thinking may well constitute the general pattern of the discussion. This method is widely used in the study of law.

A somewhat different application of the case method is made when groups proceed as though they were a committee of the State Senate or the Board of Directors of some business concern. Such imaginary situations may have some values for certain groups, but we recommend that they be used sparingly, if at all.

D. Methods for Co-acting Groups.

We have explained the co-acting group as one in which the members of the group are responding to some central source of stimulation as in a lecture, for example. While the face-to-face arrangement is greatly to be preferred in learning groups, the size of the class may prohibit its use. In such case the panel discussion, dialogue, symposium, or forum-lecture method explained in Chapter

XVI, or some variation of these methods, may be employed.

IV. PLANNING AND CONDUCTING A CONFERENCE

By a conference we here mean a large learning group of from fifty to a hundred or more members assembled, usually for two or three days, to discuss one or more problems relating to some central question or theme.[11] Most such conferences have been, and still are, conducted on the basis of a series of lectures. We shall be primarily interested here in methods of discussion which may be employed in the conference for the purpose of organizing it on a "group thinking" basis.

We may take as an example the annual St. Charles Conference sponsored by the Y.M.C.A. and Y.W.C.A. organizations at Northwestern University. About one hundred to one hundred fifty University students, faculty members, and other invited lecturers and discussion leaders assemble at the Baker Hotel in St. Charles, Illinois, about thirty miles from the Evanston Campus. The conference convenes on a Friday afternoon at five o'clock and adjourns the following Sunday noon. The following is the program of the Eighth Annual Conference.

Program

Friday, February 26th

5:00 P.M.—Registration
6:00 P.M.—Dinner—Baker Hotel
7:30 P.M.—Evening Program
       1. The Honorable Philip F. La Follette, Governor of Wisconsin—"After the Sheepskin—What?"
       2. Forum Discussion
       3. Acquaintance Period

[11] For an excellent account of methods and procedures for conferences and conventions see Harrison S. Elliott, *The Process of Group Thinking* (New York: Association Press, 1932), pp. 198-221.

Saturday, February 27th

8:00 A.M.—Breakfast—Baker Hotel

9:00 A.M.—Address

Professor W. C. Allee, Professor of Zoology, University of Chicago—"Meeting the Issues"

10:00 A.M.—Round Tables

12:30 P.M.—Lunch—Baker Hotel

2:00 P.M.—Address

Dr. Elmer L. Williams, Chicago Minister and Editor of *Lightnin'*—"What's Behind the Headlines"

3:00 P.M.—Recreation

5:30 P.M.—Dinner—Baker Hotel

7:00 P.M.—Evening Program

1. Mr. William A. McKenney, Chairman, Emergency Peace Campaign, Chicago, and Mr. Philip C. Lovejoy, Secretary, Rotary International—"Theories Into Practice"
2. Panel Discussion—Messrs. McKenney, Lovejoy, Merriam, Williams, and Schilpp
3. Entertainment—Dancing—Informal

Sunday, February 28th

8:00 A.M.—Breakfast—Baker Hotel

9:00 A.M.—Round Tables

11:00 A.M.—Plenary Session for Round Table Reports and Discussion

12:15 P.M.—Summary Address—Dr. Tracey E. Strevy, Assistant Professor of History, Northwestern University

1:00 P.M.—Dinner—Baker Hotel

The general theme of this conference was "Life Begins at Commencement," or stated as a problem: What can the University do to help its students become effective citizens in a democracy? All the addresses were planned as forum-lectures and designed to present aspects of this problem. The Saturday evening lectures were followed by a panel composed of some of the earlier conference speakers and members of the University faculty.

All of the forum discussions were presided over by student chairmen.

The most vital part of these conferences is the student round tables or commissions. These consist of groups of ten or fifteen students who meet as face-to-face groups for the purpose of discussing problems relating to the general theme of the conference. The round tables in the Eighth Annual Conference were organized into seven groups dealing with College, Religion, Social Relationships, Human Relationships, Political Trends, Economic Trends, and Leisure Time. Students are assigned to these groups on the basis of their own preferences, and each group is in charge of a student chairman with one or more members of the faculty or other persons present as "resource" experts. Each group phrases a problem appropriate to its special area of discussion and the general theme of the conference. A secretary is named to keep a record of the discussion and efforts are made to reach conclusions of practical significance to the conference and the University. The following advice for the round tables is printed on the program:

The real work at the conference is done in the commissions. Through these, each representative at the conference will have a part in group thinking. While the addresses of speakers are designed to give resources and stimulate thought, the round tables provide opportunity for students to crystallize their own points of view. The effectiveness of the conference will depend on the quality of student thinking done in these round table groups.

Each commission is expected to present to the plenary session a set of conclusions as to the problems discussed and possible remedies, and also a set of recommendations as to specific action suggested.

One of the distinguishing features of conferences of this sort is the alternation of general conference assemblies with small group meetings. This permits an interplay of ideas between the conference as a whole and the commissions, and serves to knit together the entire con-

ference. The members of the commissions have the benefit of the forum-lectures and, in the forum periods which
follow, their contributions will in turn bring into the
deliberations of the larger group much of the thought
of the commissions. The final general assembly, or
"plenary session," consists of reports from each of the
commissions, discussion of these reports, and a final summing up by a speaker who has been present for the
duration of the conference, sitting in as many of the
round tables as possible for short periods of time, and
attending the general meetings. The function of this
speaker is to get "the feel" and general drift of the conference, to note conflicts and agreements, to assemble
recommendations, and to report them to the group in a
brief final summary.

Every St. Charles Conference has as its motto, "The
Conference does not end at St. Charles." Attempts are
made to carry the results of the conference back to the
campus. Recommendations of the conference concerning
social and educational matters have many times had a
rather direct influence on University policy. The conference commissions often continue as discussion groups
on the campus.

The St. Charles Conference has been taken as an example because of its splendid organization and genuine
vitality.[12] It is attended by many of the finest students
and campus leaders in the University. The preparations
for the conference are started months in advance and
so far as possible are made by the cooperative efforts
of the students meeting as committees. While the general pattern of the conference has remained essentially
the same, many variations are made from year to year
in an attempt to improve the methods. This general pattern is typical of conferences organized on a "group

[12] Mr. Claude C. Shotts, Executive Secretary of the Y.M.C.A.,
Northwestern University, is largely responsible for the organization
of this conference.

thinking" basis and may easily be adapted to suit the needs of almost any large group gathering of this sort.

EXERCISES

1. Adopt a book or article for class discussion. Discuss the book or article, employing the developmental method described in this chapter. Work from an outline of the material.

2. Prepare a set of facts involving some moral issue in which you can raise the question: Was this individual's conduct reprehensible under these circumstances? Adopt this as a case for class discussion.

3. Prepare a brief course of study or discussion syllabus for a high school class in civics, social studies, or literature in which the discussion method is to be used.

4. Organize and conduct a student conference such as that described in this chapter. Divide the class into small groups for round-table discussions, each group dealing with an aspect of the larger problem adopted for consideration. Alternate these round tables with meetings of the entire group.

5. The following series of discussion programs was broadcast over station WBBM, Chicago, by Northwestern students. Conduct one or more discussions of this type. Use radio equipment if available.

   a. Round-table discussion: A face-to-face group discussing the European crisis relative to the demands of Germany in the Sudeten area. The question: What is the desirable solution to the Sudeten problem?

   b. Symposium-forum: The symposium consisted of three short talks on the Illinois parole system. The question: What should be done about the Illinois parole problem? These talks were given immediately before the program went on the air. The announcer explained that the talks had been given and cut the program in at the point where the leader of the forum was summing up the talks. The ensuing forum period was then broadcast.

   c. Jury-trial discussion: The question: Should universities pay their athletes? The program opened with the cross-examination of two witnesses by two members of the group. The object was to get the necessary facts and information before the group. The jury deliberations followed under the direction of the jury chairman.

d. Case-study discussion: The group studied the problem: Should the several states adopt uniform marriage and divorce laws? The program began by the presentation of a specific case, a set of facts, an incident. This case had been prepared in advance by the leader but not revealed to the group. The case served as the basis for the discussion which followed.

e. Project-discussion: The group studied the problem: Should the National Youth Administration be continued? In preparation for this discussion a systematic survey of NYA activities in the University was made, reported in the discussion, and used as the basis for the discussion.

f. Headlines discussion: Another discussion of some interest was one in which the group raised the question: What's going on at Northwestern? Employing a developmental approach, the headlines of the *Daily Northwestern* were used as a basis for the discussion of a number of related campus problems.

SELECTED BIBLIOGRAPHY

Bryson, Lyman, *Adult Education*. New York: The American Book Company, 1936.

Dashiell, J. F., "Experimental Studies of the Influence of Social Situations on the Behavior of Individual Human Adults," in *A Handbook of Social Psychology*, edited by Carl Murchison. Worcester, Massachusetts: Clark University Press, 1935. Pp. 1125-1140.

Elliott, Harrison S., *The Process of Group Thinking*. New York: Association Press, 1932. Appendix II.

Lindeman, Eduard, *Social Education*. New York: New Republic, Inc., 1933. Chapter XIII.

Hunt, E. E., *Conferences, Committees, Conventions, and How to Run Them*. New York: Harper and Brothers, 1925.

Hyde, S. B., "Using Group Discussion in Conferences of Youth," *Religious Education*. Vol. 30, 1935, pp. 130-132.

Shipley, G. T., *Evaluation of Guided Study and Small-Group Discussion in a Normal School*. New York: Bureau of Publications, Teachers College, Columbia University, 1932.

CHAPTER XV

DISCUSSION IN POLICY-DETERMINING GROUPS

A policy-determining group is one seeking to arrive at a decision which can be translated into group action. The very nature of its function distinguishes it from the learning group in the fact that it must reach a conclusion which can be set down as the decision of the group. Failing in this, the group fails in the very purpose which brought it into being and which justifies its existence. What we have to say in this chapter, then, has to do with this matter of reaching decisions through discussion.

I. NEGOTIABLE DECISIONS

The term "decision" requires some interpretation. A learning group, for example, may conclude a discussion very much in disagreement and yet be said to have reached a decision in one sense of the word. The conferees may have decided to disagree. Every discussion can profitably be brought to some kind of conclusion in the sense of summing up what has been done. But the policy-determining group has to do more than this. The group must reach a decision which can be recorded as the will of the body and be so communicated to other interested persons and groups. This is what we mean by a *negotiable decision*. It is something definite and tangible which can be passed from one person to another. Such decisions take the form of resolutions, specific recommendations, plans of action, bills and laws. Except in very informal groups where the decision does not affect others and the memory of the members can be relied upon, the decisions of policy-determining groups are carefully worded and recorded.

II. DISCUSSION, DEBATE, AND PARLIAMENTARY PROCEDURE

The typical policy-determining method is parliamentary debate. Most of us have had some experience with this process; motions are made, seconded, debated, amended if necessary, and voted upon. It requires a sizable volume to set forth all of the intricacies of parliamentary procedure, and many such volumes have been written. While many legislative assemblies have worked out their own procedural rules, *Robert's Rules of Order* are usually accepted as standard by most groups. It should be understood, however, that the deliberation which takes place under the rule of such procedure *is debate and not discussion!* Nothing but confusion can result from any other defining and labeling. Debate is a competition between opposing or logically inconsistent *outcomes of thought* (or propositions accepted as the outcomes of thought) to which the debaters are committed either by desire or by the nature of the circumstances. The reasoning process in such a competition is intentional and designed specifically to secure acceptance and victory. No proposal can even get before the group under accepted parliamentary rules until a motion is properly made and seconded. Such a motion is a proposition or proposal which the maker desires to see adopted by the group. The defense which he and others present and the attacks which others make *are* debate.

When the term "debate" is used many people seem to think of school debating and nothing else. Important and valuable as school debating may be, it is, as a matter of fact, a *relatively* unimportant kind of debating measured by any criteria other than pedagogical standards. Legislative, political, and judicial debates occupy the time and attention of some of our greatest minds and affect the lives and well-being of millions of people. School debates are a training ground for this larger and infinitely more significant arena. This observation is not intended to depreciate the usefulness of school debating, but rather to suggest what seems to us to be a proper perspective.

Whether or not school debating develops effective debaters need not concern us here. Properly conducted it does, we think. Nor shall we concern ourselves here with the question as to whether or not it is in the best interests of a democratic society to train effective debaters. We believe that any realistic conception of democracy must admit a place for the trained advocate. The important point for us to see is that the function of school debating *is* that of training advocates! We do not believe that it has or needs any other defense! Except as school debating teaches debate, we do not believe that it can be defended as a teaching device. While learning, other than learning how to debate, may be an incidental result of debating, it seems to us that these values can with few exceptions be secured better by other methods. This applies both to the debaters and to the audience.

We may say, then, that debating is primarily a policy-determining method and that school debate is designed to develop facility in debating. Discussion, on the other hand, is primarily a learning technique. It can play a significant role in policy-determining groups, however, and it is that role which we wish to explain in this chapter.

III. FACTORS DETERMINING METHOD

A. GROUP SIZE.

Discussion can play little or no part in large policy-determining bodies. Here, as we have said, parliamentary debate is the accepted and necessary method. It is in the small group that discussion finds its place. Often such groups can and do dispense with the complicated and cumbersome machinery of large legislative assemblies in the interests of freer and less competitive deliberation.

B. GROUP PURPOSE.

Many policy-determining groups serve what is essentially an investigative function. Usually these are small groups such as committees whose chief task is to make recommendations to some larger body which will be the final policy-determining agency. In Chapter III we pointed out that this investigative function was closely related to learning. The fact remains, however, that unlike the usual learning group, such investigative commissions must report out a decision. In groups of this sort, however we may classify them, discussion will usually be found to be a more satisfactory method than debate.

C. GROUP MEMBERSHIP.

A third factor affecting the use of discussion in policy-determining groups is the personnel of the group. No matter how small a group is or what its purpose may be, if a decision has to be reached, and the members are uncooperative, pugnacious, and garrulous, the discussion approach is not likely to prove satisfactory. Here the deliberations must be harnessed by a method designed to control pugnacity and garrulity, or at least to keep them sufficiently in bounds to get a decision. Parliamentary debate takes charge of such emergencies with considerable effectiveness and dispatch.

The nature of the members' interests in the problem under consideration also has an important bearing on the application of the discussion approach. If personal interests are in strong conflict and a decision has to be reached, it will usually be necessary to resort to parliamentary procedure and debate.

IV. VALUES OF DISCUSSION IN POLICY-DETERMINING GROUPS

Thus far we have suggested that discussion can profitably be used in small policy-determining groups, especially those of an investigative type, where the character and temper of the membership are compatible with a cooperative undertaking. We have touched on the values of discussion methods for policy-determining groups in earlier chapters. Summed up briefly they are: (1) The formulative stages in the process of policy determination are brought more fully into the deliberations of the group and are thus open to their examination and criticism; (2) the final product of the deliberations is more completely a group product, i. e., the result of group thinking, and thus better understood; (3) the discussion method tends to encourage a group harmony and cooperative workmanship which make for more objective deliberation; and (4) a solution cooperatively achieved is more loyally supported and more intelligently applied.

V. METHODS FOR POLICY-DETERMINING GROUPS

A. The Straight Discussion Approach.

This method is in essence the procedure explained throughout this volume. The problem is defined and analyzed, solutions are suggested and considered reflectively, and the solution which meets with the approval of the group is discussed in relation to the practical steps which would need to be taken to place it in operation. The obvious difficulty with this method for policy-determining groups is that the members may not be able to agree on the solution. When a consensus cannot be reached by the straight discussion approach, the group will then need to turn to the combination discussion-debate procedure explained below. Such a move should not be taken prematurely, however. Every reasonable effort consistent with the time available should be made to iron out differences and conflicts before making motions, conducting debate, and taking votes.

The following suggestions will be found helpful in employing the straight discussion approach in policy-determining groups: (1) Narrow the problem for discussion to the precise question at issue; (2) define terms in relation to the immediate situation at hand; (3) be especially thorough in all phases of analysis; (4) do not permit a discussion of solutions until the problem has been thoroughly analyzed; (5) even when a discussion of solutions is in order, try to prevent premature commitments on the part of members who will find it difficult to retract their position; (6) encourage members to explain rather than argue their proposals; (7) work for conciseness rather than excursiveness; (8) request that members be recognized by the leader before speaking, if it seems advisable; (9) if time is limited, impose time limits on the speakers and invoke the "rule of the majority" in matters which are time consuming and not really vital to anyone; and (10) when a conclusion has been tentatively reached give special attention to the practical aspects of working it out.

The intent of these suggestions is to keep the group definitely on the problem, to avoid rambling and unnecessary embroilments on side issues, to prevent inept and premature proposals, and to tighten up the reins on the group in the interests of harmony and progress. In policy-determining groups the educative effect of the discussion process is important, but nevertheless subordinate to the necessity of reaching a decision. The first measure of the success of the group will be the wisdom and practical value of the policy determined. Of course, educative effects and wise decisions are not necessarily in conflict; both may very well be served by the same method.

B. THE COMBINATION DISCUSSION-DEBATE METHOD.

If the group cannot reach a consensus cooperatively, the leader may then call for a motion. At this time any member of the group is at liberty to move the adoption of any proposal which he believes will meet the problem. We assume, however, that the leader will call for motions only after it becomes apparent that an agreement cannot be reached otherwise. The combination discussion-debate method does not begin with debate; it begins with discussion and turns to debate only when it is necessary to do so.

The method of the group after motions have been called for is that provided by the usual rules of parliamentary procedure.[1] The leader will usually save time by recognizing first a spokesman of what appears from the earlier discussion to be the majority opinion. When a motion is made and seconded, it is then open for debate. During the debate this main motion or *principal motion* is subject to such *subsidiary, incidental,* or *privileged motions* as may be properly introduced. Of these, the motion to amend is the most common. Any time after the debate on the principal motion has been opened, a member may move an amendment. If the motion to amend is seconded, it is then the subject of debate until accepted or rejected by a majority vote. If accepted, the motion then before the group is the principal motion *as amended* and any further debate is in order; if rejected,

[1] See Robert D. Leigh, *Modern Rules of Parliamentary Procedure* (New York: W. W. Norton and Company, Inc., 1937). This is a useful handbook designed to modernize parliamentary procedure; the author says of it: "What seems wise and sensible in traditional parliamentary procedure is retained. But rules are simplified, revised, re-named, or omitted altogether in order to bring them into line with the practical experience of groups of all kinds." P. 17.

the debate continues on the principal motion as originally presented. By simply calling for the *question*, any member may at any time request that the debate be terminated and the motion then before the group brought to a vote; if there is no dissent, the leader will put the question and take a vote. If one or more members object to closing the debate, they may call for a vote on this point. The suggestion to close the debate then has the status of a motion (*The previous question*) and, if passed by a two-thirds vote, serves to stop debate and bring to a vote whatever motion is then before the group.

The following *Table of Parliamentary Motions* together with the explanations offered will be found useful in some policy-determining groups.[2] In most small groups only a few of these motions will need to be used except on rare occasions, and in any case they should not be made an end in themselves.

Parliamentary law may vary in the details of its rules, but underlying it all there are found four invariable foundation principles or corner stones, upon which every portion of the superstructure rests. They are (1) justice and courtesy to all, (2) one thing at a time, (3) the rule of the majority, (4) the rights of the minority.[3]

The sixteen motions listed in this table are divided into four groups and are arranged in the order of their precedence from the weakest to the strongest. Principal motions are characterized by the fact that they are never in order when there is any other question or business before the assembly. Subsidiary motions are applied to other motions for the purpose of modifying, or disposing of them, or of cutting off debate on them. It is important to note that these subsidiary motions are so arranged in the table that each one takes precedence over those preceding it in the list and yields to those following it.

[2] Reprinted from J. M. O'Neill and J. H. McBurney, *The Working Principles of Argument* (New York: The Macmillan Company, 1932), pp. 340-342.

[3] J. M. Gregg, *Handbook of Parliamentary Law* (Boston: Ginn and Company, 1910), p. 52.

TABLE OF PARLIAMENTARY MOTIONS

Motions	Need a Second?	Amend-able?	Debat-able?	Vote Re-quired	May Inter-rupt a Speaker
I. Principal Motion					
1. Any main question or any independent matter of business before the meeting	yes	yes	yes	maj.	no
II. Subsidiary Motions					
2. To amend	yes	yes	yes	maj.	no
3. To postpone indefinitely	yes	no	yes	maj.	no
4. To refer to a committee	yes	yes	yes	maj.	no
5. To postpone to a certain time	yes	yes	yes	maj.	no
6. Previous question	yes	no	no	⅔	no
7. To lay on (or take from) the table	yes	no	no	maj.	no
III. Incidental Motions					
8. To suspend a rule	yes	no	no	⅔	no
9. To withdraw a motion	yes	no	no	maj.	no
10. Question of consideration	no	no	no	⅔	yes
11. A point of order	no	no	no	chair[a]	yes
12. Appeal from decision of chair	yes	no	no	maj.	yes
IV. Privileged Motions					
13. To make a matter of business a "special order" for a given time	no	no	no	⅔	yes
14. Questions of rights and privileges	no	no	no	chair[a]	yes
15. To adjourn (unqualified)	yes	no	no	maj.	no
16. To fix time for next meeting	yes	yes	no	maj.	no

[a] Require only decision of chair; no vote unless appealed.

Incidental motions are motions that arise out of other motions and come up in an incidental way. The order in which these five appear is not significant, as these motions rarely come in contact with each other. Privileged motions arise independently of other motions and concern themselves with the needs and rights of the assembly, and therefore are of the highest rank. They take precedence over all other motions, if made following them, though they yield to certain incidental motions arising out of them, and in some cases to subsidiary motions applied to them.

Every motion we have listed has a definite purpose and is designed to meet a rather specific situation. To facilitate the use of the chart we have submitted, therefore, we are listing these same motions below with their object or objects.

Objects of Motions

1. Main motion—to bring original business before the assembly.

2. To amend—to modify a question that is before the assembly.

3. To postpone indefinitely: (1) to dispose of a question for the session without voting on it directly; (2) it is used by the opponents of a question to determine their strength.

4. To refer to a committee—to secure the advantage of action by a smaller group, or of greater freedom in debate in dealing with a question.

5. To postpone to a certain time—to defer action on a question to a certain time.

6. Previous question—to suppress debate and bring the assembly to a vote.

7. To lay on the table: (1) to postpone a subject so that it may be taken up at another time during the same session; (2) to stop debate and suppress a question for the session, providing a majority cannot be secured to take the question again from the table.

8. To suspend a rule—to make temporarily possible an action contrary to the standing rules or rules of order of an organization.

9. To withdraw a motion—to expedite business in case of a changed opinion by the maker of the motion.

10. Question of consideration—an objection to the consideration of a question to enable the assembly to avoid irrelevant, unprofitable, or contentious questions.

11. A point of order—to correct a breach of order or an error in procedure.

12. Appeal from decision of chair: (1) to invoke a rule which the chairman has ignored or misinterpreted; (2) to appeal to the assembly to overrule the chairman on any rule where an opinion or a judgment may be exercised.

13. Special order—to set a specific time to consider a certain matter of business when all other things will be set aside.

14. Questions of rights and privileges—to secure to the assembly or any of its members some right with respect to safety, comfort, dignity, reputation, or freedom from disturbance.

15. To adjourn—to bring a meeting to a close.

16. To fix a time for the next meeting—to fix a time or place for reassembling.

EXERCISES

1. Adopt for discussion a problem upon which it is possible for the group to take some action, preferably a local or campus problem, e.g., Should the members of this group take the Oxford Oath? Work for group consensus through the straight discussion approach; failing in this, resort to the combination discussion-debate approach.

2. Proceed as in Exercise 1 with some question of state or national policy in which it is the purpose of the group to report out a resolution representing a consensus or majority view.

3. Conduct a legislative debate on some question of policy

in which special attention is given to parliamentary procedure. Use this period as a drill designed to develop understanding and proficiency in the use of the Table of Motions given in this chapter.

SELECTED BIBLIOGRAPHY

Courtis, S. A., *Cooperation*. Ann Arbor, Michigan: Brumfield and Brumfield, 1934. Chapters III and IV.

Elliott, Harrison S., *The Process of Group Thinking*. New York: Association Press, 1932. Appendix I.

Gregg, F. M., *Handbook of Parliamentary Law*. Boston: Ginn and Company, 1910.

Leigh, Robert D., *Group Leadership*. New York: W. W. Norton and Company, 1936.

Leigh, Robert D., *Modern Rules of Parliamentary Procedure*. New York: W. W. Norton and Company, 1937.

CHAPTER XVI

THE PANEL, DIALOGUE, SYMPOSIUM, FORUM-LECTURE

This chapter is concerned with discussion methods for co-acting groups. The principal methods are the panel discussion, the dialogue, the symposium, and the forum-lecture. Our study of them requires that we recall the definition of discussion given in Chapter II. There we said that discussion is the reflective deliberation of problems by persons thinking and conversing together cooperatively under the direction of a leader in face-to-face or co-acting groups. We have thus far considered this definition and its implications with respect to reflective deliberation, cooperative participation, and leadership. Here we are emphasizing the last phrase: "face-to-face or co-acting groups."

In the face-to-face group the members see each other face to face, speak without going to a central point, and have no one focal point of stimulus but one which is constantly changing as various persons contribute. This is, as we have said, the typical situation for discussion. When the group becomes too large for general participation, however, it is wise to substitute a co-acting situation, in which one or more speakers appear in front of the group. Here the focal point is relatively constant, the group responds to a common stimulus, and the face-to-face situation is absent. The primary difference between the two groups is in the nature of the stimulus, whether it is constantly shifting from one member of the group to another or whether the group is responding to some relatively fixed, central source of stimulation. In a face-to-face group there is no fixed audience, because each member may be a speaker at one moment and a listener at another. In a co-acting group, however, you have one group of persons present in the capacity of listeners, thus constituting a well-defined audience, and one or more persons present in the capacity of speakers.

We have emphasized this distinction in order to deal adequately with the panel discussion, dialogue, symposium, and forum-lecture. Their use necessitates the presence of both speakers and an audience; thus they are discussion methods for co-acting groups, and must be appraised as such. Our purpose in this chapter is to describe them, indicate their values and limitations, and point out some of the problems which their use creates.

I. THE PANEL DISCUSSION

A. Description and Uses.

The panel discussion, which was originated by Professor Harry A. Overstreet, is a method of discussion in which a few persons (the panel) carry on a discussion in front of an audience, which usually participates later in a question-and-answer period. Its purpose is to reproduce as far as possible the features of a small discussion group for the benefit of a larger group.

A panel discussion includes three elements: the panel, the chairman, and the audience. The panel consists of from four to eight persons who are seated facing the audience. During the first few minutes of the discussion the chairman may present the subject for consideration and point out the relations of the panel and the audience to it, at the same time briefly describing the general procedure of the discussion. The panel then discusses the problem, conversing without set speeches in the hearing of the audience. Then when the panel has adequately developed the pattern of thought, the audience is permitted to ask questions of any one member or of the panel as a whole. The chairman guides the panel in its discussion and also serves as an adapter of this discussion to the audience. He is also in charge of the question-and-answer period.

Two points need to be emphasized. First, the members of the panel are supposed to use the problem-solving method—to develop among themselves the pattern of reflective thinking. This is discussion, and intentional reasoning has no place here. Second, the audience is permitted to direct questions at the panel only after a definite pattern of ideas has been developed.

This method of discussion has, since its inception by Professor Overstreet in 1931, been widely used in conventions, conferences, and educational groups ranging from adult education to the elementary school. In recent years it has been adopted in many state and national conventions of teachers, as well as in preconvention sessions of political parties. Its popularity as a method of conducting radio programs is seen in the response given to the University of Chicago Round Table. In the educational field it has been adopted as the regular classroom method in some situations. For example, the course in Educational Foundations at Teachers College, Columbia University, uses the panel discussion, in which the two-hour session consists of a discussion among five members of the faculty followed by a question period open to the members of the class.

B. Values and Limitations.

To appraise the panel discussion accurately, we should compare it with other methods used in co-acting groups such as the lecture and the debate.

1. *Panel Discussion and the Lecture.*—By its very nature the panel discussion insures breadth and variety, spontaneity, and freedom. Because there are several persons in the panel, there is certain to be a variety of contributions; and because set speeches are barred, the manner of contributing is almost certain to be free-and-easy and in the spirit of give-and-take. The lecture, on the other hand, is probably more orderly and compact. The lecturer is giving a report of his thinking upon the problem, and he can organize and phrase this report carefully. The panel discussion carries on the process of reflective thinking, whereas the lecture reports a process carried on at a previous time. Our appraisal of the panel discussion depends, therefore, on our answer to the question: Do we wish selection, order, compactness, and economy in presentation; or do we wish breadth, variety, and spontaneity?

Overstreet gives his answer in his description of one of the first panel discussions to be conducted. During the summer of 1931 a series of four forums was planned at the University of California at Los Angeles. They were advertised not as lectures, but as discussions. When the first forum began, six men, distinguished in their field, were seated in front of the audience. They had been asked to consider the problem before them, to converse informally among themselves, and then to participate in a question period. This is what happened:

After some moments of natural hesitation, the conversing began. With no need for making speeches, with no obligation to defend finished views, these experts began to let themselves go. They began, groping and hesitatingly at first, but with increasing vigor and clarity, to think out loud. They asked questions of one another; they ventured opinions; they expressed both agreement and disagreement.

As the hour allotted to them progressed, it was as thrilling an experience as one might well wish to have—to witness intelligent men honestly trying to think their way through a jungle of perplexities.

At the end of an hour, the audience, who had been literally sitting on the edges of their chairs, eager to break in, were permitted to join in the discussion. There was no hesitation. Question after question was fired, and suggestion after suggestion made.[1]

Overstreet believes that the reason for the success of this and the other meetings of the series lay in the operation of an important psychological principle: "They were admitting an audience to an active process of thinking." To him the fact that the audience was not being instructed but was witnessing *thought in process* made these discussions successful.

We are presenting Overstreet's observation not for the purpose of arguing the merits of the panel discussion, but to report what the originator of the method believes its values to be.

2. *Panel Discussion and Debate.*—In comparing the panel discussion and debate we are concerned with a procedure in reflective thinking and one in intentional reasoning, both carried on in a co-acting situation. The panel discussion is problem solving in approach and attempts to throw light on a question being considered reflectively. Its usefulness lies in helping an audience to explore a question from many points of view and to arrive at some conclusion as objectively as possible. Debate, on the contrary, is designed to provide the best possible case for each side of a question. Much may be said for its use in a situation where a measure has been submitted to a group for acceptance or rejection, such as a party platform or an amendment to a city charter. Here debate may be useful in arraying clearly and forcefully the arguments on the two sides. In other words, in those situa-

---

[1] Harry A. Overstreet, "Capturing the Depression Mind," *Journal of Adult Education*, Vol. 4, January, 1932, pp. 12-15.

tions in which thinking has been crystallized to such a point where a definite solution is about to be submitted to the public for an expression of opinion, debate serves a useful purpose in pointing up the arguments pro and con.

C. DUTIES OF THE PANEL AND THE CHAIRMAN.

It may be a commonplace to say that the success of a panel discussion depends upon the members of the panel and the chairman, but we are emphasizing this thought because of many misconceptions which have arisen. To many people there is a certain "magic" in the panel method. They think that it requires no particular preparation. As a result the effort is feeble, and they become convinced that the panel discussion has no merit. Without taking time to find the cause, they hastily conclude that the lecture, for example, is better. The fact is that definite obligations rest upon both the panel members and the chairman, obligations fully as great as those upon the lecturer; and any comparison must assume equally competent persons and equal preparation. To be sure, it will be a different kind of preparation; but we wish to dispel the thought that the panel discussion can make something out of nothing.

1. *The Panel.*—The members of the panel have the duty of discussing intelligently the question before them. They must prepare themselves so that they have "something to offer." Furthermore, each member should assume full responsibility for the success of the discussion lest each one, believing that the other will do so, fail to make any preparation whatsoever. During the progress of the discussion each member has the additional duties of maintaining a spirit of friendly and cooperative discussion and of keeping things moving and "on point" so that they will be interesting and meaningful to the audience. The responsibility for the maintenance of a cooperative spirit arises from the nature of reflective thinking in contrast to that of intentional reasoning. The

responsibility for the creation of an interesting discussion arises from the presence of the audience. While it is true that the panel discussion is not designed to be primarily a source of entertainment, the audience must be considered. The members of the panel need to remember this fact in selecting the materials to develop the pattern of thought and in participating in the discussion. They need to speak so that they can be heard by the audience, and they need to phrase their contributions for reception by the audience as well as by the other members of the panel. All of this makes tremendous demands upon the panel, but they are inescapable.

2. *The Chairman.*—The chairman has all of the duties described in Chapter VIII for the leader of the discussion group. In addition he has the responsibility of informing the audience as to its part in the panel method, of adapting the discussion to the audience, and of deciding the proper time for the question period to begin. Thus he has the duty of assisting the panel to deliberate most effectively and also of making this deliberation valuable to the audience. Again, these are heavy demands; but they are inescapable.

D. Conducting a Panel Discussion.

There are four major problems which pertain to the organization and conduct of a panel discussion. Arranged in a time sequence they are: (1) the selection of the panel; (2) the preparation by the members, chairman, and audience; (3) the mechanical arrangements; (4) the participation by the audience.

1. *The Selection of the Panel.*—The personnel of the panel should depend upon the question to be discussed and the capabilities of the members themselves. The number of members may be determined by the number of points of view which it may seem wise to develop or by the number of representatives of important points of view that can be secured. Fansler believes that "in general the more gifted the panel members in thought and expression

the smaller the number needed," although he says that "four is the minimum number and eight the maximum."[2] The members should be well informed, should be able thinkers, and should be able to express themselves clearly and quickly. They need all the qualities of the participants in a discussion group plus the ability to converse well in front of an audience.

2. *The Preparation by the Members, Chairman, and Audience.*—The general preparation which a member of a panel should make is similar to that described in Chapter VI. Likewise, the leader should prepare himself as described in Chapter VIII. In addition, they should be concerned with the need for special preparation which they will make together. The extent of this preparation will depend upon their point of view as to the wisdom of doing more than prepare themselves individually. Some people believe that there should be no "rehearsing" of the discussion and that the panel and the chairman should not try to formulate a plan of procedure in advance. Overstreet takes this view:

One mistake frequently made is to have a "rehearsal" ahead of time. A nervous chairman will think something in the nature of a program must be agreed upon beforehand. He will therefore gather his panel about him and conduct a kind of preliminary discussion. No worse procedure can be imagined. The stimulation and the intellectual value of the panel method lies in its sheer spontaneity, for it is in the atmosphere of spontaneity that the best flashes of insight frequently come . . .[3]

Other persons who hold a similar view say that a "rehearsal" may cause differences to develop and become crystallized, with the result that the desired spontaneity may not be forthcoming in the discussion in front of the audience.

[2] Thomas Fansler, *Discussion Methods for Adult Groups* (New York: American Association for Adult Education, 1934), pp. 105-106.
[3] Harry A. Overstreet, "On the Panel," *Occupations*, Vol. 13, February, 1935, p. 427.

The other view is that a conference before the discussion is useful in permitting the members and the chairman to become acquainted and to formulate a tentative pattern. This pattern will not be concerned with the substance of the discussion, but with the steps in reflective thinking and the general means of procedure. One successful "professional" chairman of a series of panel discussions held in different cities uses this method. Because the membership of each panel is different, he believes it wise to become acquainted with the members and to talk over methods with them. He arranges a dinner before each meeting, encourages each member to express himself informally, and suggests a broad pattern for the panel to follow. He is not dogmatic about this pattern, however, often revising it to suit the wishes of the group.

When you are dealing with a group of experts and the discussion is in the field of their specialization, quite obviously there is no need for direct preparation. These people can rely on their wide background. But a different situation arises when a group of laymen or ordinary people are going to discuss a problem. Here experience has shown the wisdom of some direct preparation. By this direct preparation *we do not mean a rehearsal*, but rather study of the problem in advance of the discussion.

The amount and kind of preparation which the *audience* may make will depend on their general interests, their relations to the discussion, and the plans of the chairman. If the audience can be reached in advance—as in a series of meetings, where announcements and plans can be made from week to week—and if the chairman believes the plan to be useful, he may provide study-guides and reading materials such as those described in Chapter VIII. In the case of a regularly scheduled course a syllabus may be provided and regular preparation made by the class.

3. *The Mechanical Arrangements.*—In arranging the panel, one needs to consider both the relations of the

panel to the audience and the relations of the members
of the panel to one another. The panel should be placed
where it can be easily seen and heard. Also, the audience
should be seated as near as possible to the panel so that it
will have no difficulty in hearing and also so that the informality of the panel will not be disturbed by excessive
distances between it and the audience.

The seating of the panel should provide for the maximum of informality and the development of unity in the
group. For this reason the members should preferably be
seated in a semicircle with the chairman midway from
each end. If possible, they should be seated at a table and
be so arranged as to keep the panel from breaking up
into groups of two and three persons.

Some experimenters with the panel method advise
placing those members with the most divergent points of
view at the extreme positions, not to mark them as extremes but to take advantage of the fact that much of the
discussion will probably pass between them and necessarily will reach the others. A possible danger in this
arrangement may be the causing of unnecessary conflict
by appearing to array the supporters of one side against
the other.

Another plan is to place at the ends those members
who are likely to participate most freely. In this way the
entire panel will be included when these members speak,
and "side conversations" will be avoided at least in part.

The above diagrams suggest how these ideas can be
adapted to typical seating plans. The placing of the persons will depend, of course, upon the opportunity for the
chairman to know the characteristics of the members of
the panel and also upon the plan which he may wish to
follow.

4. *The Participation by the Audience.*—It is customary for the panel discussion to provide a question-and-answer period following the development of the pattern of reflective thinking. In preparation for this period the chairman may, if necessary, briefly summarize the discussion, then invite participation by the audience. At the end of the question period he should close the meeting in the way that best fits the spirit of the occasion. It may be best to adjourn at once, or a brief summary may be needed. Upon another occasion it may be desirable to resume the panel discussion for a few minutes in order to enable the members of the panel to adapt their earlier discussion to the questions and answers. Because this question period is primarily a forum, we are reserving more detailed consideration of it for Chapter XVII.

II. THE DIALOGUE

The dialogue is a method of discussion in which two persons, using the question-and-answer method primarily, discuss a problem in front of an audience, which participates later in a period of questions directed at one or both of the speakers. Ordinarily one of the speakers serves as chairman and questioner, and the other as respondent. Frequently the chairman not only asks questions but also discusses briefly some of the replies of the respondent.

The ideal chairman is well versed in the problem under consideration, knows the level of information and interest of the audience in the problem, and is an expert at asking questions both to develop the pattern of thinking and to follow up the replies of the respondent to his questions. A chairman like this can stimulate interest in the topic, can give pattern to the dialogue, and can draw from the respondent the information particularly needed to help the audience. The ideal respondent is an expert on the problem being discussed, is keen-minded enough to be able to reply quickly and yet fully, and is conscious enough of the audience to adapt his knowledge to it.

This type of respondent can bring to the audience a large body of material and can present it in a useful form.

The dialogue is used to some extent in public forums and in centers for adult education. Probably its greatest use is on the radio, where several well-known programs consist of a dialogue between a chairman and a subject-matter expert in some field. In fact, the radio is perhaps a better situation for the dialogue than is a meeting in an auditorium, where the participants must speak loudly enough to reach all members of the audience and thus lose some of the informality of a conversation.

The dialogue is useful in giving an audience the opportunity of listening to an expert being questioned by a skillful chairman who knows both the resources of the expert and the needs of the listeners. Our experience has shown us that in some instances the dialogue is more useful than the lecture in that it relates the contributions of the expert more fully to the needs of the audience than is the case when the lecturer prepares his material in advance with only a general knowledge of the audience. This is particularly true when the chairman knows the needs of the audience and can direct the discussion in terms of those needs. Another important value of the dialogue rests in the variety provided by the interplay which develops from a series of questions and answers. The spontaneity and direct clash make it ordinarily more interesting and lively than even the most animated lecture, although not necessarily as orderly, compact, and well phrased.

Audience participation is ordinarily limited, as in the panel discussion, to the period following the development of a pattern of thought by the speakers. In preparation for this period the chairman may, if necessary, summarize the dialogue, then invite questions. Like the chairman of the panel discussion, he should close the meeting in the manner most satisfying to the audience, using an additional summary or resuming the dialogue for a brief period only if needed.

III. THE SYMPOSIUM

A. DESCRIPTION AND USES.

The symposium is a method of discussion in which two or more persons, under the direction of a chairman, present in separate speeches the various phases of a problem. The audience is permitted to participate vocally only in the question-and-answer period which follows the speeches. The purpose of the symposium is to investigate a problem from several points of view, not to give a series of argumentative speeches. In its ideal form it consists of from three to five experts, each of whom presents a ten- to fifteen-minute speech, and of a chairman who introduces the question to the audience, provides a transition from one speech to another, briefly correlates the contributions, and takes charge of the question-and-answer period. In some instances the several speeches are presented during the same session, and in others one session is devoted to one speech, with additional speeches being given at later periods. In the latter case the continuity should be preserved by the chairman and so far as possible by the speakers themselves.

The subject of each speech may in general be determined by one of two methods. One is to ask each speaker to present his point of view upon the main problem; the other is to assign a phase of the problem to each speaker and ask him to limit himself to that phase. In the former case the sponsor of the symposium will attempt to secure speakers with reasonably divergent points of view, but he will make no attempt to assign special subjects. In the latter case the sponsor of a symposium considering, for example, "The Policy of the United States in the Far East" will assign to one speaker the policy of isolation, to another the policy of cooperation with China, and to another the policy of cooperation with Japan.

The symposium is one of the most widely used of the discussion methods for co-acting groups. It is constantly employed in educational conferences, conventions of state and national organizations, and preconvention meetings of political parties. In some colleges and universities it has been adopted as the method for conducting certain courses and occasional public meetings.

B. Values and Limitations.

To appraise the symposium adequately, we should compare it with such other methods used in co-acting groups as the lecture, panel discussion, and debate.

1. *Symposium and Lecture.*—In providing for the discussion of several phases of a problem, the symposium overcomes what is often the greatest weakness of the single lecture—the presentation of only one phase or side of a question. On the other hand, the speeches of the symposium may suffer from sketchiness and a lack of continuity, although this deficiency can often be overcome by a conference between the speakers and the chairman.

2. *Symposium and Panel Discussion.*—Both of these discussion methods are useful in providing several speakers and the opportunity for the development of several points of view. The contrast lies in the higher degree of organization in the symposium, with its series of speeches, than in the more informal, spontaneous, impromptu procedure of the panel. The one places a premium upon careful organization of speeches in advance; the other places a premium upon spontaneous adaptation of the several contributions at the moment when the pattern of thought is being constructed before the audience.

3. *Symposium and Debate.*—Both of these methods insure the discussion of the problem from more than one point of view. The contrast appears, however, in the purposes of the speeches. Whereas the symposium is investigative, the debate is designed to be persuasive, presenting the best possible case for each side. As we observed in our comparison of the panel discussion and debate, the discussion method is useful in exploring a problem from many points of view and in encouraging

objective conclusions. Its method is not applicable, however, to the situation which requires the arraying of
arguments on two sides and the using of persuasive methods to make the arguments appealing. To some persons,
who see in the symposium the arraying of divergent
points of view, this may appear to be an erroneous statement of the differences between the symposium and
debate. There is in reality a major distinction, even
though the form of the two methods may appear to be
much the same.

We repeat that the symposium should be investigative,
representing *thought in process*, and the several speeches
should develop phases of the problem in order to assist
the audience to arrive objectively at a conclusion. These
speeches are designed to present all the possible information, not to provide only those arguments which seem
necessary to win, as in the case of some debates. This is
not a criticism of debate, but a statement of differences
between the two methods, a statement which must be
emphasized lest the purpose of the symposium be misunderstood and it cease to be a method of discussion.

C. DUTIES OF MEMBERS.

The speakers in the symposium have an important responsibility in addition to being well informed and able
to speak creditably. They have the duty of contributing
in such a way that the primary purpose of the symposium
will be preserved and the session will not become a series
of persuasive speeches arguing the merits of a case. The
symposium speakers should use essentially the same
method of contributing as that suggested for the participant in the discussion group—a fair, objective treatment
of the problem. They should attempt to explain what
their points of view are and why they feel as they do
toward the problem. (See Chapter VII.)

The chairman has certain duties in addition to opening
and closing the meeting and serving as the leader of the
question-and-answer period. He should learn in advance

the points of view of the speakers and should arrange the program to provide for the greatest possible sequence and continuity. In addition, he should keep the symposium as coherent as possible by providing if necessary a brief transitional statement between the speeches and a brief summary before the question period begins. Finally, he should make every effort to preserve the investigative character of the symposium and to keep it from becoming a debate. He can do this in a pre-session conference with the speakers or if necessary in his remarks between the speeches.

IV. THE FORUM-LECTURE

The forum-lecture is a method of discussion in which one person presents a speech followed by a question-and-answer period participated in by the audience. The purpose of the lecture is to explore a subject and to inform the audience concerning one or more phases of it. It is not intended to be a persuasive speech nor should it be an example of intentional reasoning. The speaker may present his own point of view here, but the explanatory denotative or empirical method of contributing should be employed.

The forum-lecture is probably the most widely used of the discussion methods available to the regularly established forums. Several reasons may be assigned for this fact, among these being the comparative ease of securing one expert and also the comparative inexperience of any large number of persons with the panel, the dialogue, or the symposium. In many cases, however, the panel method is being used in the federal forum projects.[4]

The values of the forum-lecture exist largely in the opportunity it presents for an authority on the subject to give a systematic discussion of material which he has selected from his extensive thought and experience. It is

[4] J. W. Studebaker and Chester S. Williams, *Choosing Our Way,* United States Department of the Interior, Office of Education, Bulletin 1937, Misc. No. 1, p. 27.

ordinarily more compact and more coherent than the symposium, and more systematic than the dialogue and the panel discussion. On the other hand, it is limited by the presence of only one person and by the absence of the spontaneous, informal development of the subject characteristic of the dialogue and the panel discussion. The forum-lecture ordinarily finds its greatest usefulness when the group wants facts and wants them as quickly and systematically as possible from an authority, perhaps so that its members can profitably carry on one or more discussions among themselves. This circumstance is often observed in the programs of conferences and conventions, in which a lecture by an expert is followed by a number of round tables in which various aspects of the main topic are developed informally.

The question-and-answer period may be conducted by the lecturer himself or by the chairman of the meeting. Both plans have obvious advantages, determined largely by the lecturer's familiarity with the members of the audience and his ability to lead a forum. The procedure for this period will be discussed in some detail in Chapter XVII.

EXERCISES

1. Write 300-500 words upon one or more of the following: (a) the nature and use of the panel discussion; (b) the nature and use of the dialogue; (c) the nature and use of the symposium; (d) the nature and use of the forum-lecture. In preparing these essays, use material found in the bibliography at the end of this chapter.

2. Criticize the "Round Table" in Appendix B as a specimen of the panel discussion. Comment upon such points as: (a) the contribution made by each member; (b) the spirit of the discussion; (c) the interestingness of the discussion; (d) the clarity of the discussion; (e) the organization of the discussion.

3. Criticize the panel discussion in *Discussion Methods*

for Adult Groups by Fansler, pp. 111-132, with respect to the points given in Exercise 2.

4. Criticize each of the seven panel discussions in the *Journal of Adult Education* and each of the two panel discussions in *Religious Education* as cited in the bibliography at the end of Chapter VIII, with respect to the points given in Exercise 2.

5. What changes would have to be made in the discussion in Appendix A to make it suitable for a panel discussion? Why? Be specific.

6. What changes would have to be made in the group discussion in *Discussion Methods for Adult Groups* by Fansler, pp. 82-99, to make it suitable for a panel discussion? Why? Be specific.

7. Record a panel discussion. Play this back and criticize it with respect to the points given in Exercise 2.

8. If a radio is available, arrange a meeting of the class at a time when a discussion such as the "University of Chicago Round Table" is to be broadcast. Criticize the discussion.

9. Observe a panel discussion and a symposium. Explain their procedures and briefly summarize their contents. Appraise them separately and comparatively.

10. Observe a panel discussion and a forum-lecture. Explain their procedures and briefly summarize their contents. Appraise them separately and comparatively.

11. Observe a symposium and a forum-lecture. Explain their procedures and briefly summarize their contents. Appraise them separately and comparatively.

12. Conduct a panel discussion in class. Experiment with different methods of selecting the panel, of preparing the members of the panel, and of seating the panel. Criticize each of these methods.

13. Criticize the forum-dialogue in *Discussion Methods for Adult Groups* by Fansler, pp. 29-51, with respect to: (a) the relation of Mr. A to Professor B; (b) the pattern of the discussion; (c) the clarity of the discussion; (d) the difference between this and a lecture.

14. Conduct a dialogue in class. Criticize the work of the chairman and that of the expert being questioned by the chairman.

15. Compare and contrast the symposium and the debate

with respect to: (a) purposes; (b) materials; (c) procedures.

16. Criticize the forum in Appendix C as a specimen of the symposium. Comment upon such points as those given in Exercise 2.

17. Conduct a symposium in class in which each person presents an aspect of the problem. Conduct a symposium in which each person presents his own point of view on the problem. Criticize these methods, the work of the speakers, and the work of the chairman.

18. Criticize the forum-lecture in *Discussion Methods for Adult Groups* by Fansler, pp. 7-25. Comment upon such points as: (a) the purpose and spirit of the lecture; (b) the usefulness of the lecture in stimulating discussion; (c) the relation of the lecture to the question-and-answer period.

19. Present a ten- to twelve-minute speech suitable for a forum-lecture. The important feature of this exercise is to construct a speech which stimulates reflective thinking and which avoids affective identification with a particular point of view. Each person in the class may profitably perform this exercise. Criticize the speeches.

SELECTED BIBLIOGRAPHY

Cartwright, Morse A., "Panel," *Journal of Adult Education.* Vol. 5, January, 1933, pp. 37-42.

Fansler, Thomas, *Discussion Methods for Adult Groups.* New York: American Association for Adult Education, 1934. Parts I and III.

Leigh, Robert D., *Group Leadership.* New York: W. W. Norton and Company, 1936. Pp. 79-82.

Overstreet, Harry A., "Capturing the Depression Mind," *Journal of Adult Education.* Vol. 4, January, 1932, pp. 12-15.

Overstreet, Harry A., "On the Panel," *Occupations.* Vol. 13, February, 1935, pp. 425-427.

Pellegrini, Angelo M., and Stirling, Brents, *Argumentation and Public Discussion.* Boston: D. C. Heath and Company, 1936. Pp. 95-102.

Sheffield, Alfred D., "Discussion, Lecture-Forum, and Debate," *Quarterly Journal of Speech.* Vol. XVIII, November, 1932, pp. 517-531.

CHAPTER XVII

THE FORUM

No survey of contemporary America is complete without a consideration of the forum, a significant sign of democracy and also probably one of the most practical means of maintaining it. The fact that more than seven hundred forums were listed in a bulletin published by the Office of Education of the United States Department of the Interior in 1937, and that probably several hundred more are unlisted, shows something of the widespread use of this institution by the American people.[1]

The forum as conducted in the United States consists of an organization, either public or private, which conducts meetings using one or all of the methods of discussion for co-acting groups described in Chapter XVI, and somewhat less frequently other discussion methods. The usual procedure is to devote the first part of the session to the presentation of information and lines of thought by means of the panel discussion, dialogue, symposium, or forum-lecture. The second part consists of a question-and-answer period in which the audience participates, this being ordinarily the only time when the audience is permitted to participate vocally.

The term "forum" is commonly used with two differ-

[1] J. W. Studebaker and Chester S. Williams, *Choosing Our Way*, United States Department of the Interior, Office of Education, Bulletin 1937, Misc. No. 1.

ent meanings. It may describe the forum in an over-all sense as an institution, much as we would speak of the school or the church; or it may describe the discussion method most commonly used in this institution. We shall take the two meanings of this term as the basis of the organization of this chapter.

I. THE FORUM AS AN INSTITUTION

A. BRIEF HISTORY.

The forum movement in America can be charted by a survey of the New England Town Meeting, the Lyceum, the Chautauqua, the private or self-constituted forum, and the public or planned forum.

1. *The New England Town Meeting.*—The system of complete, or pure, democracy in existence in many of the New England towns of the pre-Revolutionary era gave rise to the organization and development of the Town Meeting. Both as a place for the exchange of opinion and as a means of determining policies of government, this type of forum had a useful and practical function. The selectmen of the town ordinarily called the meeting, at which issues and policies were outlined and discussed by all the townspeople who wished to attend. In this forum the early citizens not only received much of their training in self-government, but also crystallized opinions which later became the platform of the Revolutionists.[2]

2. *The Lyceum.*—The Lyceum, organized in 1826, carried on the tradition and method of the Town Meeting. Its first purpose was to provide a place for the discussion of the problem of public education. Later it became a means of giving part-time education to many people who could not attend schools, of assisting in the training of school teachers, and of giving opportunities to all citizens to discuss political issues. Beginning with Josiah Holbrook's plan for the organization of a Lyceum in 1826, the institution developed until at one time several

[2] *Ibid.,* pp. 1-7.

thousand units were in existence. Upon the extension of public education, however, the original purpose of the Lyceum was gone; and after continuing for some years as an organization for adult education, it disappeared. During its period of existence it was a powerful agency for the creation of enlightened public opinion and for the spread of sentiment favorable to public education.

3. *The Chautauqua.*—In 1874 there arose another institution prominent in the history of America's forums. The Chautauqua was organized to provide means of training teachers, especially Sunday-school teachers; and it rapidly developed into a strong influence. Both at Chautauqua, New York, and at the two hundred or more Chautauquas throughout the country there were conducted lectures and discussions which did much to spread a broader understanding of public affairs. Even if some of the traveling Chautauquas did deviate from the educational program of the original institution, they frequently met a need in bringing to small communities the opportunities for thought and study which we today regard as commonplace. And even if in many cases the forum feature was absent, the Chautauqua at least provided the audience with the information necessary to carry on more enlightened discussions among themselves.[3]

4. *The Private or Self-constituted Forum.*—Under the leadership of persons who saw in the forum the means of promoting democratic principles, a number of private forums sprang up in the years following 1859, the year of the opening of the Cooper Union building in New York. In New York, Boston, Chicago, Dallas, Hartford, and other cities several score of forums have been organized by church, racial, and other groups and by persons vitally interested in providing means of discussion for citizens of all economic levels. Many of these forums have continued in existence for more than fifty years,

[3] See Hugh A. Orchard, *Fifty Years of Chautauqua* (Cedar Rapids, Iowa: Torch Press, 1923).

and today are popular and influential centers of public discussion.[4]

5. *The Public or Planned Forum.*—Supplementing the work of the private forums, a number of public forum projects have been developed in recent years by cities and the federal government. Today probably the outstanding example of the city-administered forum is that in Des Moines, Iowa. It was organized by Dr. J. W. Studebaker, who later as United States Commissioner of Education also developed the present extensive federal forum project.

B. Representative Forums of Today.

The more than seven hundred listed forums in the United States today can best be classified on the basis of their sponsorship and degree of self-organization. One group is privately sponsored and may be said to be self-starting and self-constituted; these forums arose more or less spontaneously in response to a need felt by some church, racial, labor, or other group. The other type of forum is publicly sponsored and may be said to be a planned group set up for the use of a community if the citizens wish to participate in it.

1. *The Private or Self-constituted Forum.*—Included in this group are the oldest and some of the most influential forums in the United States. The oldest of these is the Cooper Union Forum, or People's Institute, established in 1897. It met a need which had been only partly met by the various unrelated meetings held in the Cooper Union building since 1859. This forum now attracts hundreds of people to its sessions, which are addressed by experts in various fields.

The city of Boston is represented by two influential forums, Old South Forum and Ford Hall Forum. The former, which meets in the Old South Meeting House,

---

[4] See Reuben L. Lurie, *The Challenge of the Forum—the Story of Ford Hall and the Open Forum Movement* (Boston: Richard A. Badger, Publisher, 1930), pp. 139-148, "The Spread of the Open-Forum Movement."

serves a constituency different from that of Ford Hall, which has been characterized as being more cosmopolitan and more informal. Each of these forums normally has more than five hundred persons in the audience, and Ford Hall frequently attracts a thousand people.[5]

Chicago is noted for a variety of well-established forums such as the Chicago Forum, under the direction of the Adult Education Council; the Social Science Institute, often called Hobo College; and the Sinai Temple Forum and the Anshe Emet Forum, both under the auspices of Jewish organizations. Dallas, Texas, has its Open Forum; Springfield, Massachusetts, and Hartford, Connecticut, have their Public Forums and Public Lectures, respectively; there is a Florida Forum at Daytona Beach; and many other cities are represented by church forums, labor organization forums, and forums organized by racial groups.

Of great interest, also, is America's Town Meeting of the Air held in the Town Hall of New York and broadcast over a nation-wide network. This forum ordinarily has more than a thousand people in the audience at Town Hall each Thursday evening, and also attracts several hundred to its daily morning meetings, which are not broadcast.[6]

2. *The Public or Planned Forum.*—Included in this group are the widely known Des Moines, Iowa, forums and those of the federal public forum project which was instituted in 1936. The Des Moines forum project, which was organized in 1932, is the result of the decision of the American Association for Adult Education to conduct in that city a five-year experiment in adult civic education. Financed by a grant of $125,000 from the Carnegie Corporation and directed by Dr. J. W. Studebaker, then superintendent of the Des Moines schools, the project developed to the point where it included one city-wide

[5] *Ibid.*

[6] See Mary L. Ely, *Why Forums?* (New York: American Association for Adult Education, 1937).

forum, five central forums, and more than twenty neighborhood forums. The project has been expanded from time to time to include study groups, credit-bearing courses, and provisions for reading by those people who wish to avail themselves of study-guides and other materials. In fact, at one time or another nearly every feature suggested for use in forums has been tried in the Des Moines project. Other city-administered forums are located in Portland, Oregon; Minneapolis, Minnesota; and San Diego and San Pedro, California.[7]

The federal forum project, which was undertaken in 1936 under the direction of Dr. Studebaker, now United States Commissioner of Education, began with ten forum districts and later was extended to other areas. At the present writing there are nineteen districts in nineteen states, extending from New Hampshire to Georgia in the East and from Washington to California in the West, and representing either city or county projects. In the nineteen districts more than five hundred forum centers have been established, and during the year 1936-1937 these held 10,451 meetings with an attendance of 1,104,384.

The administration of the forums in these districts is in control of the local city or county superintendent of schools; and the local board of education or the representatives of several boards have complete jurisdiction over all plans. They select the local directors and forum leaders, the subjects for discussion, and the places for meeting; and they are responsible for all details of organization of the local meetings.

The discussion methods used in these forums during the year 1936-1937 were largely the panel discussion and the forum-lecture. "Visual aids, charts, graphs, film strips, and motion pictures were used to supplement the oral presentations." The average meeting was one hour

---

[7] For a detailed explanation of the Des Moines forum project see John W. Studebaker, *The American Way* (New York: McGraw-Hill Book Company, Inc., 1935).

and thirty-one minutes, of which forty-six minutes were devoted to the presentation of the problem, thirty-seven minutes to the question-and-answer period, and eight minutes to announcements. The forum curriculum included such subjects as international relations, social problems, national legislation, education, economic problems, state and local problems, and religion and social change.[8]

II. THE FORUM AS A METHOD

In this section of the chapter we shall briefly survey the methods used in the forum to present the problem to the audience; then we shall consider in greater detail some of the problems of the question-and-answer period.

A. METHODS OF PRESENTING THE PROBLEM.

The forum, as we have said previously, ordinarily uses the panel discussion, dialogue, symposium, or forum-lecture method to present the problem to the audience. The specific problems related to these methods were considered in Chapter XVI. Occasionally, however, the forum as an institution may use the face-to-face discussion method, in which case the periods of presenting the problem and of conducting questions and answers do not exist. In many forums as institutions opportunities are provided, apart from the regular forums, for smaller groups to meet for round-table discussions.

B. THE QUESTION-AND-ANSWER PERIOD.

This part of the forum method has four principal uses and values: (1) to permit the audience to secure further information and to correlate ideas upon the problem; (2) to protect the audience from being misled by a presentation which may create erroneous impressions unless subjected to questioning; (3) to permit the introduction of material which might otherwise not be included in the

[8] See J. W. Studebaker and Chester S. Williams, *Choosing Our Way*, pp. 9-15, 28-30, 68.

discussion; (4) to give the audience an opportunity to participate—a value in itself over and above the other uses and values. Under the guidance of a skillful chairman and with an audience which is interested in a thorough examination of the problem, these values can be achieved with little difficulty.

Certain limitations may arise, however, when some persons attempt to start a series of arguments between the speaker and the audience or when they persist in asking irrelevant questions. These misuses have been found to arise invariably in those forums where the chairmen are relatively inexperienced or the audiences have not been trained to regard the forum as a place for a frank discussion of problems. Both the chairman and the audience, as well as the person or persons presenting the subject, can by their manner and their contributions make the forum a useful institution and method.

We are outlining here some of the duties and responsibilities of the three groups responsible for the proper conduct of the question-and-answer period: the chairman, the questioners, and the person or persons who presented the problem. In the event that there is no chairman—as is frequently the case, especially when a lecturer presents the subject—his duties will, of course, be assumed by the lecturer himself in the capacity of leader.

1. *The Duties and Responsibilities of the Chairman.*— The first major duty of the chairman is to decide whether participation by the audience is to be limited to written or oral questions, and whether expressions of opinion in addition to questions will be permitted. In the case of written questions he will also have to decide whether they are to be submitted at once or at any time during the question-and-answer period. Unless there is a standing rule or tradition governing this provision, the chairman should arrive at a decision and be careful to state the procedure at the beginning of the period. Otherwise misunderstandings may arise, and he may be charged with being discriminatory when he first invokes the rule.

Each of these plans of submitting questions has its merits. The method of presenting written questions at one time generally has the advantage of being somewhat more orderly. On the other hand, oral questions will probably be more timely and will arise more spontaneously from the course taken by the give-and-take of the previous questions. The chairman should also consider the advisability of permitting the audience to express opinions. In coming to a decision on this matter, he should consider time limits, the spirit of the audience, and the nature of the subject. Some chairmen permit brief comments from the first five or six persons who express a willingness to speak, while others permit comments only if there is time available after all questions have been asked. In any event, if comments from the audience are permitted, rigid time limits should be invoked for the common good.

The second duty of the chairman is to be ready to stimulate the audience to ask questions. If this is necessary—and in some instances this constitutes a very real problem for the chairman—he may do so by summarizing the presentation of the subject and by emphasizing several important implications arising out of it. This summary may often be in the form of a series of challenging questions. Another method is for him to ask the first question himself, thereby getting the period started. Upon some occasions he may call upon an experienced member of the audience to ask a question in order to stimulate others who are less experienced or more reticent. Another means is to ask a question of some member of the audience and help him to answer it if necessary. After the questioning has once started, the chairman can keep it going if necessary by giving credit to each person as he asks a question, using the person's name and judiciously complimenting him on the value of his question. The chairman should not force the questions from the audience. On the other hand, he should prefer to close the meeting after only one or two questions rather than to prolong the period if no real interest is shown. He needs to be alert and tactful to perform this duty skillfully.

The third duty of the chairman is to encourage the phrasing of brief and clear questions. By his own example he can encourage the audience to make the oral questions, in particular, brief and to the point. If necessary, he should rephrase those which are long and involved, and upon some occasions he may wisely interrupt the questioner and help him phrase his question more clearly.

His fourth duty is to keep the number of questions and the length of the period within reasonable limits. He should carefully watch the audience to see if it is maintaining interest and is spontaneous in its responses to the questions and answers. In the majority of cases he will probably do well to set a definite hour for closing even though interest may be fairly high. A number of forum chairmen follow the rule of limiting the entire meeting to one hour and a half, closing the question-and-answer period approximately by the clock. The federal forums, it will be remembered, averaged one hour and thirty-one minutes, with the question period averaging thirty-seven minutes. The chairman needs to exercise great care in controlling the length of this period both because the period itself will benefit and because the audience will receive a good final impression of the forum session. A long and dull period, artificially stimulated, can destroy the effectiveness of a good lecture or panel discussion, and can leave the audience with a bad impression of the values of the forum method.

Above all, the chairman should exercise ingenuity in making the period lively and varied and in bringing it to a satisfying close. He should be familiar with the various methods of concluding the period, such as a brief summary from himself, a brief summary from the lecturer, panel, or members of the symposium, or a mere dismissal of the audience after the answer to the last question. The clarity of the pattern of the discussion, the interest of the audience, and the time available should be considered by him before he decides upon the method to use. Ordinarily he should avoid any method which merely restates material which was clearly presented by the lecturer or thoroughly considered in the question-and-answer period.

2. *The Duties and Responsibilities of the Questioner.*— The first of the major responsibilities which the questioner has is to ask those questions which will be most useful to himself and to the occasion. He should ask questions designed to verify facts mentioned in the presentation of the problem, to produce additional facts, to clarify statements made in the lecture or other discussion, or to correlate various phases of the problem. If he wishes to open up new areas of thought, he should avoid asking questions which will start irrelevant arguments. By using good judgment and exercising self-restraint in this matter, he can do much to assist the chairman by avoiding misunderstandings and unpleasant or tense situations. Too frequently a chairman is faced with the charge of discrimination if he attempts to reject an irrelevant question even though his action is in the best interests of the group.

The questioner also has the responsibility of phrasing his questions and speaking in a manner that will maintain goodwill even in the midst of earnest discussion on controversial issues. He should avoid making the question period combative in spirit or a series of maneuvers between himself and the leader. He should refrain from "riding a hobby"; he should be fair and considerate; and he should honestly try to keep prejudice and strong feeling out of the discussion. He should realize that the average member of the audience would prefer adjournment to a continuation of an argument which issues largely from prejudice or an unyielding opinion. This responsibility cannot be too strongly emphasized. We have observed upon several occasions the near-disruption of forums by the insistence of members of the audience in diverting every phase of the subject to their favorite panacea. One person interrupted at frequent intervals a discussion of "America's Policy in the Orient" with references to Direct Credits as a remedy for all ills, and another insisted that a change in the economic order was the only solution for maladministration of city governments. In the first case a number of the others in the audience left the meeting in disgust, and in the other instance the leader risked being charged with high-handedness by suggesting to the offending member that he would be denied further privileges of this forum session. In either case the questioner could have saved trouble for himself and the chairman, and could have maintained the spirit of the forum on a higher plane if he had been more fair and considerate.

3. *The Duties and Responsibilities of Those Being Questioned.*—The persons being questioned can make the period profitable by paying careful attention to the phrasing of their replies and to their manner of speaking. They must be more than good lecturers or members of a panel. They must be quick-witted, alert to the interests of the audience, and interested in making the question-and-answer period more than a demonstration of their knowledge.

The following are some of the specific responsibilities concerning the phrasing of his replies which the person being questioned will do well to remember. First, he should briefly rephrase the question so that all persons in the audience can hear it. This may, of course, be unnecessary if the chairman has done so; but the person replying should take pains to see that it is done by somebody. Second, he should answer briefly. He should not give a speech even if the question may prompt extensive treatment. After all, the greatest values of this period ordinarily come from the asking of a number of questions and from participation by many people in the audience, not from another speech or symposium. Third, he should keep to the point of the question, relating it only briefly to the entire subject. There may be other questions waiting upon other phases, and he should not interfere with them. Fourth, he should leave the way open for further questions. This does not put a premium upon incompleteness, but stresses the need of stimulating the audience to explore the question further.

The manner of replying will also do much to determine the spirit of the occasion. The person being questioned should be friendly and cooperative, always encouraging the audience to participate. He should give credit to the questioner's knowledge and use it wherever possible, building his replies upon it and being quick to compliment good questions. Experienced forum leaders have discovered that this means of encouraging participation has two definite values. For one thing it stimulates this person and other persons to ask more questions. Also it encourages the members of the audience to emulate that type of phrasing and that manner of speaking which receive the most credit and attention from the leader. There are exceptions, of course, and this method is open to abuse by a leader who handles it to his selfish advantage; but in the hands of a sincere person it is a useful means of keeping the spirit of the question period on a high plane.

Above all, the person replying should not become angry at an antagonistic or impertinent member of the audience. He should attempt to deal with this person or his question solely on the merits of the case, then proceed to other questions. His own manner can often avoid embarrassment for himself and possible disruption of the forum. If he makes a curt reply, he will probably find himself confronted with an antagonistic audience, whereas invariably he will win the support of at least the majority if he deals diplomatically with a troublesome questioner.

EXERCISES

1. Present arguments for and against the forum method. Show why a panel discussion, a dialogue, a symposium, or a lecture is or is not adequate without a forum.

2. Observe a forum in operation. Describe its procedure. Appraise its usefulness. (Too much emphasis cannot be placed upon the values of having students of the technique of the forum attend an actual forum. Even if it should be necessary to travel to a different community to attend a forum, the time and effort spent in this project will bring abundant returns.)

3. In a well-organized essay present the arguments for and against the public or planned forum. Emphasize its values and limitations. Use material found in the bibliography at the end of this chapter.

4. Observe and appraise the work of a forum-chairman with respect to: (a) the stimulation of questions; (b) the encouragement of the proper phrasing of questions; (c) the proper spirit and length of the question-and-answer period; (d) the method of bringing the forum to a close.

5. Observe and appraise the work of a questioner and of one being questioned with respect to: (a) the content of their remarks; (b) the manner of their speaking.

6. Listen to a radio broadcast of a forum, for example a broadcast of a "Town Meeting of the Air." Criticize the following aspects of the question-and-answer period: (a) the work of the chairman in relation to the duties described in this chapter; (b) the work of the questioners in relation to the duties described in this chapter; (c) the work of the person being questioned in relation to the duties described in this chapter. See also Appendix C.

7. Criticize the question-and-answer period of each of the following discussions in *Discussion Methods for Adult Groups* by Fansler: (a) Forum-Lecture, pp. 7-25; (b) Forum Dialogue, pp. 29-51; (c) Panel Discussion, pp. 111-132. Comment upon the following: (a) the work of the chairman; (b) the work of the questioners; (c) the work of the person being questioned.

8. Criticize the question-and-answer period of each of the two discussions in *Religious Education* cited in the bibliography at the end of this chapter. Comment upon the following: (a) the work of the chairman; (b) the work of the questioners; (c) the work of the person being questioned.

9. Conduct forums in class following panel discussions, dialogues, symposiums, and lectures. Criticize the question-and-answer periods in the manner described in Exercise 6.

10. Prepare an eight- to ten-minute forum-lecture on some topic and be prepared to submit to questioning.

SELECTED BIBLIOGRAPHY

Artman, J. M., and Others, "The Problems Brought to Religious and Character Education by the Socio-Economic Debacle," *Religious Education*. Vol. 29, June, 1934, pp. 266-270. (A panel discussion.)

Courtis, Stuart A., and Others, "The Function of Education in Achieving and Maintaining a Social Order of Integrated Persons," *Religious Education*. Vol. 29, June, 1934, pp. 271-281. (A panel discussion.)

Eggersten, Claude, "Forums Then and Now," *School and Society*. Vol. 44, September 26, 1936, pp. 412-416.

Ely, Mary L., *Why Forums?* New York: American Association for Adult Education, 1937.

Fansler, Thomas, *Discussion Methods for Adult Groups*. New York: American Association for Adult Education, 1934.

Grant, Percy S., "The Open Forum Movement," *North American Review*. Vol. 203, January, 1916, pp. 81-92.

Grigsby, Rall I., "Ideas Have a Chance in Des Moines," *Progressive Education*. Vol. 11, April-May, 1934, pp. 283-287.

Lurie, Reuben L., *The Challenge of the Forum—the Story of Ford Hall and the Open Forum Movement*. Boston: Richard R. Badger, Publisher, 1930.

Lyman, R. L., "The Forum as an Educative Agency," *Quarterly Journal of Speech*. Vol. 1, April, 1915, pp. 1-8.

Orchard, Harry A., *Fifty Years of Chautauqua*. Cedar Rapids, Iowa: Torch Press, 1923.

Studebaker, John W., *The American Way*. New York: McGraw-Hill Book Company, Inc., 1935.

Studebaker, J. W., and Williams, Chester S., *Choosing Our Way*. United States Department of the Interior, Office of Education, Bulletin 1937, Misc. No. 1.

Studebaker, J. W., and Williams, Chester S., *A Step Forward for Adult Education*. United States Department of the Interior, Office of Education, Bulletin 1936, No. 16.

Studebaker, J. W., and Williams, Chester S., *Education for Democracy: Public Affairs Forums*. United States Department of the Interior, Office of Education, Bulletin 1935, No. 17.

Wooddy, Carroll H., "Forum Facts," *Journal of Adult Education*. Vol. 7, July, 1935, pp. 290-296.

CHAPTER XVIII

DISCUSSION IN SPEECH EDUCATION

In this chapter we shall be concerned with the role of discussion in speech education: What should be the place of discussion in the speech curriculum? We shall consider: (1) courses in discussion; (2) discussion as a tool in an integrated speech curriculum; (3) discussion as a tool in other speech courses; and (4) discussion in extra-curricular speech activities.

I. COURSES IN DISCUSSION

A course in discussion is one which aims to teach the principles and methods of discussion. It has as its primary objective the dissemination of knowledge concerning discussion and the development of skills in discussion. It aims to train good participants and leaders in informal discussion groups and to provide at least the rudimentary techniques for successful membership on a panel, in a dialogue, or in a symposium.

The usefulness of courses in discussion can be measured in terms of both social and individual needs. As we have repeatedly said in preceding chapters, democratic society presupposes critical thinking, freedom from exploitative propaganda, and careful deliberation in the spirit of cooperation. It needs citizens who can attack social problems in the same way that scientific problems are met, citizens who are willing and able to approach their common problems reflectively and cooperatively. It needs citizens who recognize the difference between propaganda and education, and between intentional reasoning and discussion. It is here that courses in discussion can be useful. By means of the philosophy and practice which they provide, the scientific point of view can be implanted and the proficient practice of discussion can be provided in a manner that is both systematic and practical. It is probably not too much to say that speech education can do as much in the training of critical thinkers and conferees as it can in the training of capable advocates, a function in which its usefulness is well established.

Courses in discussion can meet the two types of individual needs which confront speech education: (1) the needs of the prospective teachers of speech and (2) the needs of the average students in the typical school and after-school speech situations.

That the first of these needs is no imaginary possibility may be seen from a survey of nearly every textbook in the high school or college field. In some respect, either by title or by the contents of the chapters, the recent books are incorporating some of the features of discussion. Even texts in argumentation are being tempered by the point of view of discussion. This trend raises an important question as to the proper training ground for the teachers of these modified courses or of the courses in discussion which will probably follow inevitably this trend toward modification. Shall these teachers be prepared solely in public speaking and argumentation? Shall they teach the theory and practice of discussion by personal experimentation and whatever assistance they can receive from the textbooks? We submit that the properly trained teacher of speech should be as familiar with the field of discussion and as competent in its methodology as with any other aspect of speech education.

The second need becomes self-evident when one considers the typical school and after-school speech situations in which the student finds himself. After all, only a comparatively small percentage of high school and college students deliver public speeches in school or after-school situations. On the other hand, every person participates in discussions in the home, the school, and the community. The applications of discussion are almost as broad as speech itself. As was said in Chapter II, "Every person has a responsibility to himself and to society to develop knowledge, attitudes, and skills which will enable him to grow to his full stature in ability to cooperate with others for the attainment of common and reciprocal ends."

This is a need for more than the spirit of discussion. It is also a need for more than random, trial-and-error methods of developing skills in discussion. It is a need for a systematic procedure which will provide a complete and well-organized body of information about discussion together with opportunities for practice with criticism. This need can be met best by directed experiences in discussion which provide a systematic approach to the principles of discussion and—more important—provide the means of securing skills by actually participating in discussions under the guidance of an informed teacher and critic.

II. DISCUSSION AS A TOOL IN AN INTEGRATED SPEECH CURRICULUM

There are in general two fairly distinct conceptions of the curriculum today: one, commonly called the traditional or subject-matter curriculum, and the other, the progressive, activity, or integrated curriculum. The organization of the first is in terms of human knowledge, such as history, English, and geography. Briefly, it consists in passing on to the student more or less compartmentalized areas of information on the theory of preparing the individual for adult life by equipping him with a knowledge of our cultural heritage.

The so-called integrated or activity curriculum is organized with respect to the guided interests of the student and consists in a program of directed activities with emphasis on the growth of the student in his capacity to think and act intelligently in problem situations. Any single activity may involve experiences which elicit information and help from a large number of the usual subject-matter fields. In other words, the curriculum becomes the experiences of the individual organized with respect to democratically planned and executed activities and conducted under the guidance of competent teachers. Knowledge of the cultural heritage is developed as it is requisitioned by the interests and needs of the learners working in problem situations.

While students in a core or integrated curriculum will need development in all types of speech skills, the peculiar application of discussion to the needs of such a curriculum is clearly indicated. The broad objectives of an activity program and those of discussion are essentially identical in many respects, such as criticism, cooperation, and communication; and what is more, the group meetings in the integrated curriculum are discussion situations. Here problems are discussed, projects planned and reported in the spirit and method of reflective thought and cooperative group work. Is it not possible for the teacher of speech to capitalize upon these speech experiences for the purpose of teaching the accepted fundamentals of speech? Few would deny the possibility of contributing to the development of students in basic speech skills in such a program.

The activity program aims at individual growth in terms of ability in thinking and responsible acting. Such thinking and acting must of necessity be done in cooperation with others. The need for competence in communication is at hand at every turn. The planning of activities involves group deliberation, and "growth" must certainly include the development of language skills. As soon as people begin to think and act in social situations, there is constant occasion for speech. The very thinking which goes into the planning for action must of necessity be intimately associated with language. Thought becomes socially operative only when it is communicated. The speech teacher can and must render invaluable assistance in any activity program at its most central and crucial point—the point where the activity is being planned. Speech is inevitable at this point, and the success of the planning cannot help but be importantly conditioned by the nature and character of the deliberations which take place. What is our chief interest here is the inevitable importance in such a program of knowledge about and proficiency in discussion.[1]

III. DISCUSSION AS A TOOL IN OTHER SPEECH COURSES

Here we are concerned with the use of discussion as a tool in the fundamentals course and in courses in public speaking and in argumentation. In these cases the purpose is not primarily to provide training in discussion for the sake of discussion, but to aid other speech courses better to realize their purposes. There is much to be said for the usefulness of discussion as a tool in teaching the fundamentals of speech as well as in courses in public speaking and in argumentation, not to divert these to new purposes but to make them more effective in the tasks which they now have.

A. THE FUNDAMENTALS COURSE.

The first, or foundation, course in any speech curriculum is ordinarily the fundamentals course. It is not designed to concentrate on public speaking, argumentation, or interpretation, but usually is presented to

[1] Quoted with some revisions from James H. McBurney, "Speech Education in an Integrated Curriculum," *The Southern Speech Bulletin*, Vol. II, October, 1936, pp. 11-12.

provide knowledge and training in the fundamentals of speech which can be applied to any specialized field. It ordinarily is concerned with two major things: (1) the development of the individual as a person, a thinking and feeling being, in so far as a course in speech can do so, and (2) the training of competence in the rudiments of oral communication. It thus attempts not only to provide training in speech skills, but also to inspire an intellectual and an emotional point of view which will make the student a good thinker and a keen analyst as well as one who is appreciative of the highest values in society. It thus aims to provide an introduction to many fields other than the more limited skills in voice and bodily action, and at the same time to train the student to secure reasonable confidence and poise, directness, effective bodily action, vocal control, and some competence in oral composition.

This course has normally been taught by means of platform exercises, drills, and textbook work, with the platform work consisting of exercises in public speaking or interpretation, together with individual or group drills in bodily action and voice.

The question is now raised: Can discussion be a useful tool to supplement, not supplant, either or both of these other tools in the fundamentals course? In order to answer this question it is necessary to consider the purposes of this course, the methods which may be used, and the values and limitations of discussion in this situation.

If we accept as a working basis for our discussion here the statement of purposes provided by Sarett and Foster in *Basic Principles of Speech*, we shall conceive of this course as being the means of "setting up good speech habits." It will have two main objectives, one pertaining to the broad development of the individual, the other concerned with the development of specific speech habits and skills. The broad objective, which is concerned with the training of the mind and the development of the character, is expressed by Sarett and Foster as follows:

The setting up of good speech habits trains the mind in many ways. Efforts to speak well force a man to clarify his more or less nebulous thoughts, to strike out the irrelevant, to synthesize materials, to subordinate minor points, to drive at the heart of issues, and to state them without waste of words. . . .

Training in speech—the right kind of training—develops character. By character we mean those attributes which give color, beauty, vivacity, and strength to personality. They are as the sands of the sea. They are not confined to the "noble virtues." They include the qualities of a man's mind, its keenness or dullness, its depth or shallowness; the qualities of his heart, tolerance or intolerance, compassion or ruthlessness; his aspirations, high or low; his balance, courage, initiative—these and countless other attributes.[2]

To this broad objective there is added the more specific purpose of gaining competence in the fundamentals of speech: "voice, bodily action, melody, time, force, construction, diction, and style."[3]

That the traditional methods of teaching this course can do much to achieve these objectives there can be no doubt. The use of public speaking as a tool trains the student to grapple with a problem, analyze it, organize materials concerning it, and communicate these materials in the best possible manner. Similarly, the use of interpretative reading should develop mental powers of discrimination and analysis, good taste and fine balance, and competence in many of the more specialized speech skills.

Discussion may also be a useful tool in helping to achieve these objectives. It should aid in training the mind. The very act of thinking reflectively according to the logical pattern influences one to think in an orderly

[2] Lew Sarett and William Trufant Foster, *Basic Principles of Speech* (Boston: Houghton Mifflin Company, 1936), p. 6.
[3] *Ibid.*, p. 16.

manner. There is also training in careful definition and analysis of a problem, including attention to values which are desired in any proposal. In addition, there is careful treatment of proposed solutions and there is reasoning as to their validity. The very process of reflective thinking forces one to phrase his thoughts exactly, and the process of group deliberation encourages economical and exact phrasing in order to make one's contributions clear and meaningful to the group.

Similarly, discussion should aid in training what Sarett and Foster call the *character*. Reflective thinking requires keenness of mind in order to penetrate into a problem to determine its causes and to speculate as to the solutions. It is probable that group deliberation in the manner of reflective thinking will more quickly than any other means of expression expose shallow and dull thinking, because here there is no opportunity for finely conceived proofs and appeals to do more than the credentials of the thought itself would indicate should be done. Tolerance and compassion can be cultivated through discussion if anywhere. Participation in a group where ideas are presented and rejected in a spirit of cooperative search for a solution to a problem should cultivate at least some measure of concern for the attitudes of other persons. Finally, discussion should cultivate that fine balance of initiative and concern for others which Sarett and Foster stress as a quality of the well-trained person. Discussion means cooperation and group responsibility. It should exert an influence in the direction of a balance between individualism in thinking and group effort in pooling contributions toward a common outcome.

What is more, the discussion approach serves a useful purpose in introducing the student to vital contemporary problems and in developing critical attitudes toward the ideas which he attempts to communicate to others.

Discussion may not always cultivate the more specific speech skills as fully as may public speaking and interpretation, although in some instances it has been very effective in teaching good habits in voice and diction. Discussion should provide some means of achieving skill in the organization of ideas and in the cultivation of a style which is clear and forceful, even if different in all other respects from that of the persuasive speech. It may not always accomplish as much in bodily action, melody, time, and force as platform work can; and in this respect it needs other tools to supplement its contributions to the full development of the student of speech.

The procedure which will probably use to best advantage both the methods of platform speaking and those of discussion includes informal discussion, the more formal methods for co-acting groups, a few drills in voice and pronunciation, and discussions and examinations on the textbook if one is used. The schedule should ordinarily provide for informal conversations at the outset, followed by more systematic group discussion, in turn followed by all of the other forms, as the panel discussion, the dialogue, the symposium, and the lecture. These in turn would lead into assignments in platform speaking and/or interpretative reading. Thus the two methods, discussion and platform work, can supplement each other to achieve the objective of the course which attempts to cultivate broad intellectual and "character" qualifications as well as meet the more specific speech needs.

These theoretical values of discussion have been verified at least in a limited way by several teachers who have experimented with units of discussion in certain courses in fundamentals. Even if sometimes subjective and not always broad enough to be conclusive, these experiments disclose some significant results and point to the usefulness of discussion as a tool.

One experiment, in particular, is suggestive of the possibilities which lie in this direction. The experimenter, a teacher in a Southern college, attempted to use adequate controls and objective methods throughout. Using a "control group," which was conducted on the traditional basis, and a parallel "experimental group," which used discussion as a supplementary tool, the experimenter administered several tests of personality, attitudes, scientific thinking, knowledge of contemporary affairs, and skills in voice, bodily action, and diction. A comparison of the results obtained from the tests administered at the beginning of the experimental period with those obtained from the later tests showed that the group using discussion gained more knowledge than did the other group, that the group using discussion developed the scientific attitude more completely, and that this group also gained some of the attributes of the person described by Murray as the "objective introvert," attributes which are regarded by many observers as ideal for all persons except those whose duties particularly require extroversion.[4]

This experiment showed that growth in the specific speech skills was about evenly divided between the two groups. The platform-speaking group appeared to have made greater gains in the improvement of posture, manner of walking, and bodily action, whereas the experimental group made greater gains in voice and diction.[5]

The possibilities of increasing usefulness in discussion as a tool in the fundamentals course remain to be explored and tested by further experimentation, but experience seems to suggest many opportunities for the coordination of the discussion and platform methods.

B. Courses in Public Speaking and Argumentation.

In those speech courses which are designed to train advocates there is also a place for discussion. To the extent that discussion can make the trained advocate think logically and scientifically in his exploration of the problem and to be accurate and critical, this method should be useful in a course in public speaking or argumentation.

[4] Elwood Murray, *The Speech Personality* (Philadelphia: J. B. Lippincott Company, 1937), pp. 78-80.
[5] This experiment was conducted by Miss Alma Johnson and reported by her in a paper entitled "An Experimental Study of Group Discussion as a Method of Teaching Certain Fundamentals of Speech" (unpublished study, Northwestern University).

For example, the exploratory stages of investigation and analysis, even if upon a predetermined proposition, will in all probability be more valuable with the aid of discussion than if performed at random.

We recognize the importance of the trained advocate in a democratic society; but we also recognize the fact that the social justification of persuasion and advocacy will be much clearer when we know that the advocate has reached his conclusion reflectively. Here discussion admirably supplements persuasion and argumentation.

IV. DISCUSSION IN EXTRA-CURRICULAR SPEECH ACTIVITIES

For several decades extra-curricular activities in speech have consisted of debates, extemporaneous speaking contests, and oratorical contests designed to assist in the training of advocates. Their educational justification has rested in the fact that through them students are motivated to put into practice the knowledge and skills studied and practiced in the classroom. And this is justification enough, because there can be little question as to the value of the motivation arising from contests, whether intramural or interscholastic.

During the past few years, however, a number of educators have concluded that the changing emphasis in classroom teaching should be accompanied by a changing emphasis in extra-curricular activities. They have attempted to correlate the exercise which trains the advocate with the exercise which trains the investigator or reflective thinker. They have wished to motivate the training of both intentional, or projective, reasoners and reflective, or investigative, thinkers. They have sought to place as much emphasis upon working *to* a proposition as upon working *from* a proposition. Consequently, they have proposed several modifications of traditional debate and other contests in public speaking to include wherever possible certain elements of both discussion and persuasion.

In some cases the modification has been slight. Frequently the basic point of view of debate has been retained, but provision has been made for a slightly broader treatment of the proposition together with some participation by the audience. In other cases the emphasis is about evenly divided between reflective thinking and intentional reasoning, with both discussion and persuasion included in that order in a given exercise or project. In these cases the attempt has been to construct an exercise which begins with a problem, analyzes it, proposes solutions, and argues the merits of these solutions. Here discussion in method and spirit is used until the final step, when persuasion or argumentation becomes the method.

In describing these plans, we are not attempting a rigid classification into discussion or persuasion. To do so would be unwise, because several of the plans can be placed in either category depending upon the emphasis which an observer places on one feature or another of the plans. Rather, we are presenting a continuum, with one pole representing pure advocacy (debate, oratory, etc.) and the other discussion; and we are arraying a number of plans along that line. Our purpose is to call attention to both the existence of these plans and their relations to discussion and persuasion.

The typical debate, with its two teams upholding the two sides of a proposition, is too well known to require description here. It is an example of pure advocacy, of presenting the best possible case for each side of the predetermined proposition. It ordinarily limits the discussion to a consideration of the two sides of the proposition, the only exception being in the case of argument over a counter-proposition submitted by the negative.

A slight modification is seen in the three-sided debate, which has three teams, each upholding a solution or plan. The proponents of this form of debate believe that, as there are ordinarily more than two sides to a proposition, thorough treatment requires the consideration of at least three plans. Here is a slight movement toward discussion.

While the element of intentional reasoning remains, there is a breadth of approach which is nearer that of discussion than that of the traditional debate.[6]

A further slight modification is observed in the "direct clash" plan of debate. Here the number of persons on a team is flexible—two to five—and the duties of the members of the two teams are somewhat different from the traditional duties. The first affirmative speaker defines the terms, explains the affirmative proposal, and explains the issues of the debate. The first negative speaker then replies, indicating the issues accepted for a clash and those admitted. The debate must then be limited to those issues upon which there is disagreement. The purpose of the preliminary speeches is to outline the issues, present the affirmative plan and the negative counter-plan—if there is one—and prepare the way for the introduction of proofs in the subsequent speeches. While this plan is, of course, primarily debate, it does have some features of discussion, such as: (1) the provision for a period of definition; (2) the provision for explanation of issues and solutions before argument takes place.[7]

A further modification is observed in the cross-question type of debate. Whether it is a dialogue, the court technique, or the typical "Oregon Plan," it has greater variety and adaptability than the traditional debate. It is still an example of intentional reasoning, and the two sides of a proposition are present; but it has some of the features of discussion.

A very important modification is seen in four plans which have several features in common: (1) The Debate

[6] See: Raymond F. Howes, *Debating* (New York: D. C. Heath and Company, 1931), p. 138; James M. O'Neill and James H. McBurney, *The Working Principles of Argument* (New York: The Macmillan Company, 1932), p. 356; Carroll P. Lahman, *Debate Coaching* (New York: H. W. Wilson Company, 1936), p. 41; Robert Young, "Debate at Washington University," *The Gavel*, Vol. XIV, May, 1932, pp. 18-19.

[7] See Edwin H. Paget, "Rules for the Direct Clash Plan," *The Quarterly Journal of Speech*, Vol. XXIII, October, 1937, pp. 431-433.

Symposium; (2) The Co-operative Investigation; (3) The Intercollegiate Forum; and (4) The Problem Solving Debate.

The Debate Symposium provides for four teams of two members each. The first speaker for each team states his team's position, and the subsequent speakers may amplify their colleagues' remarks, may cross-question any of the speakers of the other teams, may refute any of the preceding arguments, or may restate and summarize the positions which they are upholding. Ordinarily the audience is invited to participate in an open forum at the conclusion of the speeches of the debaters.[8]

The Co-operative Investigation provides for the analysis of a problem in a manner similar to that of Dewey's steps in problem solving, each speaker of the six in a group being assigned to a topic. The first three speeches are in a category called "Understanding the Problem," and the others pertain to "Suggested Solutions." The first three speeches are explanatory and investigative, whereas the last three are argumentative and advocatory.[9]

The Intercollegiate Forum provides for a group of four speakers, the first explaining the background and present status of the problem as a basis for the proposals of the other speakers. Each of the other speakers then presents a proposal as a solution to the problem, then continues with a speech of restatement or refutation of the plans submitted. There is no premium placed upon the maintenance of the point of view originally held; in fact, a speaker may withdraw his proposal and proceed to defend the point of view of another speaker if he wishes. The features of this Forum in the direction of discussion are several: (1) It provides for orderly definition and analysis of the problem; (2) it provides for the introduction of several proposals; and (3) it

[8] See H. F. Harding, "A Debate Symposium," *The Speaker*, Vol. XX, May, 1938, p. 6.

[9] See H. L. Ewbank, "The Wisconsin Public Discussion Contest," *The Gavel*, Vol. XX, May, 1938, p. 54.

makes provision for a modification of one's original position.[10]

The Problem Solving Debate provides for three sets of speeches (analysis, solution, and evaluating) by two teams of two or three speakers each. The duty of the first speaker on each team is to present an unbiased analysis of the problem. His function is to give all the facts necessary to an understanding of the situation which has produced the problem, to discover the factors involved in the solution of the problem, and if possible to set up certain criteria by which the solutions may be judged. The duty of the second speaker is to present the solution which he and his teammates believe to be the best one, and to show why this solution is the best and why it would solve the problem. The duty of the third speaker on each team (in the case of two-speaker teams the first speaker usually presents the third speech also) is to weigh the solutions presented by both sides, agreeing or disagreeing as the case may be. He may question any of the previous speakers, and they must answer briefly and to the point. His conclusion may agree or disagree with that of his colleague; his aim should be to discover the best solution regardless of his past beliefs. He may even offer a new solution if it seems warranted.

The three sets of speeches are judged upon the following bases: (1) analysis speeches—unbiased approach, adequate presentation of facts, successful discovery of difficulties, adequate criteria for judgment, effective presentation; (2) solution speeches—freedom from prejudice, cooperative effort, logical argument, adequacy of solution to meet analyzed difficulties, effective presentation; (3) evaluating speeches—fair and judicial attitude, analysis and comparison of solutions presented, soundness of conclusions, cooperative effort, effective presentation.

The features of the Problem Solving Debate in the di-

[10] See A. B. Williamson, "A Proposed Change in Intercollegiate Debating," *The Quarterly Journal of Speech*, Vol. XIX, February, 1933, pp. 192, 200-202.

rection of discussion are several: (1) It provides for orderly definition and analysis of the problem, including attention to criteria for the judging of solutions; (2) it provides for the introduction of several proposals; (3) it provides for the informal give-and-take of discussion through questions and answers; and (4) it provides for a modification of one's original position, even to the point of disagreeing with that of one's colleague.[11]

The next modifications constitute significant departures from traditional debate. In the Forensic Experience Progression and the Intercollegiate Debate Convention each participant proceeds through several stages in essentially the method and spirit of discussion. He engages first in a round-table or informal discussion group, then proceeds to a panel discussion and perhaps a symposium, and finally to legislative or contest debate. In the respect that each person uses all these procedures, these plans represent probably the most extensive modifications of traditional debate and contests in persuasion in the direction of discussion.

The Forensic Experience Progression has been described by its originator as follows:

Objectives of the progression. The Forensic Experience Progression has been developed as a method to help make the Social studies more functional in the lives of students and citizens: The chief aim is to promote a series of speech experiences which will, (1) encourage growth in both co-operative skills and powers of independent critical evaluation, (2) deepen and widen knowledges and insights in relation to the particular vital question in the social order selected for the experiences, and (3) enhance effectiveness in the human relations and social adjustment of the students participating.

General plan of the progression: The plan may be used to take the place of a forensic tournament, or an extra-curricular activity, or a classroom unit of learning. Panels

---

[11] See Frederick W. Orr and Albert L. Franzke, "The University of Washington Plan of Problem Solving Debate," *Bulletin of the University of Washington* (Extension Series), No. 8, January, 1938.

of four or six speakers may enter a single progression. The amount of time required is flexible. The entire progression may be run off in the time allowed for a two or three day conventional forensic tournament. In this case exhaustive preparation will have been undergone during several preceding months. Or, considerable time may elapse between the presentation of each stage. A number of progressions may be run off simultaneously according to the number of students participating and schools represented. Separate progressions may be arranged for students grouped homogeneously according to abilities, sex, academic levels, etc.

Extemporaneous speaking, discussion, and debate are integrated in a functional order following Dewey's, "How We Think" sequence of problem, solution, action. The Progression is centered on a proposition which takes the form of a question for action such as, "What should be done to improve effectiveness of state legislatures?" or other questions to be formulated according to the interests of individuals or groups concerned. The speech experiences include the preparation and presentation of three forum panel discussions, one extemporaneous talk, and six one speaker team debates. Those speech experiences are organized around five sub-topics inherent in each proposition as outlined below.

Standards of achievements are set up throughout the progression with a means of rating carried on the cumulative record card of each speaker entering a progression. Throughout the progression each student will have the stimulation of other minds working intensely and sincerely on a problem the significance of which constantly increases to him. At each stage the speaker is required to formulate his own particular point of view, to defend it, or to change it, according to his own convictions as the truth is revealed to him. At no point will the student feel himself in competition with others; he will at all times have a constant challenge to a more intelligent and effective achievement. Standards are designated such as to discourage any form of rivalry or exhibitionism. The following is a description of each stage of the progression with the designation of standards of achievement.

First stage. Problem phase. Forum panel discussion on the sub-topic, "What is the problem and to what extent is it significant?" Each speaker presents a five to seven minute forum talk in which he gives a critical evaluation of the significance of the problem. He analyzes, defines, and interprets. The outline of his talk should include, (1) a statement of the facts and evidence showing the nature, scope, and extent of the problem. This should include, (a) a clear-cut statement of the position taken toward the problem by the groups who have the largest "stakes" in it, and (b) an analysis of where these interest-stakes agree and where they disagree. The talk should furthermore include, (2) a projection of the problem into the future and an indication of its effect in the social order, and (3) its effect upon the speaker as a member of that social order.

After the round of forum talks each speaker is given five minutes in which he criticises the viewpoints of other members of the panel, defends his own viewpoint, or modifies it if his convictions change. If there is any misunderstanding of terms he defines and analyzes as may be necessary; if there is confusion of views he clearly draws the issues. All talks after the first forum talk should take direct cognizance of viewpoints in preceding talks, state clearly the extent of agreement or disagreement and the reasons therefor. Where a speaker's views coincide with a previous speaker he should not repeat what has already been said, but add fresh supporting materials to the views agreed to.

After the constructive talks, at all stages, the chairman should allot about one-half hour for questions and brief comments by the audience. The chairman will keep the discussion to the point and will summarize from time to time whatever consensus is arrived at or what clear-cut differences remain.

Second stage. Problem phase continued. Formal panel discussion on the sub-topic, "What are the most important causes of the problem?" The speaking procedure is the same as in the first stage. The analysis begun in the first stage is continued to deeper levels. Here the speaker traces the causes of the problem as he conceives them to be as the result of his reading, conferences with authorities, and his own particular meditation. He must be able to trace sequences of cause and effect and to reason by analogy and example. His talk makes the following points: (1) the origin of the problem and the influences which have contributed to it, (2) the factors which all agree must be met in any solution of the problem, and (3) the factors on which there is disagreement and which must be accommodated in any solution of the problem. He evaluates the causes as presented by the other members of his progression. He is concerned with forces and principles which operate in the social order and their relation to the problem discussed.

Third stage. Solution phase. Extemporaneous talk on subtopic, "What are the solutions to the problem?" Each speaker on the progression will have five to seven minutes. The solutions are to be outlined, but not argued about in this stage. The object of the talk is to require the student to give evidence that he is informed about the chief alternatives in solution of the problem. He (1) states what he conceives the solutions to be, (2) explains them clearly and lucidly, and (3) rates them in the order of his present preference. Where a preceding speaker has clearly explained a solution which the student intends to support, he should either add fresh materials or merely mention the plan without repeating or rehashing materials already given.

Fourth stage. Solution phase continued. Debates on subtopic, "What is the best solution to the problem?" Immediately after the third stage the director or critic or judge of the progression meets with the speakers to formulate the several debate propositions which will constitute the debate series. A chief object of the debates is to require the student to commit himself definitely on a practical question as faced by a citizen who must make similar "yes" or "no" decisions in everyday life. Alternatives representative of the chief schools of thought and interests at stake should be worked out in a general discussion session. For instance, if the question pertains to improvement of state legislatures, the alternatives for debate might be, "Resolved, that educational requirements for the legislature should include the B. A. degree," and "Resolved, that the unicameral form of legislature should be adopted," and "Resolved, that the split session legislature (as in California) should be adopted," and, "Resolved, that legislature representation should be on the basis of occupation (as in Italy)," and, "Resolved, that the initiative and referendum should be adopted," etc. All negative counter plans to any proposition set up should be included as additional propositions at this point.

Each speaker may suggest the alternative which he wishes to advance and for which he is willing to assume the burden of proof. Each speaker will be required to take the affirmative in favor of his alternative for three debates and the negative against one, two, or three of the other alternatives for three debates. This schedule pertains to the six debates. After each debate for the affirmative he may change to the affirmative of another alternative according as his convictions change, provided that opponents can be found and the series of debates may proceed. Persons who have not formulated their convictions are assigned to fill in as may be necessary to administer the series.

Throughout these debates the speaker will connect the propositions defended or attacked from the standpoint of the causes and interests which must be accommodated if the problem is to be solved and which were arrived at in stage two. In case a speaker finds himself in partial agreement with an opponent care should be taken at the outset to make explicit the exact points of agreement and disagreement between the two sides.

Establishment of burden of proof for a proposition advanced will, in many cases, require the outlining of a plan. As in conventional debate all questions of constitutionality will be waived. But this should not necessarily be done in the action phase in the next stage.

Either one speaker or two speaker teams may be used although the one-speaker method is preferable in this case. Each one-speaker team debate will usually be one-half hour in length. The affirmative will have three periods of six, six, and three minutes respectively. Interspersed will be the two negative talks of eight and seven minutes respectively.

Fifth stage. Action phase. Forum panel discussion on sub-topic, "What, as citizens, will be our program to put into effect the necessary remedies?" This is probably the most important stage of the progression and the aspect of learning which in other educational procedures is most frequently neglected. It provides a necessary and valuable followup into the life of the student as a citizen.

The speaking procedure is the same as for the first two stages. Each forum talk will include the following in its outline: (1) a summary of the effect upon the speaker's thinking of experience in preparing and presenting the projects in this progression, (2) an explicit statement summarizing what measure or measures the speaker regards should be put into effect to solve the problem according to his present thinking, (3) a statement of what the speaker considers to be the chief obstacles in the acceptance of the program outlined, (4) an outline of proposed procedures to overcome these obstacles, (5) a statement of what special means, if any, the speaker proposes to undertake to make himself competent to do his part as a citizen in solution of this particular problem.

The work in stages one, two, and five may be simplified by reducing the main topics in each stage to a number of sub-topics. This would be done by the teachers, coaches, and experts on the question. Each student may then draw a sub-topic and prepare and deliver his talk as in the conventional extemporaneous speaking contests.

Criticisms and scores. After each stage a criticism of the work of each speaker should be given by a speech teacher or other person competent in discussion and speech technics. He will also give a rating to be entered on the cumulative record card for each student in the progression. At the end of the progression each student will be given his score card. The names of those doing superior work, or showing the most development through progression may be announced.[12]

The Intercollegiate Debate Convention has been described as follows:

The original Intercollegiate Debate Convention held at Syracuse University in the spring of 1933, exceeded everyone's expectations. Said Dr. Russell Wagner of Cornell, "It

[12] Elwood Murray, "The Forensic Experience Progression," *The Gavel*, Vol. XX, May, 1938, pp. 56-58. Reprinted in full by permission of Professor Murray.

is exciting, stimulating, intensive, realistic."[13] There were about one hundred fifty debaters, representing seventeen colleges and universities of New York, in attendance.

The second Convention, held in April 1934 at Colgate University, was attended by all schools who participated in the first one, plus six more. There were one hundred eighty debaters present. The 1935 Convention was entertained by the New York State College for Teachers at Albany. Student Assemblies were held in the chambers of the New York State Legislature, heightening the realism of the debates. Two hundred debaters, representing twenty-six institutions, attended. Buffalo University was host for the 1936 meeting. It was feared that the lack of central location might seriously reduce attendance, but twenty-six schools sent two hundred delegates. The 1937 Convention is to be held in Syracuse.

The plan seems to be spreading to other parts of the country. In 1934, the Northeast Ohio Debate Conference sponsored a Convention which has since become an annual event for schools in that state.[14] In March 1936, a Convention was held at Pennsylvania State College, most of the schools of that state being represented.[15]

Each of our New York Conventions has managed to improve upon the technique of its predecessors in some respect. Since the original Syracuse Convention, which the author has described,[16] a number of important changes have been made. Our present procedure is as follows:

Early in January, shortly after the State Legislature convenes, we ask Governor Lehman to suggest a list of the most important problems which will face the legislature during the coming session. From this list, a committee of coaches selects three. The committee then words the topics, using this general form: "What should the State of New York do about the problem of highway safety?" Announce-

---

[13] Russell H. Wagner, "An Experiment in Discussion," *The Emerson Quarterly*, Vol. 15, No. 2, January, 1935.

[14] W. Roy Diem, "Student Conference on Public Affairs," *The Gavel*, Vol. XVIII, January, 1936.

[15] "News and Notes," *The Quarterly Journal of Speech*, Vol. XXII, December, 1936, pp. 710-711.

[16] Milton Dickens, "Intercollegiate Convention Debating," *The Quarterly Journal of Speech*, Vol. XX, February, 1934.

ment of these questions reaches all schools by early February. The director of debate at each school immediately divides his squad into three groups, assigning one of the topics to each group. The students spend the next several weeks unearthing all possible facts relating to their topics. Next, the students in each group try to agree upon an answer to the question, "In view of these facts, what is the best solution for the problem?" If they can agree, the final step in preparation is the drawing up of a bill, following a prescribed form. Bills are limited to a maximum length of one typewritten page. As the date of the Convention approaches, the coach selects those who have done the best work to be his official delegates. Each school is entitled to a maximum of three delegates on each of the three topics. In addition, a coach may send as many alternates or observers as he desires.

The Convention itself occupies two days, a Friday and Saturday. The official events are in this order: Opening Assembly, Preliminary Committee Meetings, Main Committee Meetings, Informal Banquet, Social Event, General Assembly.

The Opening Assembly is called to order by a Temporary Chairman at eleven o'clock Friday morning. About an hour is required to elect a student chairman and secretary; hear the address of welcome and special messages; make announcements.

The Preliminary Committee Meetings require less than an hour. They are held at noon, immediately following the Opening Assembly, the three Committees meeting simultaneously in different rooms. Each Committee elects a chairman and secretary. Bills, which have been submitted by any of the delegates, are then read and, if necessary, explained, but may not be debated or acted upon at this meeting. These preliminary sessions are a recent invention and save endless time.

After lunch, the *Main Committee Meetings* convene. It is the job of each group to discuss and debate its topic, reach a majority agreement as to a solution, put that solution into form of a bill. The students may adopt or alter one of the bills offered by a particular delegation, or construct an entirely new bill. As soon as a majority of the

Committee have agreed upon the basic contents of a bill, they elect a sub-committee to word it properly, and a majority leader to arrange for its defense on the floor of the General Assembly next morning. Meanwhile, if there is a militant minority, they will meet and agree upon a minority proposal to be presented from the floor in the form of an amendment. They also elect a sub-committee to draft the amendment, and a leader to organize its defense.

All delegates gather at six-thirty for an *informal banquet*, featured by one-minute after-dinner talks by a delegate from each school.

Following the banquet, students on sub-committees set to work drafting bills or amendments. Delegates, whose work is done, are provided with a *social event*. Throughout the evening, however, majority and minority leaders may be observed circulating among the other delegates trying to gain votes for their measures.

Sometime between nine and ten o'clock Saturday morning the *General Assembly* is called to order by the student Chairman. He summarizes the rules, announces the order in which the Committees shall report, and calls for the reading of the majority report of the first Committee on the list. Following the reading of the bill, the majority leader is given ten minutes in which to explain and defend the bill. Next, all minority groups are given an opportunity to present amendments and minority leaders are given five minutes to defend their proposals. When the floor is thrown open to general debate, the Chair limits each speaker to two or three minutes and recognizes majority and minority speakers alternately. Total debate on each topic is limited to about an hour. There is a short recess between the Committee reports. This means that the Assembly will complete its work and adjourn sometime between one and two o'clock.

To conclude this description of procedure, it should be mentioned that a rather complete set of rules guides the work in all the various meetings. These rules were drawn by a faculty committee in 1934, assisted by the Clerk of the New York Legislature, and are based upon the *Clerk's Manual*. The rules are revised after each Convention. Mimeographed copies are studied by all participants during the preparation period. (The author will be glad to send copies of these rules to those interested.)

To give an example of the form in which the student bills are drafted, I have selected one from the Albany Convention to be reproduced in full. I chose this one chiefly because it is shorter than most.

"An ACT to Reapportion the Senate and Assembly Districts of New York State.

"The Students of the Colleges and Universities of New York State, in Assembly represented, do enact as follows:

"Whereas, Reapportionment is long overdue, and the inequalities of representation must be corrected at once; and

"Whereas, A special election to decide whether a constitutional convention should meet would entail great and unnecessary delay; and

"Whereas, It is the only bill which has any chance of being adopted at the present time:

"*Section* 1. We advocate the passage of the Dunnigan-Streit Bill for Reapportionment of Senate and Assembly districts; provided, however, that the Wilcox Formula shall be used as the formula for Assembly apportionment in the enactment of the bill.

"*Section* 2. The power of apportionment shall be withdrawn from the State Legislature and placed in the hands of a commission.

"*Section* 3. This commission shall consist of three members: one to be appointed by the Governor, one by the Senate of the State of New York, and one by the Assembly of the State of New York. These appointments shall be exclusive of the membership of these groups, and said Assembly apportionments are to be made every ten years, starting in the year of one thousand nine hundred forty.

"*Section* 4. Apportionment shall be made by the commission herein provided for, according to the Wilcox Formula for Assembly reapportionment.

"*Section* 5. The apportionment of Senatorial districts shall be based on the existing laws as formed in the Constitution of the State of New York with the exception of the fact that the commission herein provided for shall be given the power of apportionment now held by the State Legislature.

Passed by the Assembly of the Colleges and Universities of the State of New York, May 11, 1935.

(Signed) J. L. Brown, Hamilton, Speaker
Mary Keeler, St. Rose, Clerk"

In the General Assembly, a bill is sometimes passed quickly with little opposition. The bill reproduced above is an example of this, as witness the minutes of the Secretary:

"Mr. Crawford of St. Lawrence read the Reapportionment Bill and Mr. Flattery of Syracuse spoke in its defense. Mr. Dughi of Cornell explained the Wilcox Formula upon which the bill was based. There was scattered debate, including the offering of one amendment."

One way to evaluate the convention plan would be simply to list its advantages and difficulties, but this has already been done by several observers.[13, 14, 16] A more fundamental approach, probably would be to raise the question, what should be the place of convention debating in relation to the rest of the intercollegiate debate program? Contrasting answers to this question are found in two recent publications. One picture of the modern debate situation is given by Nichols and Baccus,[17] as the following excerpts will show:

"The [Convention] plan is a practical adaption for educational purposes of convention or legislative procedure. It requires a knowledge of parliamentary law, skill in group discussion for the committee meetings, and persuasive speaking and argumentative advocacy or partisanship in presenting and opposing bills before the house. It has practical speaking training and educational value in the handling of public questions." p. 79

"[The convention plan] is perhaps the best form of debate to use if one wishes to merge the teaching of parliamentary law with argumentative practice." p. 46

"The tournament is the most recent development in debate organization and perhaps the most significant." p. 87

[17] E. R. Nichols and J. H. Baccus, *Modern Debating* (New York: W. W. Norton and Company, 1936).

"Nor should [the student] be allowed to regard himself too highly as a social benefactor, for there is nothing so tragic, educationally speaking, as a youthful demagogue or social egotist. To a great extent it has been all right for debate to acquire a social consciousness, but it is not necessary for it to do so. . . . Debate should be looked upon as an educational means and not as a social end." p. 41

"Debate is an educational process conducted as a game or sport, whose incidental purpose is to set forth the truth about both sides of a controversial problem, and whose primary purpose is the personal development of the persons participating." p. 34

An entirely different point of view is suggested in a recent article by O'Brien:[18]

"The season would have as its climax not a debate tournament, but a state debaters' convention. . . ." p. 587

"At Pennsylvania State College we have evolved a method which we term the Parliamentary Session, which seems to us, for campus purposes, superior to other forms of group discussion and the symposium with which we have experimented. The method, on a smaller scale, is essentially that employed in the New York Debaters Convention." p. 583

"Is the primary function of extra-curricular speech that of presenting a highly polished exercise in forensic skills, or that of bringing home to the audience the vital implications of the social problems of the day? The author is forced to the conclusion that if extra-curricular speech is to survive as a significant activity the latter must take precedence." p. 582

". . . new frontiers in adult education are just opening up for those of our profession versed in the technique of the presentation of controversial problems before popular audiences. No more convincing evidence of the growing importance of this field can be found than that of the success of the Des Moines Public Forums . . ." p. 585

Thus, according to Nichols and Baccus, the emphasis in debate should be upon developing the student through

[18] Joseph F. O'Brien, "The Place of Extra-Curricular Speech in the College or University of Today," *The Quarterly Journal of Speech,* Vol. XXI, November, 1935, pp. 582-587.

standardized intellectual exercises. Audiences are unnecessary and, if they happen to attend a debate, are regarded more or less as guinea pigs upon which the debaters may practice. Large decision-tournaments are the season's climax. The idea of debaters trying to influence the actions of the campus or community regarding social problems is toned down. In such a scheme, the convention plan is merely one of several minor variants, and is chiefly useful as a technique to practice parliamentary procedure.

On the other hand, according to the view presented by O'Brien, the emphasis should be upon getting across the social message, rather than an argumentative method. The audience is as important as the speaker; in fact, the debate squad has the duty of constructing a program which will appeal to its campus, thus creating interested audiences. Ordinary platform debates would be changed in many cases to Parliamentary Sessions. In this scheme, the convention becomes the main event of the season.

Such contrasting pictures indicate that the eventual contribution of the convention plan cannot yet be gauged. When I consider the increased stature and strength of intercollegiate debating in New York since the advent of our annual Convention, it seems likely to me that the plan will gradually spread to other parts of the country. Various state and sectional conferences will probably experiment with conventions, adapting them to their particular needs. Until this has happened, and a greater number of schools have experimented with the plan and contributed to its improvement, we will not know whether to regard the convention merely as a temporary variant, or as a major change in technique opening the way for a more realistic participation by debaters in campus and community life.[19]

SELECTED BIBLIOGRAPHY

Frizzell, John H., "The Parliamentary Discussion," *The Gavel*. Vol. XVIII, November, 1935, p. 7.
The Gavel, Vol. XIX, May, 1937. (Several articles.)

[19] Milton Dickens, "Intercollegiate Convention Debates in New York," *The Gavel*, Vol. XIX, May, 1937, pp. 51-54. Reprinted in full by permission of Professor Dickens.

The Gavel, Vol. XX, May, 1938. (Several articles.)

Howes, Raymond F., *Debating*. Boston: D. C. Heath and Company, 1931.

Lahman, Carroll P., *Debate Coaching*. New York: H. W. Wilson Company, 1936.

Miller, Orville C., *The Speech Tournament and the Congress of Human Relations*. Nashville, Tennessee: Vanderbilt University, 1938.

Millson, William A. D., "New Forms of Debate," *The Gavel*. Vol. XIV, May, 1932, p. 20.

Morris, D. W., "The Intercollegiate Forum," *Quarterly Journal of Speech*. Vol. XXIV, April, 1938, pp. 212-220.

O'Neill, James M., and McBurney, James H., *The Working Principles of Argument*. New York: The Macmillan Company, 1932. Chapters XVII and XVIII.

Orr, Frederick W., and Franzke, Albert L., "The University of Washington Plan of Problem Solving Debate," *Bulletin of the University of Washington* (Extension Series), No. 8, January, 1938.

Sheffield, Alfred D., "Discussion, Lecture-Forum, and Debate," *Quarterly Journal of Speech*. Vol. XVIII, November, 1932, pp. 517-531.

Summers, H. B., "Student Legislative Assembly," *The Forensic of Pi Kappa Delta*. Series 22, October, 1936, pp. 21-24.

Williamson, A. B., "A Proposed Change in Intercollegiate Debating," *Quarterly Journal of Speech*. Vol. XIX, February, 1933, pp. 192, 200-202.

APPENDIX A

A STUDENT DISCUSSION[1]

WHAT SHOULD BE THE ROLE OF THE FEDERAL GOVERNMENT IN CONTROVERSIES BE-TWEEN CAPITAL AND LABOR?

Critical Notes

1. MR. FRANKEL, Leader: The question for discussion as you know is: What should be the role of the Federal Government in controversies between capital and labor? Time and again this question has presented itself to the American people. The rise of the sit-down strike has doubtlessly sharpened the issue in the minds of many people. Is controversy between capital and labor inevitable? Is it on the increase? What causes these disputes? Does the Federal Government have any responsibility in the matter? If so, what course of action should it take? These are some of the questions we shall probably want to consider. What do you think about the problem?

The leader makes a short introductory statement. The group is well acquainted and familiar with discussion methods. Note the series of questions.

No attempt is made to start the discussion with any particular issue.

[1] The following students at Northwestern University participated in this discussion: Stanley Frankel (Stan)—Leader, Stephen Ladd (Steve), Yager Cantwell, Robert Babcock (Ollie), Robert Waggoner (Bob), John Frank, Robert de Kieffer (Curly), Marion Plevney, Margaret Johnston, Howard O'Leary, and William Hammond. The students were undergraduates, mostly sophomores, enrolled in the course *Discussion Methods*. The preparation for this discussion was the same as that made for other class discussions. The discussion, one hour in length, was recorded and is reproduced here from the records.

2. MR. LADD: Well, as we all know, the main controversial problem between capital and labor is the industrial strike. Now the situation briefly in the last four years, not counting 1938, is this: We had approximately 10,000 strikes in those four years, which is the largest number of strikes in four years that we have ever had with the possible exception of the world war era. Now the main problem in connection with industrial strikes is the loss of pay envelopes to workers, the lost business activity, and the great financial losses to the general public; the Senate Labor Committee estimates that in 1936 strikes meant a final loss to the public of a billion dollars. In addition to this we have the great amount of bitterness between the two sides with a result which breeds further strikes, and we have lost lives such as occurred in the South Chicago massacre. Since the Wagner Labor Act which was passed in 1935, it is interesting to note that the American Federation of Labor and the C.I.O. respectively have approximately doubled and trebled their membership. Professor Paul Douglas found after careful study that increase in union organization means increased labor trouble; and so, if we get out of this business recession which we are in now and which generally holds down the number of strikes, we can expect a great deal of labor trouble in the

This rather long opening contribution involves both definition and analysis. It is mainly analytical in character, however, presenting the "effects" or evidences of the problem. Later developments show that a little more attention to definition would have helped at this point.

Authority cited.

future, and that's why we're discussing this problem today.

3. MR. CANTWELL: Paralleling too, Steve, that increased organization of labor, we might take into consideration the fact that since 1881 strikes have increased regularly through the period from 1881 to 1935, have gone up 100% and even 400%. So far as the number of strikes is concerned, we have 400% more strikes in each succeeding four-year period and that tendency, that trend, cannot be emphasized too much.

4. MR. FRANK: I should like to mention to Mr. Ladd that one of the most important reasons for the passage of the National Labor Relations Act was interstate commerce and the dangers in this area brought on by strikes. Railroad strikes and the like impair the efficiency and safety of operation; they disrupt the flow of raw materials and arrest employment, wages and so on, in many industries. They peculiarly affect the interest and well-being of the entire public. I have reference especially to public utilities of an interstate character. Since our question concerns what action the Federal Government should take, will we not be primarily concerned with these interstate strikes? After all we have to stick to the constitution.

Mr. Frank tries to define the limits of the discussion. He recognizes the need for further definition.

5. MISS PLEVNEY: The important thing to me in this whole problem is the loss of life, human suffering, and tremendous economic losses to both capital and labor caused by

Miss Plevney ignores Mr. Frank's contribution and brings the discussion back to "effects."

strikes. Homes are disrupted, children have to leave school, and the community is turned into an armed camp. These are the things we should seek to avoid.

6. MR. BABCOCK: You all are outlining strikes but at the same time you're putting most of the blame at the present time, as I see it, upon the laborer. And you're not seeing the fact that while he is striking he is also being exploited. I think that is an existing evil as much as anything else.

Mr. Babcock shows where he stands and suggests a possible cause.

7. LEADER: I think we all agree that the strikes are bad and I think we can also agree that the outer manifestations of labor disputes are strikes and all that strikes imply. The social unrest, the financial unrest and everything else the strikes produce we would like to avoid if possible. Now Mr. Babcock has led us into the discussion of causes. I think maybe we can probe a little deeper into these strikes and see what the causes are. What do you think?

The leader feels that the group is pretty much in agreement on "effects" and suggests a consideration of "causes." Should he have asked for discussion on Mr. Frank's point?

8. MISS PLEVNEY: Well, in investigating the subject I found that among the causes there are really two, the organizational type and then the strikes over wages and hours. And under this organizational type of dispute we find that there is the kind between the two factions, the A.F. of L. and the C.I.O., who are really battling with each other, and then there is this matter of the laborers seeking to

Miss Plevney begins her contribution with the inevitable "well."

have dealings with employers. In the *Monthly Labor Review* for October, 1937, it is stated that over 60% of these strikes are due to these organizational disputes.

Facts cited and source indicated.

9. MR. CANTWELL: Don't you think, Miss Plevney, that due to the subject under discussion we can outlaw, perhaps, I don't know, it depends upon what the group wants to do with it, but can't we exclude the organizational type of strike between unions because this is a discussion concerning disputes between capital and labor, as I understand it.

Mr. Cantwell considers the advisability of limiting the area of discussion.

10. LEADER: Yes, what do you think about that? Should we, for this discussion, limit the discussion to disputes between capital and labor and not include inter-labor or inter-capital disputes? Curly.

11. MR. DE KIEFFER: I think that would be a very good idea to exclude the differences between the C.I.O. and the A.F. of L. as long as we're talking about capital and labor.

Curly has indicated that he wishes to speak. The leader recognizes speakers in this way throughout the discussion.

12. LEADER: All right, if it is agreed then, I think we'll omit this A.F. of L.-C.I.O. dispute, as it is inter-labor. Mr. Frank.

The group agrees to this limitation under the guidance of the leader.

13. MR. FRANK: I'd like to sum up Miss Plevney's point by quoting what John L. Lewis said concerning the Labor Relations Board in a lecture given here in Chicago. He says that the Labor Board as we now have it was set up primarily to implement collective bargaining.

In other words, this collective bargaining is just one thing that labor is trying to get.

14. LEADER: Okey, then, that is one of the causes of strikes, the attempt to get collective bargaining. All right. Mr. Hammond.

Labor's attempt to secure collective bargaining is agreed upon as one causal factor.

15. MR. HAMMOND: I think we ought also to consider the use of lockouts and the boycott in labor disputes because, as Mr. Babcock says, the employer sometimes strikes against the worker just as much as the worker strikes against the employer. Cannot action of this sort on the part of the employer be considered as a causal factor?

Mr. Hammond thinks that the employer sometimes contributes to the controversy.

16. LEADER: I think we can assume that this is one of the causes of labor disputes, because as Mr. Hammond points out, the fact that the employer locks out his employees shows that there is a dispute existing there. Whether or not this can be called a cause of strikes, however, might be open to some question.

The leader admits this "cause" with some reluctance. Should there have been further discussion of the matter?

17. MR. CANTWELL: Mr. Frankel, before we go on I think we should recognize one fact: While we can't deal with it here and while we have excluded it, the fact remains that there are organizational disputes and we must recognize the fact that these organizations—the C.I.O. and the A.F. of L.—are both formed as opposition to capital and therefore most of the disputes between them are a direct result of the differences between capital and labor. While we have excluded it, I think

Mr. Cantwell is still thinking about the organizational disputes which he thought might be outside the limits of this discus-

we should recognize the fact that labor has organized into two great unions to protect itself against capital; therefore any disputes between them are really an effect of disputes between capital and labor.

18. LEADER: You say then that that might be one of the evils of the disputes?

19. MR. CANTWELL: Yes, yes.

20. LEADER: Well, that's a good point to bring up. I think now that we should keep on this track of causes. We've had one good cause here that Miss Plevney brought up. Mr. Babcock.

21. MR. BABCOCK: I'd like to speak on a little different type of lockout. As I understand it at the present time, in Ford's plant he is working his men at better hours and better wages than any other man in the automobile industry in the United States. He is applauded and put up as a high example of what a man can do in paying good wages and he is respected by everybody but his employees. And the reason that he is respected by everyone but his employees is the fact that Henry Ford at the present time is guilty of more than striking. He is guilty of overworking his men. He has his plant so mechanized that he can produce in six months more cars than he can sell, than the United States can buy. So he runs his plant six months of the year, makes enough cars, actually pays his men higher wages than anybody else does, but he only pays

Critical Notes

sion a few minutes before. Now he is not sure that this limitation was wise.

The leader brings the discussion back to "causes." He mentions "one good cause"; what has happened to Mr. Hammond's suggestion about lockouts?

Mr. Babcock insists on the employer's responsibility in the matter. Cites an example.

them for six months of the year, so actually, in reality, he is paying less than General Motors or any other automobile industry. So, is he not then guilty, or I mean, let me put it differently, I won't say guilty, is he not a contributing cause to dispute between labor and capital?

22. LEADER: I think we can recognize that. Mr. Ladd.

23. MR. LADD: Can't we sum up the causes of the controversies between capital and labor simply by stating that because of the nature of our economic system the interests of capital and labor are opposed? The employer wants to make more profit and the worker wants to get higher wages, and those two things are opposed. Now couldn't we just leave the causes at that as the basic causes?

24. MR. BABCOCK: Do you honestly believe that labor and capital are unalterably opposed to each other?

25. MR. LADD: Well, I think there is a sort of fundamental, basic conflict and capital wants to be the winner and so does labor. It seems to me you'll always have this basic, fundamental disagreement; that is, they both want to win.

26. MR. CANTWELL: There is one important thing which we should take into consideration before going on. If we could educate—which is the old bromide, I guess, for all the troubles of mankind—if we could make both capital and labor see that ultimately they both

Notice the attempt to avoid the emotionally toned word "guilty."

Mr. Ladd thinks the "causes" can now be summed up, and inadvertently raises a new issue which adds considerably to the analysis. Mr. Babcock sees the point.

want the same thing, they both want prosperity, they both want security, they both want an even-flowing, smooth-working productive system—if we could accomplish this, I think we might have some hope of doing away with what has been called a fundamental conflict between capital and labor. Personally, I do not believe that they need to be unalterably opposed. If we can awaken the social consciousness of each of these classes, now superficially opposed, we will have, I feel, the most satisfactory basis for working on a solution of this problem.

Mr. Cantwell thinks that this new factor may give the group a cue as to the direction which the "solution" should take.

27. LEADER: I think that's a very good point. Nevertheless we appear to be agreed that at present, on the surface at least, capital and labor are unalterably opposed. It looks like they are going to go on that way. Mr. Cantwell has brought out the fact that this discussion here this evening is possibly an attempt by this group to get in and find out what can be done to make capital and labor more cooperative. May we not accept the present opposition as one cause of strikes? Another cause has been the demands for collective bargaining. Labor demands collective bargaining. Another, of course, has been the speed-up used by employers with resulting unemployment and insecurity for the laborer.

The leader tactfully incorporates Mr. Cantwell's idea into the thought of the group and sums up the "causal factors." This time he includes the employer's responsibility.

Now let's probe just a little deeper into this matter of collective bargaining. What do they want

Suggests further analysis of causes along a specific line.

collective bargaining for? Then I think we have the causes analyzed.

28. MR. BABCOCK: I think that behind the demands for collective bargaining is the conviction on the part of the laborer that he is not being paid enough or that his hours and working conditions are unsatisfactory. I mean, he feels it in relation to capital who is getting a huge income while he is being paid a small wage per hour very much below the cost of living in the section where he is working. He feels that his share isn't coming out right, especially after the publication of some of the bonuses paid in this country, Sloan for example getting something like $400,000 a year. Why, such publications as these prove to the worker that the surplus is not coming back to the laborer and he has a right to insist on collective bargaining. So I think fundamentally the causes go back to wages and hours.

We know now that labor has a friend in court.

29. LEADER: Do you think therefore that collective bargaining is sought by the laborer in order to aid him in gaining what he considers fair wages, and fair hours, and possibly leisure time when he wants it, or something like that? Is that agreed by the group? All right, now what other causes can we set down?

Collective bargaining as a "cause" is analyzed more fully and fundamentally.

30. MR. WAGGONER: I might mention the attempt by the employees to organize and their attempt to do something about the

unemployment problem. Don't you think that this enters in?

31. MR. CANTWELL: Yes! Indeed I do—the unemployment problem in relation to these cyclical slumps and booms which are one of the dominating features of our social order. I think we should take that into consideration because they very definitely interfere with the security of both the employer and the employee. I think we have here a fundamental cause.

Mr. Cantwell suggests what he thinks is a fundamental cause.

32. MR. LADD: How does this line up with the historical fact that we've had more strikes during the periods of rising prosperity when the worker is secure and fewer strikes during periods of business recession when a worker is insecure, and doesn't dare go out on a strike for fear of losing his job?

Doesn't Mr. Ladd answer his own question?

33. LEADER: Can you answer that, Mr. Hammond?

34. MR. HAMMOND: Well, that's because in periods of prosperity the worker has to get as much as he can get, because in periods of depression he will have to give it up; but if he were given a year-round job and a decent salary, why, there wouldn't be that feeling of insecurity.

Mr. Hammond has given indication that he wants to speak. The leader gives him an opportunity.

The word "decent" is emotionally toned; "adequate" would have been better.

35. MR. FRANK: It is true also that workers are realizing now that whether we are in a period of prosperity or depression, there's always going to be several million men out of work; that's why he wants to make sure he's organized.

36. MR. LADD: I think that this

is also true that when a worker finds he is getting just a little more he is more willing to try to reach out and grasp just a little beyond his reach and always, no matter how much a worker has, he always wants just a little more so he can reach out and grab that. I believe that is fundamental also.

37. LEADER: All right. Mr. Cantwell.

38. MR. CANTWELL: We have to be careful, Steve, in relation to the point you brought up. Aren't you reasoning after the fact, "therefore because"? I think it has been beautifully brought out here. The fact that there are less strikes in periods of downswing and more in periods of upswing does not appear to me to prove what you imply; you have to be kind of careful in attributing that. I mean there is a general rise and fall and where the strikes come doesn't have an awful lot to do with our problem, I think.

39. LEADER: I wonder if we cannot now sum up this matter of causes? First, is labor's demand for collective bargaining and all that that implies; labor wants this collective bargaining as a means to insure him or help him get fair wages and fair hours. A second cause of friction and strikes is the speed-up; I have reference here to Ollie's point—the fact that some employers work their men very hard for six months and then lay them off. Then, there is this matter of unemployment and the consequent in-

Mr. Ladd reacts to Mr. Hammond's contribution with some show of heat.

The leader, perhaps wisely, gives Mr. Cantwell a chance to get back to his original point. Mr. Cantwell then disposes of Mr. Ladd's objection. Suggests Mr. Ladd has fallen into a fallacy.

An excellent summary by the leader.

security. All of these factors seem to boil down to this matter of insecurity: The laborer doesn't think that he is getting his share of profits nor is he certain of a steady income. As a result he organizes and strikes, if necessary, to improve his condition. I think that we could use some facts here on the actual conditions, that is, wages, hours, and working conditions, but perhaps we had better go on. There seems to be pretty general agreement, at least by implication, that many laborers have a right to be dissatisfied. What is your attitude on this? What should be our attitude toward the strike in relation to all the parties involved? We will have to set up some standard or criterion of value in these matters before we go much farther.

Suggests need for more facts.

40. MR. HAMMOND: I think one of the criteria should be that the interests of all the people of the United States as well as the working class and capitalists should be considered.

The group moves on to the second phase of analysis—a consideration of standards of value. Mr. Hammond makes the first suggestion.

41. LEADER: In other words, you mean the greatest good to the greatest number?

42. MR. HAMMOND: Yes.

43. LEADER: Is there an argument on that? Mr. Babcock.

44. MR. BABCOCK: I'd like to find out what he really means by the majority, the greatest good to the majority. Because you realize in making that statement who the majority is. I believe that in all cases the majority is the laborer.

Mr. Babcock is still thinking about the interests of labor.

Critical Notes

45. MR. LADD: Perhaps this is a restatement of Mr. Hammond's criterion, but I would suggest that the desirable thing would be to remove the necessity for industrial strikes and lockouts and at the same time not be unfair to either of the parties concerned.

Later developments will show that Mr. Ladd here has in the back of his mind the solution which he plans to present.

46. MR. CANTWELL: That's pretty fundamental. Whatever our conclusion is, we want that conclusion to include abolishing strikes, because we feel that strikes are not to the greatest good of the greatest number. Is that a fair statement of the group's opinion?

An attempt to sum up "values."

47. MR. DE KIEFFER: May I say right along that line, if you can remove the fundamental differences between capital and labor, then you will eliminate the strikes because little is accomplished by trying to put your foot down after a strike has occurred. I think you have to nip it in the bud, before the strike occurs.

Mr. de Kieffer expresses what he believes to be the fundamental "value" when he suggests that any solution to the problem must remove the basic causes of strikes.

48. LEADER: All right. Will someone state that in little more specific terms? When you say remove the fundamental disputes do you mean to do something about wages and hours and things like that?

49. MR. DE KIEFFER: Exactly! If you can get down to the fundamental sources of these conflicts, you may hope to eliminate or at least largely do away with strikes—and I gather that the elimination or reduction of strikes with all the evils which they bring is what we are trying to get at.

50. MR. FRANK: Hadn't we bet-

Critical Notes

ter modify this attitude toward strikes a bit? Remember we are discussing possible courses of action for the *Federal Government* to take. Now the policy of the Federal Government as represented in the Wagner Act is not one of outlawing strikes. This Act does not actually interfere with or impede in any way the right to strike. What is more, I should like again to point out that the range of activities of the Federal Government is necessarily limited to interstate strikes. They have no jurisdiction in purely local squabbles.

Mr. Frank unintentionally confuses the issue a bit by interpreting the "elimination of strikes" to mean the "outlawing of strikes."

51. MR. DE KIEFFER: Granting all that you have said, John, the fact remains that in so far as the Federal Government is competent to do anything about this problem, it seems to me that it ought to work in the direction of removing the causes of strikes. Whether this means outlawing strikes is another question.

Mr. Frank still believes the term "Federal Government" in the question for discussion imposes certain limits on the discussion. (See his contribution 4.)
A discerning reply well stated.

52. MR. FRANK: All right. I'll accept that for the moment at least. Let's go on.

Mr. Frank is not satisfied, but he does not wish to impede the discussion by his insistence.

53. MR. CANTWELL: Now I don't know how this will fit into the ideas of the rest of the group but I would say that we are considering the salve rather than the basic remedies, to use a trite analogy. That is, I think that if we want to do away with and abolish the fundamental conflict as it has been termed, we should get at basic remedies such as trying to stabilize the business cycle, things that have bothered economists and sociolo-

Mr. Cantwell agrees with Mr. de Kieffer (see 46 and 48).

gists for decades. I think we should consider in this discussion these basic things that will do away with this conflict, such as I suggested earlier, an educational program to awaken a social consciousness if that is possible and other such things; unemployment insurance, for instance, has been advocated as a possible remedy. Then there are all the various means of stabilizing the business cycle which have been proposed from time to time. Now do we want to go into these matters or do we want to deal with methods of handling strikes after they occur?

Asks an important question.

54. MR. WAGGONER: In other words, the Federal Government might undertake sweeping social reforms designed to bring better things for the laboring man and thus remove the causes which produce strikes—that is one way of looking at this problem. Another way is to consider the role of the Federal Government in dealing with disputes between capital and labor under existing conditions. While I should not wish to speak against fundamental reform, I am inclined to believe that we will get farther here by concerning ourselves more specifically with methods of dealing with strikes. Put through all the reforms you care to and we will still have *some* strikes. Our question is: How shall the Federal Government deal with these strikes?

Mr. Waggoner states the issue clearly and takes a position. Notice how this contribution shapes up the discussion which follows.

Is this a discussion of values or one of definition and limitation?

55. LEADER: Bob has drawn an

issue here. Which way do we want to go?

56. MR. FRANK: I'll admit I'm a little mixed up here, but I am still convinced that if we are to consider the role of the Federal Government at all realistically, we will have to stick to the constitution.

57. LEADER: You do appear to be a little mixed up, John [Laughter], but I understand you to mean that you are interested in the role of the Federal Government in dealing with strikes over which it has legal jurisdiction. Apart from the matter of jurisdiction, this would appear to line you up with Bob; that is, you feel that the immediate problem of dealing with strikes rather than social reform is our chief concern.

58. MR. LADD: I agree. If we get to talking about how you can eliminate the business cycle and how you can eliminate these basic causes, I'm afraid we'll stray pretty far away from our subject as stated: "How should the government deal with the controversies between capital and labor?" Now there is one point I'd like to bring up here, and that is that in order to do something for this problem you don't necessarily have to get at the basic causes. Now we have our courts of common law which are machinery for settling disputes between individuals. Now those courts do solve the problem to a great extent but they don't get at the basic causes, this basic human nature tendency

Mr. Frank is insistent even if slightly confused.

The leader tries to straighten Mr. Frank out. He does this in a fine spirit and tactfully gives credit to Mr. Waggoner (Bob) for his contribution 54.

Mr. Ladd also agrees with Mr. Waggoner and sheds further light on the issue in an excellent contribution.

Draws an analogy.

which brings about disputes between human beings.

59. LEADER: All right then, you don't especially agree with the idea of getting down to the bottom. You think the most important, the direct thing, is to get at the strike now?

60. MR. LADD: Under this particular question, that is my idea.

61. LEADER: All right. How many agree? Is this the consensus of the group? How many feel that for purposes of this discussion at least we should limit ourselves to such direct steps as the Federal Government can take to deal with controversies between capital and labor? [Takes vote.] This seems to be the wish of the majority. Do you object, Ollie?

The leader resorts to a vote to ascertain the wishes of the g r o u p . Remember that the group started out to discuss values; is this a vote on values or on limitation of the field of discussion? Aspects of both appear to be involved.

62. MR. BABCOCK: I'd like to know right now how much you want to do in regard to this issue. You say prevent the strikes. Well, how far are you willing to go to prevent the strikes? I can give you a solution right now to prevent the strikes!

Mr. Babcock objects and shows some impatience.

63. LEADER: All right. Let's have it. What do you want to do to prevent these strikes?

64. MR. HAMMOND: Well, I'd like to say before Ollie speaks that all these different solutions that we are going to propose must really deal with basic causes because the only way that you can settle strikes is by dealing with the basic causes. You can't satisfy strikers by handing them a few crumbs off the table.

Mr. Hammond again raises the question which has just been voted upon. "A few crumbs off the table," as used by Mr. Hammond, is question begging. This position should have been

65. MISS JOHNSTON: Isn't the point this: No matter how far the government might go in eliminating the basic causes of strikes, it is reasonable to believe that some strikes and lockouts will still occur. What we want to know is what the government can do to help the situation when these strikes do occur. Perhaps socializing all industry would get at the basic causes, but even so we still face the problem of deciding what the government should do in the event of a strike or the threat of strike. This latter issue seems to me to be worth discussing.

66. MR. WAGGONER: I agree. I see no reason why we need to take a question concerning the role of the Federal Government in labor disputes as an excuse for overhauling our entire economic system.

[Several people try to talk at once.]

67. LEADER: Just a minute here now! I'll ask for a vote on this again. Do we want to discuss this question within the general framework of our present economic and political system, the capitalistic system and our present constitution, or . . . [Mr. Babcock breaks in.]

68. MR. BABCOCK: No, sir!

69. LEADER: Now wait a minute. I want a vote on this. How many say we do? [Takes vote.] The majority appears to favor keeping within the bounds of our present constitution.

stated more objectively and judiciously.

Miss Johnston speaks for the first time. She restates Mr. Waggoner's position effectively. An excellent contribution.
A shrewd guess at what Mr. Babcock is driving at. She has been in other discussions of economic and political questions with Mr. Babcock.

Mr. Waggoner takes advantage of the situation to score a point for "his side." In doing so he destroys Miss Johnston's valiant attempt to placate Mr. Babcock.

The leader steps in; suggests another vote on the same question.

Mr. Babcock is now thoroughly aroused.

The leader rightly insists on order, but puts the question badly.

70. MR. BABCOCK: We can amend the constitution, can't we?!!

This statement is sarcastic and in bad taste.

71. LEADER: Pardon me, Ollie. I'll be arbitrary here and say that we will act at the present time within the constitution. Now we won't argue the constitutionality of other questions. We can't do that. But we will aim in this discussion to work within that constitution.

The leader handles the situation politely but firmly. His explanation isn't very clear, however.
Ollie capitulates.

72. MR. BABCOCK: Right.

73. LEADER: I think that we can sum up by saying that we are looking for a government labor program which is designed to secure the greatest good for the greatest number, and one that will prevent or deal with strikes in such a way as to reduce to a minimum the distress and inconvenience resulting from strikes. Now I think that we can go ahead with solutions. What do some of you have to say about that? Mr. Babcock.

An excellent summary of the discussion of "values." We know now what we want the solution to this problem to do. The leader now addresses Ollie as "Mr. Babcock."

74. MR. BABCOCK: Well, I'd like to bring up one. The one that I had chosen as a matter of fact myself, the *constitutional* cooperative society in the United States. I think that this could be done through the present constitution. I see no reason why you'd have to do more than is done now through any other cooperative society. Make the laborer think that he is a member of the firm or the industry for which he is working. Why would he strike if he is a member of it? If he strikes his stock goes down and if his stock goes down he has lost twice.

I think Mr. Babcock knows that he is violating the wishes of the group in suggesting this solution. The majority has twice indicated its desire to confine this discussion to direct activities of the Federal Government in dealing with strikes. Note the play on the word "constitutional."

75. LEADER: Now just a minute.

This question has to do with what should the Federal Government itself do to settle disputes. You are suggesting that the Federal Government should set up these cooperative societies?

76. MR. BABCOCK: Yes.

77. LEADER: That of course has an implication. We'll have to rule out your suggestion because that is of course socialism and that cannot be done within the confines of our constitution, that is, in our present capitalistic system. I'm sorry but I think we'll have to.

The leader does not mean to argue against socialism. He means that this is not the place to discuss it, in view of the wishes of the group. He should have made this clear.

78. MR. BABCOCK: Well, if it's already ruled out, I'd like to ask a question.

79. LEADER: Yes, I think we'll have to rule that out. Don't you agree with me—that your scheme is socialistic? Beyond the confines of the agreed limits of the discussion?

Tries to make Mr. Babcock see the point.

80. MISS JOHNSTON: It certainly is if the government is going to set it up.

81. MR. BABCOCK: I am proposing an extension of consumers' cooperatives, encouraged and managed by the Federal Government. If that is socialism or communism, then make the most of it! I'm for it!

Resorts to an old stratagem.

82. MISS JOHNSTON: That isn't the point, Ollie. You have a perfect right to believe in socialism if you want to; nor have the rest of us meant to indicate a position in this matter. Consumers' cooperatives would be a good subject for discussion next week perhaps, but

Miss Johnston again adopts the role of conciliator. An excellent contribution.

for the moment we are discussing what the Federal Government should do in disputes between capital and labor.

83. MR. BABCOCK: Well, I think that there are two extremes in this matter of government action. One is complete socialization, complete ownership and operation; the other one is the old laissez-faire, hands-off policy. Now I think that the desirable solution is somewhere between these two extremes.

Mr. Babcock sees the point.

84. LEADER: All right. That's good. That gives us something to work by. Now I think that the Wagner Act is somewhere between these two extremes. Does anyone care to discuss that? Steve Ladd.

The leader tactfully commends Mr. Babcock, but takes precaution to see that the discussion is directed elsewhere. Notice how the leader turns the discussion to the Wagner Act—probably justified under the circumstances.

85. MR. LADD: Well, it has been thought for a long time by certain government officials, etc., that collective bargaining is the best way to settle industrial disputes. That is, to have the workers have their representatives meet with the representatives of their employer on an equal footing. And through an investigation it has been found that employers have generally done a great deal to prevent workers from organizing, workers from obtaining equality in collective bargaining; so the purpose of the Wagner Act is merely to define the rights of the laborer, that is, the rights to organization and the right to collective bargaining, and to outlaw any attempt on the part of the employer to interfere with this prospect. Now the question is, will these

Mr. Ladd explains the Wagner Act as he sees it.

disputes be settled if both sides are on an equal footing with respect to collective bargaining? Now it doesn't seem that this Wagner Act has solved the problem because in the first six months of 1937 we had the greatest number of strikes we have ever had in six months and that was after the Wagner Act was passed. And even after it was declared constitutional we had the biggest steel strike in twenty years.

Mr. Ladd believes the Wagner Act to be inadequate.

86. MR. HAMMOND: I think a great many of those strikes were due to the fact that the workers had to strike in order to get their rights under the Wagner Act because their employers refused to grant them.

87. MISS PLEVNEY: The N.L.R.B. has successfully enforced over 300 rulings against employers to date.

Miss Plevney makes her third remark. (See 5 and 7.) We haven't heard from Mr. O'Leary as yet. Should the leader have done something about this?

88. MR. CANTWELL: Then might we go on with our discussion, Steve, and say that we are likely to extend the powers of these mediation boards? Or do you think the Wagner Act is sufficient?

Mr. Cantwell helpfully "draws out" Mr. Ladd.

89. MR. LADD: No. I don't. I wouldn't necessarily . . . I mean . . .

90. MR. CANTWELL: In what way would you say . . .

91. MR. LADD: Well, I think that giving labor power which is compatible with capitalistic power isn't going to solve the problem. It's just going to make the strikes all the more bitter, hard fought and longer and more costly.

92. MR. CANTWELL: In other words, this Wagner Act as I understand it sets the fine for certain unlawful and unfair labor practices. Secondly, it requires capital and labor to sit down around a table and talk. Thirdly, and one of the most important things, it doesn't outlaw the strike and it doesn't compel agreement. Do you feel that's where it doesn't go far enough?

A good contribution.

93. MR. LADD: The Wagner Act is a step in the right direction but I don't think it will solve the problem.

94. LEADER: Are we agreed that the Wagner Act is a step in the right direction? Can I assume that? From all of you?

The leader consolidates a position. "Can I assume that? From all of you?" is hardly called for.

95. SEVERAL VOICES: Yes.

96. LEADER: All right. Mr. Cantwell.

97. MR. CANTWELL: Before we go on I'd like to ask something in relation to what Ollie brought up. You stamped his cooperative scheme as socialistic. Now would, under the criteria by which you stamped that socialistic, would unemployment insurance be socialistic too? May we consider that?

Mr. Cantwell runs the risk of stirring up "extrinsic conflict" again.

98. LEADER: Let's talk about this Wagner Act a little bit more first, if you don't mind. We've decided the Wagner Act goes pretty far and is a trend in the right direction, but is not quite far enough. Now what is far enough? Mr. O'Leary.

The leader keeps the discussion on the point.

99. MR. O'LEARY: If we put in a clause in the Wagner Act declar-

Mr. O'Leary speaks for the first time. His

ing strikes illegal, maybe that will help.

100. MR. FRANK: I don't think that should be done because a strike is the only weapon the worker usually has to fight the accumulated wealth of industry and he has to have something to use.

101. MISS JOHNSTON: Recent legislation dealing with labor certainly gives evidence of a more liberal point of view on the part of Congress and the Supreme Court. I think that is all to the good, but I doubt the advisability of outlawing the strike completely. I think that would be a reactionary step out of line with the spirit of the Wagner Act and present tendencies.

102. MR. DE KIEFFER: I agree. The Wagner Act does not take away labor's right to strike and I think that we are getting on dangerous ground when we talk about laws to abolish strikes. Can't the Federal Government provide machinery of some kind for arbitration or mediation? I know the Wagner Act aims at this, but I think that more might be done in that direction.

103. MR. LADD: Well, the extreme intervention-set-up is one, and is what you usually think of as compulsory arbitration. You set up a court and you say any strike anywhere or any lockout is absolutely illegal and this court is to settle any disputes that come along. Well, now I have a suggestion. It won't go quite that far; it limits

first contribution is number 99.

An excellent contribution.

An excellent contribution.

Mr. Ladd proposes a solution. He explains

the right to strike, and, in limiting it, I believe, takes away the necessity of strikes and yet does not outlaw strikes. That is the general system that they have on the railroads in this country and on the airways industry, and in Canada to a certain extent. It calls for compulsory investigation. Capital and labor, either one, has to give a thirty-day notice if it wants to make a change in contract. Strikes are illegal during that period. In all railroad industries collective bargaining takes place during those thirty days and if it fails the national mediation board steps in and tries to bring the two parties together and if that fails the President can appoint a special arbitration committee which investigates the dispute and hands down the decision. And strikes are illegal only for thirty days after this decision is made. And after that they can strike all they want to, but in the 12 years the system has been in effect there has not been a single strike and the important thing is that both sides have been treated fairly. They have a cooling off period, and a chance for an intelligent investigation.

104. MR. O'LEARY: I see. Thirty-day period of illegal strikes. That is, strikes are illegal during thirty days.

105. MR. HAMMOND: I think we ought to discuss something that would make the employer give something to labor because, after

his position clearly. An excellent contribution. Mr. Ladd is well informed.

An excellent contribution. A fair ques-

all, if labor gives up its right to strike and submits to any agreement like that, why, there ought to be something constructive from capital. Doesn't Mr. Ladd's proposal demand heavy concessions from labor without corresponding demands from the employers?

tion which should have been considered.

106. MR. CANTWELL: Right along that line I'd like to bring up the matter of unemployment insurance; for two reasons: One, because it spreads the burden of unemployment, and two, if the employer knows that he has to pay the laborer when he is not employed he will try his best to keep that laborer employed. Even after that laborer has gone out of his concern he'll have to keep paying that person until he gets employment. Therefore he'll try as hard as he can to get a job for his former employee.

Mr. Cantwell breaks into the pattern of thought with a "pet idea." He should have postponed this proposal.

107. LEADER: Well, let's take time out for just a second. Now what do you think of unemployment insurance? Then we'll get back to Steve's question. Do you all favor that generally?

The leader defers to Mr. Cantwell's interruption.

108. SEVERAL VOICES: No!

109. MR. HAMMOND: Well, I want to tell you something about a liberal employer in New York. It was a broker's firm and they had to lay off 20 men recently during the recession because of a lack of sales of stock. And one of the partners of this firm was delegated to the job of getting employment for these men. It took him six months

Mr. Cantwell gets a loud "No!" The group did not like the interruption.

An example cited.

but he saw to it that those men were employed, before they were let off. That's a real capitalist.

110. LEADER: Well, that's good. That is on the point. But now what do you think about this unemployment insurance? Shall we put this in? Who is against it? Ollie.

111. MR. BABCOCK: Well, I think you're running around the point, not getting at it. Your unemployment insurance is fine but that still doesn't raise the wages or help the hours of the present worker. The employer says, "All right, now you have imposed unemployment insurance on me and I've got to pay. All right, but I'll lower your wages so you can't work anyway and then you'll quit."

An excellent contribution from Mr. Babcock.

112. LEADER: Well, just a second. Can we say, though, that unemployment insurance is good in so far as it goes but it doesn't go far enough? Is that the feeling of the group?

113. SEVERAL VOICES: Yes.

114. LEADER: All right then, we can incorporate unemployment insurance among our final solutions. That will not be the main solution. Now let's get back to Steve's proposal. I haven't heard any destructive criticism yet on compulsory investigation. Miss Plevney.

Mr. Cantwell now gets a "Yes." Why this sudden change in the attitude of the group?

The leader restores the discussion to the original issue.

A good question.

115. MISS PLEVNEY: In this compulsory investigation, after the thing has been investigated and in case the two parties don't agree, what happens then, Steve?

116. MR. LADD: They are free to strike after such a period, but it has been very successful in removing this necessity for strikes because if you investigate it with intelligent arbitrators—there are plenty of industrial relations experts—and have an intelligent decision and a cooling-off period, they usually don't strike. Now in Canada for 31 years, from 1907 to 1938, this compulsory investigation act has been over 95% effective in peacefully settling the disputes which have been handled.

An informed answer.

117. MR. HAMMOND: That's all very interesting, but I'd like to know what does that offer constructively as a plan for the entire nation? I mean, after all, you've got to take into consideration many different kinds of business and you couldn't work that into this system. We are not concerned just with the railroads.

Mr. Hammond's opening words tend to imply that Mr. Ladd has not offered much.

118. MR. LADD: I think that we could work this plan on any interstate industry under our constitution, and that, after all, is the main problem. I mean most of this billion dollars which we lost in '36 was due to interstate industries as defined in the Wagner Act.

A good answer.

119. LEADER: All right. Is there anything else relative to that question?

120. MR. O'LEARY: This is just a suggestion, that we make a law saying that a decision must be reached through these investigations and in that way get around

Mr. O'Leary returns to his original suggestion (99).

the strikes without saying definitely you can't have them.

121. MISS PLEVNEY: I don't believe we ought to have a compulsory agreement because if labor or capital is at fault, no matter which one, and you are going to have a compulsory agreement, you're going to have a strike eventually anyway.

Miss Plevney gets back into the discussion.

122. MR. FRANK: In this connection I'd like to say that in this railroad act, the reason that it's so successful is that the workers are so well organized. They've had a union for 40 or 50 years and they know how to run one. Now this is the proposal I was thinking of. Instead of making these boards of the government so powerful, why not make the labor unions incorporate; after all the laborers are more interested in wages and hours; they could be sure that they got good wages and hours; why not make the labor unions a legal entity? You see? That will give the unions the same legal status which the employer now has. Both will be responsible.

Mr. Frank submits a proposal.

123. LEADER: All right. That's a good suggestion.

The leader interrupts prematurely.

124. MR. FRANK: Let me finish. Then, don't you see we won't need national labor boards at all because you have courts. Then when the union and employers, the two entities, bargain collectively and can't come to an agreement, take them to the court.

125. MR. CANTWELL: The trouble with that as I see it, John, is that you're going to put too much power in the hands of labor. Labor is out after all that it can get. History shows that they keep wanting more and more. John L. Lewis has done that. Now if they do want more and more and more, and keep going after more than capital can actually give them, then you're going to have all kinds of trouble.

A good exchange between Mr. Frank and Mr. Cantwell.

126. MR. FRANK: I have just mentioned that instead of having a national labor board you have a regular law court and unless the law court and judges are bribed by labor they won't get more and more. They'll get as much as is coming to them.

127. MR. CANTWELL: Who's going to determine how much they get?

128. MR. FRANK: Well, don't you see, they'll have their own court. They're both legal entities. It will be a regular law case.

129. MR. CANTWELL: In a regular law case you have two scrapping people, both of whom claim they want what overlaps the other.

130. MR. FRANK: Well, what have we got now? I'm trying to get rid of the strike.

131. LEADER: All right. Mr. Ladd.

132. MR. LADD: Mr. Frank is suggesting compulsory incorporation of labor unions. Now he wants that so unions can be sued. Well, they can be sued right now in 35

out of 48 states of the Union and there are only three industrial states in the Union in which they can't be sued. Now I am interested in this proposal that we should do away with the boards and have the disputes settled in our ordinary law courts. Now disputes between capital and labor are not common lawsuits, they are not equity suits. You'd have to set up new statutes which would amount to compulsory arbitration with our regular courts as the arbitrators.

An excellent contribution.

133. MR. FRANK: May I ask, then, if our regular courts can't take care of them under the act as it is, why are the cases sent up to the United States Supreme Court of Appeals for final decision?

A good exchange between Mr. Frank and Mr. Ladd.

134. MR. LADD: Questions going to the Supreme Court have been those in which the issue is whether or not the employers have infringed upon the right of labor as defined in the Wagner Act. Now if you want compulsory arbitration you should certainly set up special boards and committees rather than handle it through our regular law courts.

135. MR. FRANK: You mean for efficiency?

136. MR. LADD: They're already so overcrowded that you can't get cases heard.

137. MR. FRANK: All right, I'd agree there, yes.

138. MR. CANTWELL: It's whole-hog compulsory arbitration; that's

Mr. Frank agrees. Mr. Frank's plan is given a name.

the point. I don't think it's necessary.

139. LEADER: Do any of you believe in this so-called wholehog compulsory arbitration? That is, the other extreme of the field? Do any of you believe that?

140. MR. FRANK: I'm not so sure that I'm proposing wholehog compulsory arbitration and I'm certain that I don't like the label. [Laughter]

141. MR. BABCOCK: Well, if I were going to work on that basis I'd go further and say that the personnel of your mediation boards would have to be from the laboring class or some disinterested party, for I feel any bureau in the government which would act upon this would be political in character, and as we all know, politicians are controlled by capital. That's the way they get into power.

Mr. Babcock objects.

142. LEADER: Just a second. Now I think that we are generally agreed —our time is going rapidly—generally agreed that some form of arbitration, compulsory or otherwise, is desirable. We have limited it pretty well. We have said that the Wagner Act doesn't go far enough. It should go farther toward that other extreme, compulsory arbitration. And Mr. Ladd's suggestion has been one that has gone pretty far in the direction of compulsion. We have outlined the situation we want. That is, strikes not outlawed, no, but a time for cooling off and a time for investigation,

The leader reviews the discussion of solutions and takes Mr. Babcock's point as a basis for going on to Step V in the reflective thinking process. Apparently, rather general agreement has been reached on Mr. Ladd's proposal, at least tentatively.

time to bring out the facts, for seeing just what can be done, and we have also included unemployment insurance to relieve insecurity. Now I think we can go directly into the application of this problem. If you wish we can take that suggestion, compulsory investigation, and spend the rest of our time on how this could be applied. Mr. Babcock started it off when he pointed to the need for impartial investigators. Let's see how we are going to apply it. Mr. Ladd.

143. Mr. Ladd: Well, there are about 30 to 35 professional mediators in the conciliation division of the Department of Labor at present. You could set those men up as a panel of industrial relations experts and when a dispute fails to be settled by mediation each side to choose one of those, and those two could get together and choose a third chairman and those three compose an investigating, arbitrating committee.

An answer is given to Mr. Babcock's objection.

144. Mr. Waggoner: Right along that line I think it might be a good idea to put this committee under Civil Service, and in that way you could avoid your political tangle.

145. Miss Plevney: How is Civil Service going to help in choosing these investigators?

146. Mr. Waggoner: Only trained men are on Civil Service and they have spent their whole career in mediation, which means

they are impartial to any problems in the country.

147. MISS JOHNSTON: I think that the plan we are approaching is very similar to what is set up in New Zealand, Great Britain, and Australia. All three have been very successful.

148. MR. FRANK: I'd like to add another point of application. It seems to me that the C.I.O. has six or seven hundred thousand I guess, or right around that number; there are about forty million workers altogether. Now it seems to me if the government can help all those workers organize, don't you see, so that they have an instrument, a means of meeting the employers and employees, and in these courts, I think that would go a long way toward helping the disputes.

149. LEADER: Is there a discussion on that? Mr. Hammond.

150. MR. HAMMOND: Well, that's what the C.I.O. is trying to do, trying to organize the unorganized workers and yet it's being called communistic because they are trying to do that.

151. MR. DE KIEFFER: Isn't that organization being called communistic because of the opposition? I mean the capitalistic outlook?

152. MR. HAMMOND: Yes, that's what they're *trying* to label the C.I.O.

153. MR. FRANK: I don't see anything communistic about my proposal! After all, we are trying to help labor and we have decided

A second suggestion is given for making the plan effective.

A spirited exchange on Mr. Frank's suggestion.

upon an instrument. Now it seems to me that the way the labor board could help to the best advantage would be to have the workers organized so that they could present their problems to them.

154. MR. CANTWELL: All right now, you encourage strong organization, strong labor unions?

155. MR. FRANK: Exactly.

156. MR. CANTWELL: All right. Okey. Stan, I'd like to bring up one thing. I would think that you would defeat the purpose of this plan of ours by encouraging strong labor organization. It wouldn't be necessary because every laborer would have the right to bring his case before the board. I would think it would encourage a smaller organization of laborers. The tendency would be more toward more company unions rather than a sort of industrial or national union.

157. MR. FRANK: What do you mean?

158. MR. CANTWELL: Well, any laborer that has a dispute with capital, that was discriminated against, could bring his dispute up to this labor board. Am I right, Steve?

159. MR. LADD: No, I don't think so. As a matter of fact, you could say that the machinery of this plan would only be used in disputes between organized labor and capital. Now incidentally the railroad unions are among the strongest unions we have, which shows that this plan doesn't necessarily do away with unions.

160. MR. HAMMOND: That's why it's so successful, isn't it? Because they are so well organized. They can stop some of these cracks that are always being taken at labor.

161. MR. LADD: I don't think the unions exert any influence over the mediation or arbitration machinery that's used. There is one other point that should be brought up and that is under a plan of this type, where you have some compulsory features, mediation and collective bargaining usually settle most of the disputes whereas they don't otherwise; because under this plan the two parties realize that they can't just fight it out without any restraint, so they decide that they might just as well make the best of it and come together.

Mr. Ladd settles the matter.

162. MISS PLEVNEY: Well, I'd like to know about this: You say that in this investigation after a certain period they can resort to striking?

A question is asked.

163. MR. LADD: Yes.

164. MISS PLEVNEY: Well, now with labor organization getting stronger and their demands increasing, because as has been said, labor is never satisfied, they are always desiring more and more; well, would that satisfy them? I am still rather doubtful as to whether that would really stop the trouble. If they had so much power and if they knew that they had the power, wouldn't they go on with the strike afterwards?

165. MR. BABCOCK: Miss Plevney, you speak of the laborer always wanting something more. Well, labor hasn't had a fair deal since the beginning of the United States. Ever since industrialization of the U. S. they haven't had a real fair deal as yet. I mean you're getting further away the whole time from equality among the two. You're getting bigger business and you're still educating your worker. If you don't want to give your worker a break, quit educating him!

166. MR. CANTWELL: The point that Miss Plevney is driving at I think, Ollie, is that under this proposal of Steve's your labor organization is getting stronger and stronger. That means that they will be able to bring more and more pressure to bear upon the capitalists, the employer. Therefore, if they can bring more pressure and therefore get more and more out of the employer, why, then you're going to have labor demanding more. I think that's what you mean.

167. MISS PLEVNEY: Yes. More than its rightful share. Therefore I would suggest that you have economists on your board, educate your labor union and have these economists give labor only its rightful share as determined by impartial investigation and arbitration.

168. MR. HAMMOND: There's talk about labor never being satisfied, but neither is capital. Because every time that labor gives capital a chance, why, it pushes labor back

Mr. Babcock makes a spirited reply.

Mr. Cantwell comes to the rescue.

Mr. Hammond's zeal for labor persists. His consistency is commendable, but his choice of words and

several hundred years. And capital is so well organized that labor has to keep on moving all the time or she would be defeated.

169. MISS PLEVNEY: Then you say we don't have to worry about labor exploiting capital?

170. MR. HAMMOND: I think also that if everybody brings their cards and puts them on the table and spreads them out so that everybody can see, so that capital says here's the amount of profits I'm getting, here's what I'm paying for labor and here's what I'm paying for my running expenses and everything is laid on the table, I think that labor will see that they can go only so far and they will be fair enough and not try to get more than is absolutely their share.

171. MISS PLEVNEY: Then you think therefore that by an open-handed dealing we can also bring in that force of public opinion for fair play.

172. MR. HAMMOND: Absolutely.

173. MR. O'LEARY: Well, in case they don't though what are you going to do? I still stick by my idea that you should have a decision reached at the end of these investigations which is going to be put into effect. I still don't find anything wrong with that.

174. MR. LADD: Well, there are a number of objections to whole-hog compulsory arbitration. Personally I don't see why we should just jump right into such a revolutionary idea at this time. I think

way of putting his contributions are not always conducive to reflective thought. He is too combative at times.

Mr. Hammond makes an excellent contribution.

Mr. O'Leary again insists on his point.

that ultimately we may have some scheme along that line, but this system, whether it's a panacea or not, would definitely help. I can't see any question about that. And on the railroads, so far as worrying about whether they are going on a strike afterwards, they haven't struck in twelve years. If you have an intelligent decision arrived at by disinterested persons, the railroad employees don't dare strike because they know public opinion would be against them. And a union has to have public opinion in order to be successful in the long run. Some of you may say perhaps that labor didn't have public opinion with it on the sit-down strikes, but I believe that the Gallup poll will show that it did.

> Mr. Ladd replies to Mr. O'Leary and offers further material on his proposal.

175. MR. O'LEARY: The investigations of many of the strikes and lockouts found that public opinion really didn't hold when either of the two sides lost much. I mean they didn't regard public opinion; they went right on ahead and did what they desired.

> Mr. O'Leary persists.

176. LEADER: I think we're quibbling over little incidental matters here. Is there anything big up that we haven't discussed? If not, I'll try to sum this up. Yager.

> The leader thinks that it is time to summarize.

177. MR. CANTWELL: How is this board going to decide these cases? How is it going to decide what labor's rightful share is? It's a well-known fact that in the Insull case all the accountants and economists who were brought in couldn't fig-

> Mr. Cantwell raises a point which had been considered earlier in the discussion.

ure out the intricacies of Insull's, shall I say, accounting. May I say here that Insull's punishment should have been that he figure out just exactly the intricacies he had gotten himself and all his laborers into. So I think you ought to have a very high standard for these mediation boards.

178. MR. WAGGONER: Trained Civil Service plus people who are economists. That combination is pretty high, don't you agree?

179. LEADER: All right, is there any other discussion relevant to this plan? If not, I think I'll take a little bit of the remaining time. Mr. Babcock.

The leader again suggests a final summary.

180. MR. BABCOCK: I'd like to ask one thing. Are there any teeth in this proposal? Have you any ways of enforcing your decision?

Mr. Babcock has another question.

181. MR. LADD: You have ways of preventing strikes during this cooling-off period. It has been found through the injunction that by tying up union funds, if they start to go out on a strike, you can completely stop the strike right in its tracks. So that can be enforced, and you can sue the capitalists. Now the point of this whole thing is that you don't have to say arbitrarily that no strikes will ever be tolerated, because this plan affords machinery for intelligent decision and the two sides will abide by the decision of their own free will. Experience has shown that they have in the railroads and in Canada.

Mr. Ladd replies.

182. LEADER: We agree, I guess, that unless we outlaw strikes completely that strikes will occur. Our object, then, is not to hit the 100% mark, but to get as many strikes as possible off the record. Now do you agree that this plan goes a long way in doing that? It's not a panacea, a cure-all, but it does set forth certain standards which will aid us in breaking down these strikes.— Mr. O'Leary, did you have something to say?

An excellent point by the leader. He says what most members of the group appear to be thinking.

183. MR. O'LEARY: I guess not.

184. LEADER: In brief summary, then: We seem to be agreed that the strike is an unfortunate manifestation of these controversies between capital and labor and that there is every reason to believe that strikes will increase unless something is done. We have found the basic causes of the trouble to be labor's desire for collective bargaining, which, in turn, goes back to its desire for better wages, hours, and working conditions. Underlying all of this is the business cycle with its periodic depressions and consequent insecurity for both capital and labor. The fact that some of us have sought to blame the employer and others to blame labor may mean that both are partially responsible, or it may mean, as several implied, that the whole system is wrong.

Mr. O'Leary is not completely satisfied, but it is about time to adjourn.

A good summary— fair, tactful, accurate, and adequate in length.

We decided in this discussion, however, to consider what the Federal Government should do to avert or alleviate the strike or the threat of strike, in the interests of both capital and labor and the general public as well. Various proposals were offered ranging from governmentally managed cooperatives to various extensions and modifications of the Wagner Act. An extension of the Wagner Act to include compulsory investigation along the lines of the Canadian system seemed to meet with the approval of the group. At the same time most of us felt that compulsory arbitration and outlawing strikes would be a mistake. We closed with discussion of several suggestions for putting this compulsory investigation plan into operation. Is that a fair summary?

185. SEVERAL VOICES: Yes.

A PANEL DISCUSSION

THE UNIVERSITY OF CHICAGO ROUND TABLE

PROPAGANDA IN A DEMOCRACY[1]

Harry D. Gideonse, Associate Professor of Economics
Harold D. Lasswell, Associate Professor of Political Science
T. V. Smith, Professor of Philosophy, Illinois State Senator
(All three are members of the University of Chicago faculty)

MR. GIDEONSE: Well, T. V. Smith, is it propaganda to tell others what propaganda is?

MR. SMITH: If so, we are going to be guilty of propaganda in this Round Table.

MR. GIDEONSE: There ought to be some kind of distinction, then, apparently, between the propaganda that you and I think is right and which we probably call "education," and the propaganda which we think is wrong and call "propaganda."

MR. SMITH: Either way we look at it, there is propaganda to the right of us and propaganda to the left of us, and now, propaganda in front of us, since Mr. Lasswell has arrived.

MR. GIDEONSE: Did the cab get here on time, Lasswell?

MR. LASSWELL: Oh, quite so. I am greatly disappointed that I gave you a chance to define the word "propaganda" before I got here.

[1] A radio discussion broadcast from Chicago over the Red Network of the National Broadcasting Company, Sunday, August 14, 1938, at 9:30 P.M., Central Daylight Time, in cooperation with the University Broadcasting Council.

The Round Table, oldest educational program continuously on the air, is broadcast entirely without a script. Subjects are chosen because of their social, political, or economic significance. No participant has "an ax to grind," and the opinion of each speaker is his own, based on his own background of research and experience.

Reprinted by permission of the University of Chicago Round Table.

MR. SMITH: Do you have a good excuse for being late to this Round Table?

MR. GIDEONSE: He knows propaganda techniques and he knows one of the best ways of drawing attention to himself is to arrive late—to do the unusual and grab the publicity and all the rest of it, which you and I have been conferring on.

MR. SMITH: Let me answer your question while he catches his breath. There are two senses in which the term "propaganda" is used—perhaps many more, for aught I know. There is an ancient use which means anything that is propagated.

MR. GIDEONSE: Wasn't the term originally built up on the practice of the College of Propaganda of the Holy Roman Church?

MR. SMITH: I don't know, but that is a very good example. People that use propaganda in this sense suppose they are telling the truth—spreading information. I suppose that like most words it gets its bad reputation by starting right and being misused later.

MR. LASSWELL: I think we ought to agree to define the word "propaganda" for our purposes in a perfectly descriptive fashion.

MR. SMITH: We have a right, so that we won't be propagandists.

MR. LASSWELL: I think we might just as well decide to use the term in a perfectly naturalistic, descriptive sense, and go on from there.

MR. GIDEONSE: "Naturalistic, descriptive sense." Let's have it, Lasswell—what is the "naturalistic, descriptive sense" of "propaganda"?

MR. LASSWELL: I should say that that is using it as a term to describe something, in the same objective spirit in which you talk about a stone—rather than using it to express a preference. After all, in scientific circles I don't think we want to use the word in a stench-bomb sense. From that point of view, I recommend defining the term "propaganda" for our discussion here as the technique of manipulating words to modify attitudes on controversial issues.

MR. GIDEONSE: Say, for instance, that a moving picture is being made in Hollywood, and a very prominent church organization, very closely associated with the Catholic

Church, does not like some of the things that are in the moving picture while it is being produced. If they keep those things out, the country undergoes a negative form of what I would call propaganda, but I don't see very much manipulation of words. I see the excising of a lot of words and scenes. The purpose is to modify attitudes in what are, from the Church's standpoint, controversial situations.

MR. LASSWELL: There are two points involved there. The first is censorship. The ordinary use of the term "censorship" is that it is negative propaganda—that is, some sort of restriction on words, and word substitutes. The second point, as you quite properly brought out, is that in the case of the motion picture, one is dealing with pictorial representation rather than verbal. The definition would have to be enlarged to include word substitutes.

MR. SMITH: I don't want to quibble over a definition. We ought to get clear what we are talking about, but if we are going to use the word in its "naturalistic, descriptive sense," Lasswell, let's make it very clear that that is a special use for our own purpose. I think to nine Americans out of ten the word "propaganda" carries an invidious sense—something is hidden, something is being put over. And this surely ought to be said, even from the scientific point of view, that we don't ever use words without a purpose. Our purpose seldom gets fully expressed in our words. In that sense we never can tell when propaganda is a statement of facts for influencing opinion in controversial situations, and when it is the statement of something that will pass for facts but that would not stand the test scientifically.

MR. LASSWELL: I should agree with that. Speaking as social scientists, our purpose here is to use a word which would be naturalistic for our special scientific interests. Now, then, one of the principles of propaganda, which we can state naturalistically, is to use congratulatory words often, in referring to what we are doing. One of the principles of propaganda is, quite often, not to call what you are doing "propaganda."

MR. GIDEONSE: You go into a campaign to advertise, say, certain industrial techniques and the interests of the American family in those industrial techniques. But the emphasis is on the American family.

MR. LASSWELL: We can certainly draw a distinction, if we want to go into distinctions, between using words to transmit a skill and using words and word substitutes to influence a preference. It is the second, I believe, in which we are particularly interested.

MR. GIDEONSE: Well, then, could you give me some idea of what you have in mind by the kinds of propaganda that are not called propaganda by the ordinary man, but which your social scientist, with his "naturalistic, descriptive" talents, does call propaganda?

MR. SMITH: Don't let him get away with it, Lasswell. Come, come, now, Harry, you are a social scientist, yourself. Let's join in the party.

MR. GIDEONSE: It all depends on the company, T. V. I am particular.

MR. LASSWELL: I was surprised that your colleague resigned from the fraternity of social scientists so speedily. What I was going to say was that one of the most interesting specializations in our propaganda now is that of the public relations counsel. The public relations counsel is one who handles propaganda for a number of clients. That sets him off from the simple press agent.

MR. SMITH: He is the last of a long line of people who have tried to influence public opinion in these disputed situations?

MR. LASSWELL: Yes, and it has only been in rather recent times that there has been any considerable number of people who have tried to spread an idea of some kind without themselves believing in it.

MR. SMITH: Well, advertising used to do that, didn't it? That is what I think of first—what is done in newspapers. The advertisers have goods to sell—or ideas to sell, perhaps—but, they have something to sell, and they tell people about it. Isn't that an earlier form of propaganda?

MR. GIDEONSE: Incidentally, I think advertising is one of the greatest forces in the United States and in the Western World working toward a destruction of freedom—in the sense that an advertiser creates consumer discontent. If there is anything more wicked in the world than creating consumer discontent—anything that makes for more insecurity and instability, I'd like to hear of it.

MR. SMITH: Smile when you say that, Gideonse.

MR. GIDEONSE: No, I don't feel like smiling. You remember that Thoreau said that there were only two real sources of men's loss of freedom. One was the restraint of freedom by a person's equals; the other was restraint by his own wants. To keep his freedom, a person has to keep his wants down. From Thoreau's standpoint, advertising is the most vicious attack on human freedom that I know of.

MR. SMITH: I feel the world whirling under my feet, and I am transplanted back in ancient stoicism, when men were the slaves of nature. Instead of going out to get what they wanted, they learned to want what they could get.

MR. LASSWELL: Well, after this introduction of your preferences, in the form of the term "wicked," it is clear that at least you have great capacity for passing moral judgments on the world.

MR. GIDEONSE: Manipulating words to modify attitudes in controversial situations. And you heard from T. V., of course, that the situation is plenty controversial.

MR. LASSWELL: I think the term "wicked," applied to the consequences of advertising, suggests that propaganda might not be so far away from us.

MR. GIDEONSE: It meant to me that I think if you create consumer discontent, you do something wicked. I believe in people not being so discontented.

MR. LASSWELL: You would approve of using propaganda to diminish the discontent of the community?

MR. GIDEONSE: Perhaps, if I might define the term my way, as you are defining it in your way.

MR. SMITH: We are getting back now to "propaganda" in the bad sense—that it is what the other guy uses, while what we use is educational. Seriously, Lasswell, I have seen colleges and churches and political parties put on publicity campaigns for this purpose or the other. That is a form of propaganda, also, isn't it?

MR. LASSWELL: Yes, it is a part of well-recognized, modern technique. As a matter of fact, as you well know, there are several specialized agencies which devote themselves to handling propaganda to raise funds for hospitals and schools and colleges and similar institutions that require some sort of public support.

MR. SMITH: Well, every politician may soon have a press agent to keep him before the country. I suppose that is legitimate, also, in our general conception, isn't it?

MR. LASSWELL: That is taken for granted, too. There are very few public figures in modern society who haven't "ghosts" and other propagandists. I don't know, Congressman, whether you have a "ghost" yet?

MR. SMITH: Do you know, Lasswell, that Gideonse is my press agent?

MR. GIDEONSE: Yes, I find out all the nice words for him. But certainly most of us know of agencies and individuals who approach us and tell us that for twenty-five dollars a week they will see to it that we get all sorts of publicity even if we say nothing—and if we feel like saying nothing, they will find something for us to say. I again use the word "wicked." If it is propaganda to call that sort of thing wicked, all right, then, it is propaganda.

MR. SMITH: I think you have a real point there, Harry. This business of extending human wants indefinitely for people without the means of satisfying them is at the source of much modern discontent.

MR. GIDEONSE: That isn't the point, T. V. If I have a typewriter that is a magnificent typewriter and has fifteen more years of life in it, the job of an advertising manager of a typewriter company is to make me feel that it is a miserable, wicked, old-fashioned instrument and that I should want with all the want I have in me the new gadgets and the new nickel-plate or whatever it is that he has on his new machine. He wants to make me discontented with what I've got, when what I've got is excellently serviceable for the purpose for which I use it.

MR. LASSWELL: Of course, on the other side is the emphasis on creating all sorts of psychological enjoyment by the use of propaganda. I take it there is a point, which liberals used to regard as of some importance, that one could stimulate progress by stimulating a new set of demands, and in that sense, modern advertising has contributed to the creation of the type of world that some people wish could still survive.

MR. SMITH: I think that our friend Gideonse represents one attitude, and you represent another, and, of course,

I am in the middle—and right, as usual. But either of you is willing to use whatever techniques you can to spread information which will ingratiate your way of life with me— or with the public.

MR. GIDEONSE: Says he, running for office right now.

MR. LASSWELL: Of course, my role here is devil's advocate. My comments in this situation are to indicate arguments for any particular prejudice that neither of you happens to express.

MR. GIDEONSE: You didn't say anything about newspapers, incidentally. Think of all the kinds of propaganda we find in the newspapers—apart from the advertising pages and the "legitimate" propaganda on the editorial page.

MR. LASSWELL: Of course, part of the regular technique in any pressure group in modern society—whether the National Association of Manufacturers, the American Federation of Labor, or the Committee for Industrial Organization —is to do whatever it can to control these newspaper channels of publicity. But, after all, the most subtle and important propaganda in modern society is public relations. That means something rather different from the simple business of paid publicity, which is advertising, or even sending out "releases," which are rather plainly marked as coming from some special agency.

MR. SMITH: I got in great trouble with some of these public relations men not long ago when I called them "plutogogs," defining them as the voice of wealth when wealth could no longer speak respectably for itself. But that was an oversimplification, because these counsels also represent causes of peace and men who are devoted to peace as well as those devoted to war and armaments. By and large they represent any cause that comes to them, don't they?

MR. LASSWELL: They are just as willing to serve any client as a lawyer is. Their particular judge and jury is the community-at-large that they are trying to influence.

MR. SMITH: I read somewhere recently that business, when it felt itself on the defensive along about 1933, diverted its efforts from trying to sell its goods to trying to sell its ideas. It tried to propagate the notion that business is what the businessman wants it to be and to cultivate an attitude of good will. As you said, it is rather a recent thing that men will represent causes or ideas in which they don't believe.

Mr. Lasswell: I think it would be perfectly legitimate to say that public relations, in the sense in which you just referred to it, has developed on an especially large scale in our own society since 1933. The business counter-offensive got well under way at that time. Confidence in business was undermined, what with the stock market crash and depression. Consequently, a great many of the more articulate business groups—some of the major automobile corporations and some of the major trade and business associations— undertook to develop public relations policies.

The first thing they did was to adopt an advertising and publicity program, but more recently they have taken over what can truly be called public relations techniques. That seems to me to be the most important recent development. One way to illustrate what is involved is to refer rather briefly to one typical campaign of that kind, the campaign in California to beat the differential tax on chain stores.

What was done there was not, in the first place, to develop a great barrage of advertising and publicity. They tried first to find out what rather nasty things people were saying about chain stores. There was a survey of what the workers in the chain group were saying, what their wives were saying, what customers in different parts of the state were saying.

Then they began—at first within the chain store organization itself—not with publicity but with certain policies and certain rumors of policies. Gradually the employees of the chain stores began to feel that they had a stake in the enterprise as a whole. Their wives began to spread the news in the community. Then, when the large publicity techniques came into operation, there were already thousands of people feeling that their personal interests were tied up very closely with the survival of the chains.

Mr. Gideonse: But you defined propaganda as manipulating words to modify attitudes in controversial situations, Lasswell. This example in California is, in part, a modification, not of attitudes in a controversial situation, but of the controversial situation itself.

MR. LASSWELL: That is a very important point. There is a definite movement, in public relations technique, from the simple manipulation of words to the careful adjustment of policy. For instance, in that situation, the first act was not to raise wages or shorten hours of work in the stores, but simply to circulate the rumor that something of this kind might happen. Then, later, certain changes of policy did take place.

MR. SMITH: Do you mind if I express my preference that we discuss what I think is more nearly to the point now— that is, government propaganda?

MR. GIDEONSE: As Lasswell was saying, this new trend in public relations is to a large extent a counter-offensive on the part of private groups. Presumably, the counter-offensive is in answer to propaganda on the part of the government.

MR. SMITH: Here is the point. The chain stores in California resorted to this particular technique when they felt themselves in danger of being heavily taxed—that is, when they were on the defensive. Business, in general, feels itself on the defensive, not so much against the government, but against everything—the depression, the world in general.

So it resorts to public relations counsels. Many people think the government is spending a lot of money and engaging in sending out propaganda, in the neutral sense and in every other sense.

What is fair to say, I suppose, is that the government is spending more money in this regard now, because it feels itself on the defensive—feels that it doesn't get a break in the newspapers.

MR. GIDEONSE: How much propaganda is there, Lasswell, in this talk about the federal government using so much money and making so much more of an effort along propagandist lines?

MR. LASSWELL: There has been a very important increase in the deliberate use of publicity by administrative departments of the government. You may have noticed, too, that it has even affected Congress. T. V., you may discover, when you get to Washington, that the Senate has already established a press agent. That was done only last July. I don't think the House of Representatives has a press agent yet, so that is one of the possible measures that could be taken up.

Mr. Smith: Well, counting no eggs until the chickens are grown, Lasswell, let's not discuss the quarrel between government and business except to say that this matter of being on the defensive and being fearful always makes people defend themselves as best they can. What is really in the minds of the public now is whether the government has a right to defend itself against these foreign governmental groups in our midst that are propagating ideas in which they believe, but in which we don't believe.

Mr. Lasswell: That is an important point, but let me say just one more thing about the magnitude of government publicity. There was a report which was worked out by the staff of the Brookings Institution, at the request of Senator Byrd's committee last year.

This report has been rather carefully checked over by Professor McCamy. He said that when those people who had no discretionary control over what publicity they sent out were eliminated, you might find as many as 280 or 290 full-time publicity people in the federal government. That army of publicity people is relatively small, compared to the number of secretaries of trade associations and the number of hired advertisers, and so on, representing other groups in the country.

Mr. Smith: Why, the National Association of Manufacturers in 1937 spent outright and openly about eight hundred thousand dollars in a campaign just for its group alone. I am amazed at the smallness of the figures that you quote for the federal government.

Mr. Lasswell: I was quoting the numbers of persons directly employed primarily in publicity work, but, after all, these quantitative questions are much less important than the question of principle that you posed a moment ago.

How far is it consistent with democratic policy for government to spread propaganda itself, or to block propaganda directed against it?

Mr. Smith: I think we can admit at once that a democratic government is directly concerned in the most gigantic propaganda machine that it can command—its public school system. We say that it is teaching citizenship, but that means teaching people to appreciate the democratic form of government.

MR. GIDEONSE: All you have to do is look at an American school primer and compare it with a Russian or German primer, and you can see that. Of course, there are a number of other aspects there. These totalitarian governments get a great deal out of such things as marching together and wearing uniforms. And any democratic country that overlooks the effectiveness of that technique, I think, would be very foolish. I think, for instance, it would be a very defensible attitude for a democracy that intended to remain a democracy to legislate against such marching and such wearing of uniforms of non-American groups.

MR. LASSWELL: I think that democracies are justified in circulating proper democratic propaganda, but that democracies must also agree to the circulation of anti-democratic propaganda. But it is important to draw the line. I suggest that the line be drawn at the point of "incitement."

MR. SMITH: Before we draw the line, let's emphasize that a democratic government must allow propaganda against itself and its ideas, because that is one of the things democracy means. As Justice Holmes once said, "We should be eternally vigilant against attempts to check the expression of opinions that we loathe and believe fraught with death."

But there is a point beyond which it seems fairly clear we can't tolerate those who advertise their intolerance and tell us that tomorrow, if they get in power, they will stop every avenue of freedom which we extend them.

MR. LASSWELL: I think that the term "incitement" may cover situations which include the one that Gideonse referred to just a moment ago. When people start marching around in uniforms and going through military exercises, the line is overstepped. I feel that it is too dangerous for orderly and stable democratic government to permit the use of symbols in such close relationship with drill.

MR. SMITH: Our Supreme Court, you know, has drawn the distinction between advocacy of violent overthrow of government, which is allowed, and efforts to overthrow the government, which are not allowed.

MR. GIDEONSE: Of course, any rule, even the simple one about marching in uniforms, Lasswell, is likely to be distorted in interpretation and practice. For instance, marching in uniforms might be held against the Boy Scouts.

MR. SMITH: Well, we live in a very complex world, it is true, in which Gideonse's earlier notions will have to be somewhat modified. We have to allow advertising and not call it the death of freedom. We have to allow propaganda against our government. But we seem in general to agree that no government, not even a democracy, is obligated to do itself to death. I propose that we shall be tolerant to the tolerant and intolerant only to the grossly intolerant.

A SYMPOSIUM-FORUM

AMERICA'S TOWN MEETING OF THE AIR

IS OUR PUBLIC OPINION CONTROLLED BY PROPAGANDA?[1]

CHAIRMAN DENNY: Good evening, neighbors! On our program last week when we were discussing the problem of world peace, Mrs. McCormick spoke of the twilight zone in which Europeans live—"between two worlds," as Matthew Arnold said, "one dead, the other powerless to be born." We can look upon our life today as the most thrilling and exciting period in man's history, or, if we are pessimists, we can regard it as the most appalling and dangerous age mankind has ever faced. One course may lead to victory, the other harbors sure defeat. Never before in the history of the world has it been so essential for large populations of people to be honestly informed about their common problems and to act wisely on the basis of this information. Advancing science has shrunk the earth's surface and has tied it in a fabric made of varying economic, social, and political designs. This inharmonious picture reflects the public opinion of many nations, but on what is this public opinion based? Yesterday I saw a movie showing the perfect precision with which one great European country has been regimented under dictator rule. Watching this picture, I was impressed with the grave responsibility that rests upon us in the democratic countries to find our way through the welter of conflicting propagandas to a workable democracy. And I am sure this cannot be done unless we have an honestly informed public opinion. Like the Town Hall itself, this program is dedicated to the advancement of American democracy through education and an enlightened public opinion.

We present on our program this evening Professor

[1] Reprinted by arrangement with the Columbia University Press.

Hadley Cantril, of Princeton University, President of the Institute for Propaganda Analysis, who, by the way, was so much interested in America's Town Meeting of the Air during its first year of operation that he conducted an independent survey with his resources to find out the effect of these programs on our listeners; Mr. John T. Flynn, well-known journalist and author, who is not new to Town Meeting audiences; and Mr. Frank R. Kent, famous political columnist and Vice President of the *Baltimore Sun*. It is now my pleasure to present Professor Hadley Cantril, President of the Institute for Propaganda Analysis.

MR. CANTRIL: So far, in the twentieth century, propagandists have sold us everything from toothpaste to war. Never before has the world seen so many propagandas competing for the attention of the bewildered layman. One of the chief reasons for this tremendous barrage is the vast development that has taken place in the media of communication. Newspapers, the radio, and the movies all are vehicles of propaganda, and two of them in our own culture, the newspaper and the radio, depend for their very existence upon one form of propaganda which we call advertising.

What is this thing, "propaganda"? It is difficult to define since it includes so much. Our definition will be that propaganda is a deliberate attempt by interested individuals or groups to influence opinions or actions of other individuals or groups with reference to predetermined ends. This definition implies several things: first, that propaganda is positive, that it is well planned, that it is selfish, that it is one-sided, making use of suggestion and not reason, and, finally, that it may be good or bad, depending upon the point of view of the individual judging it.

How does the propagandist go about his task? There are certain simple rules and principles of propaganda the psychologist sees. The first of these propaganda principles is to connect the idea or object being propagandized with some attitude, symbol, or emotion that people already know and feel strongly about. The propagandist must, then, know people. Nazi propagandist Goebbels has one rule of propaganda: to see with the eyes of the masses. Propagandists must use symbols, that is, words standing for abstract ideals rich in their emotional meaning, symbols that appeal to broad general attitudes or sentiments which are so vague that people may be for or against them emotionally and yet not know precisely what such symbols mean. Take, for example, the often repeated symbols of justice, beauty, liberty, economy, patriotism. To these and other such attitudes, we find the propagandist connecting soaps, cigarettes, political campaigns, and appeals to join the army. Vague emotionally toned words such as "fascist," "communist," "red," "atheist," "slacker," are used to arouse us against government officials, labor leaders, and other individuals whom the propagandist freely labels. These vague words that most people like or dislike are, at the same time, little understood. Therefore, people are apt to accept the propaganda because the symbols it appeals to are not defined. What, for example, is meant by "liberty"? Liberty for whom—for workers or for business?—for radicals or for conservatives?—for you or for me? This simple rule of propaganda is so frequently used that the layman is by now more or less aware of the propagandist's trick. Hence the propagandist must resort to another technique in order to conceal his purpose or to make it socially acceptable.

This other method is to build up an attitude around a product or idea by using subtle, concealed suggestion. In using this technique, the propagandist frequently tries to get his propaganda into newspapers as news or editorial opinion. In this he is highly successful and the critical observer will see that a large proportion of the news in even the best newspapers of the country is propaganda. One paper may headline one story while another paper may carry the same story in a back page. This propaganda by emphasis depends upon the interests of those who own and edit the paper. The technique is seen every day by any person who takes the trouble to compare the way the news of the Spanish Civil War, of a strike, of a Republican or Democratic policy is reported, headlined, and pictured in different papers.

Another method for building up the public attitudes regarding someone's pet idea is to disguise propaganda as explanation. This is a device frequently employed by those already in power. Here we find, for example, the efforts of the public utilities to enlist the cooperation of educators so that the educators will teach, without knowing it, the things that would preserve the interests of those who now control utilities. Textbook writers are influenced, college professors are hired to write and speak for the interests, technical journals are used to "explain" or rationalize the selfish interests of those behind the scenes. There are many examples of such propaganda by explanation. Propagandists "explain" why we need a larger navy, why we need higher or lower tariffs, why corporations should or should not be taxed.

Since the use of this particular method is so dependent upon the situation in question and the tenor of the times, great companies, organizations, and powerful individuals now hire experts in propaganda who call themselves "public relations counsels," and whose business it is to feel the public's pulse in all classes and vocations and find out where people are most gullible. The public relations counsel, once hired, will work for his client through the newspapers, the radio, the medical journal, the school textbook, the cut-out for the kiddies.

A knowledge of the techniques of the propagandist is, however, only half the story if we really want to understand this important force in modern life. For propaganda is always directed at people. And we must ask ourselves what it is in us that makes propaganda possible and effective. Why do the techniques work?

There are several reasons for the success of propaganda. First, the great majority of the words in our language, or any other language, are freighted with emotion. Most of the time we do not react to the dictionary meaning of the word, but to a whole complex of feeling that surrounds that word. Take, for example, the word "strawberry." We know what a strawberry is, but we always think it is a "good" thing. The word "love" can hardly be mentioned without arousing a whole host of sentiments in every individual. The word "Turk" will arouse in most Americans an unfavorable attitude even though most of these same Americans have never known a Turk. We learn the attitude toward words, or society's value of words, at the same time that we learn their meaning.

A second reason why the propagandist is so successful is that most of us are unsure of ourselves. We seek a meaning for those things we do not understand. We do not want to appear ignorant on too many questions, and so we accept the judgment of some authority, of some official, of some newspaper editor, of some columnist, or some radio commentator. We feel that he must know more about the issue than we do, but we forget at the same time that the opinions of such experts are frequently elaborated rationalizations of their own points of view, rationalizations which seem to us objective, critical analyses. As life becomes more and more specialized, we are depending more and more upon other people for our judgments. The propagandist, then, gives us his meaning to satisfy our desire for a solution to problems such as, What shall I buy? How shall I vote? What shall I believe?

A third reason for his success is that most of us are anxious to preserve our own position in life, to maintain or to enhance our status. We have, therefore, a tendency to accept the type of propaganda that makes us feel superior to other individuals or makes us feel that our own status is better than the other fellow's. One race will believe it is superior to another race. The rich will think the poor are happy or irresponsible. We accept the political philosophy that best suits our interests. That is one reason why most people read a newspaper whose editorials or news slant fits their prejudices, why many people turn off the radio if a speaker's views do not fit their own.

How can we make ourselves less susceptible to propaganda? There are two chief methods: first, to understand the technique of the propagandist and the aims and goals he has in mind; second, to understand our own biases, the forces in the environment that have given us our particular status and our particular opinions and that have tended to make us reject other opinions which do not serve our own selfish interests. This means, essentially, that education is propaganda's most deadly enemy and is the reason why the propagandists themselves are frightened when they see people being educated in the methods that the propagandists use. For real education is critical, not one-sided. It appeals to reason more than to emotion and it seeks truth rather than tries to achieve some special selfish interest. And real education implies that the educator himself is not unwittingly teaching someone else's propaganda. [Applause]

CHAIRMAN DENNY: Thank you, Professor Cantril. Now we shall hear Mr. John T. Flynn, well-known author and journalist.

MR. FLYNN: I believe that public opinion is controlled by propaganda. I quite agree with Mr. Cantril that the world is so full of all sorts of propaganda that on many fronts the layman is not so much convinced as bewildered. I also agree with him that propaganda may be good or bad. After all, it is a means of propagating ideas. The saints have used it as well as the sinners. It is a method of getting ideas accepted. I think we may also say that the press and the air are so crowded with conflicting propagandas that many of them refute each other and cancel the effect.

My own concern is with certain forms of propaganda. We know, of course, that there is such a thing as the mass mind. And we know that there is an immense effort under way ceaselessly to capture and tame that monster. Now of course you cannot reach the mass mind by throwing up a window and shouting your message to the stars—nor even from the top of a soap-box. In order to carry on propaganda against the mass mind, you must have access to the instruments of propaganda. These instruments are the press and the radio and certain other forms of print. And these instruments are very expensive. You cannot use them unless you have plenty of money to pay the bills. And the result is that the only really effective instruments of propaganda are open only to those who have the money to pay the bills.

Let me give you an example. A statesman or philosopher or agitator, if he is sufficiently important, can get five or ten or fifteen minutes on the radio. But not many will tune in to hear him and as his voice roars into the living room someone quickly enough runs over to the radio to dial him out. Of course, it is not the fault of the radio company if a speaker can't get himself listened to. The radio companies do, in fact, at their own cost, give the public so free a forum as this Town Meeting of the Air, where all sides are represented. I am speaking of those bought programs where only one side is represented, and it is always the same side because only one side has the money to buy programs.

But now see effective propaganda at work on the mass mind. There is no better time to catch the monster than on Sunday evening. It is relaxed. It is in a benevolent mood. On Sunday evening the family is gathered in the living room when into their midst float the strains of music from a great symphony orchestra. In millions of homes people are listening. This goes on for half an hour. Then as the strains of some well-loved old song fade from the air and the family sits around, thoroughly softened up, there floats into the room and into the unguarded chambers of their minds the voice of the propagandist. For five or ten minutes the carefully planned infection flows into the monster. It tells of the romantic saga of business, the great achievements, the massive wisdom, the matchless courage, the civilizing alchemy of the great business man as distinguished from the selfish and narrow ignorance and wickedness of the Government—the great-souled business leader compared with the small-minded and vicious Senator.

Now that costs a lot of money. It costs a lot of money for another program sent out by certain great banks of America—another great symphony orchestra, but interrupted for those precious five minutes while an economist, notorious as an apologist for big business, pours his propaganda into the listening ears of millions. And who can afford the money to put on a counter-blast that people will listen to and do it regularly, week after week?

Now I don't believe any more than Frank Kent here that Senators and Congressmen are incapable of some splendid stupidities. But they have no corner on that. Their business brothers are at least as bad. But this propaganda about the folly and stupidity of Government is one of those deliberate propagandas which business fosters through press and radio to discredit the efforts of the Government to make it behave itself. Whatever the reason, the chief point I make is that the great cost of modern instruments of propaganda has given the commercial elements in our society almost a monopoly in pouring propaganda for their strange forms of culture over the minds of the American people. A program of music filters in through the radio. It is sentimental and sad. A chorus sings the old songs that men love. Some old actor called Uncle Jasper, with a voice like an old Southern preacher, talks to you in a strain of lugubrious sentiment and when your heart is just about broken and is welling up with human sympathy, the announcer sneaks in on you and sells you some sort of kidney medicine. And sometimes when he is selling you the kidney medicine or the motor car or the cigarette as a cure for bronchitis, he may sell you a little political or economic or social philosophy which the sponsor thinks is good for business.

Now what of the newspapers? Once there used to be Democratic and Republican and independent newspapers. But now, with a few exceptions, they are all the same. They are just commercial organs. They may differ on certain unimportant points, but when the interests of business are attacked, particularly of big advertisers, they are suddenly a unit. They print the speech of some important authority in a small paragraph on page 27 and the address of the chairman of the board of an international liverwurst company in full on page 1. There are certain areas of news beats, as editors call them, around which fences are built and over which reporters are never permitted to peek and about which little is ever printed.

And here I cannot leave out a form of propaganda for which I have an especial aversion. That is the form which is called by the name of shirt-stuffing. Big business corporations spend fortunes on publicity. One form of publicity is to exploit the name, the character, the wisdom of the head of the corporation. They build him up into a great and often a heroic figure. They write speeches for him to deliver. They compose epigrams for him to utter. They invent philosophies for him to proclaim. They even write magazine articles which appear over his name. And thus the American people have accepted the naïve illusion that because a man knows how to make a million dollars, he knows how to run a government, how to bring back prosperity, how to fashion and mold our culture, how to direct universities, and how, in fact, to control our theology and govern our churches. The result is that these stuffed shirts become useful instruments for getting space in the papers and time on the radio to spread the propaganda that is essential to their commercial objectives.

But, after all, our papers have a better record than the

radio. The newspaper still writes its own news and composes its own editorials. They do have a bias in favor of advertisers. But they do not rent their editorials to advertisers. You still do not see over the editorial page of your newspaper the legend that these editorials are coming to you through the courtesy of a crazy crystal corporation. The editor still maintains some self-respect. He still occasionally breaks out in a blast of independent opinion. And there are papers which are notable exceptions. I am happy to say that the great journal for which Mr. Kent is an ornament and official clings courageously to its liberal traditions. And I am also glad to say that I have the privilege of writing for a great chain of newspapers which opens its columns fearlessly to every side of all issues and which permits me to write without restraint my own views which, I do not have to assure you, are hardly propaganda for big business.

I liked what Mr. Cantril said about the technique of propaganda under the guise of explanation. I am reminded of one excellent illustration. The stock market, as you know, flourishes only when people are gambling in stocks. For years that institution has managed to keep itself safe from legal restraints. To do that it invented a collection of assumptions which it wanted people and lawmakers to believe. One was that what went on on its floor was not gambling. Another was that security speculation is essential to the financing of industry—a pure assumption and utterly false. Another was that brokers must be permitted to gamble for their own account—only they call it trading. So the Exchange hired a professor of English at Yale and made him the "economist" of the Exchange. Then he wrote a book about the operation of stock markets which was published by a reputable firm. As Mr. Cantril describes, it explained very sweetly all of these important assumptions. Then that book turned up in every library, in all economic departments of colleges, in college libraries, in editorial offices. It became a kind of standard work. But all the copies were bought from the publisher by the Exchange and sent around the country to libraries, colleges, teachers. It sent me three copies. The harm which that book did in poisoning the minds of the teaching and editorial world about a group of utterly false and even dangerous assumptions cannot be calculated.

These instruments are available to people with money. Groups, orders, associations without money are necessarily denied these powerful weapons of propaganda. The result is that the civilization of our society, our culture, has come to be molded disproportionately by these powerfully organized profit-seeking groups.

I have at least one suggestion to make. I agree with Mr. Cantril that the only final defense is education. We have to become a little more civilized before we can properly protect ourselves. But I would prevent advertisers from using the radio for political propaganda. Let them put on their symphony orchestras, their swing bands, their crooners, and their jokesters. But let them not be permitted to use the air, which belongs to the nation, to slip over their immature and selfish political and economic propaganda with their news crooners, their hired professors, and their highly-paid and therefore subservient commentators. Let them talk about the glories of their pills, their breakfast foods, their soaps, and their motor cars, but let them not use their advertising programs to sell their political nostrums.

I don't want to end propaganda. Men will never get over the itch to sell their ideas to the world. I merely want to protect that poor, pushed around monster, the mass mind, from being exploited only by the monied groups in our society. [Applause]

CHAIRMAN DENNY: Thank you, Mr. Flynn. And now I present Mr. Frank R. Kent, of the *Baltimore Sun.*

MR. KENT: I hold no particular brief for propaganda, and there is much in Mr. Flynn's entertaining indictment to which I agree. Nevertheless, there are certainly two sides to the question and it seems to me a great mistake to regard all propaganda as poisonous and all propagandists as evil. The simple fact is that when the propaganda is directed against the men, the measures, and the causes which we advocate, it seems wholly sinister; but when it supports our side, then it promptly becomes the dissemination of useful information and very righteous, indeed. It altogether depends upon the point of view. From one angle it is bad; from the other good. Of course, the cheap custom of so many bad losers in politics of blaming their defeat on propaganda has helped give the word a malign meaning, somewhat misleading. And this has been accentuated by one or two misguided corporate campaigns, notably that of the public utilities some years ago which, it is interesting to note, however, did them vastly more harm than good. It was a real boomerang and had much to do with creating the feeling against the utilities which has made them today the favorite targets of political demagogues in both parties.

Actually, propaganda is part of the democratic process. Without it our system would function very badly and our politics would be absurd. The term, as it is now used, has become so flexible in meaning as to cover every organization and individual actually engaged on any side of any controversial public question. Every political committee, of course, is primarily a propaganda committee. Four-fifths of all the money in a national campaign in both parties is spent on propaganda. If you telegraph or write a Congressman for or against a bill you can be, and are, called a propagandist. But, what of it? It is your right to propagandize for the things in which you believe and against those in which you do not. It is linked with the right of petition guaranteed under the Constitution and this would no longer be a free country if it were curtailed.

I do not say that harm has not been done by propaganda, that the people have not at times been misled, and that it does not contribute to the general muddy-mindedness of the public. I do say, however, that I do not see how it can be regulated without regulating free speech; and I do say that propaganda and propagandists—even paid propaganda and paid propagandists—are essential in our system, and that, making due allowances for the abuses, there is nothing inherently wicked about them; quite the contrary. How else does an interest, an industry, or an individual under attack, in Congress or in any other legislative body, defend itself or present its side except through propaganda? What other protection have they against a raid on their rights? So long as it isn't corruptly spent, what is wrong in such spending? In the fight against the court packing bill and the Reorganization Bill, there was organized propaganda certainly on the one side and great administration pressure on the other. Why is propaganda bad and political pressure good? There are, I know, people who think it was wicked to propagandize against these bills, but I do not happen to be one of them. In my opinion, that propaganda was distinctly in the national interests and an indispensable factor in the forces that fought these proposals.

I know the point is made that propaganda costs money and, therefore, the common man is at a disadvantage while the wealthy are enabled more or less to monopolize the publicity facilities. There are three reasons why I do not think this contention sound. One is that extensive propaganda on a controversial question is never one-sided very long. They rarely get away with it. Somehow or other it generates its own opposition. The well-financed Anti-Saloon League is offset promptly by the Anti-Prohibition Association; the labor organizations with their great propaganda departments bring into existence the Citizens' Committee. The propaganda of one Spanish factor inspires propaganda from the other. The public utilities propaganda was more than nullified by the Senatorial committee investigation and exposure, and so on.

A second reason is that, unless the people are ready for it, propaganda, no matter how extensive, is futile. I do not subscribe to the theory that anything can be put over by propaganda. I do not believe that a nation's thought can be wholly molded by propaganda. I think the facts disprove that idea. An instance of the futility of propaganda, I think, is that of the Communist Party in this country. Another is that of the Republican Party in the last campaign. Plenty of other instances will occur to you, instances where all the publicity, all of the newspapers, were on one side and the voters on election day on the other. Propaganda does not get anywhere unless the people are ready for it. The soil has to be ripe or it is wasted. And propaganda to stick has got to have a basis of fact and an equipment of logic. A certain number of susceptible, simple-minded people may be swung off balance by crazy propaganda, but not a majority and not for very long. Eventually they are trued up either by counter propaganda or clarifying events.

The third reason is that the ordinary man—the man without any money—unable to purchase time on the radio or space in the papers, is nothing like as helpless as he seems. He never lacks defenders. On the contrary, he is invariably well provided with them. Nine-tenths of the politicians in office and certainly nine-tenths of those who want office constitute themselves his consistent champions for the simple reason that there are so very, very many of him to vote on election day. It is, as a matter of fact, the successful, who have risen above the ordinary, who these days are without defenders in politics, which is why it is necessary for them to spend money on propaganda if they want to retain the rewards of success—and all of them do. It's the only way in this country by which they can put up a fight and the idea that the odds are with them is not well based. Really, the odds are the other way.

It is my conviction, too, that lying propaganda defeats itself, and the propagandists who deliberately misrepresent or falsely accuse are stupid in the extreme. As a rule the reaction is swift and sure. There are too many free vehicles of communication available for denials and denunciations— which always makes news—of propagandists who have laid themselves open by statements which cannot be sustained. And there are always the libel laws and the courts. Actually, when one considers the tremendous flood of propaganda, it seems to me that astonishingly little of it can be justly called vicious.

There is one form of propaganda for which, perhaps, vicious is the wrong word, but which, in my mind, is clearly bad—and that is Government propaganda as developed in the last five years. Prior to 1933 there were almost no departmental publicity directors. Today, every bureau, board, agency, and commission has its separate publicity section. The Government payrolls are literally cluttered with press agents; the volume of their product is vast and its cost runs high up in the millions. Now it is as natural and proper for an administration to propagandize in its own behalf as for the opposition to propagandize against it. But, I submit that an administration is a party affair. It is in power as the result of success at the polls of one political party. Its propaganda should be conducted through the organization of that party and with that party's funds—not through governmental agencies, nor paid for with the taxpayers' money. To this sort of thing, there are various grave objections. For one, it not only gives to the Administration an utterly unfair advantage but it is distinctly dishonest, as in using the money of the taxpayers to promote its policies and perpetuate itself, it is using the money not only of those who are for it but of those who are against it—and that, I contend, is not in the least on the level. [Applause]

CHAIRMAN DENNY: Thank you, Mr. Kent. Now we are ready for the questions. Please rise and state the name of the person to whom your question is directed.

MAN: Mr. Flynn, with respect to your condemnation of a certain rule, do you not believe in the rights of a minority as necessary to the true function of democracy?

MR. FLYNN: I do.

MAN: Mr. Flynn, you said that some groups cannot get time on the air because of the money interest. Now, isn't it perfectly all right for a business such as the Chase National Bank to put on a program to give counter propaganda to what is being handed out in Washington?

MR. FLYNN: Well, the President in Washington is just waiting for us to get off the air now, to get on the air. He has not been on the air, I think, for about seven or eight months, but these programs I have been talking about—and, mind you, I am no advocate of the President—are on every week, week after week, pouring out stuff with a hired economist into the ears of the American people and using a great symphony orchestra in order to get attention. In place of the technique the old orators used, which was the *exordium* of the orator himself—he had to tell a funny story to get you interested and then tell you what he had to say— they now have a three- or four-thousand-dollar orchestra to get you to listen to them and then they turn on the economist for five minutes to give you a form of political economy which is a propagandizing of business interest. I don't object to their doing it, but I say they can do it because they have got the money, but nobody else has. [Applause and boos]

CHAIRMAN DENNY: I am going to ask Mr. Kent if he will speak to that same question. What do you think about the right of business to have these programs such as Mr. Flynn has been attacking, to counteract what has been called Government propaganda?

MR. KENT: I think it is all right. [Applause] I think I said so in my remarks. The Government propaganda is financed out of the taxpayers' money; mostly these days it is directed against business. What possible way has business got of protecting itself except through counter propaganda? [Applause] And they have got to pay for it. Nobody will give it to them freely; it isn't like the ordinary man with every politician or nine-tenths of the politicians championing his cause. And how do they get it unless they have some money to pay for it? If they didn't have money and couldn't pay for it, they would simply be trampled in the ground and ruined. [Applause]

WOMAN: Mr. Cantril, you prescribed the remedy of education to counteract the vicious effects of propaganda, and you sort of indicted educators themselves as being propagandists, so where are we to look for reform?

MR. CANTRIL: I still think you can look for a little light from the poor educator. Your question, however, is an extremely important one and brings up the difference between the educator who realizes he is a propagandist and the educator who thinks he isn't. Most educators think, of course, that they are not propagandists, and consciously they probably are not, and we should not label them as such. However, the educator who receives the book that Mr. Flynn received and who does not have Mr. Flynn's perspective and does not know that it is sent by an interested group, who reads that book, who is convinced by it, and who teaches that to his pupils, is a propagandist from the point of view of Mr. Flynn, of myself, and others who know who sends the book. He is not a propagandist from his own point of view. So real education is essentially proportional to the ability of the educator to recognize propaganda. [Applause]

MAN: Mr. Cantril, you and Mr. Flynn both rather assume that corporate interests are behind most of what you define as propaganda. In all fairness, aren't the labor unions today, both wings of labor, as adept and efficient in its use, as witness the flood of propaganda today to sell us a little soviet, under the Pepper Bill, under the sacred name of art? That is magnificent propaganda.

MR. CANTRIL: Yes; I think definitely these labor groups as well as any other organized group or interest can be accused of propaganda. However, my illustrations, if they do not seem to be fair, were merely meant to be proportional to the amount of propaganda that comes to us. I agree rather thoroughly with Mr. Flynn that the propaganda now is rather on one side, although I definitely feel that the labor groups, if they had the opportunity, would certainly propagandize just as much.

MAN: Mr. Flynn, did the newspapers that were against the Reorganization Bill criticize the bill on its merits, or did they use it as an attack to discredit our great President, and is it a credit to a democracy where true facts shall prevail?

MR. FLYNN: I think the idea of the reorganization of the government was an excellent thing, but I think it was approached in an abominable way, and I think the newspapers are pretty nearly right in criticizing it. I am not sure that a lot of them weren't motivated by a hatred of our "great" President. The bill was bad just the same.

MAN: Mr. Kent, you spoke a little earlier about the Government driving the poor Big Business to the poorhouse. How about the advance that Big Business made from the time that there was no Government propaganda, from 1932 to 1937, when they reached their highest profits?

CHAIRMAN DENNY: You have got your dates mixed up, haven't you? Let's ask your question again now in terms of dates.

SAME MAN: I mean the period of 1933, when Roosevelt came into power, to 1937. In 1933 they were at the bottom; in 1937 they almost reached their 1929 levels despite the fact that we had this propaganda that you alluded to so unfavorably.

MR. KENT: I don't say that the propaganda that I alluded to unfavorably, which was the Government propaganda, had anything to do with that. I think that business prospered during those years in spite of Government propaganda and Government policies. And that the weight and propaganda of Government policies and Government propaganda eventually have brought about a recession. [Applause]

MAN: Mr. Kent, do you think that the opportunity for propaganda in this country today is so equal that it can't be improved, and if you think that it should be improved, how would you go about doing it?

MR. KENT: I think that is a very interesting and intelligent question, and I wish I could answer it. I don't think that opportunities are altogether equal. I would like to see them equalized, and I would like to see the abuses cut out. I don't see exactly how it can be done, and I am afraid of any curtailment because it does involve the curtailment of free speech.

CHAIRMAN DENNY: How about a lot of Town Meetings of the Air, Mr. Kent?

MR. KENT: They are bully.

MAN: Mr. Cantril, I have heard rumors that there are at present a large number of British propaganda agents among us at the present time trying to get us emotionally interested in the Middle European situation. Do you have any information on that subject?

MR. CANTRIL: I am sorry, I don't.

WOMAN: Mr. Kent, you speak of libel laws which do protect individuals and corporations from misstatement, but when the radio and newspapers, which you all admit can be bought, attack not individuals but laws and historical facts and make misstatements about them that we all recognize, if we have the education to recognize them, but which the mass mind does not recognize, and when they attack groups and countries and parties and the Government itself, who is going to sue them for libel over those misstatements? [Applause]

MR. KENT: I should first like to correct a misapprehension that you seem to be under. I did not say, and I did not agree, that either the radio or the newspapers were bought. I have nothing to do with radios, but I have had for a good many years something to do with newspapers, and I work on one that I know can't be bought, and I do not believe we monopolize all the journalistic virtue in the country. [Applause]

MAN: Professor Cantril, in articulating all that has been said tonight is the assumption that there is something other than propaganda. I should like to ask you, if like physical facts there are social facts which impartially presented can inform us through some medium other than propaganda? In other words, it is my belief that in our modern world there are no social facts, that all statements of the phenomena of society are propaganda, are opinionated, are in one sense or another a seeking towards some preconceived end, which I believe was your impression.

MR. CANTRIL: The point you raise is extremely important. I might answer it perhaps by means of an analogy. The propagandist we might regard as a gardener who plants seeds and cultivates the soil. He always has, however, the soil upon which to work. That soil, from the point of view of the propagandist, consists of all the ideas, the ideologies, the custom stereotypes, frames of reference, or what you will, that people already have, so that what the propagandist does is merely to play upon those things for a particular end. I have been interested in the discussion tonight, for example, to see how this soil has conditioned our discussion. We think here in terms of the Democratic and the Republican parties, as though those were the only two parties in the world. That is an indication of the frame of reference under which or within which we are working, within which our propaganda is assumed. [Applause]

MAN: I would like to direct a question to Mr. Cantril and perhaps have the others comment on it. Inasmuch as in a democracy it is important both to get the people to think and to act, and inasmuch as it is very difficult really to get people to do either, much less both of those things, isn't there a danger in carrying your suggestions to their logical conclusion that you will increase that state of inertia? For instance, in the Reorganization Bill, if one reads it in the manner that you suggest, by critical propaganda analysis, one can't get very much excited about it one way or another, but if one is open to the influence of a propagandist, one not only acts immediately but very vituperatively either for or against the bill, and thus it is those who are affected by propagandists who convey their opinion in the Government, and the people that you are trying to create are in such inertia that they are likely not to be a factor in a democracy.

MR. CANTRIL: Yes, I think it is very important, when we discuss this program of propaganda, to recognize or to ask ourselves what the issue is about. It seems to me that when we do not know much about a problem, such as the Reorganization Bill, then we are extremely susceptible to propaganda. However, when we do know something about the issue, then it takes much more propaganda to work us up to an opposite point of view and extremely little propaganda to turn us into action for our particular cause. That is why I think the propaganda during the election is not particularly effective, but why propaganda, for example, directed at the Turk, about whom we know little, is extremely effective.

CHAIRMAN DENNY: Thank you, Professor Cantril. I'm sorry we haven't time for more questions. This is the kind of program where we get a great many letters from listeners saying, "When Mr. So-and-So spoke, we thought he was perfectly right, he had such a perfect case there was no use listening to the other man; and when the next man spoke, his case was so perfectly presented we didn't know what to do. What do you think, Mr. Denny?" [Laughter] The answer is that you have got to think. Now, that is the purpose of the program this evening, to make us all think. In fact, that is the purpose of all of these Town Meeting programs.

A LECTURE

DISCUSSION IN THE DEMOCRATIC PROCESS

by Lyman Bryson[1]

One way of describing democracy is to call it a system that provides for the management of public business by public discussion. When the democratic experiment was new in America, when our enthusiasm for it was fresh, we talked and argued endlessly about our political affairs. We were dangerous people in those days. The world was afraid of us. Out of America people expected explosions to come, explosions that would rock the autocracies of Europe, very much as we expected a decade or so ago that the Bolsheviks of Russia would upset everything. When European observers like Tocqueville, overcoming their fear of such a wild and dangerous place, came to America to observe, they noticed above everything else our constant political talk. We may have lost some of this loquacity, but foreign observers still notice it. As long as we believe in democracy we will believe that talking things over is the best way to get our public business done.

In politics, systems are distinguished by methods, not by ends. All governments in this modern world claim to be for the good of all the people. The honesty of that claim is hard to judge. But between democracy and the various totalitarian states there is open disagreement as to the means by which the good of the people can be attained. Totalitarian states are all founded on the principle that there must be complete agreement for successful living. Complete agreement is the same as obedience to the will of some one person or some group. Dictatorships justify obedience by asserting that one man or a small group of men can decide public

[1] This lecture was delivered by Mr. Lyman Bryson, Professor of Adult Education, Teachers College, Columbia University, as a part of the Symposium in Public Speaking, Northwestern University, 1938.

425

questions more wisely than the people in whose behalf they are decided.

Democracy, however, does not require that all men shall believe the same things nor even that they must consider such unity desirable. Nor does it relieve any citizen of his responsibility to share in the burdens of government. Instead of obedience, democracies ask of their citizens responsible deliberation. If we take discussion out of a democracy, we have removed the essence of the process.

It may be wise, in these days of skepticism, to remind ourselves often that we Americans began, one hundred fifty years ago, the trend toward free self-government for all peoples. Other nations, some of which have attained democracy in some phases of their social life even more successfully than we have done, did not undertake the dangerous reforms until we had set the pace. Our situation, as much as any special virtue, made us the pioneers.

At the end of the eighteenth century, the scattered groups of colonists on the Atlantic seaboard had definite advantages for making the great attempt. They had had a century and a half of political experience under new conditions. In fact, the Declaration of Independence neatly divides the history of the United States into halves. We are likely to forget the importance of that first half of our history because of the spectacular large scale achievements of the second half in which we have been formally organized as a nation. The first advantage was this long experience in local self-government. We had the forms of British representative government, not yet worked out into anything like democracy in the home country, but adaptable through town meetings to the colonists' needs. Part of this experience led to suspicion of executive power because executive power meant the intervention of the British government in what was coming to be more and more an independent American society. This suspicion is not yet dead, and its corollary is confident reliance on legislative debate. The executive will always be suspected in a democracy unless he can be compelled to explain at every step his reasons for his conduct. In other words, the executive, by the logic of his responsibilities, is likely to be impatient with discussion. On that account his zeal and vigor may make him anti-democratic. But in spite of the fact that we acquired some prejudices, we got the practice which helped to make success possible when we were completely on our own responsibility as a nation.

Our second advantage was that we had, at the end of the eighteenth century, a high degree of social homogeneity. The colonies had striking differences in their cultures and thought proudly of themselves as national units. Nevertheless, the pervading culture was agrarian. Most men, even great leaders like Washington and Jefferson, were farmers. Men who were not actually working the land were busy with professional and mercantile affairs that depended directly on the farm prosperity. In the South, in spite of what fashionable romances have tried to tell us, the great majority of the voting citizens, the white men, made their living in the fields. Since most men worked at simple occupations, it was not difficult for neighbors to understand each other and trust in each other's political competence. Discussion was a natural social activity.

The third advantage was that our political thinking was shot through with those liberal ideas that had arisen more than a century before in England and were then fermenting in the minds of the philosophers of France. The ideas of John Locke, in their original English phrases or in their French versions, were familiar to all the leaders. Writers like Tom Paine were putting them into homely slogans that any farmer could use. Thus, we had a philosophy of independence and equality, a generally like-minded body of citizens and practice in managing our own affairs. We were lucky.

Much of this has changed. The nineteenth century produced a crisis between the farming interests and the industrial centers. The Civil War fixed the balance of power in the hands of industry. Millions of immigrants came over into the land of freedom and filled up the factories and the growing cities. The occupational pattern became more and more complicated; people worked at more and more different kinds of jobs. It is no doubt true that the coming of immigrants from all over the world did much to complicate the social pattern. These strangers had to learn American ways, and sometimes they misunderstood democracy. Sometimes they were not given a fair chance to learn. But I think it is possible to exaggerate the difficulties which came from the influx of aliens. Whether a man was a recent arrival or a descendant of the forefathers, he was subjected to the diversifying influences of the industrial order. New occupations make new languages. Men who are occupied with widely differing tasks find it harder to work in harmony and mutual trust than those who live in a simple rural society. Discussion, the method of democracy, becomes more difficult when those who are trying to reach a practical agreement have widely differing backgrounds.

At the same time, industrial development and the organization of great corporations led to the accumulation of economic power in the hands of small groups of men. The founders of the republic foresaw this danger. Jefferson, in fact, seemed to believe that a democracy could work only among men who owned and worked the land. Hordes of city dwellers would be unable, he thought, to understand or appreciate its benefits. Other men of Jefferson's time were less extreme in their views, but believed that great aggregations of wealth might make democracy impractical We are well aware now that there was truth in these predictions. Government by discussion is infinitely more difficult in a country where mass production and financial manipulation divide men into groups with different experiences and conflicting interests. Many people have come regretfully to the decision that democracy is no longer possible.

I do not share that gloomy conclusion. But it is certain that we shall have to adapt our political institutions to our economic ambitions. Equality is probably, in any complete sense, an impossible ideal. I doubt if it would be desirable. But equality of opportunity, by which men can have an equal chance to be their best selves, is an ideal worth working for. Our economic system denies and defeats democracy in so far as it defeats this ideal. We are generally agreed that we must reform our society at this point. It is not my business to discuss the technical difficulties that stand in our way. The question at the moment is this, how can we make the necessary changes by agreements openly and fairly arrived at?

We have suffered from a conflict of ideals as well as from

the complication of public business and the loss of like-mindedness. Bertrand Russell has pointed out in *Freedom versus Organization* that our political ideal of freedom has been struggling against an industrial ideal of discipline and efficiency. In the first stages of industrial progress, men and women and children were brutally sacrificed for the products of the machine. We cared more about producing things than we did about the lives of those who made them. And these early ideals of the factory system, discipline and efficiency, have seduced many thoughtful people into believing that discipline and efficiency are good for their own sake. We talk now of "industrial democracy." It may be that we shall find ways of maintaining our industrial production without sacrificing humanity. Or we may some day be wise enough to decide that we would rather have our people lead decent lives even if that means less industrial efficiency. This is a complex and subtle question about which there is a good deal of oratory and not much careful reasoning.

For our present purpose, it is enough to point out that the ideals of discipline and mechanical efficiency are not the highest ideals for us to follow in all phases of our lives. They may be necessary in industrial organization, although I doubt it. I am sure that they are inferior to the ideal of human worth in politics. In some human groups there may be good reasons for sacrificing the person to the group. It is possible that an army is most effective if every soldier follows orders with machine-like regularity. But in a family there are things more important than discipline. Or, consider a schoolroom. You have seen classes in which every child sat with stiff propriety and had nothing in his head but a guess at what the teacher was going to do next. In such a class, humanity has been sacrificed to mechanics, and education is not the product.

What kind of human institution is government? If mechanical efficiency is its proper ideal, it may well be that the dictator is the ideal solution for all our troubles. He can enforce discipline and he can regiment individuals into machine-like masses. This is not the ideal of democracy.

When someone says that a Fascist government moves more swiftly and neatly than any government by talk can do, we have to admit the truth of that claim. When it is said that a dictator can make decisions more quickly than a parliament, there is no answer—as long as the argument is based on those premises. It is my belief that decisions by the democratic process are, in the long run, wiser than those of dictators. But even if this were not so, I would still believe that democracy is the best form of government and the best social principle.

The point is that a government is not to be judged by its mechanical qualities but by what it does to the people who make up the nation. It is not efficiency in public business that distinguishes a good government from a bad one in the final test, but differences in the quality of its citizens as human beings. A democratic government compels every person to bear some responsibility in the nation's business. In doing so, it gives an opportunity for the development of personal powers. Still more it extends and expands and develops those individual powers by participation in the solution of great questions. People who have to make decisions for themselves and share in the making of decisions for their country are likely to be better human beings than those who can rest on the decisions of their rulers. At least that is an idea basic to democracy. And the method by which responsibility is shared is public discussion of public business.

Walter Bagehot said a long time ago that parliamentary government was good government because it is government by talk. We tend to form a "crust of custom" over our political and social conduct. Discussion breaks up the crust and makes rational change not only possible but also peaceable. This idea of Bagehot's, an essential truth about democracy, has been obscured in our minds under the influence of those other ideals that industrialism engenders.

We can reaffirm our faith in the political ideal of freedom but we cannot refuse to face the problems industrialism has created. Public business is more complex and more difficult than ever before. Political decisions require technical knowledge. When we began, a hundred and fifty years ago, the problems of the nation were immensely difficult but they were comparatively simple. The men of 1800 did not differ much in their technical knowledge. Since then has come a vast development of specialties, of techniques, of recondite knowledge which no one man can possibly master. And yet the special knowledge is all needed if we are to keep our system working. How can we square this difficulty with our basic idea that democracy is a good form of government because it brings to every citizen the stimulus of responsible public discussion?

It may help to look for a moment at discussion itself, the process of solving problems by talking things over. John Dewey has said that the improvement of public discussion is the most important public business we have on hand. What is the nature of this activity? It must be something more than conversation, although talk is a human activity of the highest importance, however futile it may seem at times.

Properly speaking, discussion is controversy. It is talk in which opinions are contrasted and judged. It is controversy over judgments that belong properly in the realm of opinion. Discussion is not a means, except incidentally, for discovering facts. It is a poor instrument to use if the problem at hand can easily be solved by some ascertainable fact. No amount of discussion will make the opinion of an untrained person as good as the opinion of an expert in those areas where expertness is possible. But most important questions are questions that every man has a right and a responsibility to think through for himself. Very few important questions can be settled by fact alone. When all the available facts are in, the important issues of life arise. Given these facts, what are we to do? No doubt authority plays some part in all questions, even in ethics, aesthetics, or politics. But the ultimate judgments here are judgments of value, and they must be made finally by each person for himself. It is exactly in this area that discussion belongs, and it is only by discussion that each of us can try out his own opinions against the opinions of others and learn what is of most worth.

The first question then to be decided in trying to find out how democracy can survive industrialism is this, What is the proper role of the technically trained expert in public affairs? Obviously, it will be larger today than it was in the society of one hundred years ago. Experts may have discussions among themselves, but these are beyond the scope of the ordinary citizen. He must, when they have decided, accept their judgment. But of what issues is the expert the proper judge? It is a paradox, but true, that as we have more things to talk about in public affairs, there is less that the average citizen can presume to have opinions on. More and more must be left to the judgment of technicians.

Perhaps I can illustrate this division by saying that the general public has a right to decide when and where some great municipal bridge is to be built but that the actual building, the calculation of load and stress, had better be left to the engineers. It is natural that democracies should resist the coming of technicians into public control, but it is strange that we have been so slow in giving them their proper place in public life when our private lives have been put so largely into their hands. We trust the doctor, the teacher, the engineer, and a good many other people about whose technical competence we can know very little. Above all, we trust the average workman to know how to do his job and to be faithful in his task. Otherwise, our highly mechanized lives would all go to smash together. What we have to do is to decide rationally what phases of public affairs should be taken care of in the same way.

What does this leave for the average man to do? What becomes of his share in responsibility for his country's fate? What is there left for him to discuss? As I said a moment ago, all the really important questions are still to be decided. The technician can tell us how to discover and weigh the facts, and he can tell us how to achieve our plans. He is an expert in the "how" but he cannot take from the rest of us our responsibility to decide "what." The ultimate values and the ultimate choices are still everybody's business, and everybody is challenged to be the best human being that his capacity will allow by having to face the ultimate issues.

If discussion is the instrumentality by which we are to do our part in these matters of high policy, it is worthy of our searching study. It is surprising that so important an activity has been so haphazard and so careless. Since the first days of western education, men have devoted prolonged labor and the highest skill to the problem of persuasion, the rhetorician's problem of having one's own way. But this, if democracy is what I have said it is, can be only part of the total process. The persuasive offering of one's own thought is only the first gesture in a drama in which the other man's thought must also play a part. It is a drama in which the characters are not persons but ideas and in which victory is not the triumph of a man but the general attainment of the truth. For this we must have trained minds and a willing spirit. If democracy has become difficult, we can make it work only by clarifying the process which is its essence.

BIBLIOGRAPHY

MATERIALS DIRECTLY ON DISCUSSION

BOOKS AND PAMPHLETS

Bowman, LeRoy C., *How to Lead Discussion*. New York: The Woman's Press, 1934. 31 pp.

Chancellor, John, and Williams, Chester S., *Printed Page and the Public Platform*. Washington: United States Department of the Interior, Office of Education, Bulletin 1937, No. 27. vi + 100 pp.

Courtis, Stuart S., *Cooperation*. Ann Arbor, Michigan: Brumfield and Brumfield (mimeographers), 1934. 77 pp.

Cummings, Milton C., and Walser, Frank, *Discussion Guide* (mimeographed). Hartford, Connecticut: The State Board of Education, 1936. 13 pp.

Dunn, Frederick S., *The Practice and Procedure of International Conferences*. Baltimore: The Johns Hopkins Press, 1929. xiv + 229 pp.

Elliott, Harrison S., *Group Discussion in Religious Education*. New York: Association Press, 1930. vi + 100 pp.

Elliott, Harrison S., *The Process of Group Thinking*. New York: Association Press, 1932. x + 229 pp.

Ely, Mary L., *Why Forums?* New York: American Association for Adult Education, 1937. viii + 220 pp.

Ewing, R. L., *Methods of Conducting Forums and Discussions*. New York: Association Press, 1926.

Fansler, Thomas, *Discussion Methods for Adult Groups*. New York: American Association for Adult Education, 1934. v + 149 pp.

Fansler, Thomas, *Effective Group Discussion: A Guide for Group Members*. New York: New York University, Department of Research, Division of General Education, 1936. 22 pp.

Fansler, Thomas, *Teaching Adults by Discussion*. New

York: New York University, Division of General Education, 1938. 39 pp.

Graham, Gladys Murphy, "Speech in the Service of Deliberation," in *A Program of Speech Education for a Democracy*, edited by W. A. Cable. Boston: Expression Company, 1932. ix + 595 pp.

Hayes, Cecil B., *The American Lyceum—Its History and Contribution to Education*. Washington: United States Department of the Interior, Office of Education, Bulletin No. 12, 1932. xii + 72 pp.

Hunt, Edward E., *Conferences, Committees, Conventions, and How to Run Them*. New York: Harper & Brothers, 1925. xiv + 218 pp.

Inquiry (The), *Business and Ideals: A Syllabus of Discussion Outlines for Groups of Business Employees*. New York: Association Press, 1929.

Inquiry (The), *Community Conflict: A Formulation of Case Studies in Community Conflict, with Discussion Outlines*. New York: Association Press, 1929. xviii + 156 pp.

Inquiry (The), *International Problems and the Christian Way of Life*. New York: Association Press, 1923.

Inquiry (The), *The Worker and His Job: An Outline for the Use of Workers' Groups*. New York: Association Press, 1927.

Jenness, Mary, *Twelve Negro Americans*. City-Wide Young People's Forum, Baltimore, Maryland. New York: Friendship Press, 1936. x + 180 pp.

Judson, Lyman S., and Judson, Ellen, *Modern Group Discussion*. New York: H. W. Wilson Company, 1937. 198 pp.

Leigh, Robert D., *Group Leadership*. New York: W. W. Norton & Company, Inc., 1936. xiv + 259 pp.

Leigh, Robert D., *Modern Rules of Parliamentary Procedure*. New York: W. W. Norton & Company, Inc., 1937. vi + 106 pp.

Lurie, Reuben L., *The Challenge of the Forum—the Story of Ford Hall and the Open Forum Movement*. Boston: Richard R. Badger, 1930. 218 pp.

Miller, Orville C., *The Speech Tournament and the Con-*

gress of Human Relations. Nashville, Tennessee: Vanderbilt University, 1938.

Murray, Elwood, *Argumentative Dialogue* (mimeographed). Denver: University of Denver, 1938.

Myer, Walter E., and Others, *Talking It Through, A Manual for Discussion Groups.* Washington: National Education Association, Department of Secondary School Principals, 1938. 70 pp.

Orchard, Harry A., *Fifty Years of Chautauqua.* Cedar Rapids, Iowa: Torch Press, 1923. 313 pp.

Orr, Frederick W., and Franzke, Albert L., "The University of Washington Plan of Problem Solving Debate," *Bulletin of the University of Washington* (Extension Series), No. 8, January, 1938. 68 pp.

Paget, Edwin H., *Southeastern Forensic Tournament* (mimeographed). Raleigh: North Carolina State College, 1938.

Pellegrini, Angelo M., and Stirling, Brents, *Argumentation and Public Discussion.* New York: D. C. Heath and Company, 1936. xv + 415 pp.

Sheffield, Alfred D., *Creative Discussion.* New York: Association Press, 1936. (Third Edition, Revised and Enlarged) 68 pp.

Sheffield, Alfred D., *Joining in Public Discussion.* New York: George H. Doran Company, 1932. xvii + 168 pp.

Sheffield, Alfred D., *Training for Group Experience.* New York: Association Press, 1929. xv + 105 pp.

Studebaker, John W., *The American Way.* New York: McGraw-Hill Book Company, Inc., 1935. xi + 206 pp.

Studebaker, John W., *Safeguarding Democracy Through Adult Civic Education.* Washington: United States Department of the Interior, Office of Education, Bulletin No. 6, 1936.

Studebaker, John W., and Williams, Chester S., *Choosing Our Way.* Washington: United States Department of the Interior, Office of Education, Bulletin 1937, Misc., No. 1. 118 pp.

Studebaker, John W., and Williams, Chester S., *Education for Democracy: Public Affairs Forums.* Washington: United States Department of the Interior, Office of Education, Bulletin 1935, No. 17. 74 pp.

Studebaker, John W., and Williams, Chester S., *A Step*

Forward for Adult Education. Washington: United States Department of the Interior, Office of Education, Bulletin 1936, No. 16. 28 pp.

Studebaker, John W., Sheats, Paul, and Williams, Chester S., *Forums for Young People*. Washington: United States Department of the Interior, Office of Education, Bulletin 1937, No. 25. iv + 113 pp.

United States Department of Agriculture, *Discussion: A Brief Guide to Methods*. Washington: United States Department of Agriculture, 1936. (D-1, revised) 11 pp.

United States Department of Agriculture, *How to Organize and Conduct County Forums*. Washington: United States Department of Agriculture, 1936. (D-2, revised) 6 pp.

United States Department of Agriculture, *What is the Discussion Leader's Job?* Washington: United States Department of Agriculture, 1937. (D-3) 21 pp.

Walser, Frank, *The Art of Conference*. New York: Harper & Brothers, 1933. x + 305 pp.

Wiese, Mildred, Bryson, Lyman, and Hallenbeck, W. C., *Let's Talk It Over*. Chicago: University of Chicago Press, 1936. 41 pp.

Wileden, A. F., and Ewbank, H. L., *How to Conduct Group Discussion*. Madison: Extension Service of the College of Agriculture, University of Wisconsin, Circular 276, 1935. 64 pp.

PERIODICALS

Adams, William F., "A Cross-section Round Table," *Journal of Adult Education*. Vol. 5, 1933, pp. 61-63.

Artman, J. M., and Others, "The Problems Brought to Religious and Character Education by the Socio-Economic Debacle," *Religious Education*. Vol. 29, 1934, pp. 266-270. (A panel discussion)

Bane, Charles L., "The Lecture versus the Class-Discussion Method of College Teaching," *School and Society*. Vol. 21, 1925, pp. 300-302.

Bennett, H. Arnold, "Limits of the Discussion Method," *Educational Method*. Vol. 10, 1930, pp. 104-109.

Birchall, Sara H., "The Voice in Boston's Wilderness: Being an Account of Ford Hall," *Outlook*. Vol. 111, 1915, pp. 865-870.

Bogardus, E. S., "Leaders of Panel Discussions," *Sociology and Social Research.* Vol. 20, 1935, pp. 71-74.

Bryson, Lyman, "The Limits of Discussion," *Journal of Adult Education.* Vol. 9, 1937, pp. 261-264.

Bryson, Lyman, and Others, "Recent Trends in the American Movement for Adult Education," *Journal of Adult Education.* Vol. 5, 1933, pp. 265-270. (A panel discussion)

Cambridge, Elsie G., "Farmers' Forums," *Journal of Adult Education.* Vol. 6, 1934, pp. 181-185.

Cartwright, Morse A., "Panel," *Journal of Adult Education.* Vol. 5, 1933, pp. 37-42.

Courtis, Stuart A., "Cooperation in Thinking," *Progressive Education.* Vol. 10, 1933, pp. 85-88.

Courtis, Stuart A., and Others, "The Function of Education in Achieving and Maintaining a Social Order of Integrated Persons," *Religious Education.* Vol. 29, 1934, pp. 271-281. (A panel discussion)

Dickens, Milton, "Intercollegiate Convention Debates in New York," *The Gavel.* Vol. XIX, 1937, pp. 51-54.

Dooley, R. E., "A Village Forum," *Journal of Adult Education.* Vol. 7, 1935, pp. 147-149.

Ellis, A. Caswell, and Others, "Education for Citizenship," *Journal of Adult Education.* Vol. 4, 1932, pp. 260-265. (A panel discussion)

Ewbank, H. L., "The Wisconsin Public Discussion Contest," *The Gavel.* Vol. XX, 1938, p. 54.

Fansler, Thomas, "Leaders in Training," *Journal of Adult Education.* Vol. 6, 1934, pp. 412-417.

Fansler, Thomas, "The Test of Method," *Journal of Adult Education.* Vol. 6, 1934, pp. 171-174.

Frank, Glenn, "The Parliament of the People," *Century.* Vol. 98, 1919, pp. 401-416.

Frizzell, John H., "The Parliamentary Discussion," *The Gavel.* Vol. XVIII, 1935, p. 7.

Graham, Gladys M., "Discussion Method and Speech Training," *Journal of Adult Education.* Vol. 4, 1932, pp. 404-408.

Grigsby, Rall I., "Ideas Have a Chance in Des Moines," *Progressive Education.* Vol. 11, 1934, pp. 283-287.

Harding, H. F., "A Debate Symposium," *The Speaker*. Vol. XX, 1938, p. 6.

Johnson, Roy I., "Standards in Round-Table Discussion," *School Review*. Vol. 37, 1929, pp. 44-48.

Kotschnig, Walter M., "Light from Des Moines," *School and Society*. Vol. 45, 1937, pp. 639-643.

Lawrence, James C., and Others, "Unemployment Educational and Guidance Problems," *Journal of Adult Education*. Vol. 4, 1932, pp. 266-278. (A panel discussion)

Leith, Donald M., "Implementing Democracy; the Des Moines Forums," *Religious Education*. Vol. 29, 1934, pp. 113-119.

Lindeman, Eduard C., "Social Methods for Social Problems," *Progressive Education*. Vol. 10, 1933, pp. 253-255.

McKean, Dayton D., "Debate or Conference," *Quarterly Journal of Speech*. Vol. XX, 1934, pp. 223-236.

Millson, William A. D., "New Forms of Debate," *The Gavel*. Vol. XIV, 1932, p. 20.

Morgan, Rita, "The Technique of Cooperation," *Quarterly Journal of Speech*. Vol. XX, 1934, pp. 236-241.

Morris, D. W., "The Intercollegiate Forum," *Quarterly Journal of Speech*. Vol. XXIV, 1938, pp. 212-220.

Murray, Elwood, "The Forensic Experience Progression," *The Gavel*. Vol. XX, 1938, pp. 55-58.

Overstreet, Harry A., "Capturing the Depression Mind," *Journal of Adult Education*. Vol. 4, 1932, pp. 12-15.

Overstreet, Harry A., "On the Panel," *Occupations*. Vol. 13, 1935, pp. 425-427.

Overstreet, Harry A., and Others, "Education for Culture," *Journal of Adult Education*. Vol. 4, 1932, pp. 249-259. (A panel discussion)

Overstreet, Harry A., and Others, "To What Extent Does Radio Broadcasting in the United States Need Public Regulation?" *Journal of Adult Education*. Vol. 6, 1934, pp. 278-285. (A panel discussion)

Paget, Edwin H., "Rules for the Direct Clash Plan," *Quarterly Journal of Speech*. Vol. XXIII, 1937, pp. 431-433.

Russell, James E., and Others, "Occupational Education," *Journal of Adult Education*. Vol. 4, 1932, pp. 279-284. (A panel discussion)

Scott, Elmer, and Others, "Social Values in Adult Education," *Journal of Adult Education.* Vol. 4, 1932, pp. 240-248. (A panel discussion)

Sheffield, Alfred D., "Discussion, Lecture-Forum, and Debate," *Quarterly Journal of Speech.* Vol. XVIII, 1932, pp. 517-531.

Shepard, Grace F., "Symposium Rather Than Debate," *Education.* Vol. 52, 1931, pp. 211-213.

Summers, H. B., "Student Legislative Assembly," *The Forensic of Pi Kappa Delta.* Series 22, 1936, pp. 21-24.

Wiener, Philip P., "Scientific Method and Group Discussion," *Journal of Adult Education.* Vol. 9, 1937, pp. 135-140.

Williamson, A. B., "A Proposed Change in Intercollegiate Debating," *Quarterly Journal of Speech.* Vol. XIX, 1933, pp. 192, 200-202.

Wooddy, Carroll H., "Forum Facts," *Journal of Adult Education.* Vol. 7, 1935, pp. 290-296.

OCCASIONAL PAPERS

Inquiry (The), "A Course for Group Leaders," *Occasional Papers.* January, 1927.

Inquiry (The), "Debate Is Not Discussion," *Occasional Papers.* January, 1926.

Inquiry (The), "Discussion Leaders in the Making," *Occasional Papers.* May, 1927.

Inquiry (The), "An Experiment in the Training of Discussion Leaders, Chicago Leads," *Occasional Papers.* March-April, 1927.

Inquiry (The), "Group Discussion—How and When," *Occasional Papers.* May, 1928.

Inquiry (The), "How to Get a Start (A Few Words to the Discussion Leader)," *Occasional Papers.* February, 1927.

Inquiry (The), "How to Run a Conference," *Occasional Papers.* October, 1925.

Inquiry (The), "How Your Discussion Gets Somewhere," *Occasional Papers.* May, 1927.

Inquiry (The), "Management of Discussion," *Occasional Papers.* December, 1927.

Inquiry (The), "Suggestions for Discussion Leaders," *Occasional Papers.* March, 1929.

NOTE: Additional materials in the form of Pamphlets and Occasional Papers may be secured from the United States Department of Agriculture and various state agencies. The following are representative agencies which have published such materials:

United States Department of Agriculture, Washington, D. C., *Subject-Matter Pamphlets*. (DS-1 through DS-17)

The Agricultural Extension Division of each of the following: Cornell University, University of Illinois, Ohio State University, University of Tennessee, University of Wisconsin.

The Extension Division of each of the following: Iowa State College of Agriculture, Missouri College of Agriculture, University of Nebraska, Utah State Agricultural College.

The State Department of Education of each of the following: Connecticut, Idaho, Mississippi.

MATERIALS NOT DIRECTLY ON DISCUSSION

BOOKS

Adler, Mortimer, *Dialectic*. New York: Harcourt, Brace and Company, 1927. ix + 265 pp.

Angell, Sir Norman, *From Chaos to Control*. London: Allen and Unwin, 1933. 214 pp.

Angell, Sir Norman, *The Public Mind; Its Disorders: Its Exploitation*. New York: E. P. Dutton & Company, 1927. x + 232 pp.

Bacon, Francis, *The Works of Francis Bacon*. (Based upon the complete edition of Spedding, Ellis, and Heath) Boston: Houghton Mifflin Company, 1857. xxxii + 193 + 413 + 438 pp.

Baird, A. Craig, *Public Discussion and Debate*. Boston: Ginn and Company, 1937. v + 400 pp.

Beard, Charles A., *The Discussion of Human Affairs*. New York: The Macmillan Company, 1936. vii + 124 pp.

Bernays, Edward L., *Crystallizing Public Opinion*. New York: Boni and Liveright, 1923. viii + 218 pp.

Biddle, W. W., "Propaganda and Education," *Teachers College Contributions to Education*. No. 521, 1932, 84 pp.

Boas, George, *Our New Ways of Thinking*. New York: Harper & Brothers, 1930. xxi + 194 pp.

Bogardus, Emory S., *Contemporary Sociology*. Los Angeles: University of Southern California Press, 1931. 483 pp.

Bogardus, Emory S., *Leaders and Leadership*. New York: D. Appleton-Century Company, 1934. viii + 325 pp.

Bogoslovsky, Boris B., *The Technique of Controversy*. New York: Harcourt, Brace and Company, 1928. vi + 266 pp.

Bridgman, P. W., *The Intelligent Individual and Society*. New York: The Macmillan Company, 1938. vi + 305 pp.

Bryson, Lyman, *Adult Education*. New York: American Book Company, 1936. v + 208 pp.

Burtt, Edwin A., *Principles and Problems of Right Thinking*. New York: Harper & Brothers, 1928. xii + 590 pp.

Busch, Henry M., *Leadership in Group Work*. New York: Association Press, 1934. vi + 305 pp.

Carmichael, R. D., *The Logic of Discovery*. Chicago-London: The Open Court Publishing Company, 1930. ix + 280 pp.

Chase, Stuart, *The Tyranny of Words*. New York: Harcourt, Brace and Company, 1938. xiv + 396 pp.

Clarke, Edwin C., *The Art of Straight Thinking*. New York: D. Appleton and Company, 1929. xi + 470 pp.

Cohen, Morris R., and Nagel, Ernest, *An Introduction to Logic and Scientific Method*. New York: Harcourt, Brace and Company, 1934. xii + 467 pp.

Columbia Associates in Philosophy, *An Introduction to Reflective Thinking*. Boston: Houghton Mifflin Company, 1923. vii + 351 pp.

Coyle, Grace L., *Social Process in Organized Groups*. New York: Richard R. Smith, Inc., 1930. xiv + 245 pp.

Dashiell, J. F., "Experimental Studies of the Influence of Social Situations on the Behavior of Individual Human Adults," in *A Handbook of Social Psychology*, edited by Carl Murchison. Worcester, Massachusetts: Clark University Press, 1935. xii + 1195 pp.

Dewey, John, *How We Think*. Boston: D. C. Heath and Company, 1910. vi + 224 pp. (Also, 1933 edition. x + 301 pp.)

Dewey, John, *Liberalism and Social Action*. New York: G. P. Putnam's Sons, 1935. viii + 93 pp.

Dewey, John, *Logic: The Theory of Inquiry.* New York: Henry Holt and Company, 1938. viii + 546 pp.

Dewey, John, *Philosophy and Civilization.* New York: Minton, Balch & Company, 1931. vii + 334 pp.

Dewey, John, *The Public and Its Problems.* New York: Henry Holt and Company, 1927. vi + 224 pp.

Dimnet, Ernest, *The Art of Thinking.* New York: Simon & Schuster, Inc., 1932. xii + 221 pp.

Doob, Leonard, *Propaganda, Its Psychology and Technique.* New York: Henry Holt and Company, 1935. x + 424 pp.

Evans, D. Luther, and Gamertsfelder, Walter S., *Logic: Theoretical and Applied.* New York: Doubleday, Doran & Company, Inc., 1937. xiii + 482 pp.

Follett, Mary P., *Creative Experience.* New York: Longmans, Green & Company, 1924. xix + 303 pp.

Follett, Mary P., *The New State.* New York: Longmans, Green & Company, 1926. xxix + 373 pp.

Hazlitt, Henry, *Thinking as a Science.* New York: E. P. Dutton & Company, 1916. 251 pp.

Jastrow, Joseph, *The Betrayal of Intelligence.* New York: Greenberg, Publisher, Inc., 1938. 170 pp.

Jastrow, Joseph, *Effective Thinking.* New York: Simon & Schuster, Inc., 1931. xiii + 271 pp.

Korzybski, Count Alfred, *Science and Sanity; an Introduction to Non-Aristotelian Systems and General Semantics.* Lancaster, Pennsylvania, and New York: The International Non-Aristotelian Library Publishing Company; The Science Press Printing Company, distributors, 1933. xx + 798 pp.

Lahman, Carroll P., *Debate Coaching.* New York: H. W. Wilson Company, 1936. 428 pp.

LaPiere, Richard T., and Farnsworth, Paul R., *Social Psychology.* New York: McGraw-Hill Book Company, Inc., 1936. xii + 504 pp.

Lasswell, Harold D., *Propaganda Technique in the World War.* New York: Alfred A. Knopf, Inc., 1927. 233 pp.

Lindeman, Eduard C., *The Community.* New York: Association Press, 1921. ix + 222 pp.

Lindeman, Eduard C., *Social Discovery.* New York: New Republic, Inc., 1925. xxvii + 375 pp.

Lindeman, Eduard C., *Social Education*. New York: New Republic, Inc., 1933. xix + 233 pp.

Lippmann, Walter, *The Method of Freedom*. New York: The Macmillan Company, 1934. xiv + 117 pp.

Lippmann, Walter, *The Phantom Public*. New York: Harcourt, Brace and Company, 1925. (The Macmillan Company, 1927.) 205 pp.

Lippmann, Walter, *Public Opinion*. New York: Harcourt, Brace and Company, 1922. x + 427 pp.

Lumley, Frederick E., *Means of Social Control*. New York: Century Company, 1925. xiii + 415 pp.

Lumley, Frederick E., *The Propaganda Menace*. New York: Century Company, 1933. ix + 454 pp.

Maller, J. B., "Cooperation and Competition," *Teachers College Contributions to Education*. No. 384, 1929, 176 pp.

Mannheim, Karl, *Ideology and Utopia*. New York: Harcourt, Brace and Company, 1936. xxxi + 318 pp.

Martin, Everett Dean, *The Conflict of the Individual and the Mass in the Modern World*. New York: Henry Holt and Company, 1932. 200 pp.

Mueller, A. D., *Principles and Methods in Adult Education*. New York: Prentice-Hall, Inc., 1937. xx + 428 pp.

Mulgrave, Dorothy I., *Speech for the Classroom Teacher*. New York: Prentice-Hall, Inc., 1936. xxiv + 398 pp.

Murray, Elwood, *The Speech Personality*. Philadelphia: J. B. Lippincott Company, 1937. xii + 517 pp.

Ogden, C. K., and Richards, I. A., *The Meaning of Meaning*. (Third Edition, revised.) New York: Harcourt, Brace and Company, 1930. xxii + 363 pp.

Ogg, Helen L., and Immel, Ray K., *Speech Improvement*. New York: F. S. Crofts & Co., 1936. xxv + 190 pp.

O'Neill, James M., Laycock, Craven, and Scales, Robert L., *Argumentation and Debate*. New York: The Macmillan Company, 1928. xvi + 495 pp.

O'Neill, James M., and McBurney, James H., *The Working Principles of Argument*. New York: The Macmillan Company, 1932. vii + 441 pp.

Overstreet, Harry A., *Influencing Human Behavior*. New York: W. W. Norton & Company, Inc., 1925. viii + 296 pp.

Rignano, Eugenio, *The Psychology of Reasoning*. (Translated by Winifred A. Hall) New York: Harcourt, Brace and Company, 1927. viii + 395 pp.

Robinson, Daniel S., *The Principles of Reasoning.* (Second Edition) New York: D. Appleton-Century Company, 1930. xviii + 393 pp.

Robinson, James Harvey, *The Mind in the Making.* New York: Harper & Brothers, 1921. 235 pp.

Rowden, Dorothy, *Handbook of Adult Education in the United States.* New York: American Association for Adult Education, 1934. ix + 423 pp.

Sarett, Lew, and Foster, William Trufant, *Basic Principles of Speech.* Boston: Houghton Mifflin Company, 1936. v + 577 pp.

Schiller, Ferdinand C. S., *Logic for Use.* New York: Harcourt, Brace and Company, 1930. viii + 469 pp.

Schopenhauer, Arthur, *The Essays of Arthur Schopenhauer.* (Translated and edited by T. Bailey Saunders) New York: Willey Book Company, no date. (Also, The Macmillan Company.)

Sellars, R. W., *The Essentials of Logic.* Boston: Houghton Mifflin Company, 1925. v + 369 pp.

Sidgwick, Alfred, *Fallacies.* New York: D. Appleton and Company, 1884. xvi + 375 pp.

Studebaker, John W., *Plain Talk.* Washington: National Home Library Foundation, 1936. ix + 166 pp.

Tead, Ordway, *The Art of Leadership.* New York: Whittlesey House, McGraw-Hill Book Company, Inc., 1935. ix + 308 pp.

Tead, Ordway, *Human Nature and Management.* McGraw-Hill Book Company, Inc., 1929. x + 312 pp.

Thouless, Robert H., *The Control of the Mind; a Handbook of Applied Psychology.* London: Hodder and Stoughton, 1928. v + 211 pp.

Thouless, Robert H., *Straight and Crooked Thinking.* New York: Simon & Schuster, Inc., 1932. 261 pp.

Tralle, Henry E., *Psychology of Leadership.* New York: Century Company, 1925. ix + 234 pp.

Wallas, Graham, *The Art of Thought.* New York: Harcourt, Brace and Company, 1926. 314 pp.

Wallas, Graham, *The Great Society.* New York: The Macmillan Company, 1915. viii + 383 pp.

Westaway, F. W., *Scientific Method*. London: Blackie &
Son, Ltd., 1924. xxi + 456 pp.

Wolfe, Albert B., *Conservatism, Radicalism, and the Scientific Method*. New York: The Macmillan Company, 1923.
xiv + 354 pp.

Woolf, Leonard S., *After the Deluge: A Study of Communal
Psychology*. London: L. and V. Woolf, 1931. (New
York: Harcourt, Brace and Company, 1931.) xv + 347 pp.

PERIODICALS

Allport, F. H., "The Influence of the Group upon Association and Thought," *Journal of Experimental Psychology*.
Vol. 3, 1920, pp. 159-182.

Biddle, W. W., "A Psychological Definition of Propaganda,"
Journal of Abnormal and Social Psychology. Vol. 26,
1931, pp. 283-295.

Burnham, W. H., "The Group as a Stimulus to Mental
Activity," *Science*. Vol. 31, 1910, pp. 761-767.

Chen, W. K. C., "The Influence of Oral Propaganda Material upon Students' Attitudes," *Archives of Psychology*.
Vol. 23, No. 150, 43 pp.

Dashiell, J. F., "An Experimental Analysis of Some Group
Effects," *Journal of Abnormal and Social Psychology*.
Vol. 25, 1930, pp. 190-199.

Dodge, R., "The Psychology of Propaganda," *Religious
Education*. Vol. 15, 1920, pp. 241-252.

Farnsworth, P. R., "Concerning So-called Group Effects,"
Journal of Genetic Psychology. Vol. 35, 1928, pp. 587-594.

Gordon, K., "A Study of Esthetic Judgments," *Journal of
Experimental Psychology*. Vol. 6, 1923, pp. 36-43.

Jenness, Arthur, "Social Influences in the Change of Opinion; the Role of Discussion in Changing Opinion Regarding a Matter of Fact," *Journal of Abnormal and Social
Psychology*. Vol. 27, 1932, pp. 279-296.

McBurney, James H., "The Place of the Enthymeme in
Rhetorical Theory," *Speech Monographs*. Vol. III, 1936,
pp. 49-74.

Moore, H. T., "The Comparative Influence of Majority and
Expert Opinion," *American Journal of Psychology*. Vol.
32, 1921, pp. 16-20.

Saadi, M., and Farnsworth, P. R., "The Degrees of Acceptance of Dogmatic Statements and Preferences for Their Supposed Makers," *Journal of Abnormal and Social Psychology.* Vol. 29, 1934, pp. 143-150.

Sengupta, N. N., and Sinba, C. P. N., "Mental Work in Isolation and in Group," *Indian Journal of Psychology.* Vol. 1, 1926, pp. 106-110.

Shaw, M. E., "A Comparison of Individuals, and Small Groups in the Rational Solution of Complex Problems," *American Journal of Psychology.* Vol. 44, 1932, pp. 491-504.

South, E. B., "Some Psychological Aspects of Committee Work," *Journal of Applied Psychology.* Vol. 11, 1927, pp. 348-368.

Spence, R. B., "Lecture and Class Discussion in Teaching Educational Psychology," *Journal of Educational Psychology.* Vol. 19, 1928, pp. 454-462.

Stroop, J. R., "Is the Judgment of the Group Better Than that of the Average Member of the Group?" *Journal of Experimental Psychology.* Vol. 15, 1932, pp. 550-562.

Watson, G. B., "Do Groups Think More Efficiently than Individuals?" *Journal of Abnormal and Social Psychology.* Vol. 23, 1928, pp. 328-336.

Wheeler, D., and Jordon, H., "Change of Individual Opinion to Accord with Group Opinion," *Journal of Abnormal and Social Psychology.* Vol. 24, 1929, pp. 203-206.

Whittemore, I. C., "The Competitive Consciousness," *Journal of Abnormal and Social Psychology.* Vol. 20, 1925, pp. 17-33.

Whittemore, I. C., "The Influence of Competition on Performance: an Experimental Study," *Journal of Abnormal and Social Psychology.* Vol. 19, 1924, pp. 236-253.

INDEX

Accent, stratagem of, 212
Adler, M. J., 142
All and some, stratagem of, 229
Allport, F. H., 27, 88
Allport, Gordon, 5
Ambiguity, stratagem of, 211
American Institute of Public Opinion, 187
Amphiboly, stratagem of, 212
Analogy, 184, 188
Analysis, 11 ff., 67; functions of, 168
Arbitration, 41
Aristotle, 16, 193, 194
Attitudes, 261; in discussion, 93 ff.

Bacon, Francis, 17, 208, 209
Bibliography, 84, 434 ff.
Bogardus, E. S., 24, 115
Bogoslovsky, B. B., 167, 231
Bryson, Lyman, 247, 425
Burtt, E. A., 165, 173

Case method, 267
Causal relationships, 170
Cause, 184, 188 ff.
Censorship, stratagems of, 217 ff.
Chautauqua, 308
Chicago (University of) Round Table, 394 ff.
Clarke, E. L., 175
Co-acting groups, 14, 43, 267, 287 ff.
Columbia Associates in Philosophy, 175
Combination discussion-debate method, 281
Compromise, 253 ff.
Conference, 39, 268 ff.
Conflict, 118, 129 ff.; causes of, 245 ff.; example of, 369; extrinsic, 250 ff.; intrinsic, 247 ff.; nature of, 243 ff.; resolving, 244, 248 ff.

Constructive and intentional reasoning distinguished, 3 ff., 183 ff.
Continuous variation, 7, 166 ff., 200, 230 ff.
Contributing, 87 ff.; examples of, 351 ff.
Convention debating, 242 ff.
Cooper Union Forum, 308, 309
Cooperation, 13, 260
Cooperative Investigation, 335
Courtis, S. A., 254
Criticism and propaganda distinguished, 5 ff.
Criticism blank, 110
Curriculum, discussion in, 322 ff.; integrated, 324 ff.; speech, 326 ff.

Dashiell, J. F., 11, 259, 262, 263, 264
Debate, 14, 276, 281 ff., 333 ff.; convention debating, 342 ff.
Debate Symposium, 335
Decisions, 275
Definition, 11, 67; methods of, 165 ff.; role of, 164
Democracy, 20 ff., 31, 394 ff., 406 ff., 425 ff.
Des Moines Forums, 309, 310, 311
Developmental method, 266
Dewey, John, 4, 11, 17, 18, 106
Dialectic, 17
Dialogue, 15, 297 ff.
Dickens, Milton, 343, 349
Diem, W. R., 343
Discussion, atmosphere for, 43; attitudes in, 93 ff.; bibliography on, 434 ff.; contemporary interest in, 19; courses in, 322 ff.; defined, 10 ff.; evaluating, 109 ff.; history of, 15 ff.; in extra-curricular activities, 332